STUDIO JMS PRESENTS...

SIDEKICK ™

Volume **2**

Written by:
J. Michael Straczynski

Line art by:
Tom Mandrake

Colors by:
HiFi

Letters by:
Troy Peteri

.....

Book Design, Layout
& Series Production Editing:
Phil Smith

Production:
Tricia Ramos

.....

Cover by: **Tom Mandrake & HiFi**

Original logo design by: **Jerry Ordway**

published by
**Image Comics with
Studio JMS & Joe's Comics**

IMAGE COMICS, INC.
Robert Kirkman – Chief Operating Officer
Erik Larsen – Chief Financial Officer
Todd McFarlane – President
Marc Silvestri – Chief Executive Officer
Jim Valentino – Vice-President

Eric Stephenson – Publisher
Corey Murphy – Director of Sales
Jeff Boison – Director of Publishing Planning & Book Trade Sales
Jeremy Sullivan – Director of Digital Sales
Kat Salazar – Director of PR & Marketing
Emily Miller – Director of Operations
Branwyn Bigglestone – Senior Accounts Manager
Sarah Mello – Accounts Manager
Drew Gill – Art Director
Jonathan Chan – Production Manager
Meredith Wallace – Print Manager
Briah Skelly – Publicity Assistant
Randy Okamura – Marketing Production Designer
David Brothers – Branding Manager
Ally Power – Content Manager
Addison Duke – Production Artist
Vincent Kukua – Production Artist
Sasha Head – Production Artist
Tricia Ramos – Production Artist
Jeff Stang – Direct Market Sales Representative
Emilio Bautista – Digital Sales Associate
Chloe Ramos-Peterson – Administrative Assistant
IMAGECOMICS.COM

STUDIO JMS™

JOE'S COMICS
a division of Studio JMS
for more information go to
www.studiojms.com

JOE'S COMICS™

COMIC SHOP LOCATOR SERVICE
888-COMICBOOK
888-266-4226

to find the comic shop
nearest you call:
1-888-COMICBOOK

SIDEKICK trade paperback volume 2,
ISBN: 978-1-63215-026-4, $15.99 USD. February 2016. FIRST PRINTING.
Published by Image Comics, Inc. Office of Publication: 2001 Center Street, Sixth Floor, Berkeley, CA 94704. Originally published as SIDEKICK #7-12. SIDEKICK ™ & © 2016 Studio JMS. "Sidekick," the Sidekick logos and the likeness of all featured characters are trademarks of Studio JMS. All rights reserved. Image Comics ® and its logos are registered trademarks of Image Comics, Inc. Any resemblance to actual persons (living or dead), events, institutions, or locales, without satiric intent, is coincidental. No portion of this publication may be reproduced or transmitted, in any form or by any means, without the express written permission of Studio JMS. Printed in the U.S.A. For information regarding the CPSIA on this printed material call: 203-595-3636 and provide reference # RICH – 662298. For foreign licensing and international rights contact: foreignlicensing@imagecomics.com

-Table of Contents-

- Original Edition Series "A" covers by: Tom Mandrake & HiFi -

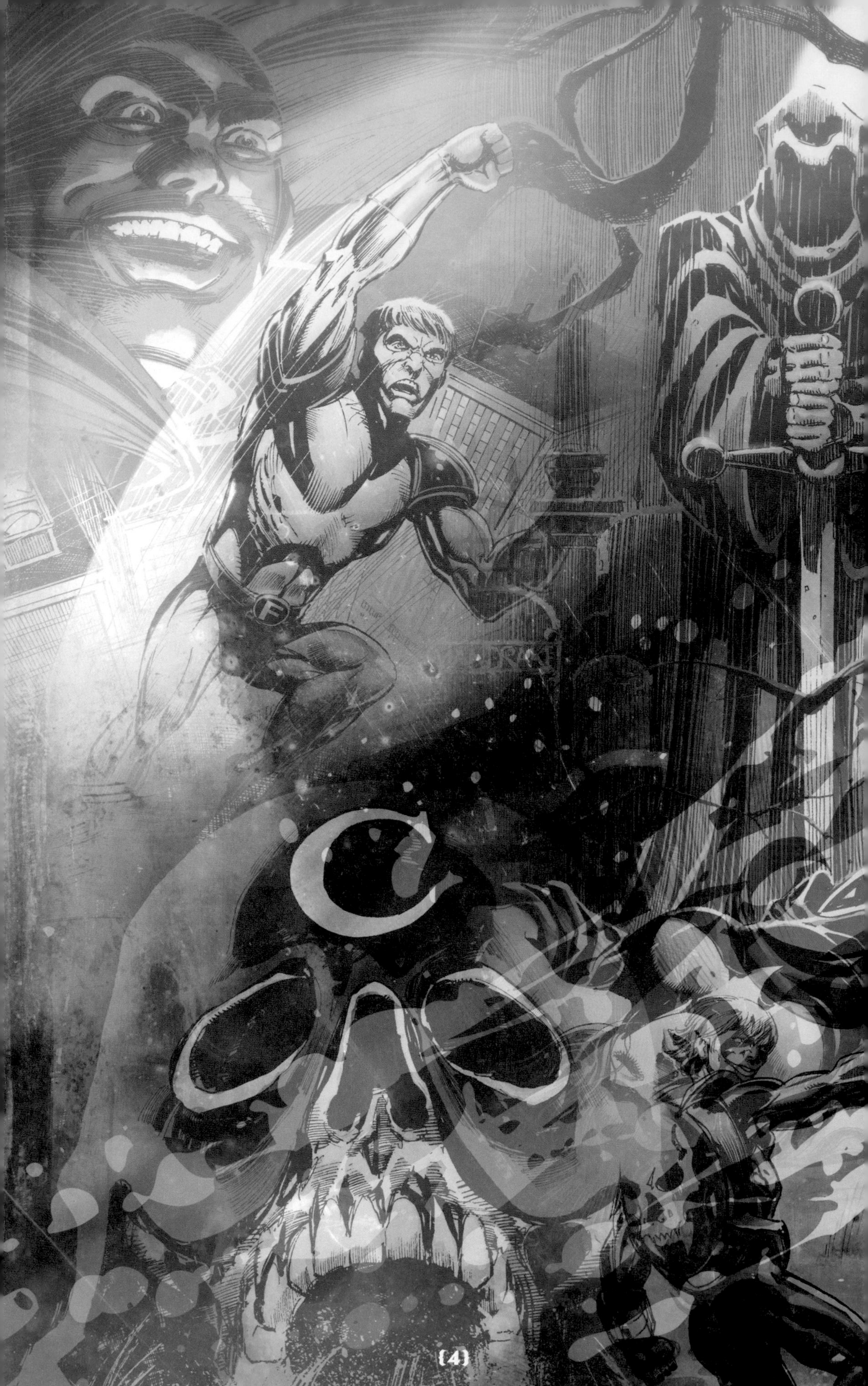

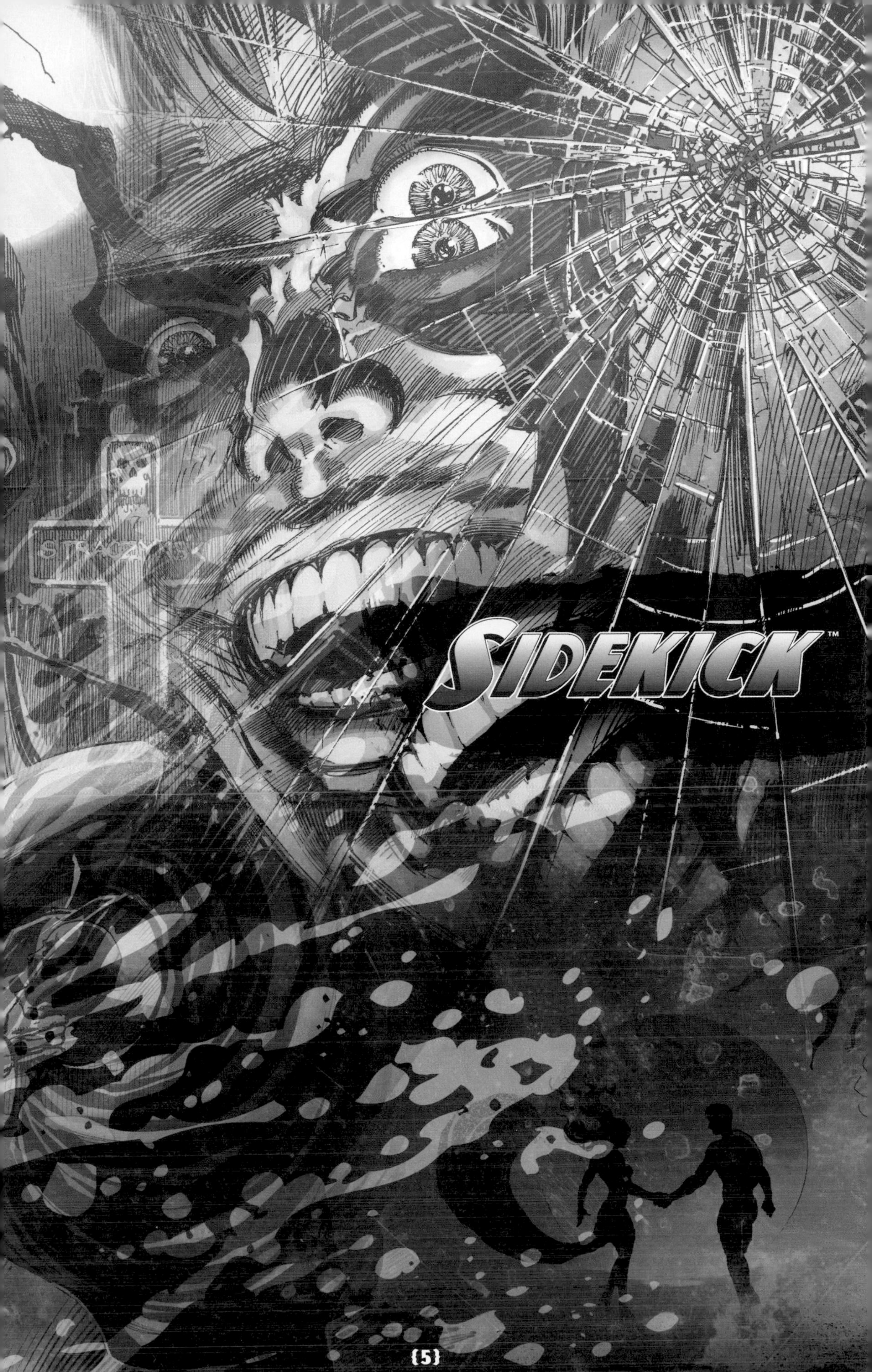
SIDEKICK™

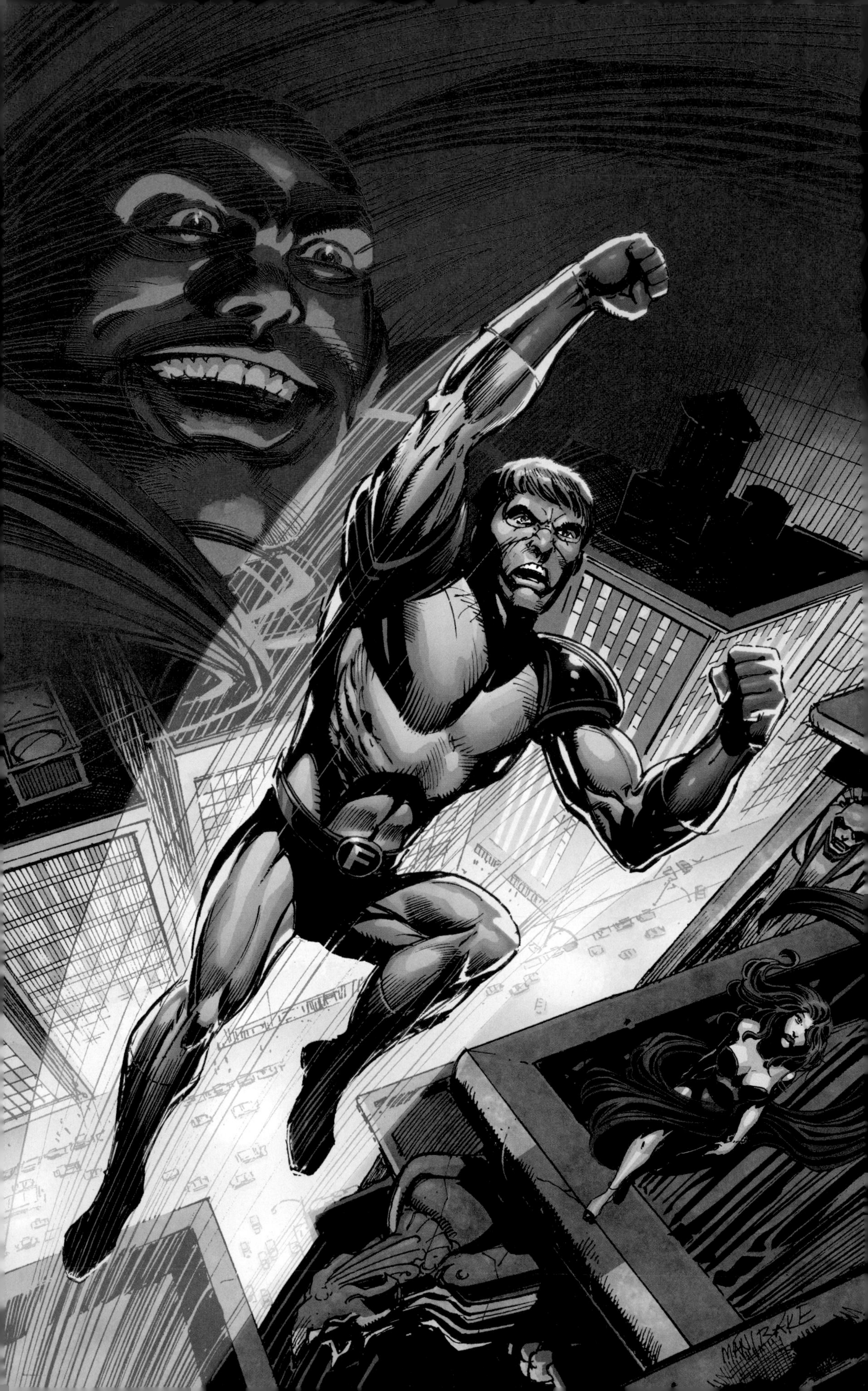

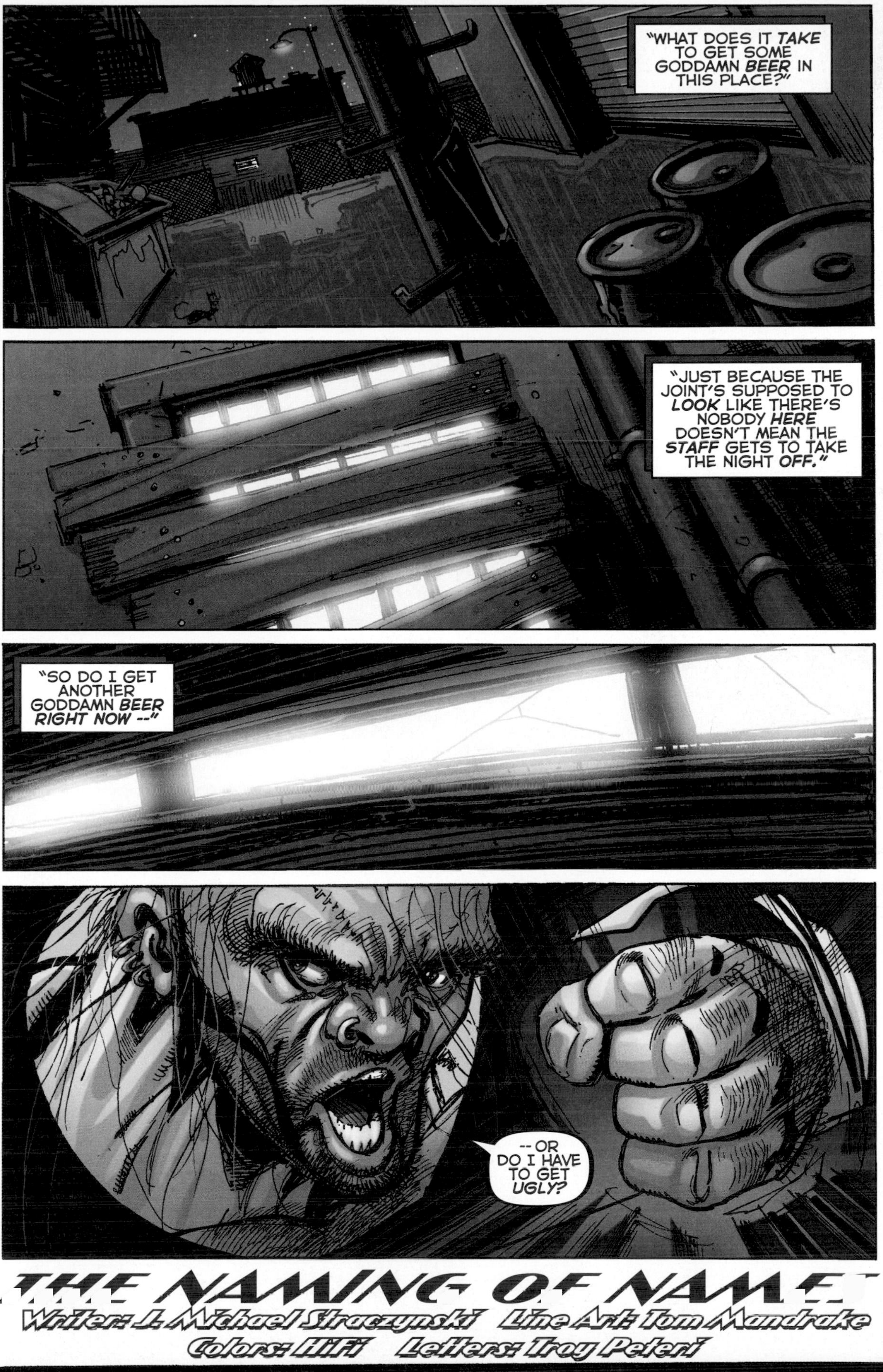
"WHAT DOES IT TAKE TO GET SOME GODDAMN BEER IN THIS PLACE?"
"JUST BECAUSE THE JOINT'S SUPPOSED TO LOOK LIKE THERE'S NOBODY HERE DOESN'T MEAN THE STAFF GETS TO TAKE THE NIGHT OFF."
"SO DO I GET ANOTHER GODDAMN BEER RIGHT NOW --"
--OR DO I HAVE TO GET UGLY?

THE NAMING OF NAMES

Writer: J. Michael Straczynski Line Art: Tom Mandrake
Colors: HiFi Letters: Troy Peteri

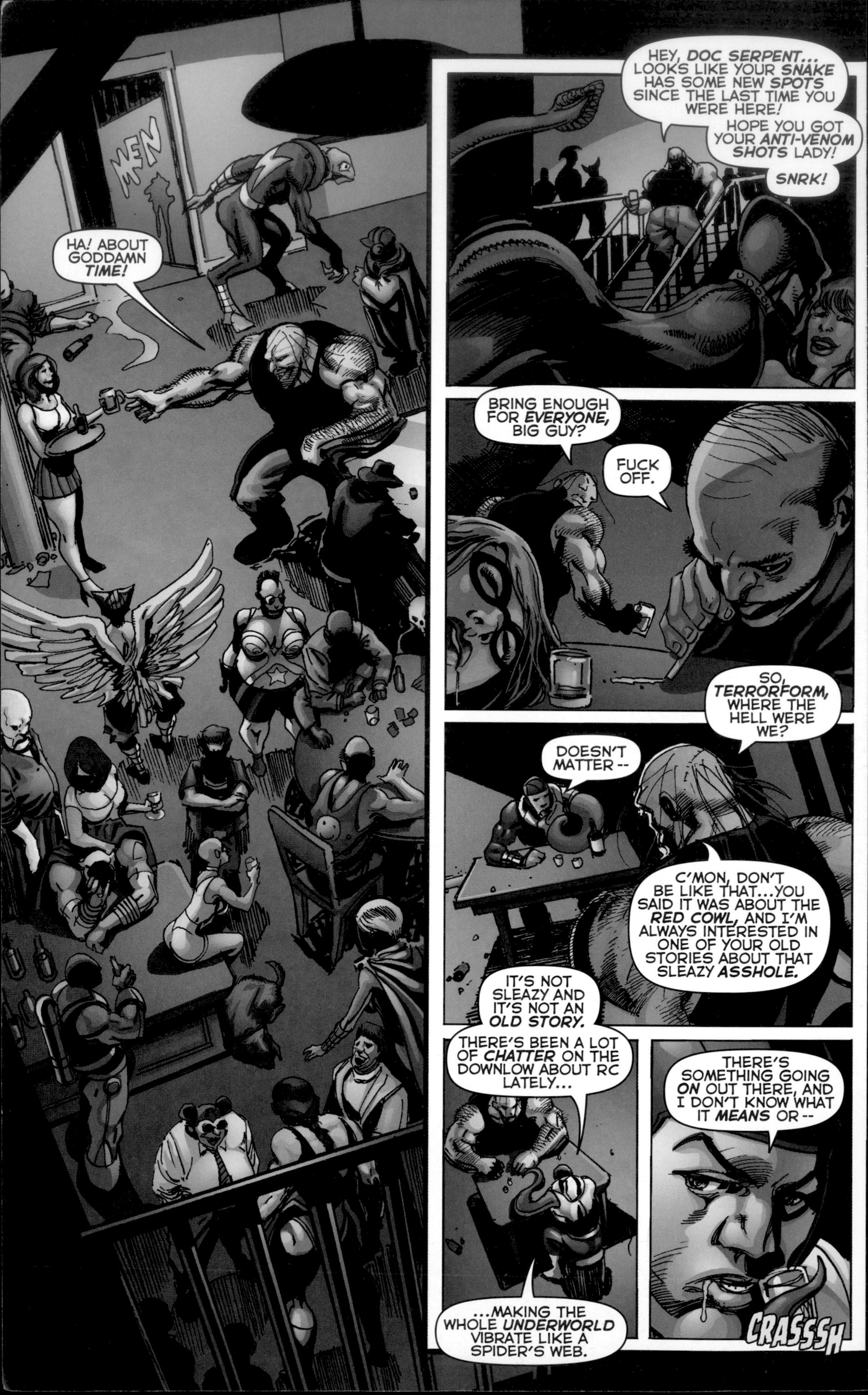

MEN
HA! ABOUT GODDAMN TIME!
HEY, DOC SERPENT... LOOKS LIKE YOUR SNAKE HAS SOME NEW SPOTS SINCE THE LAST TIME YOU WERE HERE!
HOPE YOU GOT YOUR ANTI-VENOM SHOTS LADY!
SNRK!
BRING ENOUGH FOR EVERYONE, BIG GUY?
FUCK OFF.
SO, TERRORFORM, WHERE THE HELL WERE WE?
DOESN'T MATTER --
C'MON, DON'T BE LIKE THAT...YOU SAID IT WAS ABOUT THE RED COWL, AND I'M ALWAYS INTERESTED IN ONE OF YOUR OLD STORIES ABOUT THAT SLEAZY ASSHOLE.
IT'S NOT SLEAZY AND IT'S NOT AN OLD STORY.
THERE'S BEEN A LOT OF CHATTER ON THE DOWNLOW ABOUT RC LATELY...
...MAKING THE WHOLE UNDERWORLD VIBRATE LIKE A SPIDER'S WEB.
THERE'S SOMETHING GOING ON OUT THERE, AND I DON'T KNOW WHAT IT MEANS OR --
CRASSSH

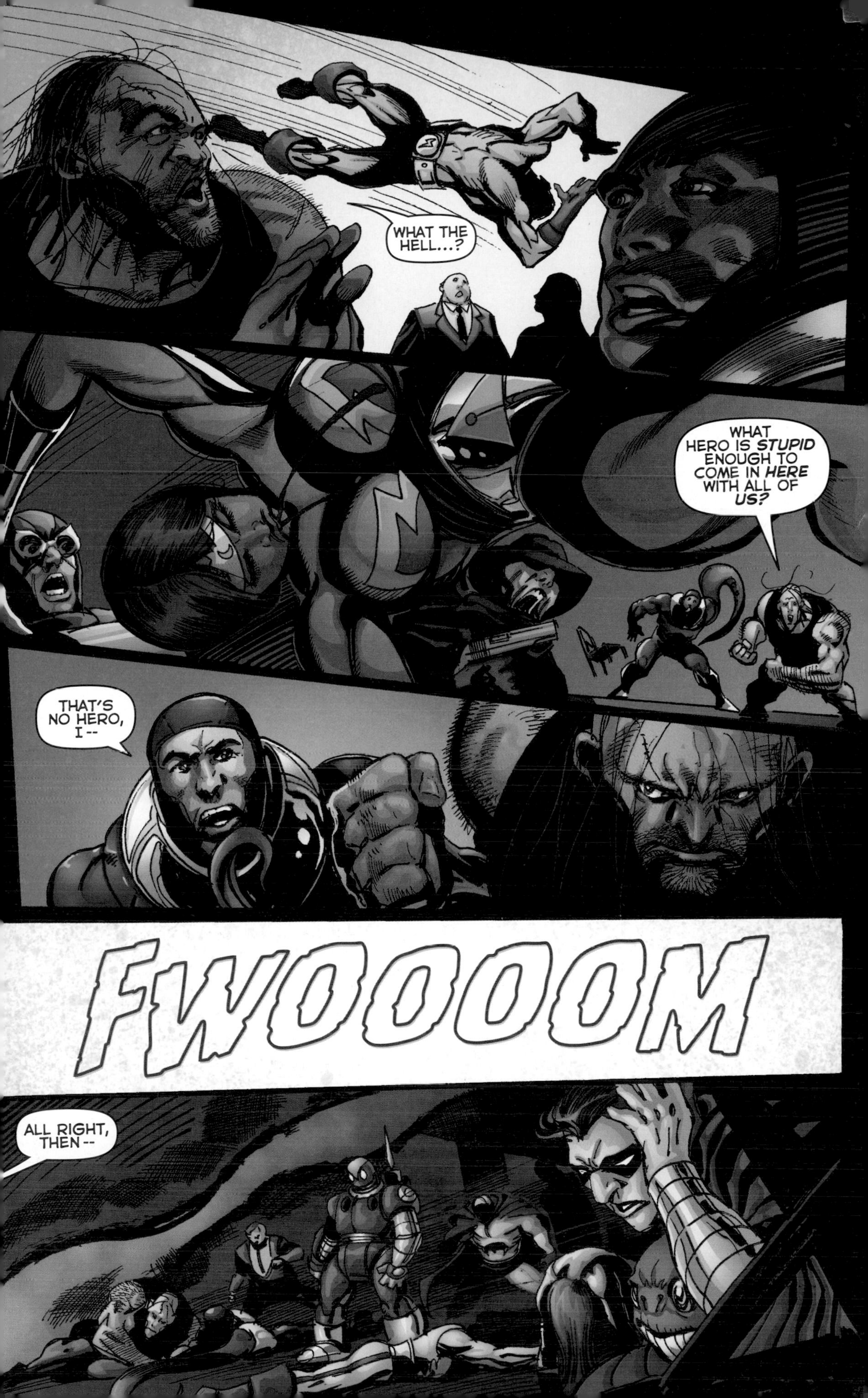

WHAT THE HELL...?
WHAT HERO IS STUPID ENOUGH TO COME IN HERE WITH ALL OF US?
THAT'S NO HERO, I --
FWOOOOM
ALL RIGHT, THEN --

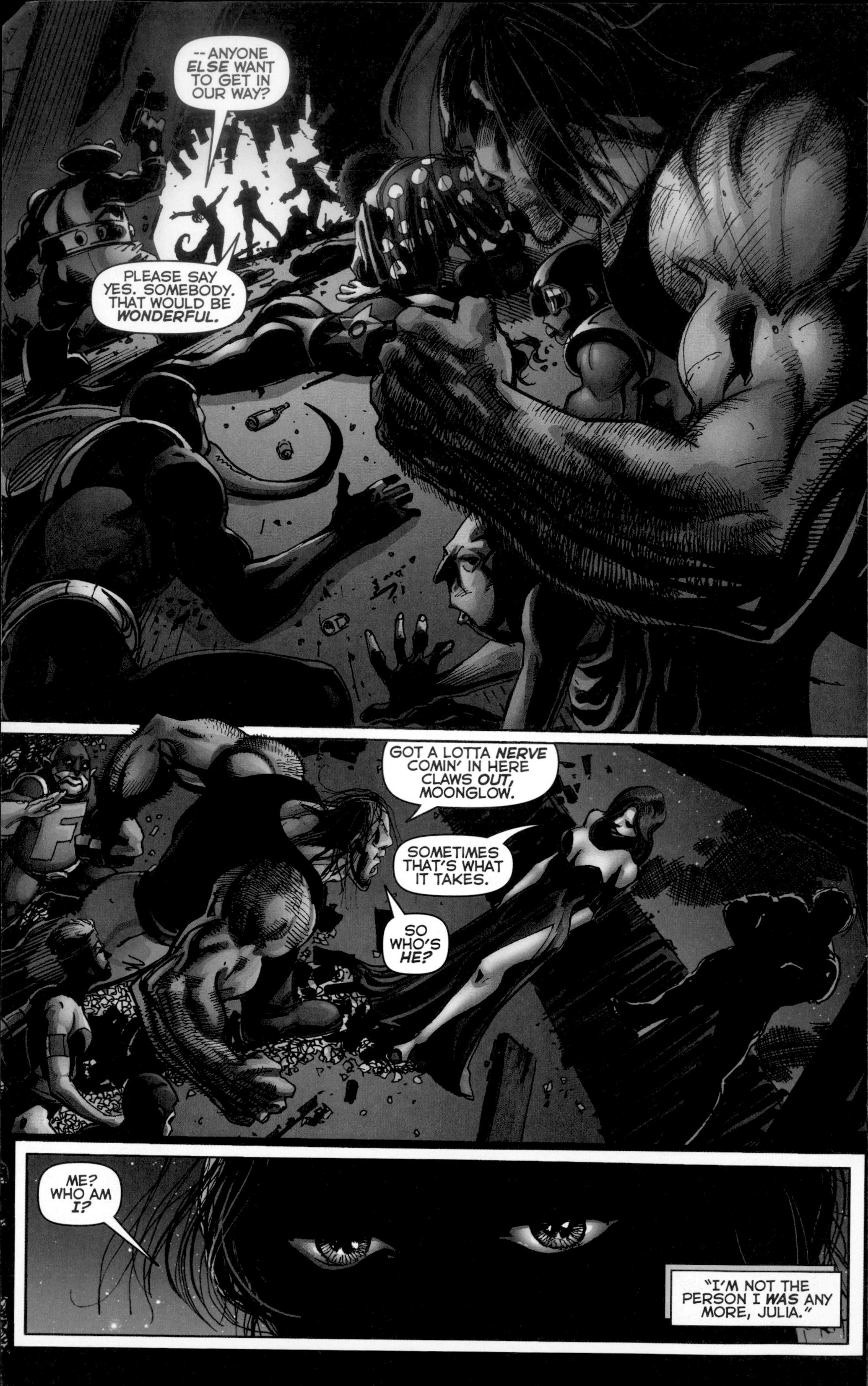
-- ANYONE ELSE WANT TO GET IN OUR WAY?
PLEASE SAY YES. SOMEBODY. THAT WOULD BE WONDERFUL.
GOT A LOTTA NERVE COMIN' IN HERE CLAWS OUT, MOONGLOW.
SOMETIMES THAT'S WHAT IT TAKES.
SO WHO'S HE?
ME? WHO AM I?
"I'M NOT THE PERSON I WAS ANY MORE, JULIA."

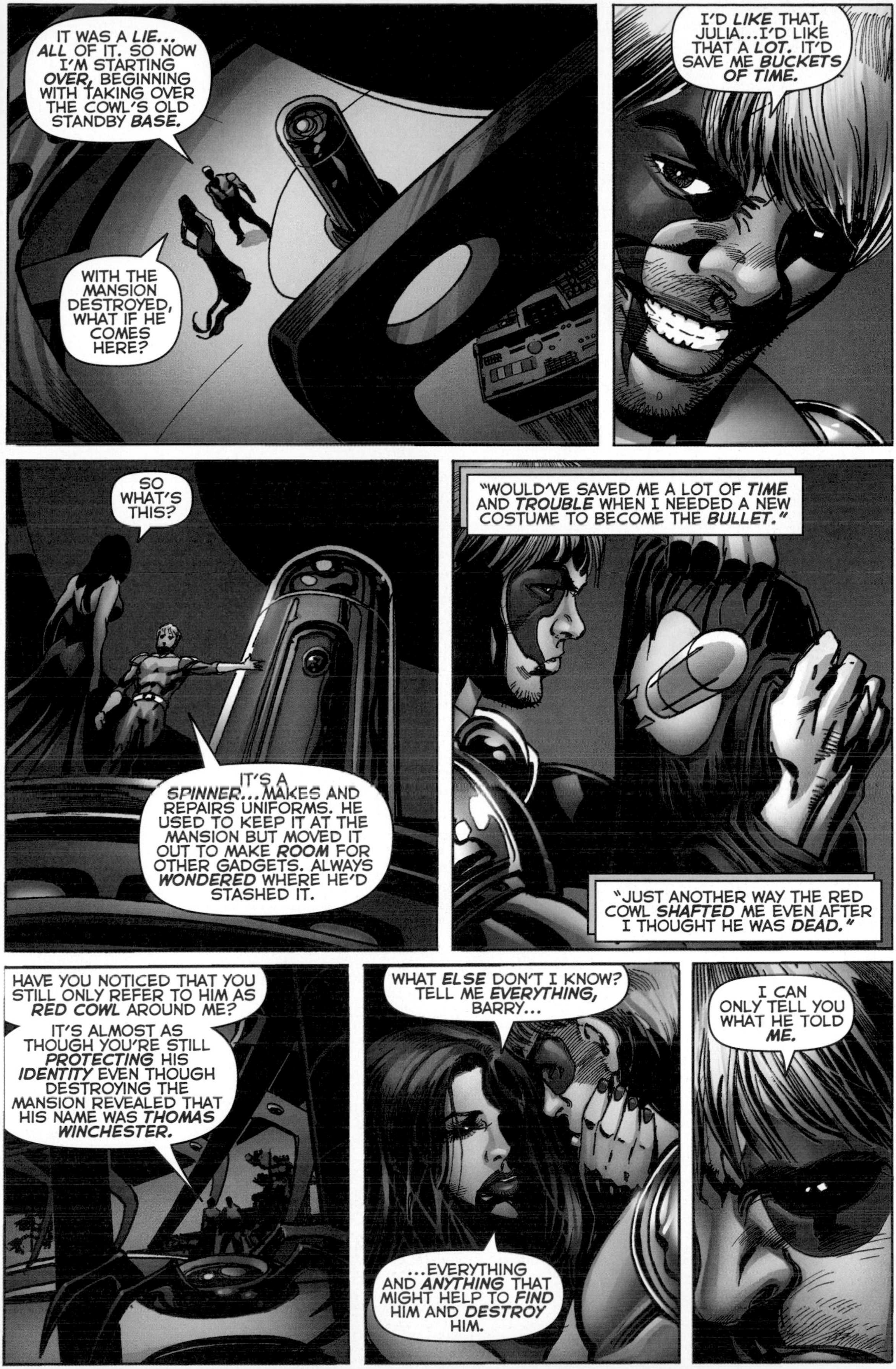
IT WAS A LIE... ALL OF IT. SO NOW I'M STARTING OVER, BEGINNING WITH TAKING OVER THE COWL'S OLD STANDBY BASE.
WITH THE MANSION DESTROYED, WHAT IF HE COMES HERE?
I'D LIKE THAT, JULIA...I'D LIKE THAT A LOT. IT'D SAVE ME BUCKETS OF TIME.
SO WHAT'S THIS?
IT'S A SPINNER...MAKES AND REPAIRS UNIFORMS. HE USED TO KEEP IT AT THE MANSION BUT MOVED IT OUT TO MAKE ROOM FOR OTHER GADGETS. ALWAYS WONDERED WHERE HE'D STASHED IT.
"WOULD'VE SAVED ME A LOT OF TIME AND TROUBLE WHEN I NEEDED A NEW COSTUME TO BECOME THE BULLET."
"JUST ANOTHER WAY THE RED COWL SHAFTED ME EVEN AFTER I THOUGHT HE WAS DEAD."
HAVE YOU NOTICED THAT YOU STILL ONLY REFER TO HIM AS RED COWL AROUND ME?
IT'S ALMOST AS THOUGH YOU'RE STILL PROTECTING HIS IDENTITY EVEN THOUGH DESTROYING THE MANSION REVEALED THAT HIS NAME WAS THOMAS WINCHESTER.
WHAT ELSE DON'T I KNOW? TELL ME EVERYTHING, BARRY...
...EVERYTHING AND ANYTHING THAT MIGHT HELP TO FIND HIM AND DESTROY HIM.
I CAN ONLY TELL YOU WHAT HE TOLD ME.

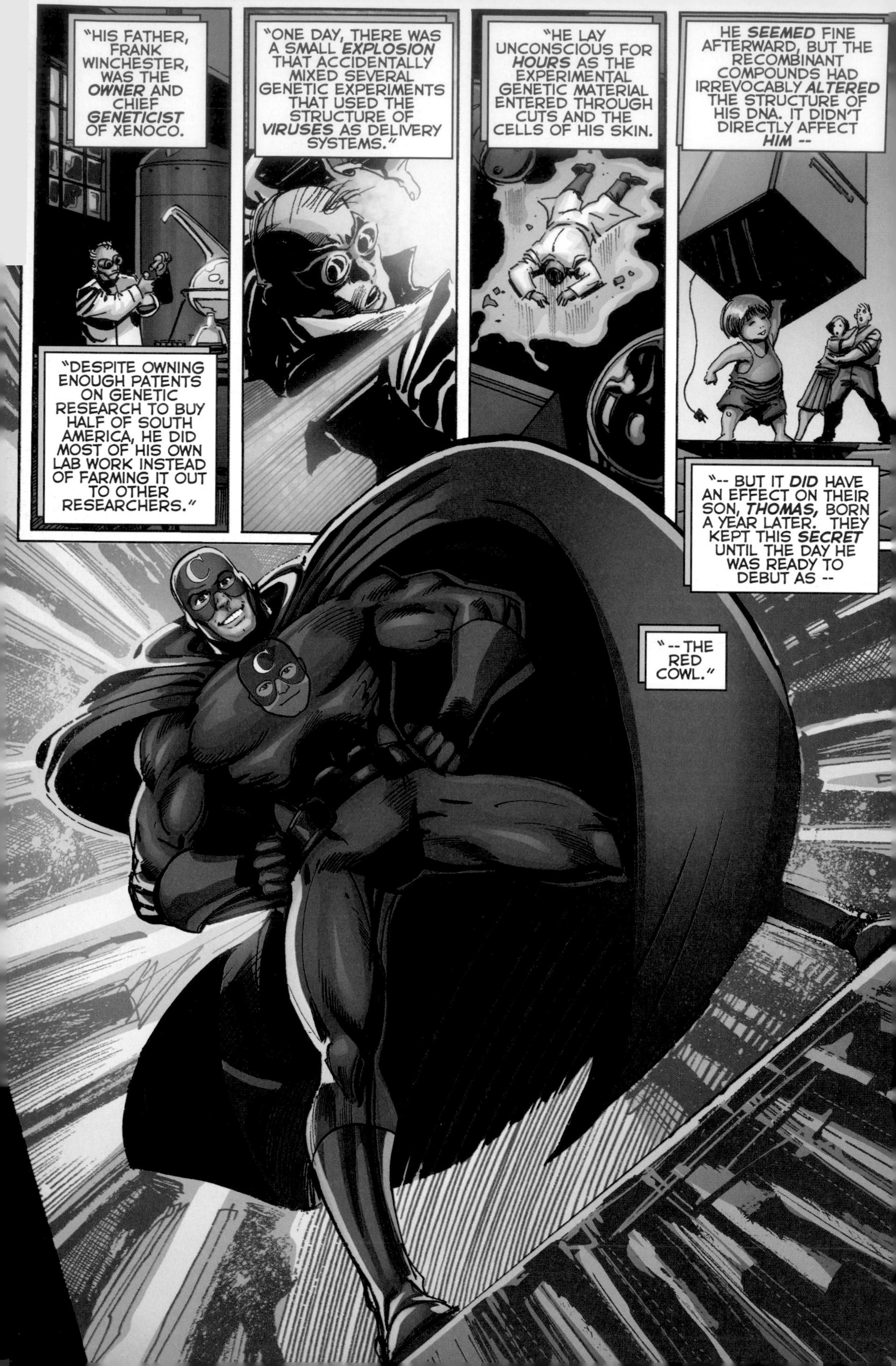
"HIS FATHER, FRANK WINCHESTER, WAS THE OWNER AND CHIEF GENETICIST OF XENOCO.
"DESPITE OWNING ENOUGH PATENTS ON GENETIC RESEARCH TO BUY HALF OF SOUTH AMERICA, HE DID MOST OF HIS OWN LAB WORK INSTEAD OF FARMING IT OUT TO OTHER RESEARCHERS."
"ONE DAY, THERE WAS A SMALL EXPLOSION THAT ACCIDENTALLY MIXED SEVERAL GENETIC EXPERIMENTS THAT USED THE STRUCTURE OF VIRUSES AS DELIVERY SYSTEMS."
"HE LAY UNCONSCIOUS FOR HOURS AS THE EXPERIMENTAL GENETIC MATERIAL ENTERED THROUGH CUTS AND THE CELLS OF HIS SKIN.
HE SEEMED FINE AFTERWARD, BUT THE RECOMBINANT COMPOUNDS HAD IRREVOCABLY ALTERED THE STRUCTURE OF HIS DNA. IT DIDN'T DIRECTLY AFFECT HIM --
"-- BUT IT DID HAVE AN EFFECT ON THEIR SON, THOMAS, BORN A YEAR LATER. THEY KEPT THIS SECRET UNTIL THE DAY HE WAS READY TO DEBUT AS --
"-- THE RED COWL."

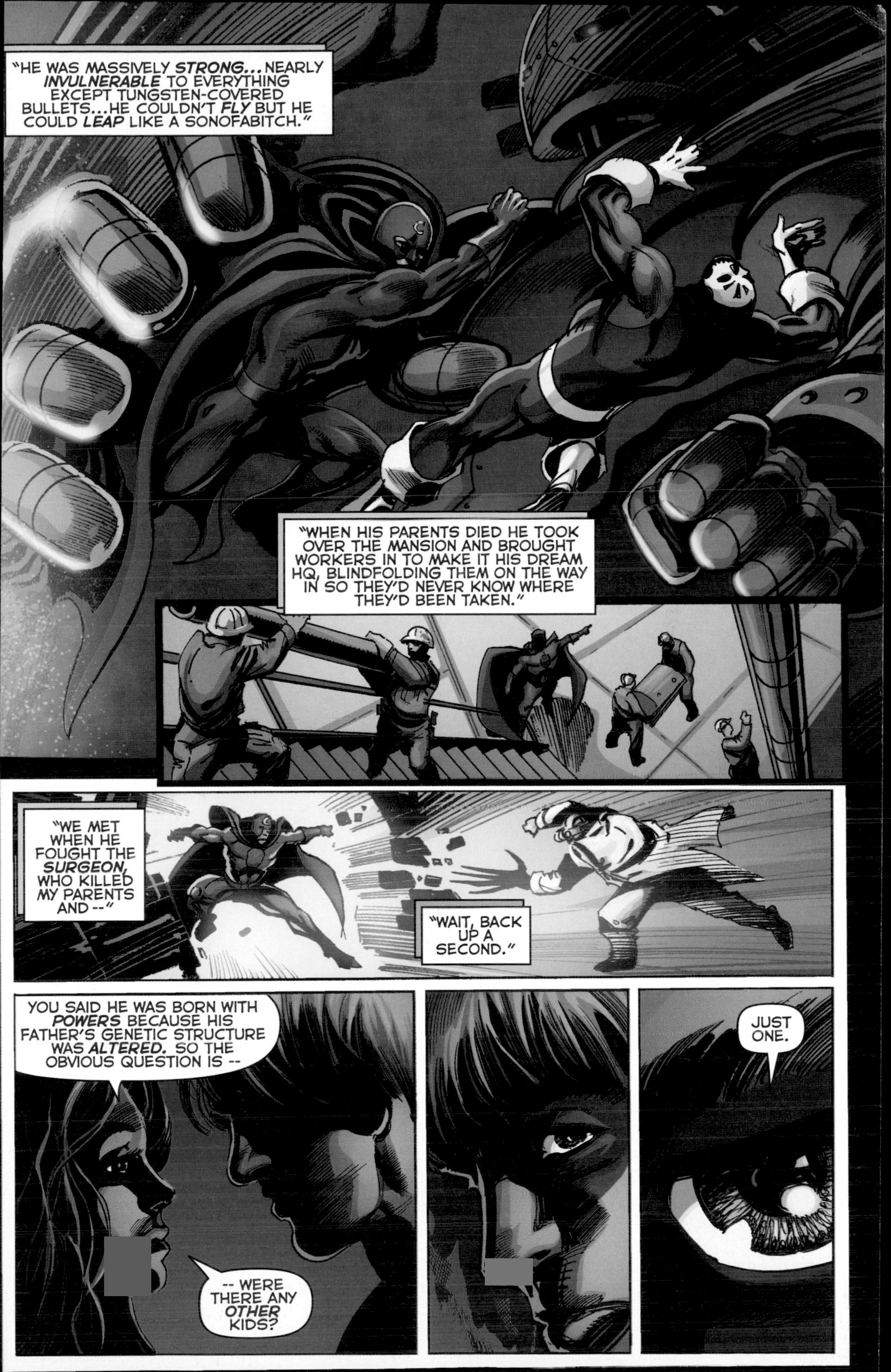
"HE WAS MASSIVELY STRONG... NEARLY INVULNERABLE TO EVERYTHING EXCEPT TUNGSTEN-COVERED BULLETS...HE COULDN'T FLY BUT HE COULD LEAP LIKE A SONOFABITCH."
"WHEN HIS PARENTS DIED HE TOOK OVER THE MANSION AND BROUGHT WORKERS IN TO MAKE IT HIS DREAM HQ, BLINDFOLDING THEM ON THE WAY IN SO THEY'D NEVER KNOW WHERE THEY'D BEEN TAKEN."
"WE MET WHEN HE FOUGHT THE SURGEON, WHO KILLED MY PARENTS AND --"
"WAIT, BACK UP A SECOND."
YOU SAID HE WAS BORN WITH POWERS BECAUSE HIS FATHER'S GENETIC STRUCTURE WAS ALTERED. SO THE OBVIOUS QUESTION IS --
-- WERE THERE ANY OTHER KIDS?
JUST ONE.

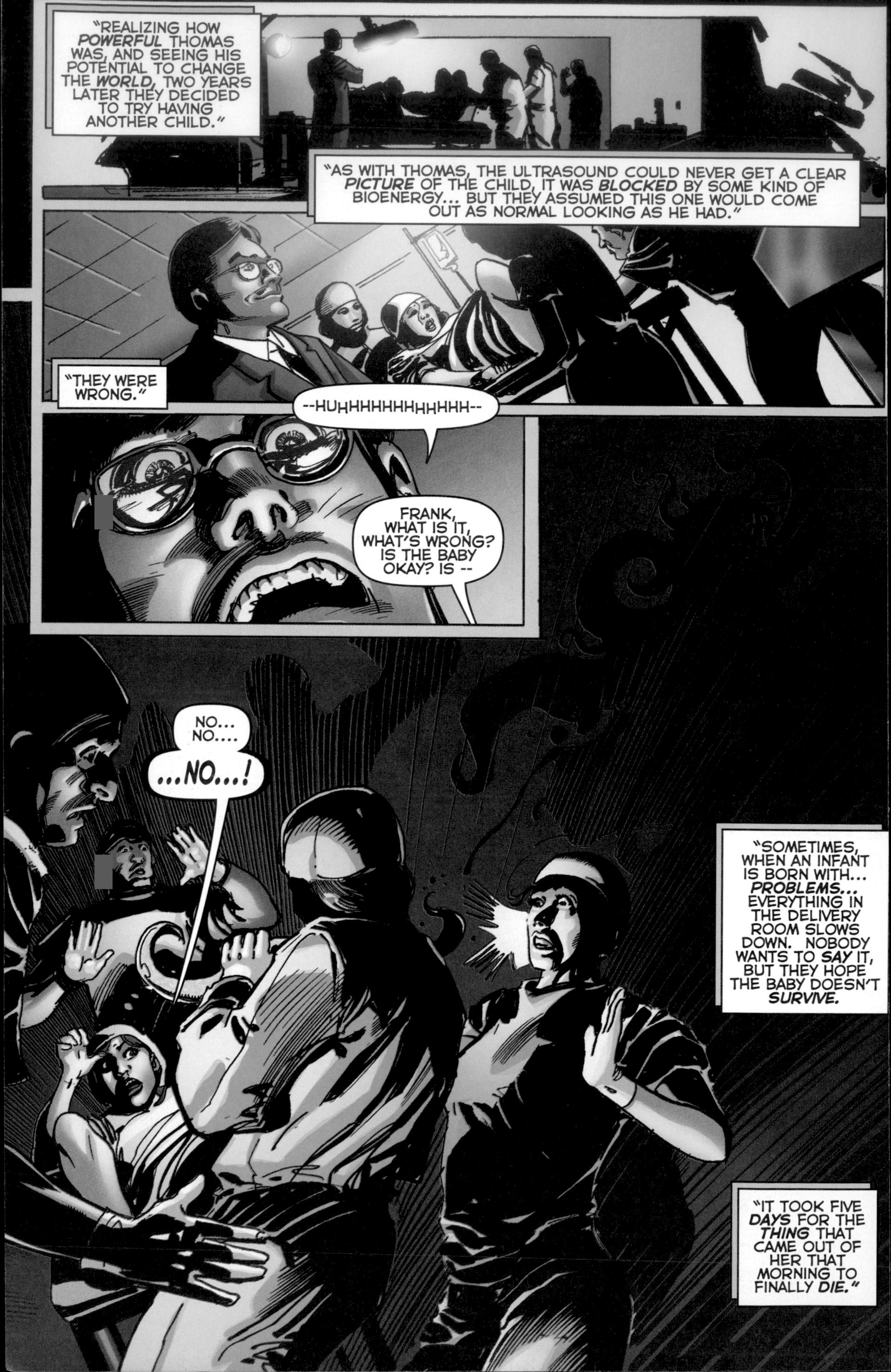
"REALIZING HOW POWERFUL THOMAS WAS, AND SEEING HIS POTENTIAL TO CHANGE THE WORLD, TWO YEARS LATER THEY DECIDED TO TRY HAVING ANOTHER CHILD."
"AS WITH THOMAS, THE ULTRASOUND COULD NEVER GET A CLEAR PICTURE OF THE CHILD, IT WAS BLOCKED BY SOME KIND OF BIOENERGY... BUT THEY ASSUMED THIS ONE WOULD COME OUT AS NORMAL LOOKING AS HE HAD."
"THEY WERE WRONG."
--HUHHHHHHHHHHHH--
FRANK, WHAT IS IT, WHAT'S WRONG? IS THE BABY OKAY? IS --
NO... NO....
...NO...!
"SOMETIMES, WHEN AN INFANT IS BORN WITH... PROBLEMS... EVERYTHING IN THE DELIVERY ROOM SLOWS DOWN. NOBODY WANTS TO SAY IT, BUT THEY HOPE THE BABY DOESN'T SURVIVE.
"IT TOOK FIVE DAYS FOR THE THING THAT CAME OUT OF HER THAT MORNING TO FINALLY DIE."

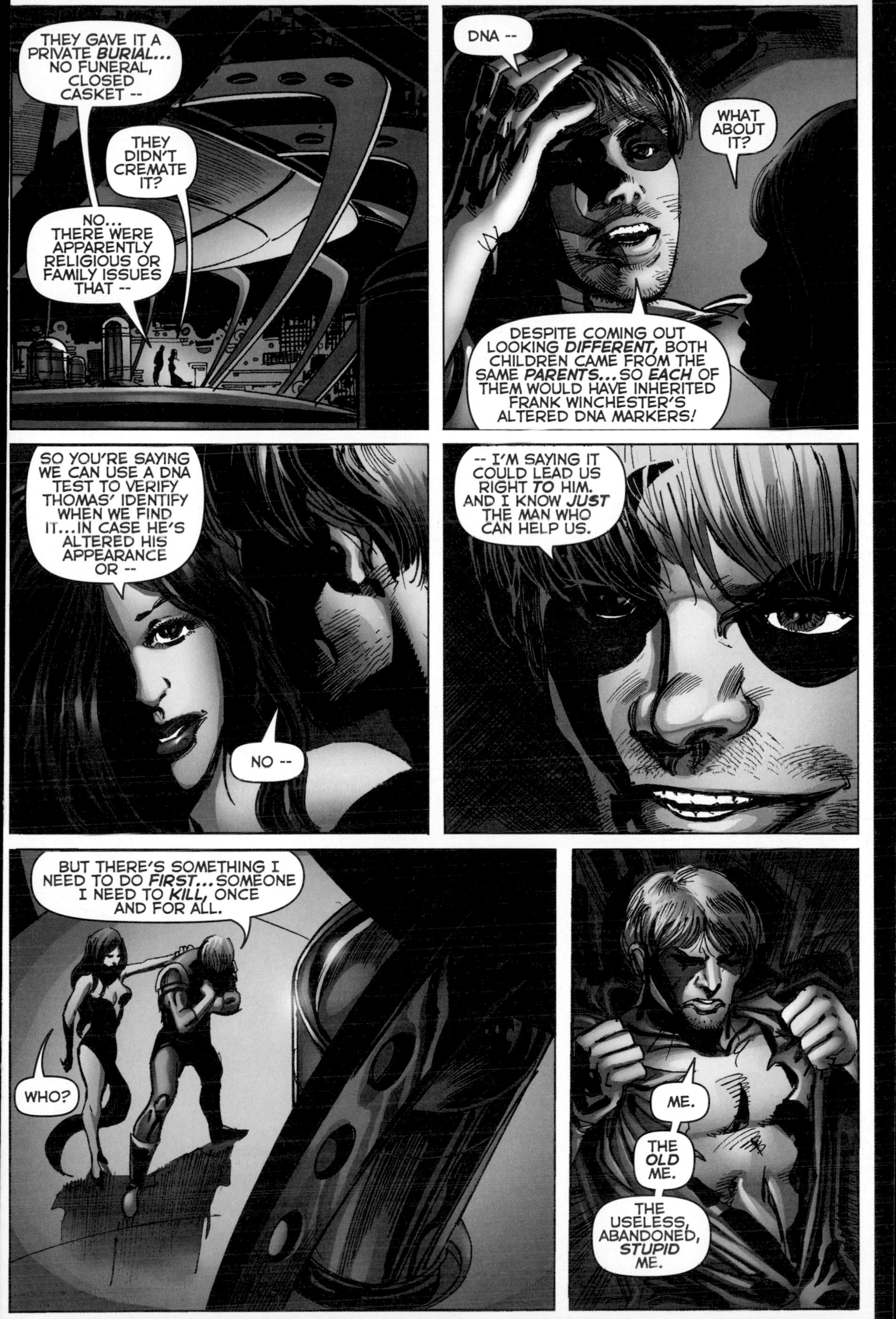
THEY GAVE IT A PRIVATE BURIAL... NO FUNERAL, CLOSED CASKET --
THEY DIDN'T CREMATE IT?
NO... THERE WERE APPARENTLY RELIGIOUS OR FAMILY ISSUES THAT --
DNA --
WHAT ABOUT IT?
DESPITE COMING OUT LOOKING DIFFERENT, BOTH CHILDREN CAME FROM THE SAME PARENTS... SO EACH OF THEM WOULD HAVE INHERITED FRANK WINCHESTER'S ALTERED DNA MARKERS!
SO YOU'RE SAYING WE CAN USE A DNA TEST TO VERIFY THOMAS' IDENTIFY WHEN WE FIND IT...IN CASE HE'S ALTERED HIS APPEARANCE OR --
NO --
-- I'M SAYING IT COULD LEAD US RIGHT TO HIM. AND I KNOW JUST THE MAN WHO CAN HELP US.
BUT THERE'S SOMETHING I NEED TO DO FIRST... SOMEONE I NEED TO KILL, ONCE AND FOR ALL.
WHO?
ME.
THE OLD ME.
THE USELESS, ABANDONED, STUPID ME.

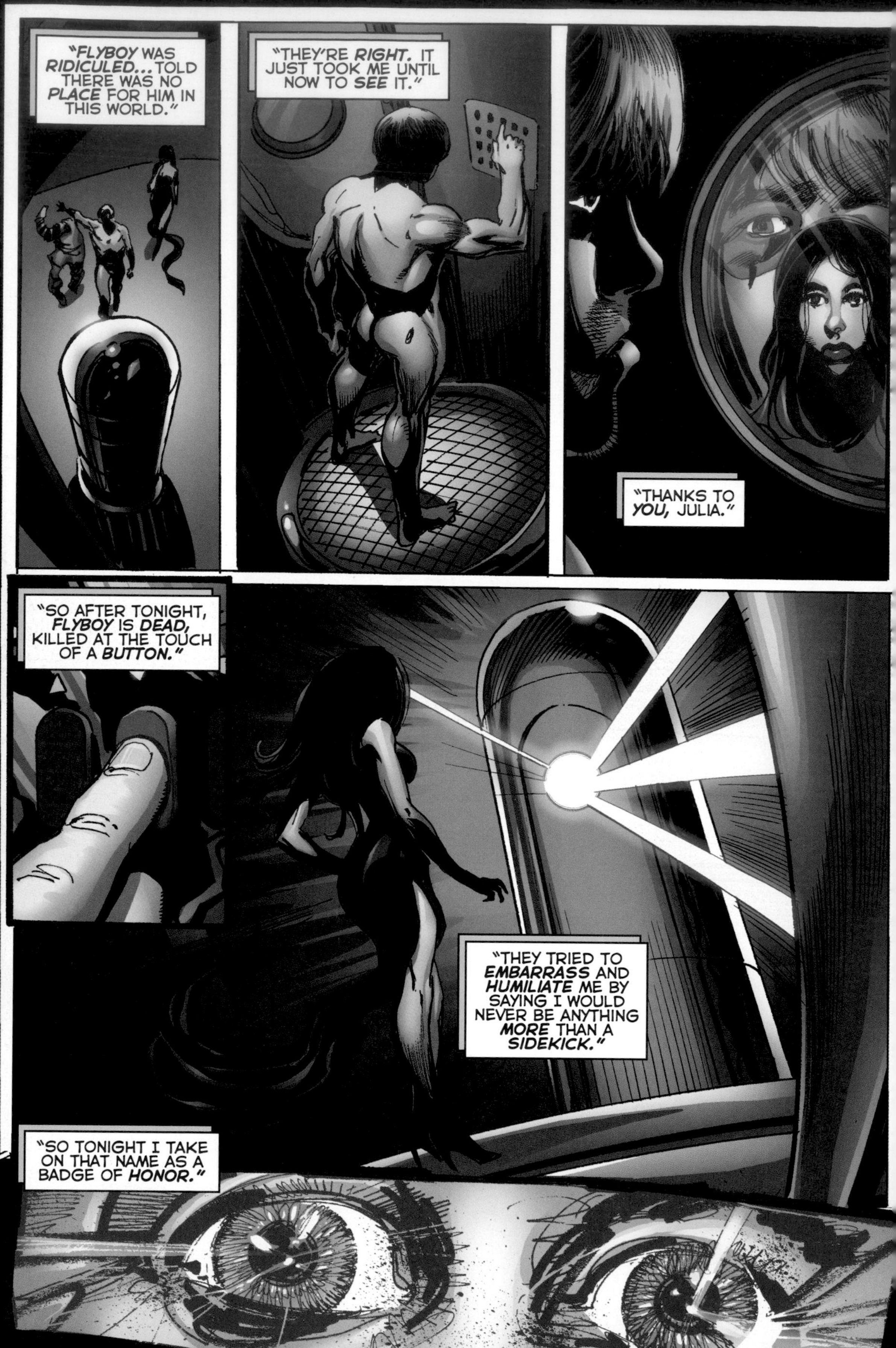
"FLYBOY WAS RIDICULED... TOLD THERE WAS NO PLACE FOR HIM IN THIS WORLD."
"THEY'RE RIGHT. IT JUST TOOK ME UNTIL NOW TO SEE IT."
"THANKS TO YOU, JULIA."
"SO AFTER TONIGHT, FLYBOY IS DEAD, KILLED AT THE TOUCH OF A BUTTON."
"THEY TRIED TO EMBARRASS AND HUMILIATE ME BY SAYING I WOULD NEVER BE ANYTHING MORE THAN A SIDEKICK."
"SO TONIGHT I TAKE ON THAT NAME AS A BADGE OF HONOR."

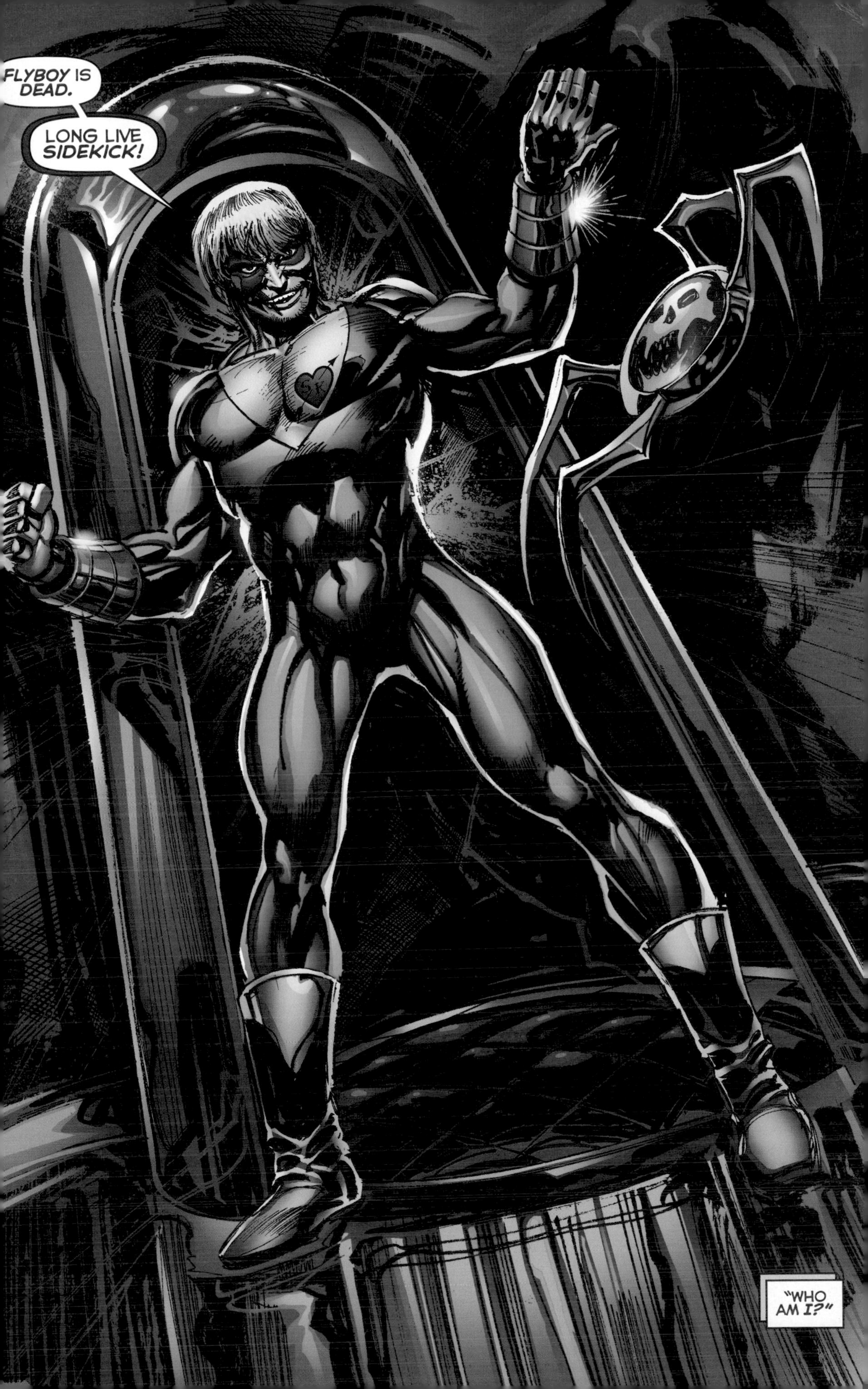
FLYBOY IS DEAD.
LONG LIVE SIDEKICK!
"WHO AM I?"

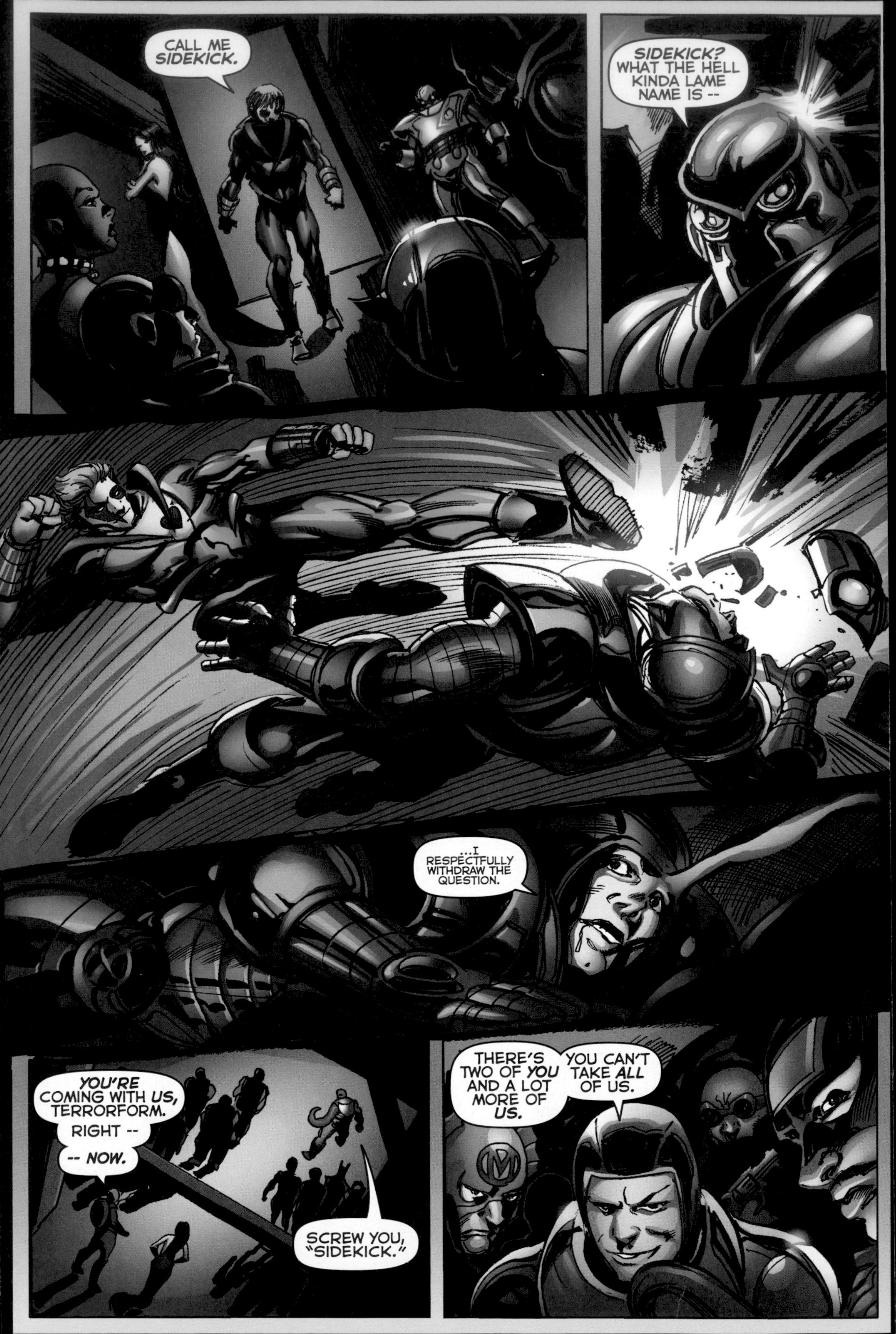
CALL ME SIDEKICK.
SIDEKICK? WHAT THE HELL KINDA LAME NAME IS --
...I RESPECTFULLY WITHDRAW THE QUESTION.
YOU'RE COMING WITH US, TERRORFORM.
RIGHT --
-- NOW.
SCREW YOU, "SIDEKICK."
THERE'S TWO OF YOU AND A LOT MORE OF US.
YOU CAN'T TAKE ALL OF US.

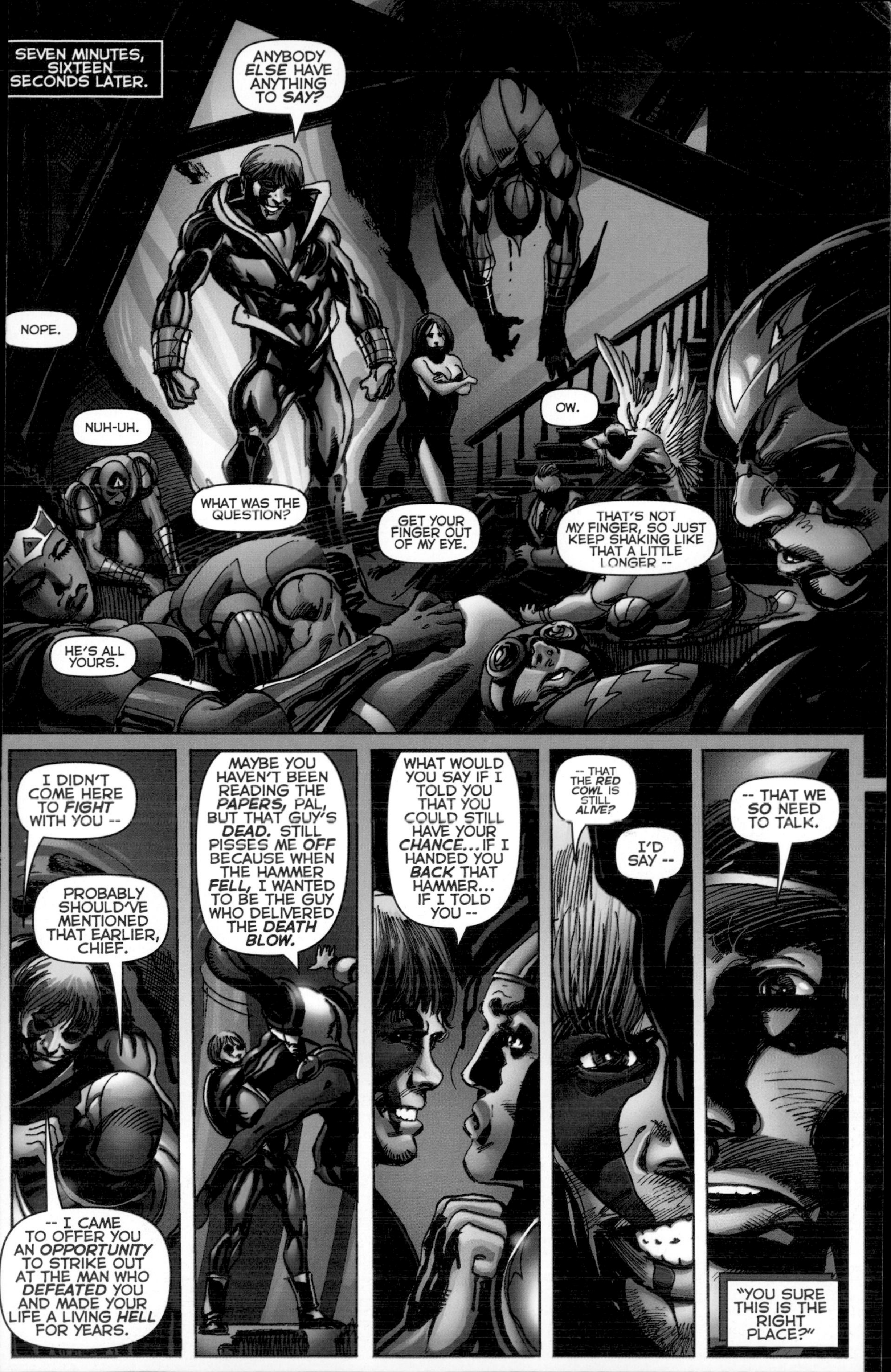
SEVEN MINUTES, SIXTEEN SECONDS LATER.
ANYBODY *ELSE* HAVE ANYTHING TO *SAY?*
NOPE.
NUH-UH.
OW.
WHAT WAS THE QUESTION?
GET YOUR FINGER OUT OF MY EYE.
THAT'S NOT MY FINGER, SO JUST KEEP SHAKING LIKE THAT A LITTLE LONGER --
HE'S ALL YOURS.
I DIDN'T COME HERE TO *FIGHT* WITH YOU --
PROBABLY SHOULD'VE MENTIONED THAT EARLIER, CHIEF.
-- I CAME TO OFFER YOU AN *OPPORTUNITY* TO STRIKE OUT AT THE MAN WHO *DEFEATED* YOU AND MADE YOUR LIFE A LIVING *HELL* FOR YEARS.
MAYBE YOU HAVEN'T BEEN READING THE *PAPERS,* PAL, BUT THAT GUY'S *DEAD.* STILL PISSES ME *OFF* BECAUSE WHEN THE HAMMER *FELL,* I WANTED TO BE THE GUY WHO DELIVERED THE *DEATH BLOW.*
WHAT WOULD YOU SAY IF I TOLD YOU THAT YOU COULD STILL HAVE YOUR *CHANCE...* IF I HANDED YOU *BACK* THAT HAMMER... IF I TOLD YOU --
-- THAT THE *RED COWL* IS STILL *ALIVE?*
I'D SAY --
-- THAT WE *SO* NEED TO TALK.
"YOU SURE THIS IS THE RIGHT PLACE?"

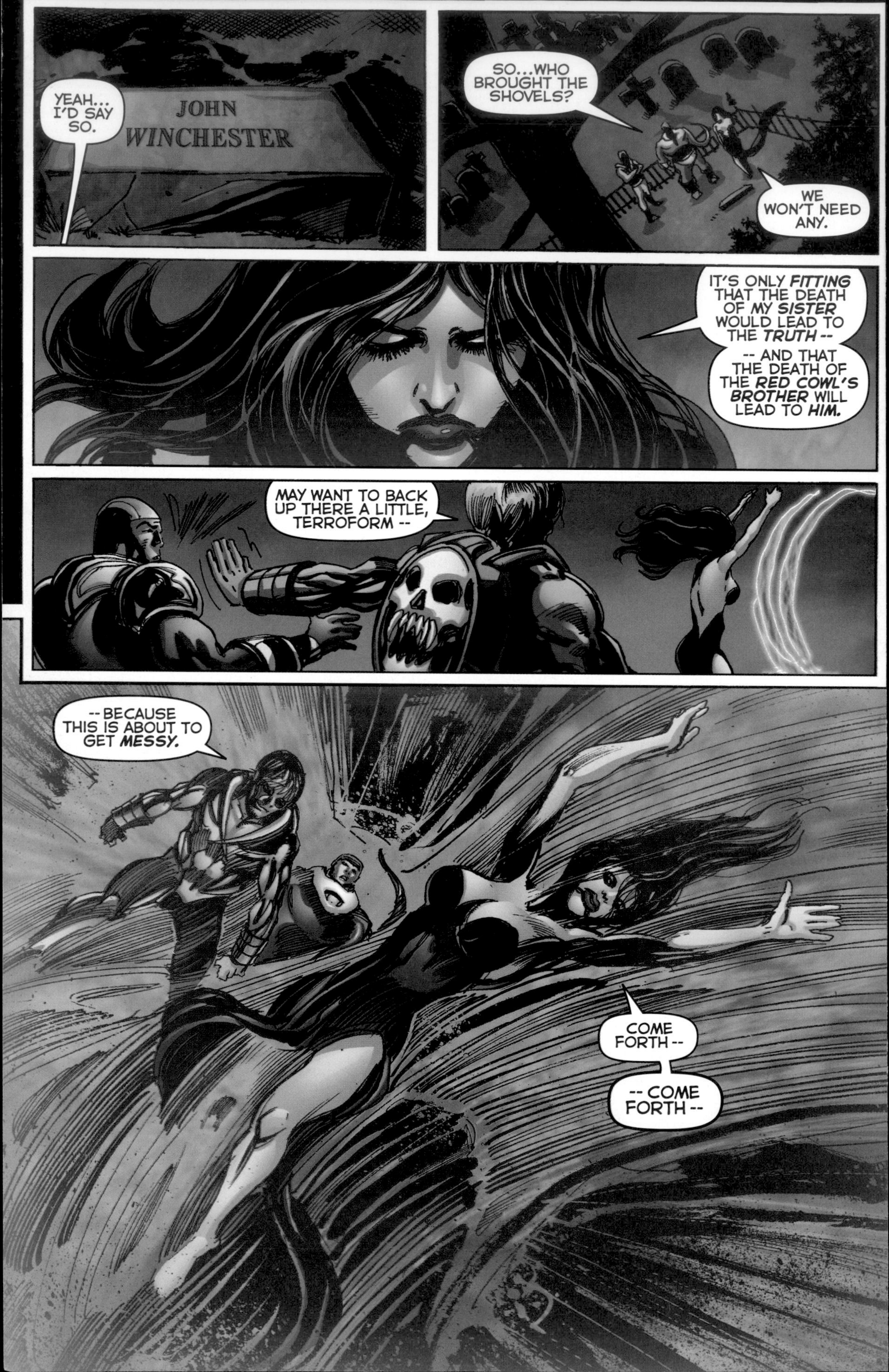
JOHN WINCHESTER
YEAH... I'D SAY SO.
SO...WHO BROUGHT THE SHOVELS?
WE WON'T NEED ANY.
IT'S ONLY FITTING THAT THE DEATH OF MY SISTER WOULD LEAD TO THE TRUTH --
-- AND THAT THE DEATH OF THE RED COWL'S BROTHER WILL LEAD TO HIM.
MAY WANT TO BACK UP THERE A LITTLE, TERROFORM --
-- BECAUSE THIS IS ABOUT TO GET MESSY.
COME FORTH --
-- COME FORTH --

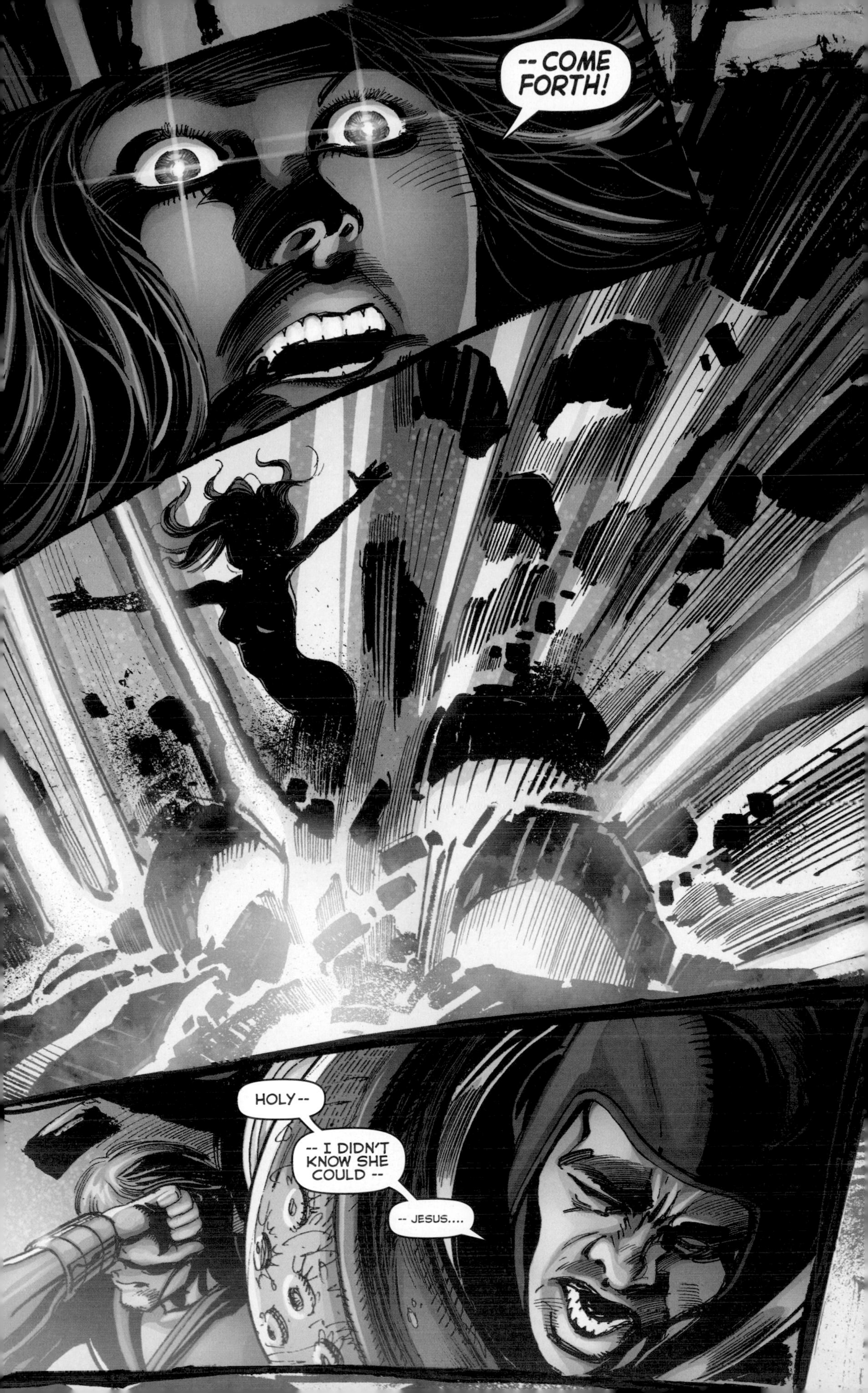
--COME FORTH!
HOLY--
-- I DIDN'T KNOW SHE COULD --
-- JESUS....

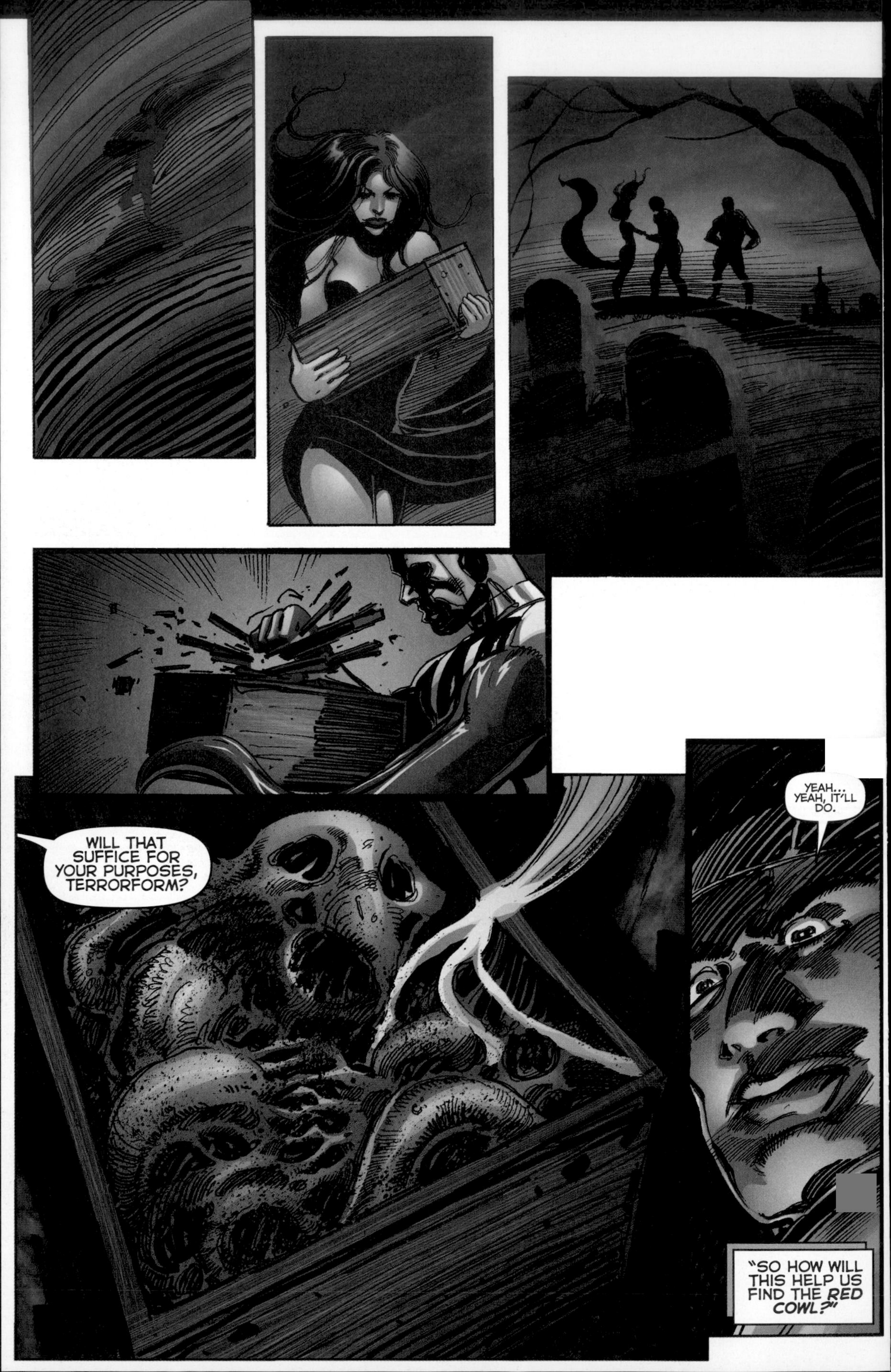
WILL THAT SUFFICE FOR YOUR PURPOSES, TERRORFORM?
YEAH... YEAH, IT'LL DO.
"SO HOW WILL THIS HELP US FIND THE *RED COWL?*"

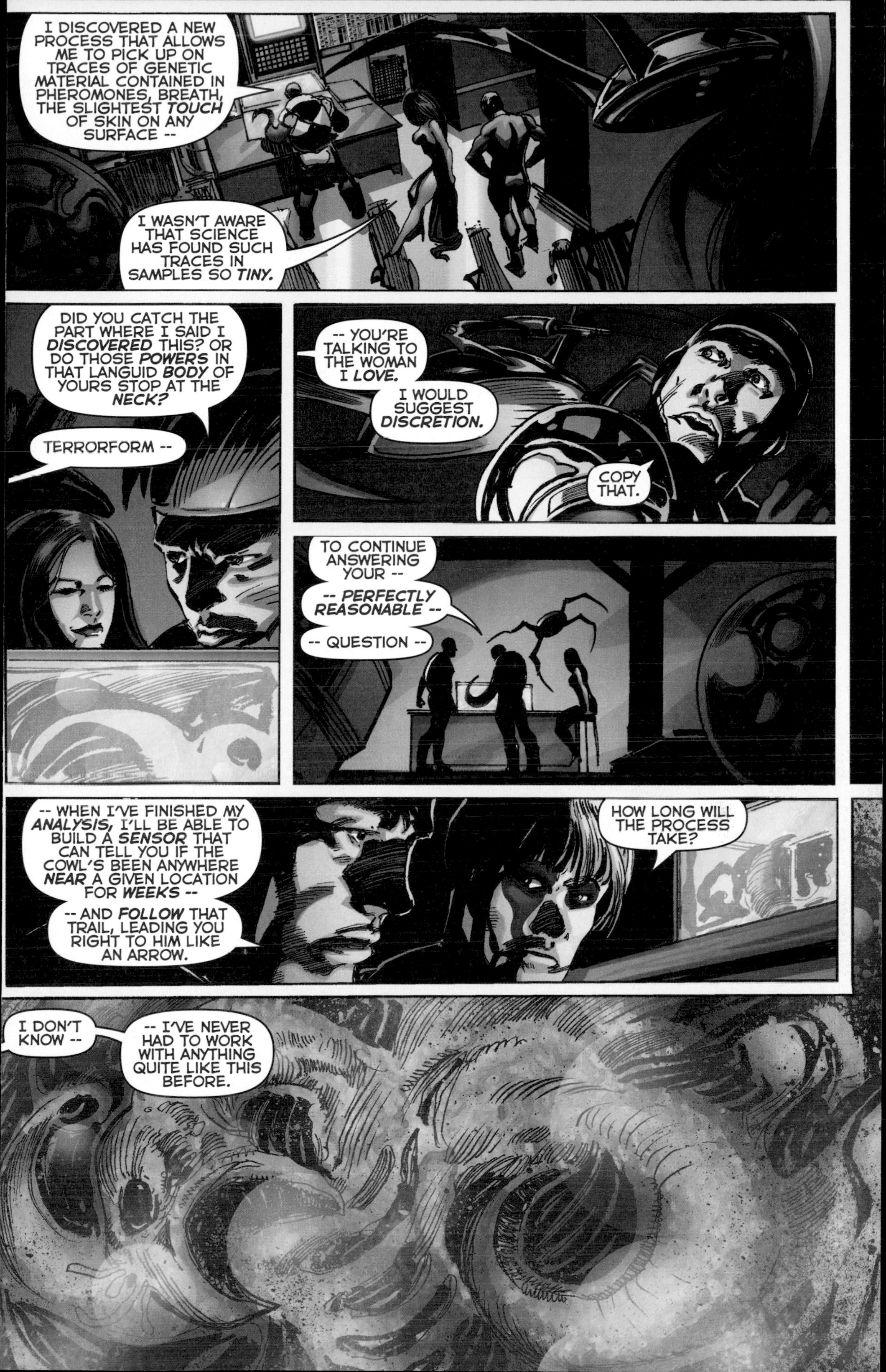

I DISCOVERED A NEW PROCESS THAT ALLOWS ME TO PICK UP ON TRACES OF GENETIC MATERIAL CONTAINED IN PHEROMONES, BREATH, THE SLIGHTEST TOUCH OF SKIN ON ANY SURFACE --
I WASN'T AWARE THAT SCIENCE HAS FOUND SUCH TRACES IN SAMPLES SO TINY.
DID YOU CATCH THE PART WHERE I SAID I DISCOVERED THIS? OR DO THOSE POWERS IN THAT LANGUID BODY OF YOURS STOP AT THE NECK?
TERRORFORM --
-- YOU'RE TALKING TO THE WOMAN I LOVE.
I WOULD SUGGEST DISCRETION.
COPY THAT.
TO CONTINUE ANSWERING YOUR --
-- PERFECTLY REASONABLE --
-- QUESTION --
-- WHEN I'VE FINISHED MY ANALYSIS, I'LL BE ABLE TO BUILD A SENSOR THAT CAN TELL YOU IF THE COWL'S BEEN ANYWHERE NEAR A GIVEN LOCATION FOR WEEKS --
-- AND FOLLOW THAT TRAIL, LEADING YOU RIGHT TO HIM LIKE AN ARROW.
HOW LONG WILL THE PROCESS TAKE?
I DON'T KNOW --
-- I'VE NEVER HAD TO WORK WITH ANYTHING QUITE LIKE THIS BEFORE.

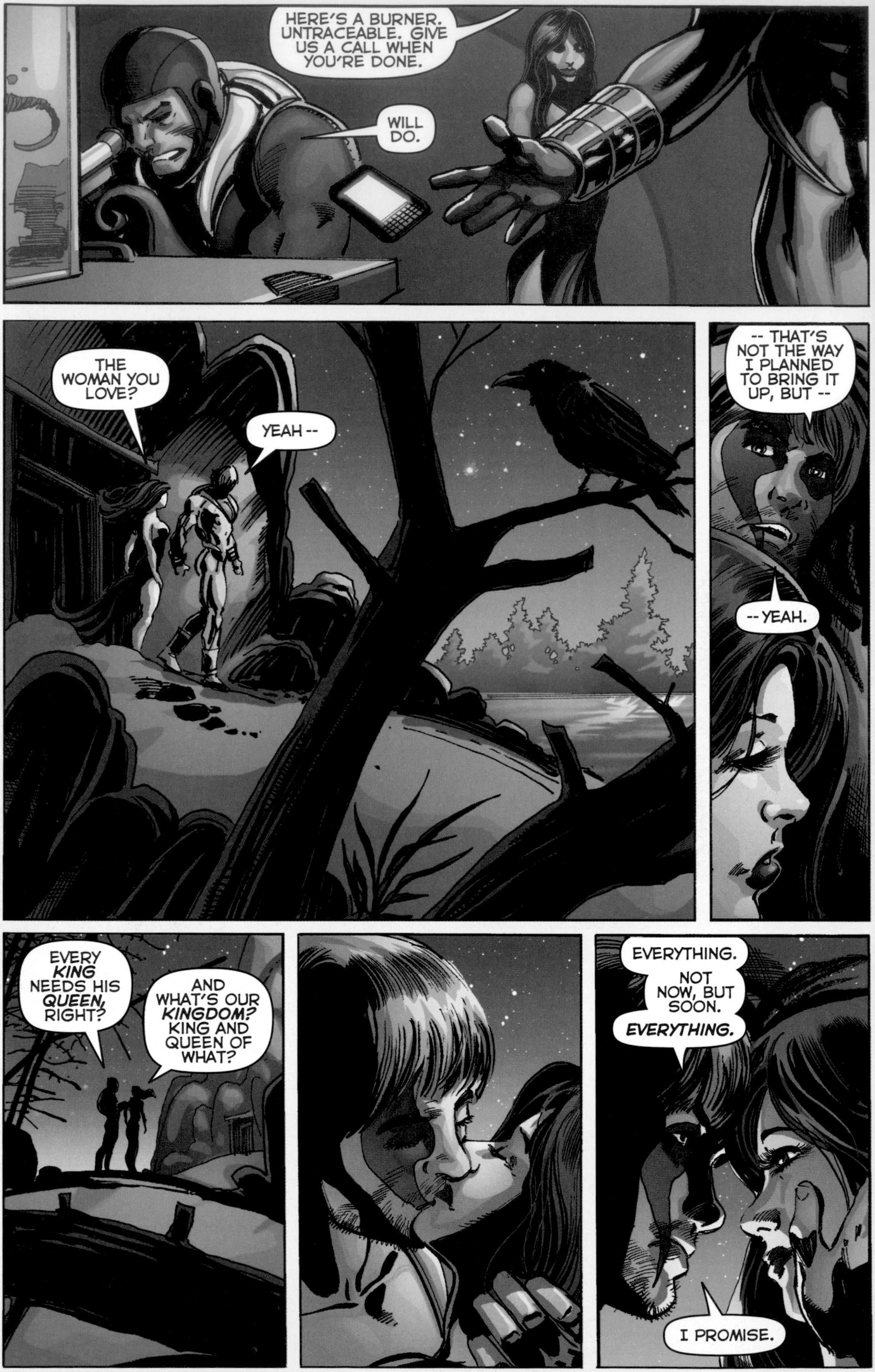
HERE'S A BURNER. UNTRACEABLE. GIVE US A CALL WHEN YOU'RE DONE.
WILL DO.
THE WOMAN YOU LOVE?
YEAH --
-- THAT'S NOT THE WAY I PLANNED TO BRING IT UP, BUT --
-- YEAH.
EVERY *KING* NEEDS HIS *QUEEN,* RIGHT?
AND WHAT'S OUR *KINGDOM?* KING AND QUEEN OF WHAT?
EVERYTHING.
NOT NOW, BUT SOON.
EVERYTHING.
I PROMISE.

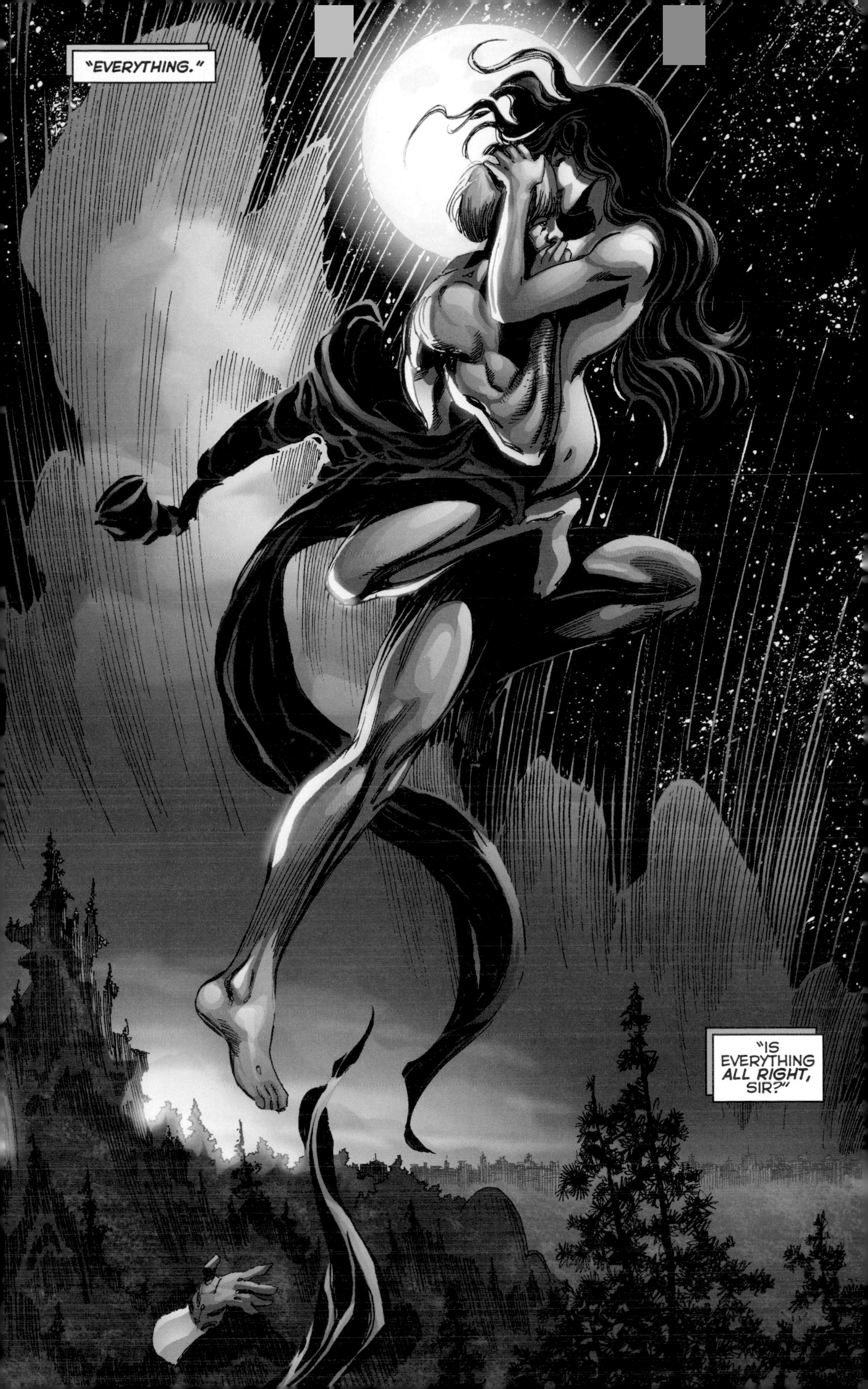
"EVERYTHING."
"IS EVERYTHING ALL RIGHT, SIR?"

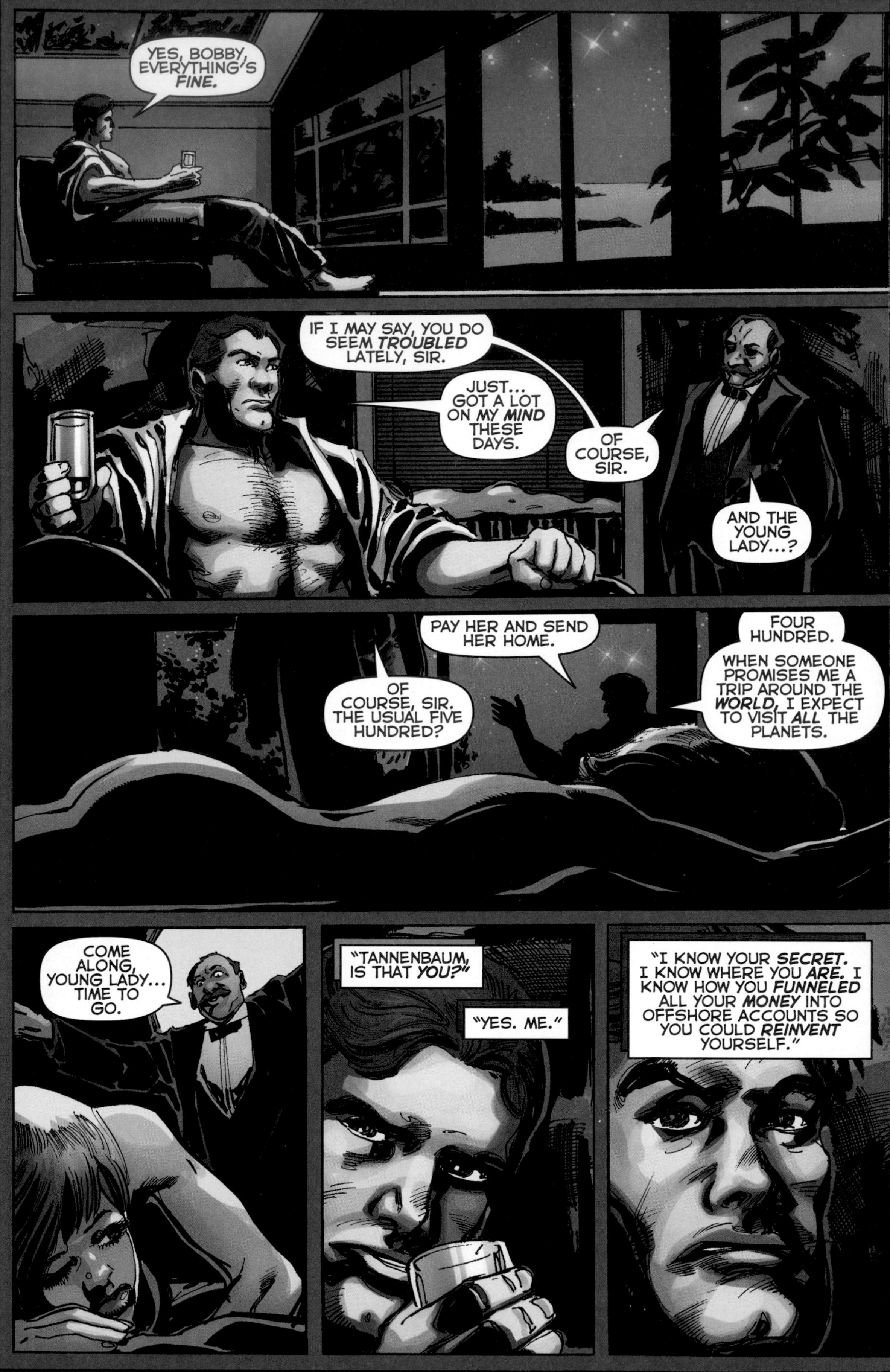
YES, BOBBY, EVERYTHING'S *FINE.*
IF I MAY SAY, YOU DO SEEM *TROUBLED* LATELY, SIR.
JUST... GOT A LOT ON MY *MIND* THESE DAYS.
OF COURSE, SIR.
AND THE YOUNG LADY...?
PAY HER AND SEND HER HOME.
OF COURSE, SIR. THE USUAL FIVE HUNDRED?
FOUR HUNDRED.
WHEN SOMEONE PROMISES ME A TRIP AROUND THE *WORLD,* I EXPECT TO VISIT *ALL* THE PLANETS.
COME ALONG, YOUNG LADY... TIME TO GO.
"TANNENBAUM, IS THAT *YOU?*"
"YES. ME."
"I KNOW YOUR *SECRET.* I KNOW WHERE YOU *ARE.* I KNOW HOW YOU *FUNNELED* ALL YOUR *MONEY* INTO OFFSHORE ACCOUNTS SO YOU COULD *REINVENT* YOURSELF."

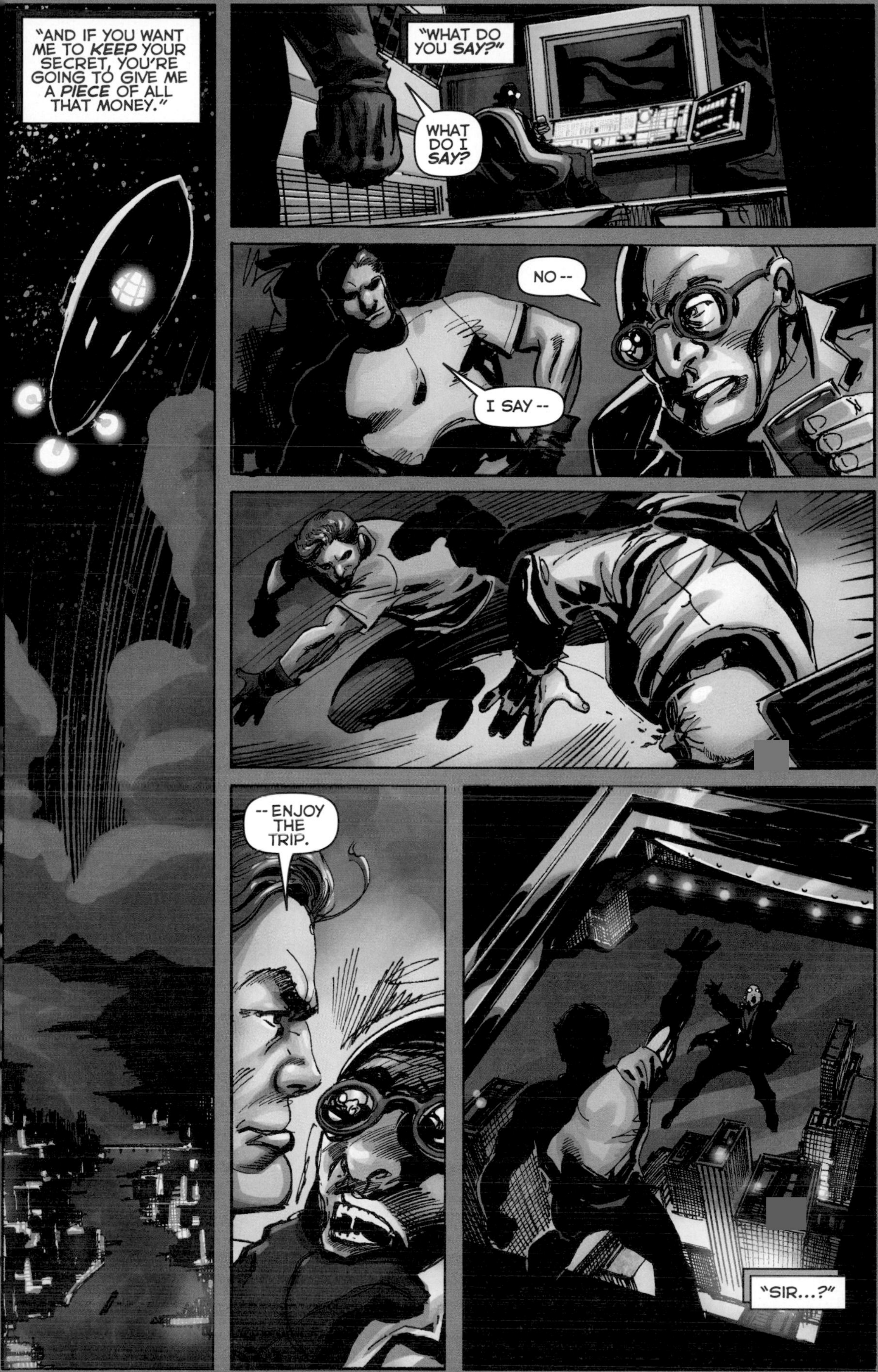

"AND IF YOU WANT ME TO KEEP YOUR SECRET, YOU'RE GOING TO GIVE ME A PIECE OF ALL THAT MONEY."
"WHAT DO YOU SAY?"
WHAT DO I SAY?
NO --
I SAY --
-- ENJOY THE TRIP.
"SIR...?"

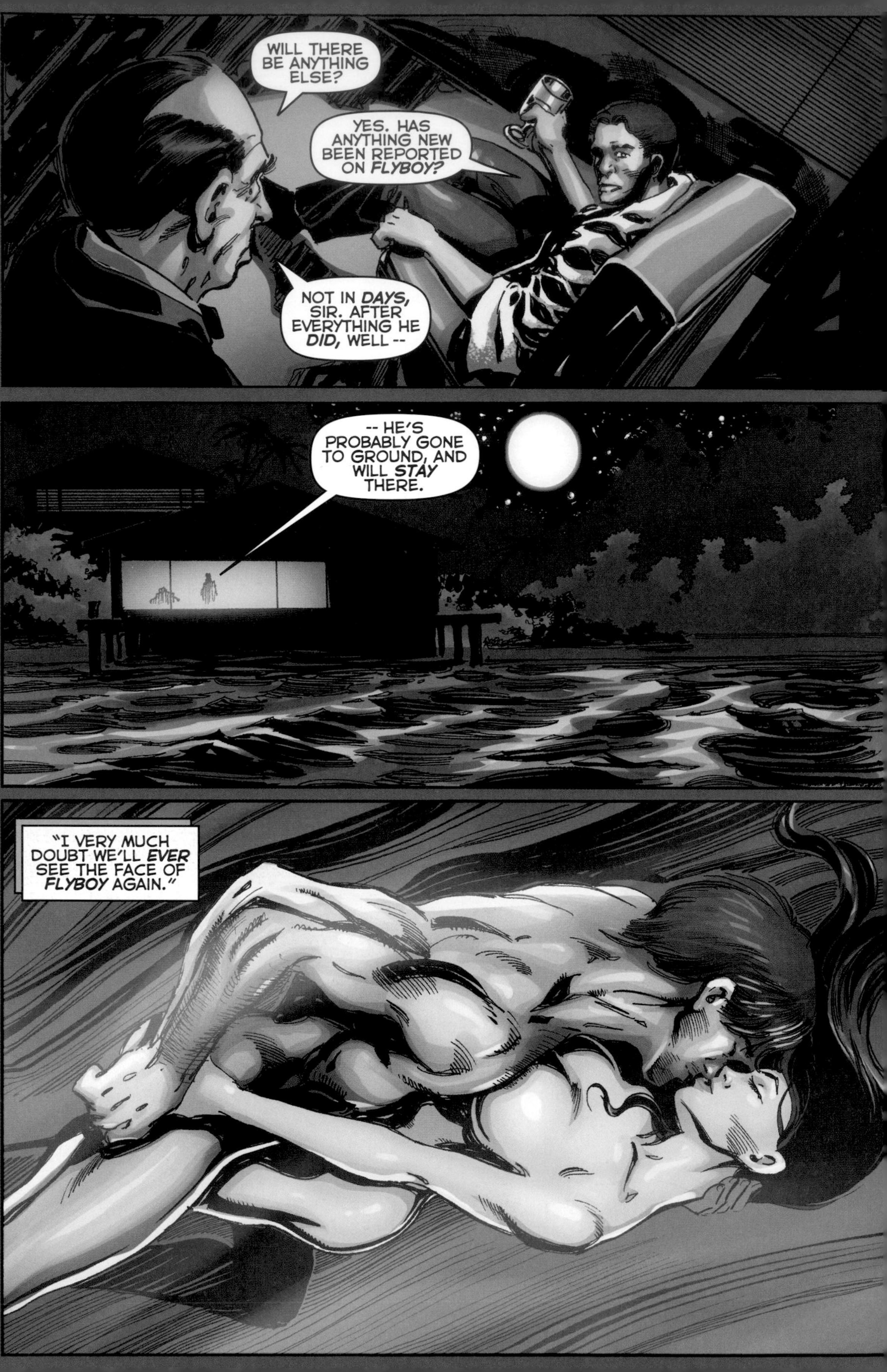
WILL THERE BE ANYTHING ELSE?
YES. HAS ANYTHING NEW BEEN REPORTED ON *FLYBOY?*
NOT IN *DAYS,* SIR. AFTER EVERYTHING HE *DID,* WELL --
-- HE'S PROBABLY GONE TO GROUND, AND WILL *STAY* THERE.
"I VERY MUCH DOUBT WE'LL *EVER* SEE THE FACE OF *FLYBOY* AGAIN."

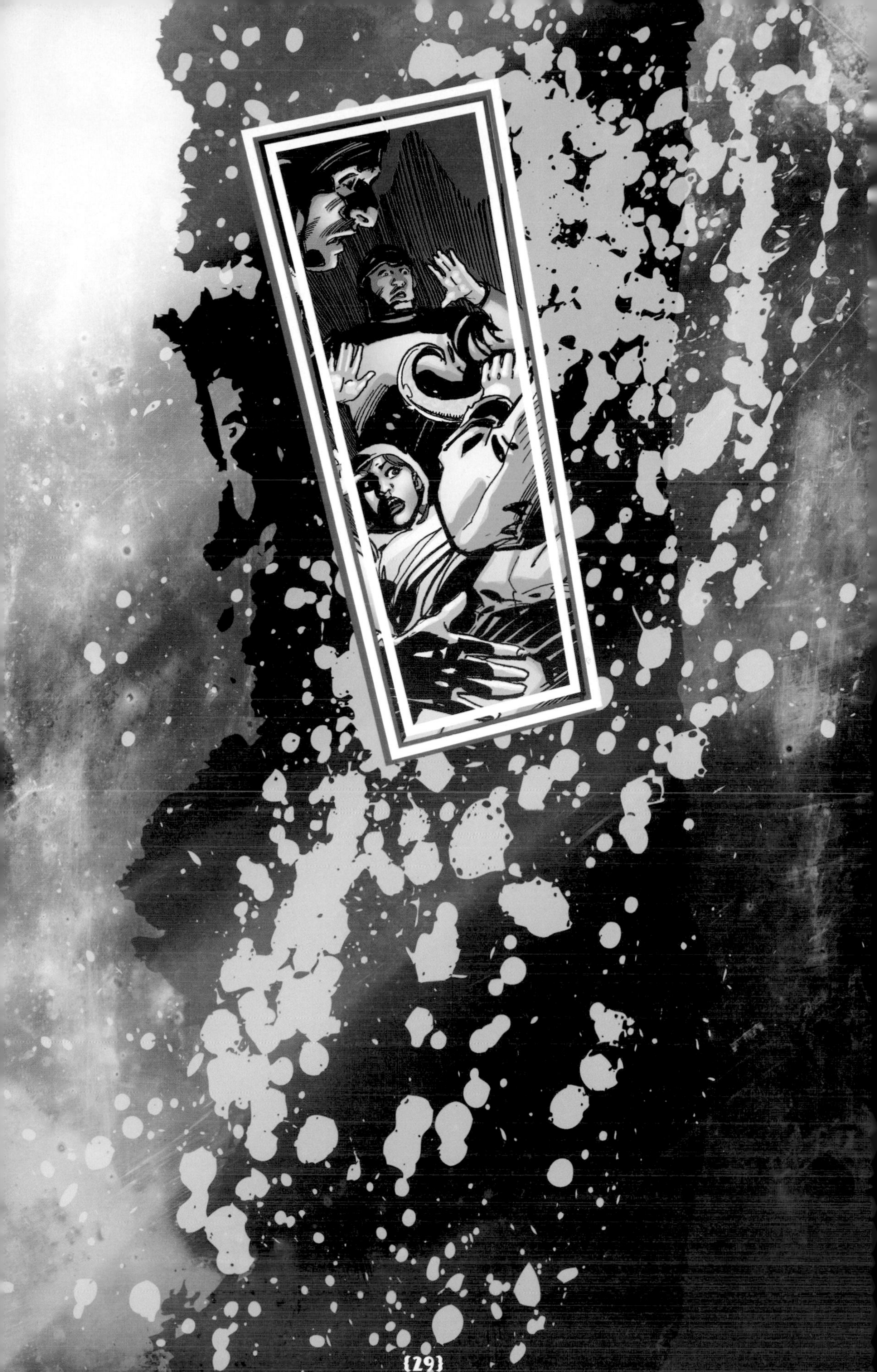

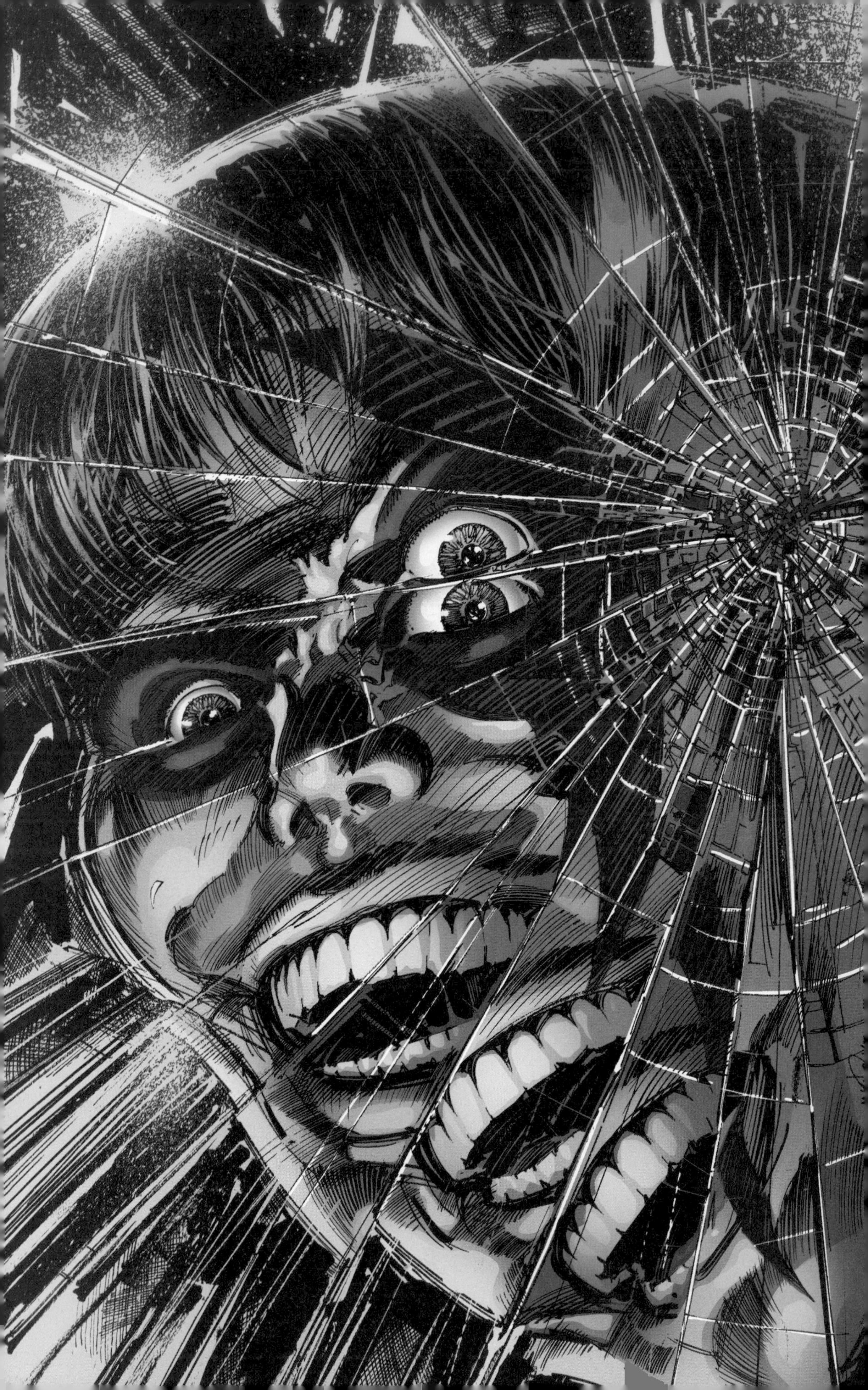

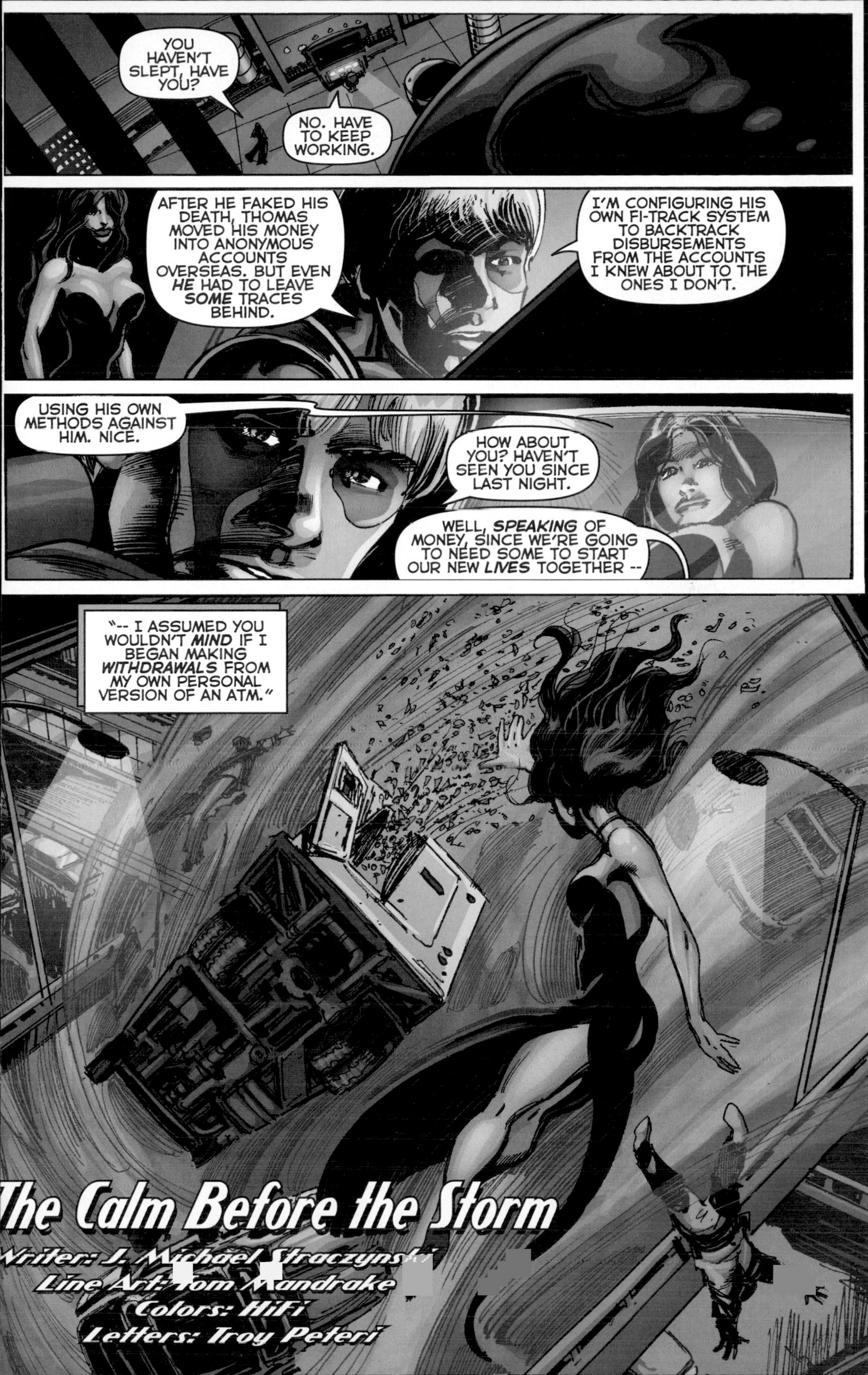
YOU HAVEN'T SLEPT, HAVE YOU?
NO. HAVE TO KEEP WORKING.
AFTER HE FAKED HIS DEATH, THOMAS MOVED HIS MONEY INTO ANONYMOUS ACCOUNTS OVERSEAS. BUT EVEN HE HAD TO LEAVE SOME TRACES BEHIND.
I'M CONFIGURING HIS OWN FI-TRACK SYSTEM TO BACKTRACK DISBURSEMENTS FROM THE ACCOUNTS I KNEW ABOUT TO THE ONES I DON'T.
USING HIS OWN METHODS AGAINST HIM. NICE.
HOW ABOUT YOU? HAVEN'T SEEN YOU SINCE LAST NIGHT.
WELL, SPEAKING OF MONEY, SINCE WE'RE GOING TO NEED SOME TO START OUR NEW LIVES TOGETHER --
"-- I ASSUMED YOU WOULDN'T MIND IF I BEGAN MAKING WITHDRAWALS FROM MY OWN PERSONAL VERSION OF AN ATM."
The Calm Before the Storm
Writer: J. Michael Straczynski
Line Art: Tom Mandrake
Colors: HiFi
Letters: Troy Peteri

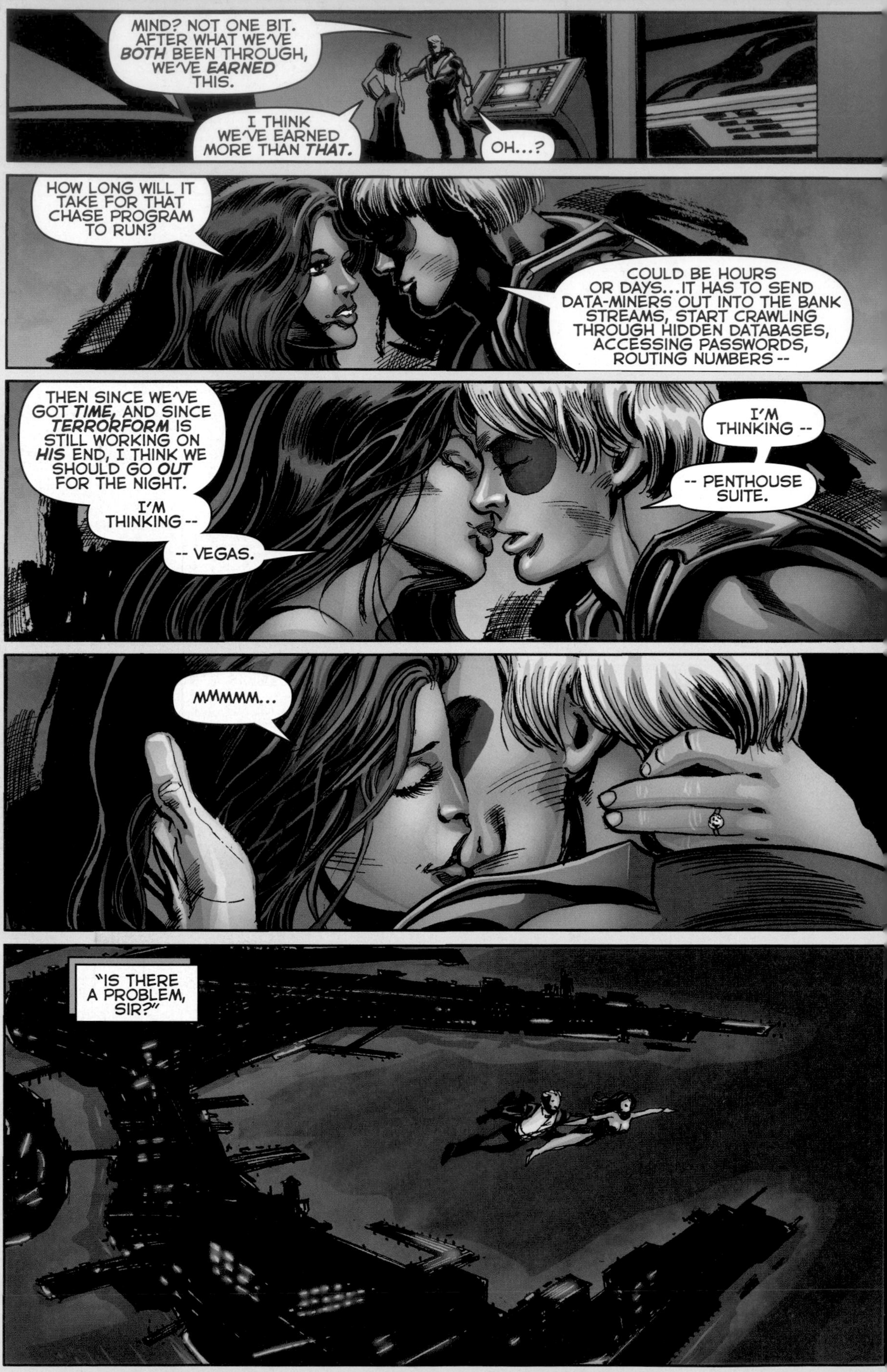
MIND? NOT ONE BIT. AFTER WHAT WE'VE *BOTH* BEEN THROUGH, WE'VE *EARNED* THIS.
I THINK WE'VE EARNED MORE THAN *THAT.*
OH...?
HOW LONG WILL IT TAKE FOR THAT CHASE PROGRAM TO RUN?
COULD BE HOURS OR DAYS...IT HAS TO SEND DATA-MINERS OUT INTO THE BANK STREAMS, START CRAWLING THROUGH HIDDEN DATABASES, ACCESSING PASSWORDS, ROUTING NUMBERS --
THEN SINCE WE'VE GOT *TIME,* AND SINCE *TERRORFORM* IS STILL WORKING ON *HIS* END, I THINK WE SHOULD GO *OUT* FOR THE NIGHT.
I'M THINKING --
-- VEGAS.
I'M THINKING --
-- PENTHOUSE SUITE.
MMMMM...
"IS THERE A PROBLEM, SIR?"

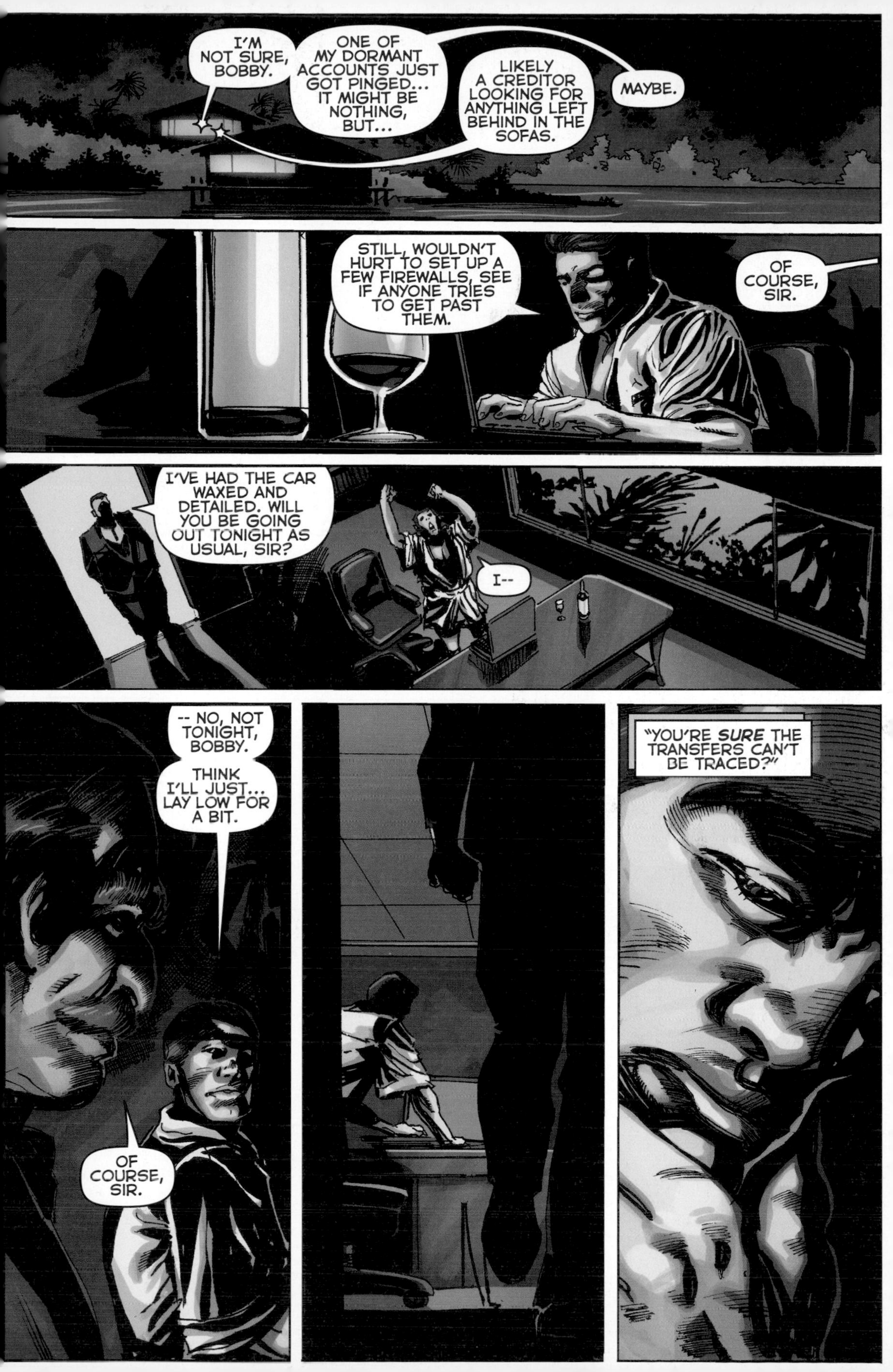
I'M NOT SURE, BOBBY.
ONE OF MY DORMANT ACCOUNTS JUST GOT PINGED... IT MIGHT BE NOTHING, BUT...
LIKELY A CREDITOR LOOKING FOR ANYTHING LEFT BEHIND IN THE SOFAS.
MAYBE.
STILL, WOULDN'T HURT TO SET UP A FEW FIREWALLS, SEE IF ANYONE TRIES TO GET PAST THEM.
OF COURSE, SIR.
I'VE HAD THE CAR WAXED AND DETAILED. WILL YOU BE GOING OUT TONIGHT AS USUAL, SIR?
I--
-- NO, NOT TONIGHT, BOBBY.
THINK I'LL JUST... LAY LOW FOR A BIT.
OF COURSE, SIR.
"YOU'RE *SURE* THE TRANSFERS CAN'T BE TRACED?"

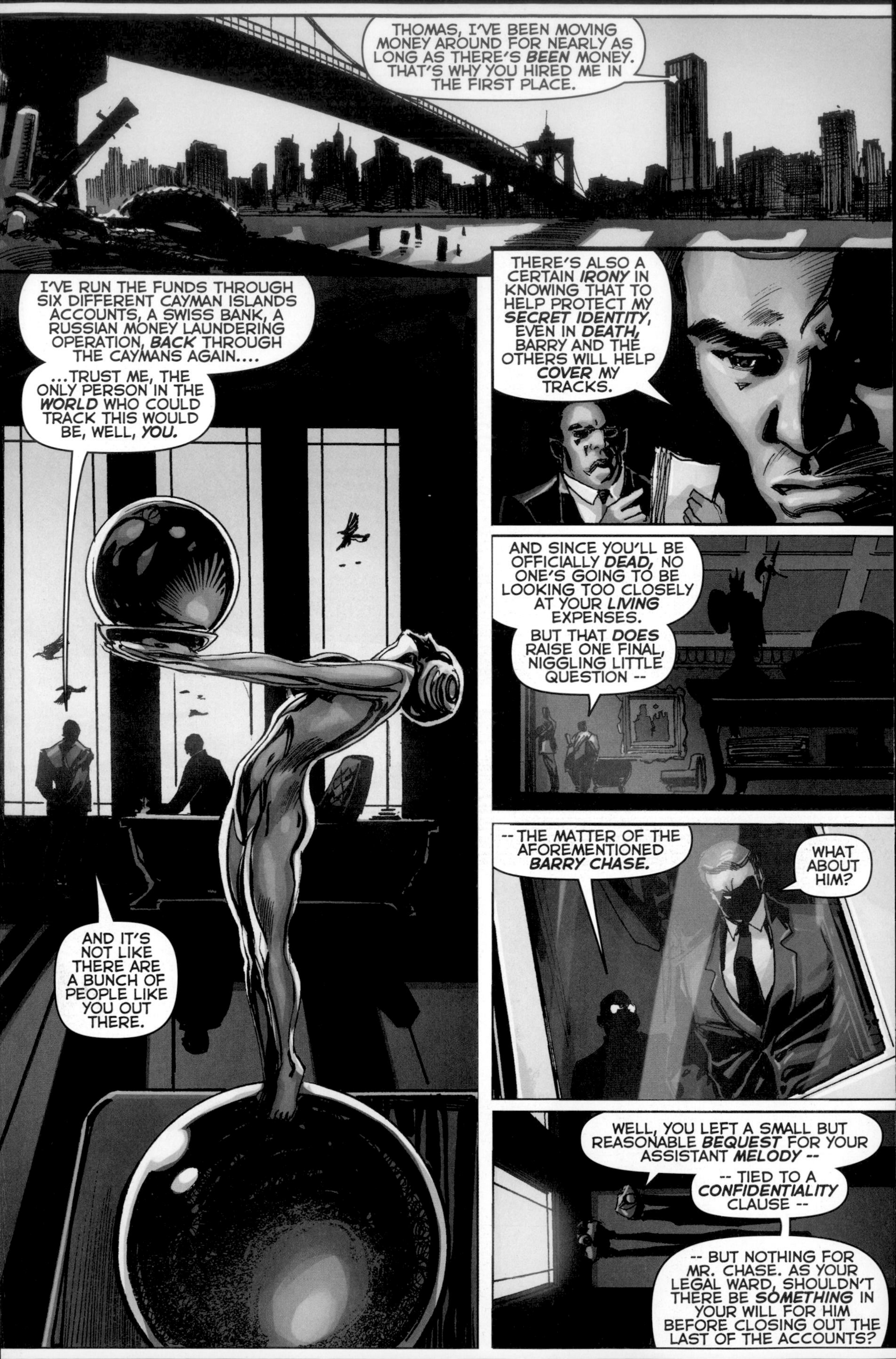
THOMAS, I'VE BEEN MOVING MONEY AROUND FOR NEARLY AS LONG AS THERE'S BEEN MONEY. THAT'S WHY YOU HIRED ME IN THE FIRST PLACE.
I'VE RUN THE FUNDS THROUGH SIX DIFFERENT CAYMAN ISLANDS ACCOUNTS, A SWISS BANK, A RUSSIAN MONEY LAUNDERING OPERATION, BACK THROUGH THE CAYMANS AGAIN....
...TRUST ME, THE ONLY PERSON IN THE WORLD WHO COULD TRACK THIS WOULD BE, WELL, YOU.
AND IT'S NOT LIKE THERE ARE A BUNCH OF PEOPLE LIKE YOU OUT THERE.
THERE'S ALSO A CERTAIN IRONY IN KNOWING THAT TO HELP PROTECT MY SECRET IDENTITY, EVEN IN DEATH, BARRY AND THE OTHERS WILL HELP COVER MY TRACKS.
AND SINCE YOU'LL BE OFFICIALLY DEAD, NO ONE'S GOING TO BE LOOKING TOO CLOSELY AT YOUR LIVING EXPENSES.
BUT THAT DOES RAISE ONE FINAL, NIGGLING LITTLE QUESTION --
-- THE MATTER OF THE AFOREMENTIONED BARRY CHASE.
WHAT ABOUT HIM?
WELL, YOU LEFT A SMALL BUT REASONABLE BEQUEST FOR YOUR ASSISTANT MELODY --
-- TIED TO A CONFIDENTIALITY CLAUSE --
-- BUT NOTHING FOR MR. CHASE. AS YOUR LEGAL WARD, SHOULDN'T THERE BE SOMETHING IN YOUR WILL FOR HIM BEFORE CLOSING OUT THE LAST OF THE ACCOUNTS?

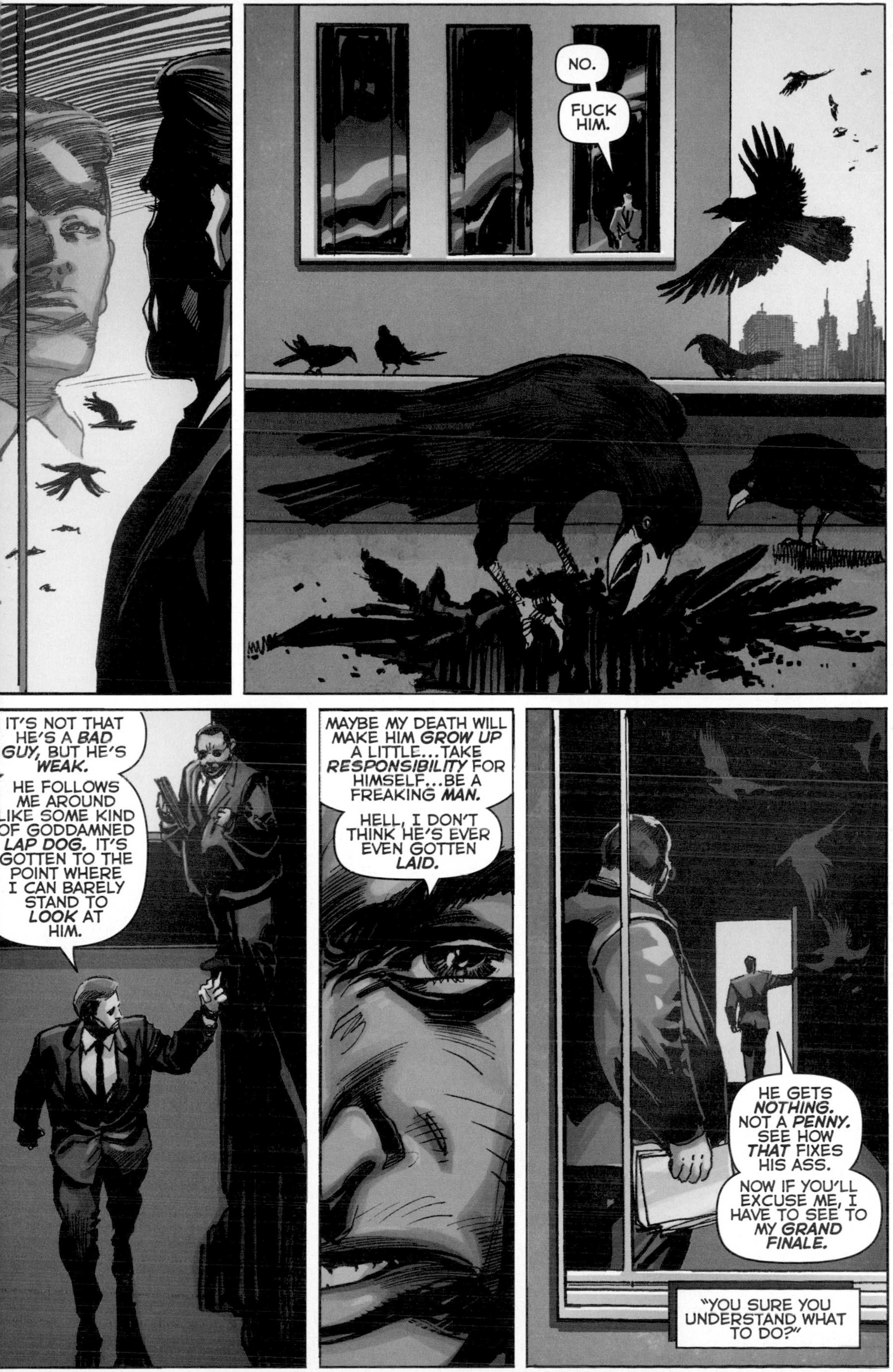
NO.
FUCK HIM.
IT'S NOT THAT HE'S A *BAD GUY,* BUT HE'S *WEAK.*
HE FOLLOWS ME AROUND LIKE SOME KIND OF GODDAMNED *LAP DOG.* IT'S GOTTEN TO THE POINT WHERE I CAN BARELY STAND TO *LOOK* AT HIM.
MAYBE MY DEATH WILL MAKE HIM *GROW UP* A LITTLE...TAKE *RESPONSIBILITY* FOR HIMSELF...BE A FREAKING *MAN.*
HELL, I DON'T THINK HE'S EVER EVEN GOTTEN *LAID.*
HE GETS *NOTHING.* NOT A *PENNY.* SEE HOW *THAT* FIXES HIS ASS.
NOW IF YOU'LL EXCUSE ME, I HAVE TO SEE TO *MY GRAND FINALE.*
"YOU SURE YOU UNDERSTAND WHAT TO DO?"

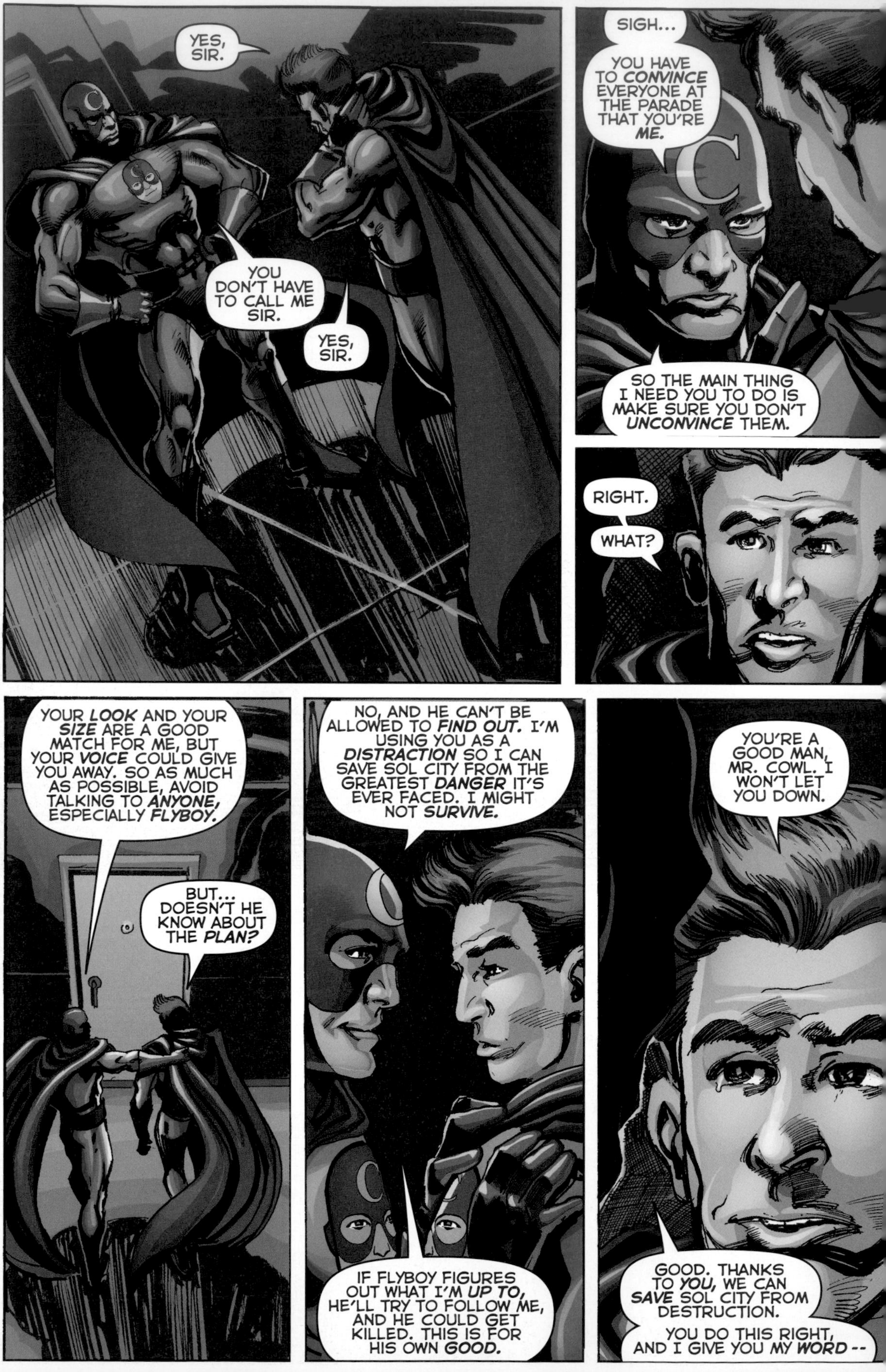
YES, SIR.
YOU DON'T HAVE TO CALL ME SIR.
YES, SIR.
SIGH...
YOU HAVE TO CONVINCE EVERYONE AT THE PARADE THAT YOU'RE ME.
SO THE MAIN THING I NEED YOU TO DO IS MAKE SURE YOU DON'T UNCONVINCE THEM.
RIGHT.
WHAT?
YOUR LOOK AND YOUR SIZE ARE A GOOD MATCH FOR ME, BUT YOUR VOICE COULD GIVE YOU AWAY. SO AS MUCH AS POSSIBLE, AVOID TALKING TO ANYONE, ESPECIALLY FLYBOY.
BUT... DOESN'T HE KNOW ABOUT THE PLAN?
NO, AND HE CAN'T BE ALLOWED TO FIND OUT. I'M USING YOU AS A DISTRACTION SO I CAN SAVE SOL CITY FROM THE GREATEST DANGER IT'S EVER FACED. I MIGHT NOT SURVIVE.
IF FLYBOY FIGURES OUT WHAT I'M UP TO, HE'LL TRY TO FOLLOW ME, AND HE COULD GET KILLED. THIS IS FOR HIS OWN GOOD.
YOU'RE A GOOD MAN, MR. COWL. I WON'T LET YOU DOWN.
GOOD. THANKS TO YOU, WE CAN SAVE SOL CITY FROM DESTRUCTION.
YOU DO THIS RIGHT, AND I GIVE YOU MY WORD --

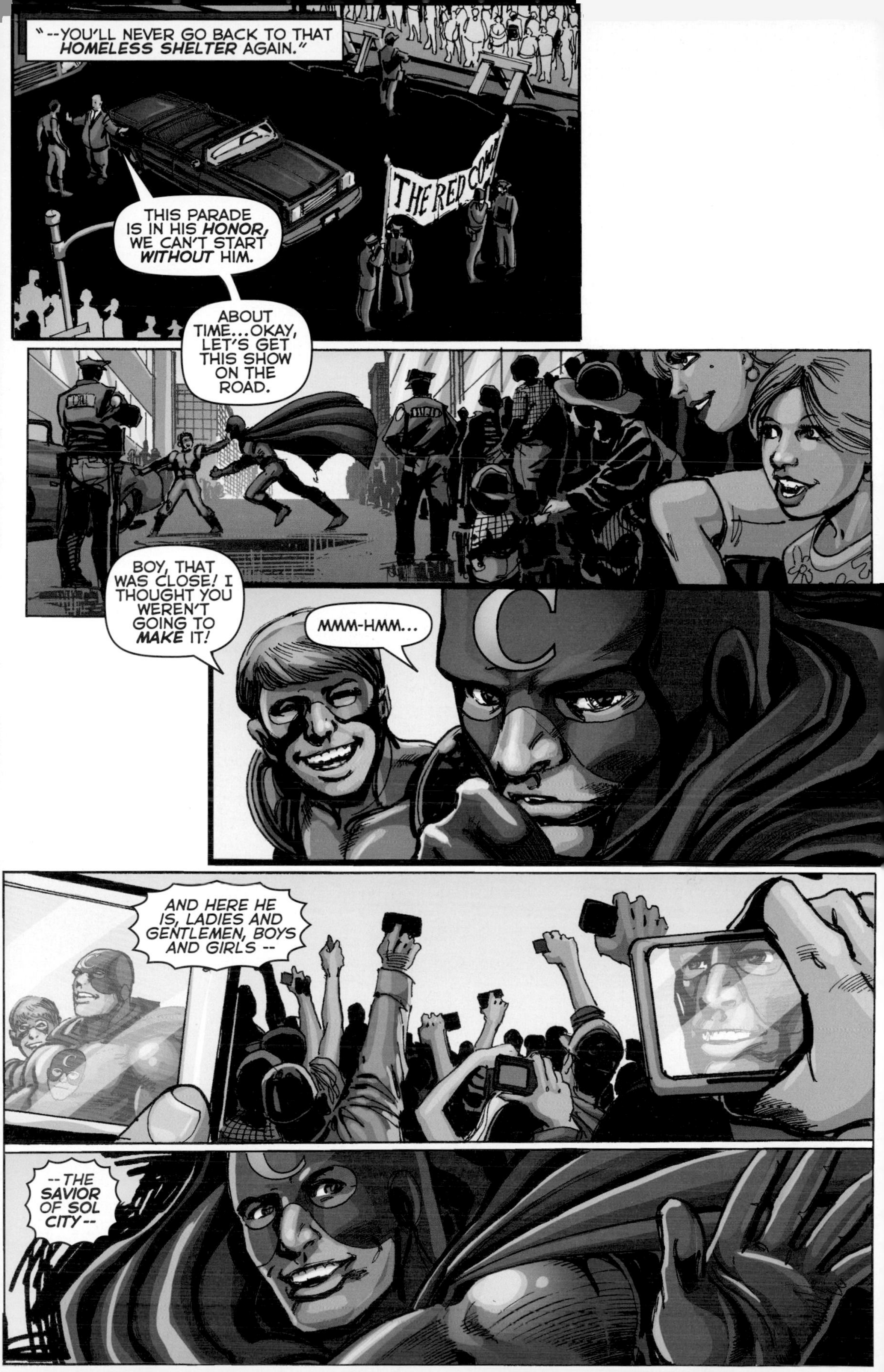
"--YOU'LL NEVER GO BACK TO THAT HOMELESS SHELTER AGAIN."
THIS PARADE IS IN HIS HONOR, WE CAN'T START WITHOUT HIM.
THE RED CO
ABOUT TIME...OKAY, LET'S GET THIS SHOW ON THE ROAD.
BOY, THAT WAS CLOSE! I THOUGHT YOU WEREN'T GOING TO MAKE IT!
MMM-HMM...
AND HERE HE IS, LADIES AND GENTLEMEN, BOYS AND GIRLS --
--THE SAVIOR OF SOL CITY--

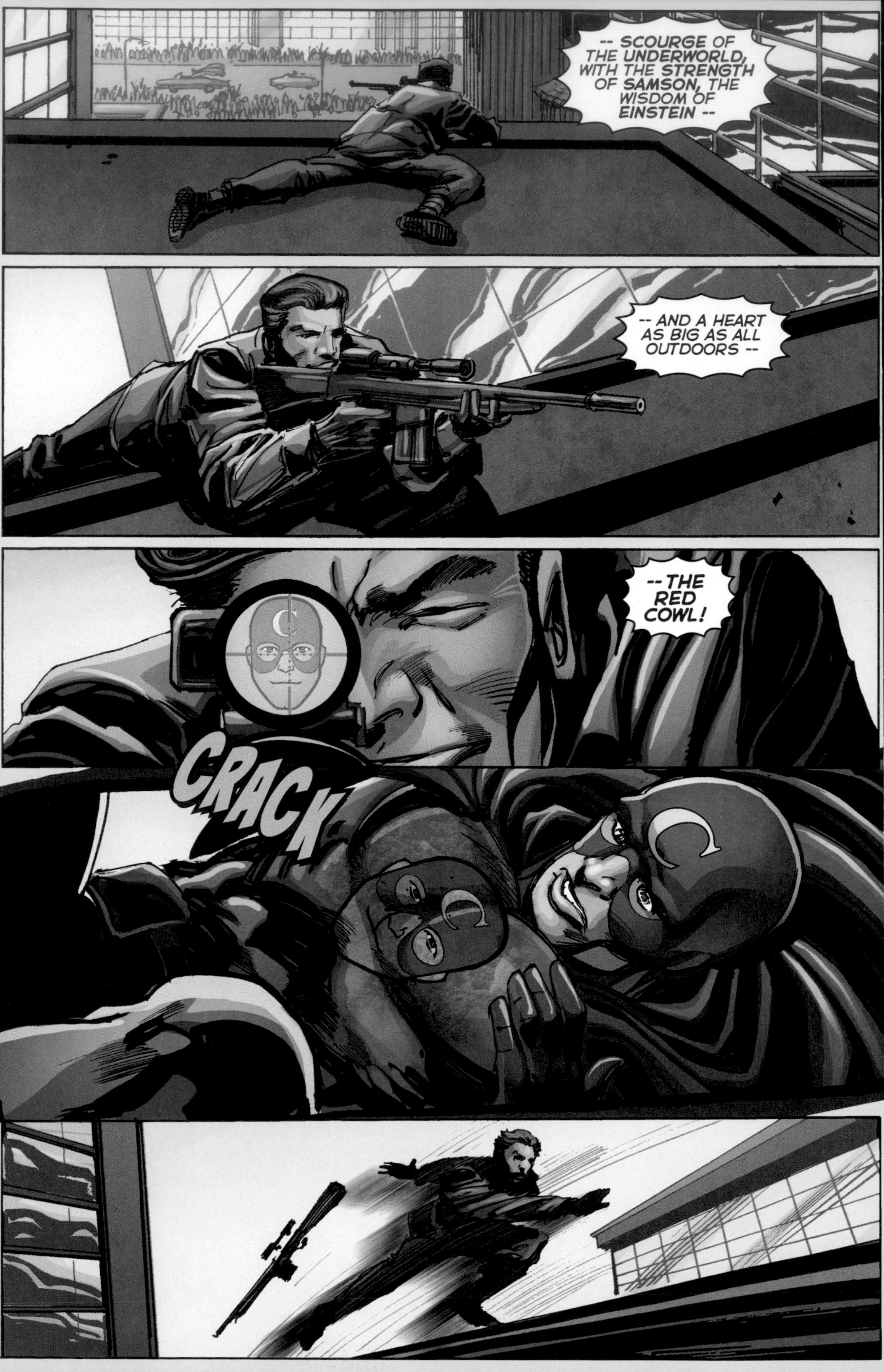
-- SCOURGE OF THE UNDERWORLD, WITH THE STRENGTH OF SAMSON, THE WISDOM OF EINSTEIN --
-- AND A HEART AS BIG AS ALL OUTDOORS --
-- THE RED COWL!
CRACK

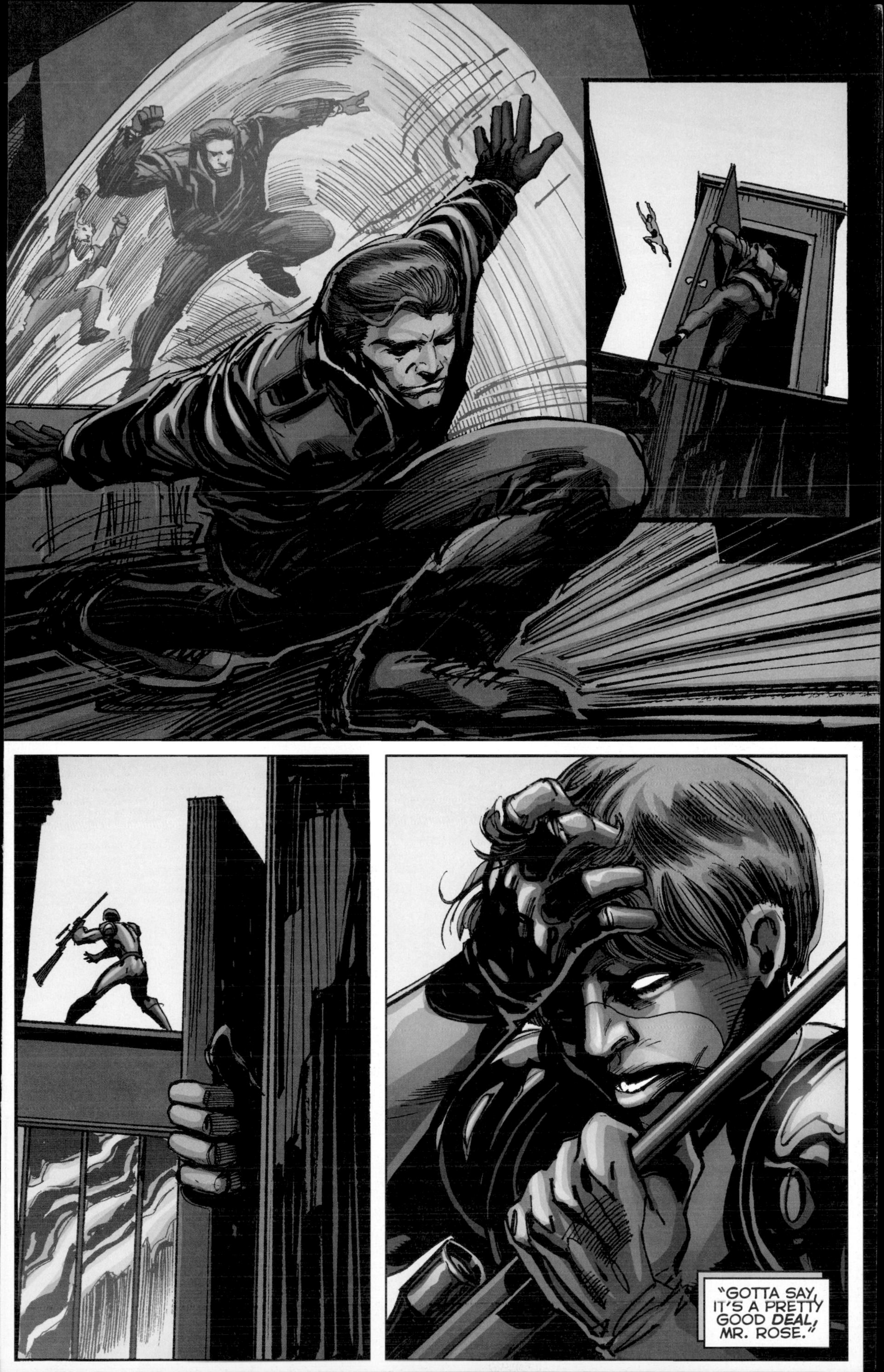
"GOTTA SAY, IT'S A PRETTY GOOD *DEAL*, MR. ROSE."

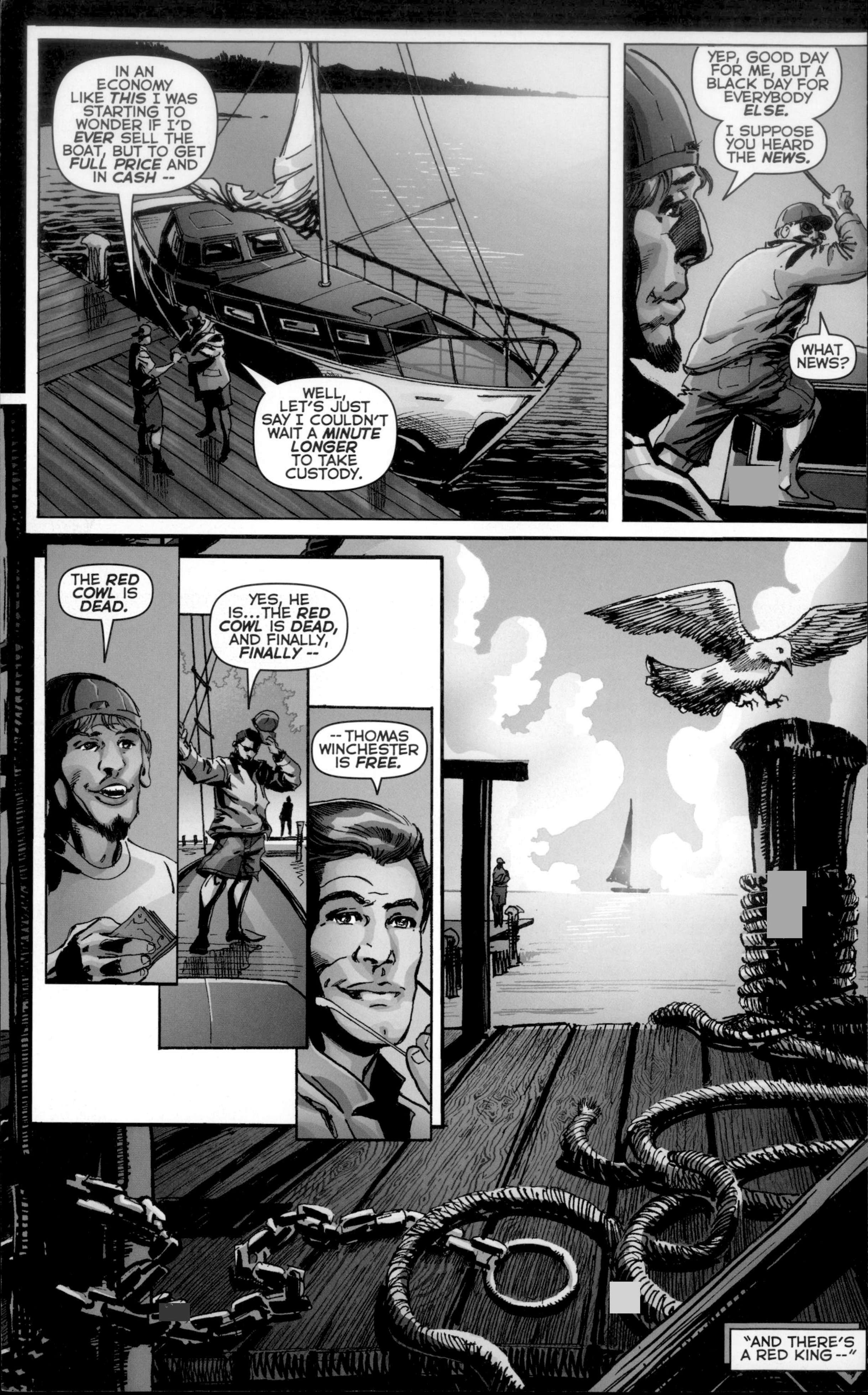
IN AN ECONOMY LIKE THIS I WAS STARTING TO WONDER IF I'D EVER SELL THE BOAT, BUT TO GET FULL PRICE AND IN CASH --
WELL, LET'S JUST SAY I COULDN'T WAIT A MINUTE LONGER TO TAKE CUSTODY.
YEP, GOOD DAY FOR ME, BUT A BLACK DAY FOR EVERYBODY ELSE.
I SUPPOSE YOU HEARD THE NEWS.
WHAT NEWS?
THE RED COWL IS DEAD.
YES, HE IS...THE RED COWL IS DEAD, AND FINALLY, FINALLY --
-- THOMAS WINCHESTER IS FREE.
"AND THERE'S A RED KING --"

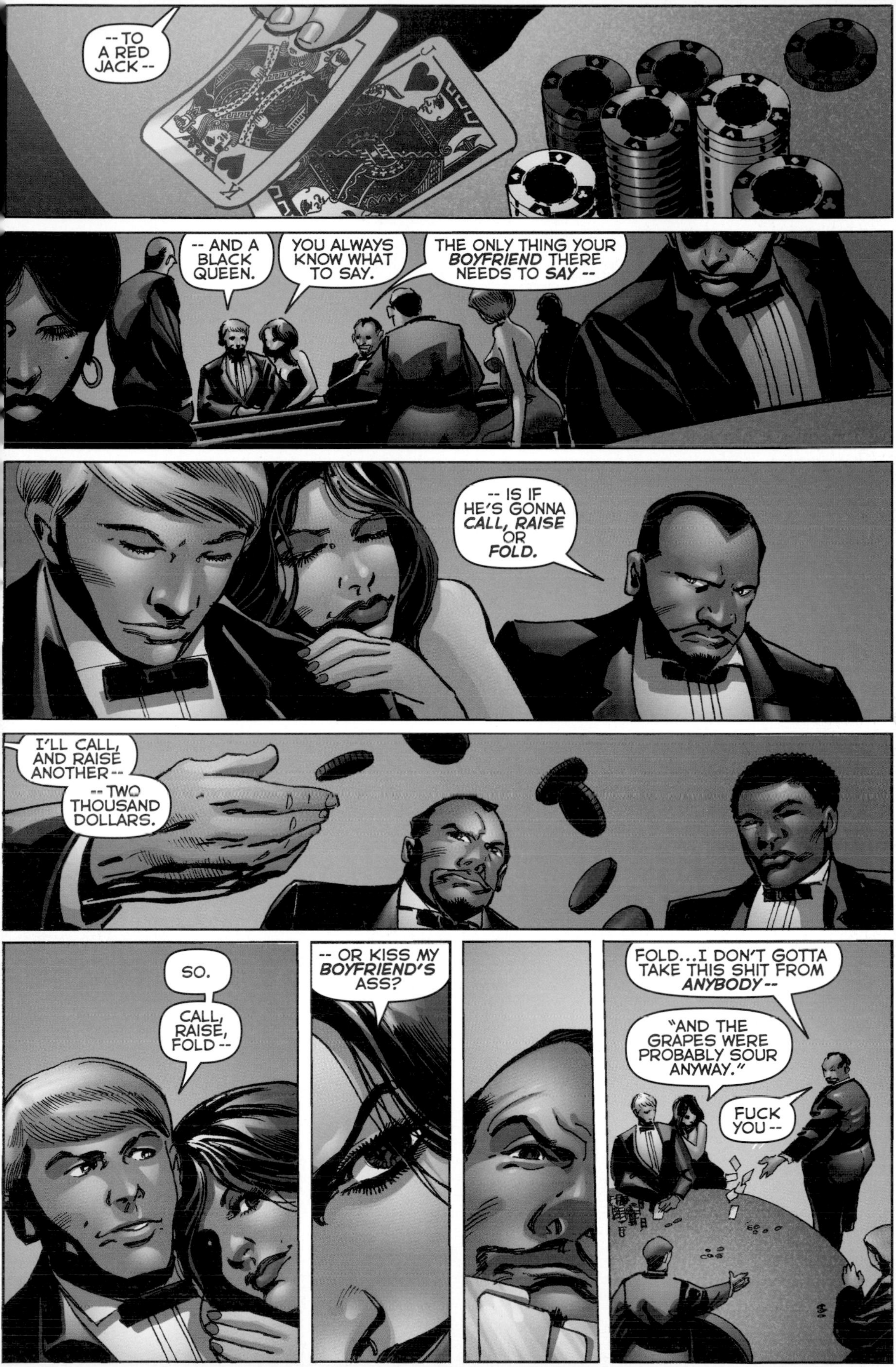
-- TO A RED JACK --
-- AND A BLACK QUEEN.
YOU ALWAYS KNOW WHAT TO SAY.
THE ONLY THING YOUR BOYFRIEND THERE NEEDS TO SAY --
-- IS IF HE'S GONNA CALL, RAISE OR FOLD.
I'LL CALL, AND RAISE ANOTHER --
-- TWO THOUSAND DOLLARS.
SO.
CALL, RAISE, FOLD --
-- OR KISS MY BOYFRIEND'S ASS?
FOLD...I DON'T GOTTA TAKE THIS SHIT FROM ANYBODY --
"AND THE GRAPES WERE PROBABLY SOUR ANYWAY."
FUCK YOU --

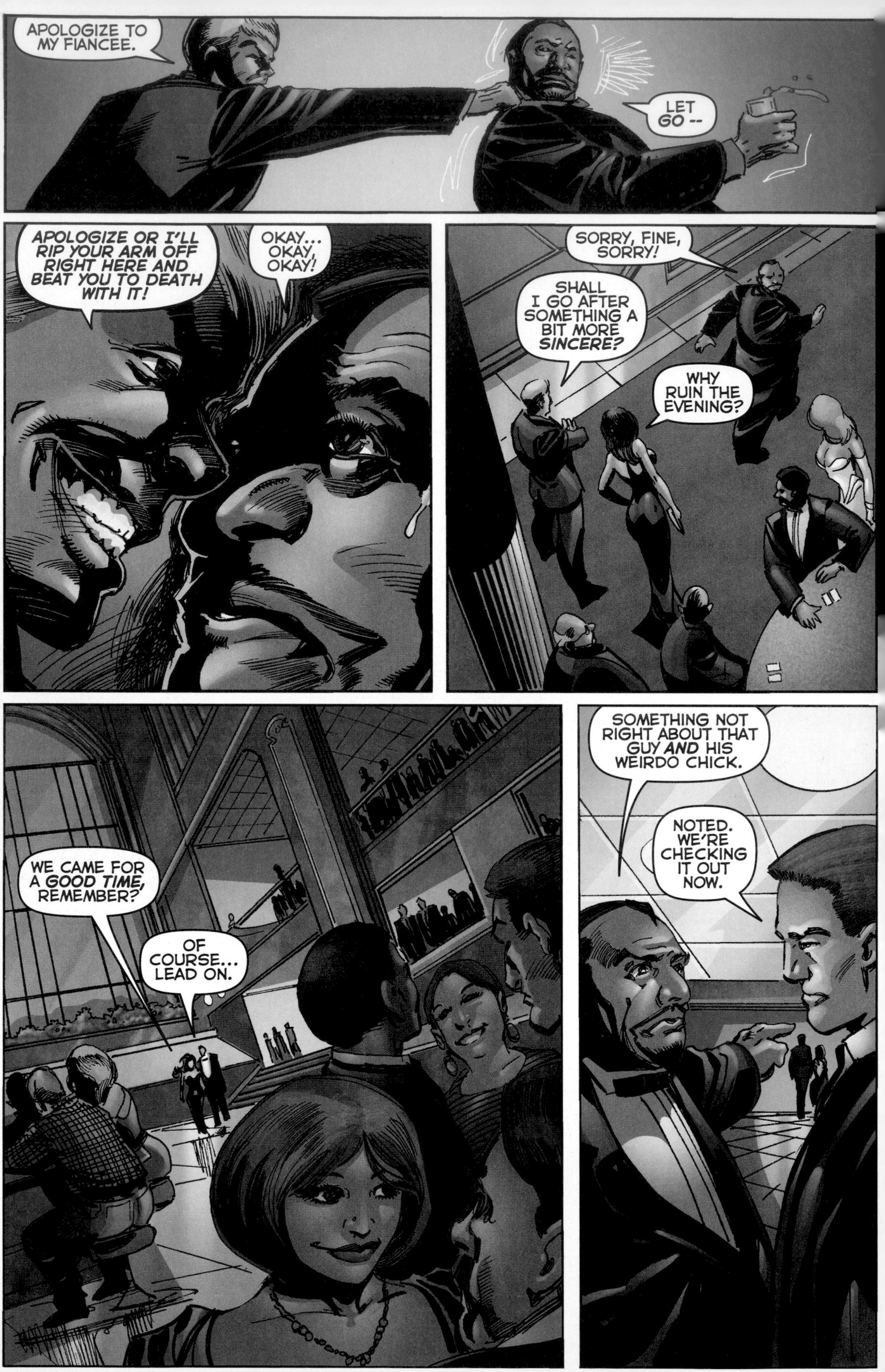
APOLOGIZE TO MY FIANCEE.
LET GO --
APOLOGIZE OR I'LL RIP YOUR ARM OFF RIGHT HERE AND BEAT YOU TO DEATH WITH IT!
OKAY... OKAY, OKAY!
SORRY, FINE, SORRY!
SHALL I GO AFTER SOMETHING A BIT MORE SINCERE?
WHY RUIN THE EVENING?
WE CAME FOR A GOOD TIME, REMEMBER?
OF COURSE... LEAD ON.
SOMETHING NOT RIGHT ABOUT THAT GUY AND HIS WEIRDO CHICK.
NOTED. WE'RE CHECKING IT OUT NOW.

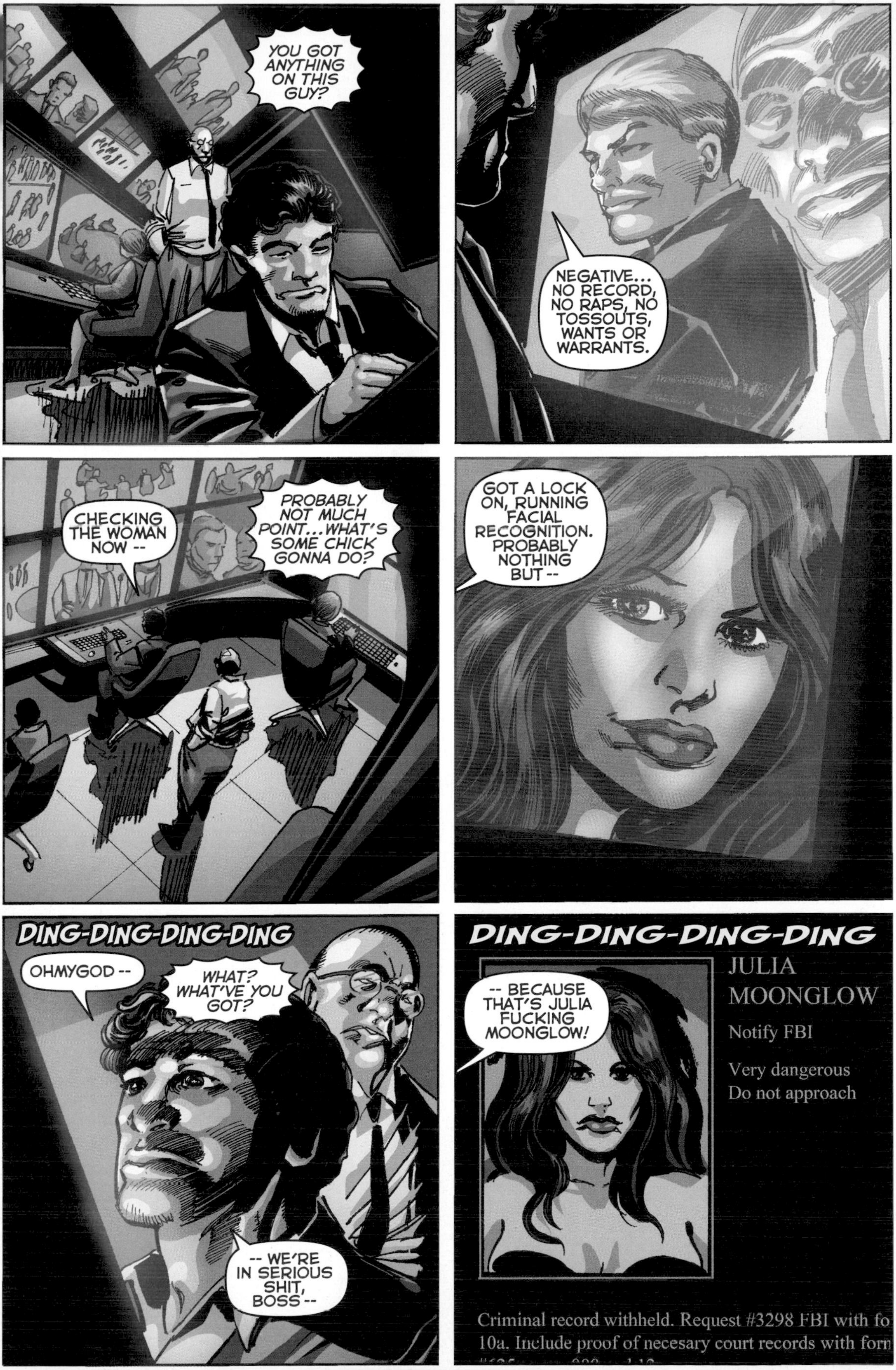
YOU GOT ANYTHING ON THIS GUY?
NEGATIVE... NO RECORD, NO RAPS, NO TOSSOUTS, WANTS OR WARRANTS.
CHECKING THE WOMAN NOW --
PROBABLY NOT MUCH POINT...WHAT'S SOME CHICK GONNA DO?
GOT A LOCK ON, RUNNING FACIAL RECOGNITION. PROBABLY NOTHING BUT --
DING-DING-DING-DING
OHMYGOD --
WHAT? WHAT'VE YOU GOT?
-- WE'RE IN SERIOUS SHIT, BOSS --
DING-DING-DING-DING
JULIA MOONGLOW
Notify FBI
Very dangerous
Do not approach
-- BECAUSE THAT'S JULIA FUCKING MOONGLOW!
Criminal record withheld. Request #3298 FBI with fo
10a. Include proof of necesary court records with forn

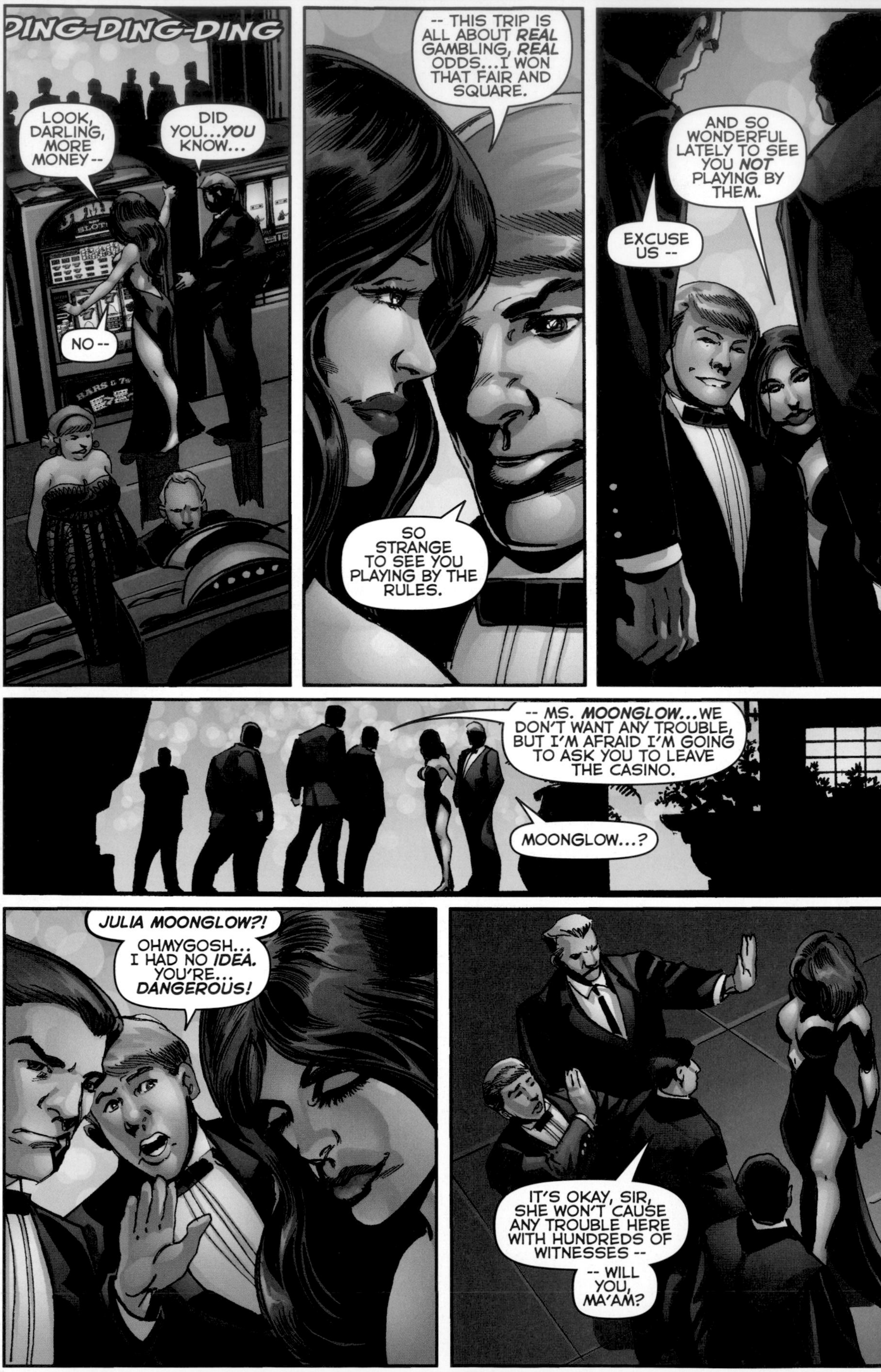
DING-DING-DING
LOOK, DARLING, MORE MONEY --
DID YOU...YOU KNOW...
NO --
-- THIS TRIP IS ALL ABOUT REAL GAMBLING, REAL ODDS...I WON THAT FAIR AND SQUARE.
SO STRANGE TO SEE YOU PLAYING BY THE RULES.
AND SO WONDERFUL LATELY TO SEE YOU NOT PLAYING BY THEM.
EXCUSE US --
-- MS. MOONGLOW...WE DON'T WANT ANY TROUBLE, BUT I'M AFRAID I'M GOING TO ASK YOU TO LEAVE THE CASINO.
MOONGLOW...?
JULIA MOONGLOW?!
OHMYGOSH... I HAD NO IDEA. YOU'RE... DANGEROUS!
IT'S OKAY, SIR, SHE WON'T CAUSE ANY TROUBLE HERE WITH HUNDREDS OF WITNESSES --
-- WILL YOU, MA'AM?

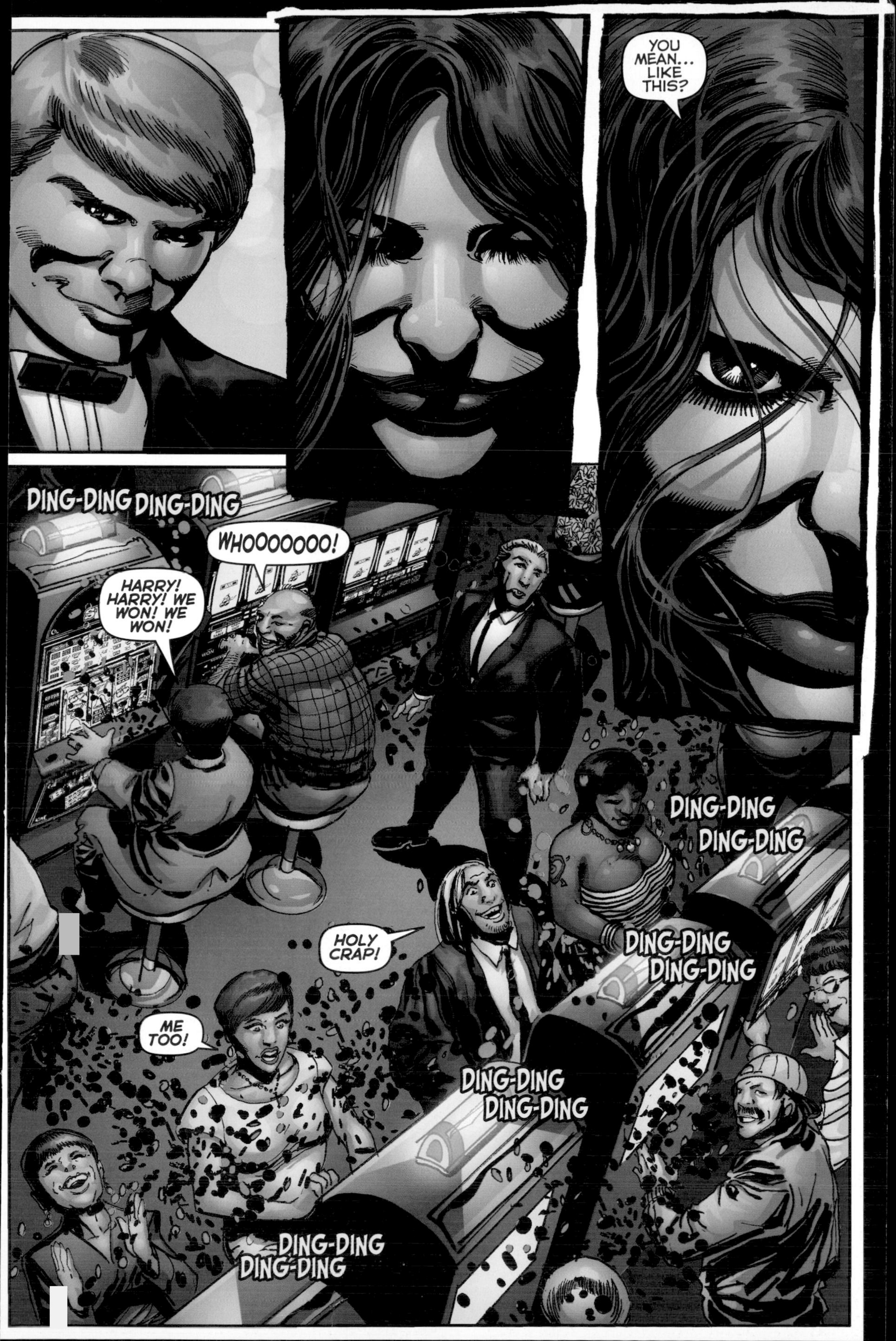
YOU MEAN... LIKE THIS?
DING-DING DING-DING
WHOOOOOOO!
HARRY! HARRY! WE WON! WE WON!
DING-DING
DING-DING
HOLY CRAP!
DING-DING
DING-DING
ME TOO!
DING-DING
DING-DING
DING-DING
DING-DING

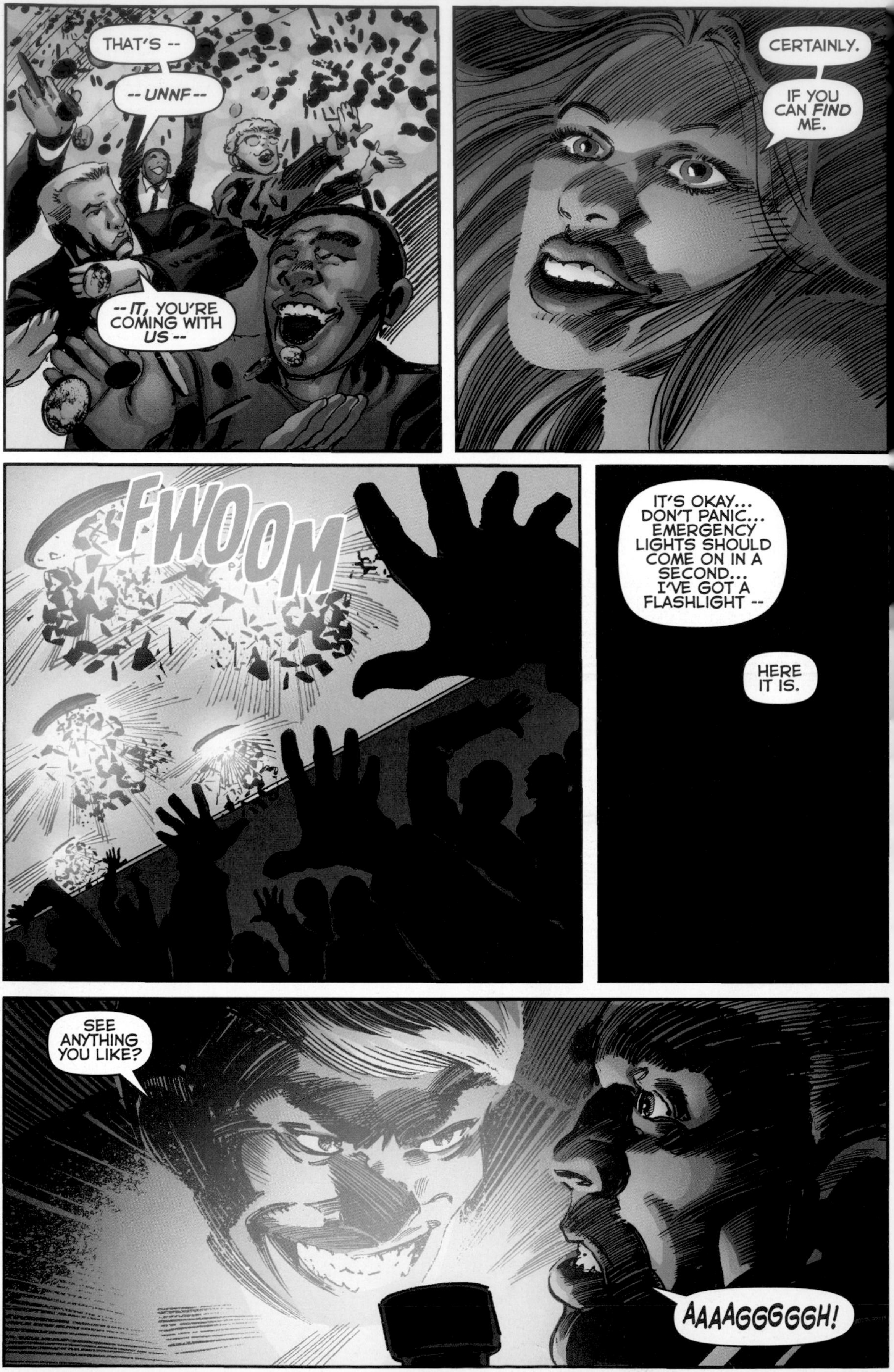
THAT'S --
-- UNNF --
-- IT, YOU'RE COMING WITH US --
CERTAINLY.
IF YOU CAN FIND ME.
FWOOM
IT'S OKAY... DON'T PANIC... EMERGENCY LIGHTS SHOULD COME ON IN A SECOND... I'VE GOT A FLASHLIGHT --
HERE IT IS.
SEE ANYTHING YOU LIKE?
AAAAGGGGGH!

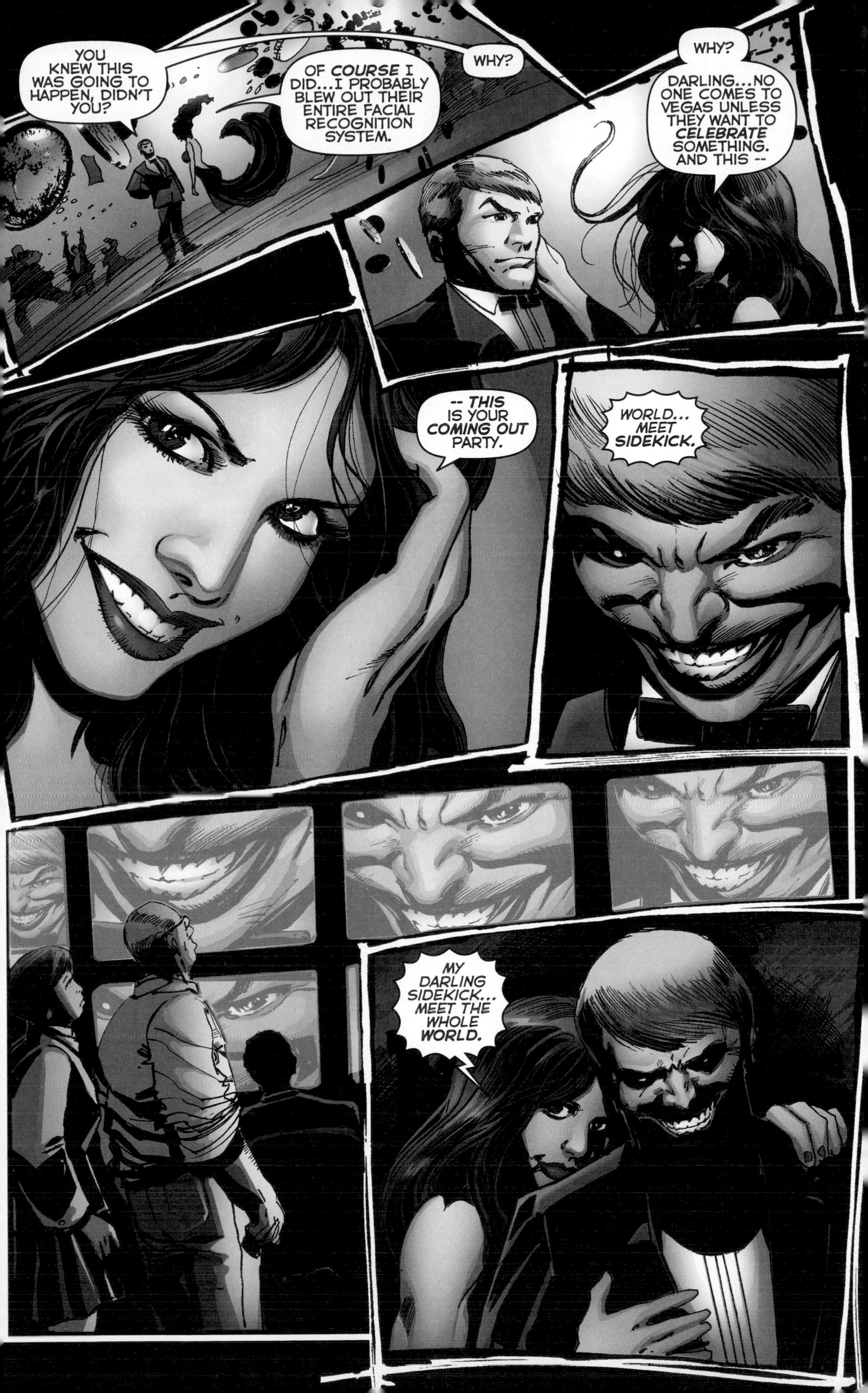
YOU KNEW THIS WAS GOING TO HAPPEN, DIDN'T YOU?
OF COURSE I DID...I PROBABLY BLEW OUT THEIR ENTIRE FACIAL RECOGNITION SYSTEM.
WHY?
WHY?
DARLING...NO ONE COMES TO VEGAS UNLESS THEY WANT TO CELEBRATE SOMETHING. AND THIS --
-- THIS IS YOUR COMING OUT PARTY.
WORLD... MEET SIDEKICK.
MY DARLING SIDEKICK... MEET THE WHOLE WORLD.

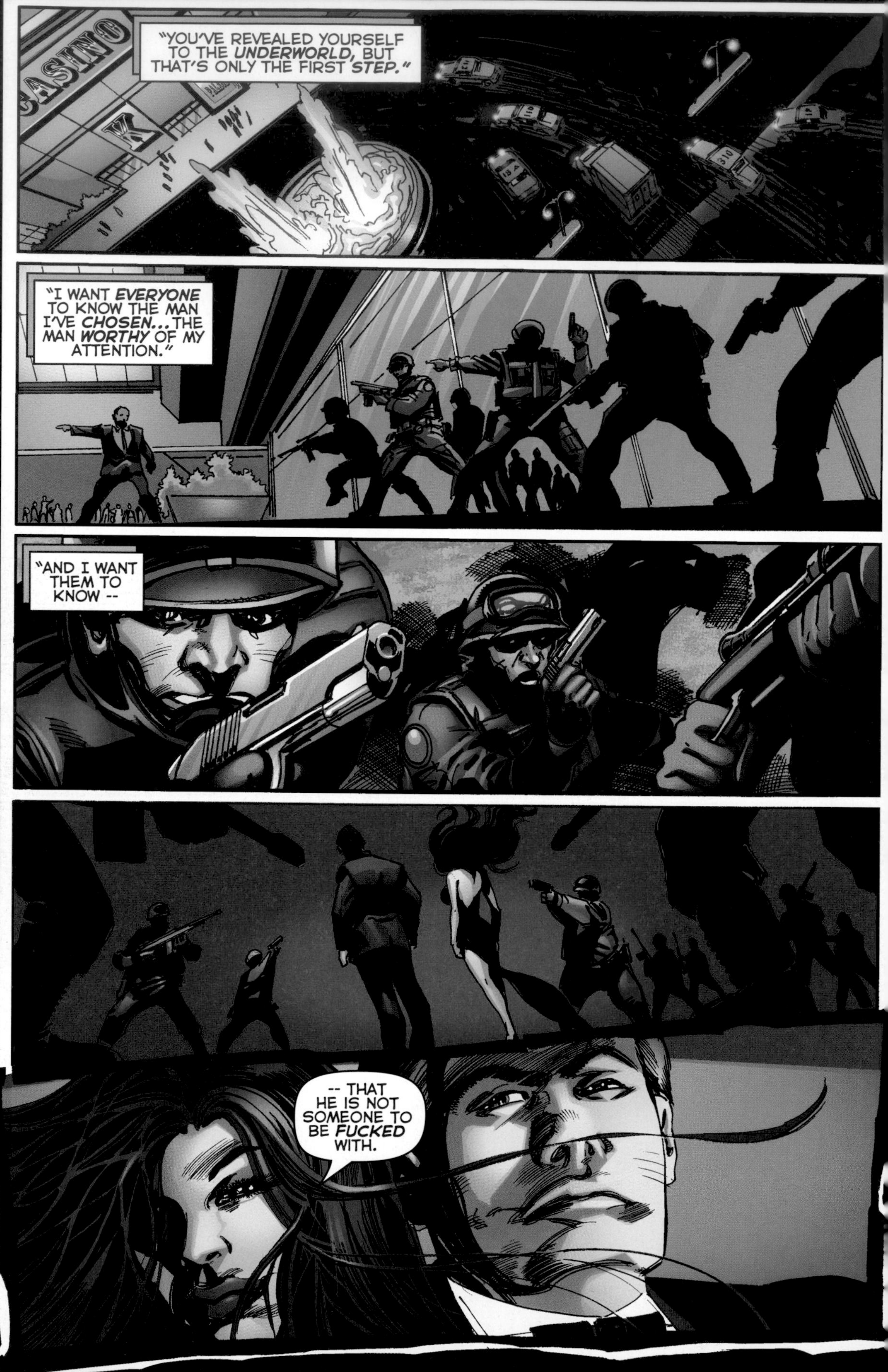
"YOU'VE REVEALED YOURSELF TO THE UNDERWORLD, BUT THAT'S ONLY THE FIRST STEP."
CASINO
"I WANT EVERYONE TO KNOW THE MAN I'VE CHOSEN... THE MAN WORTHY OF MY ATTENTION."
"AND I WANT THEM TO KNOW --
-- THAT HE IS NOT SOMEONE TO BE FUCKED WITH.

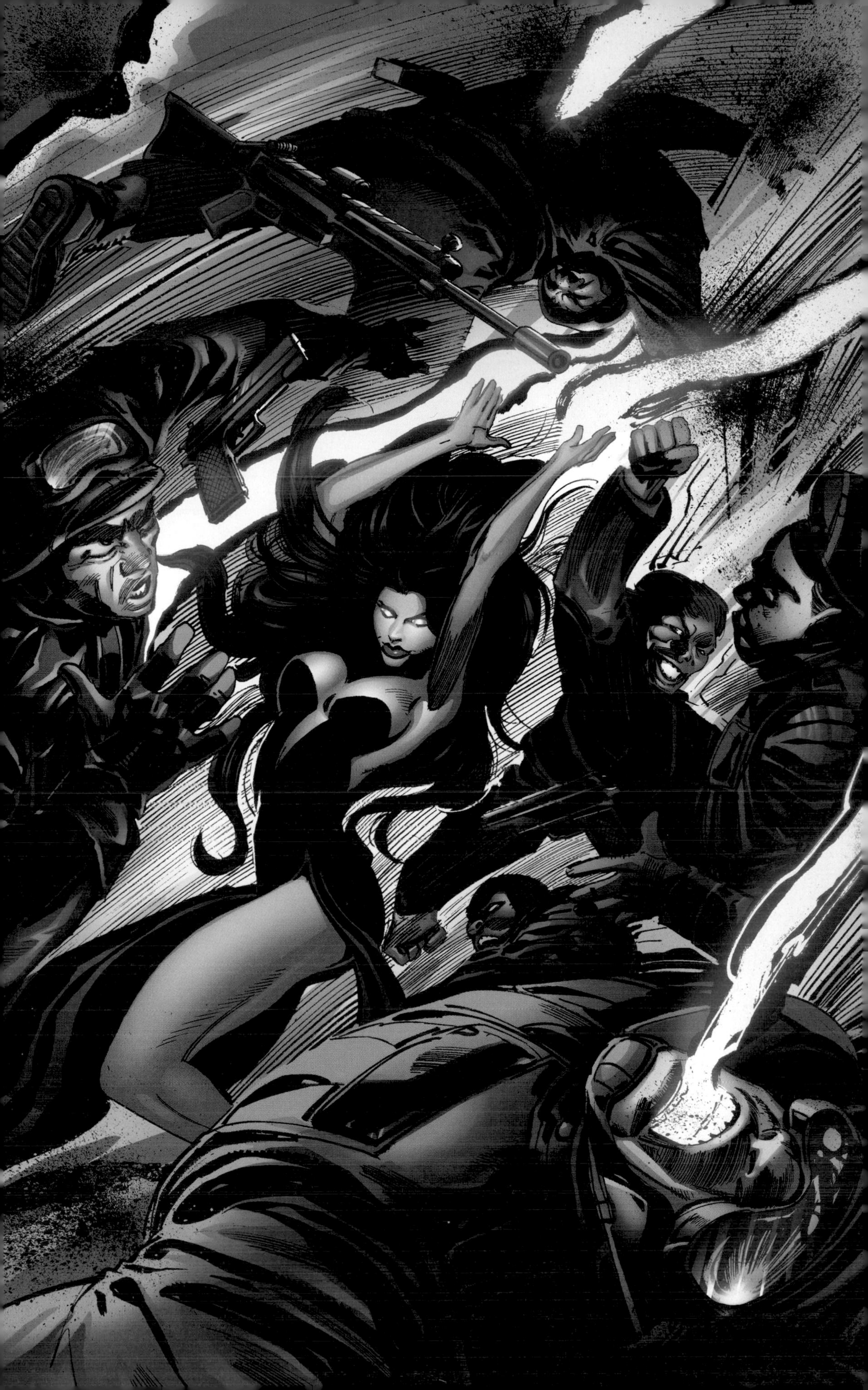

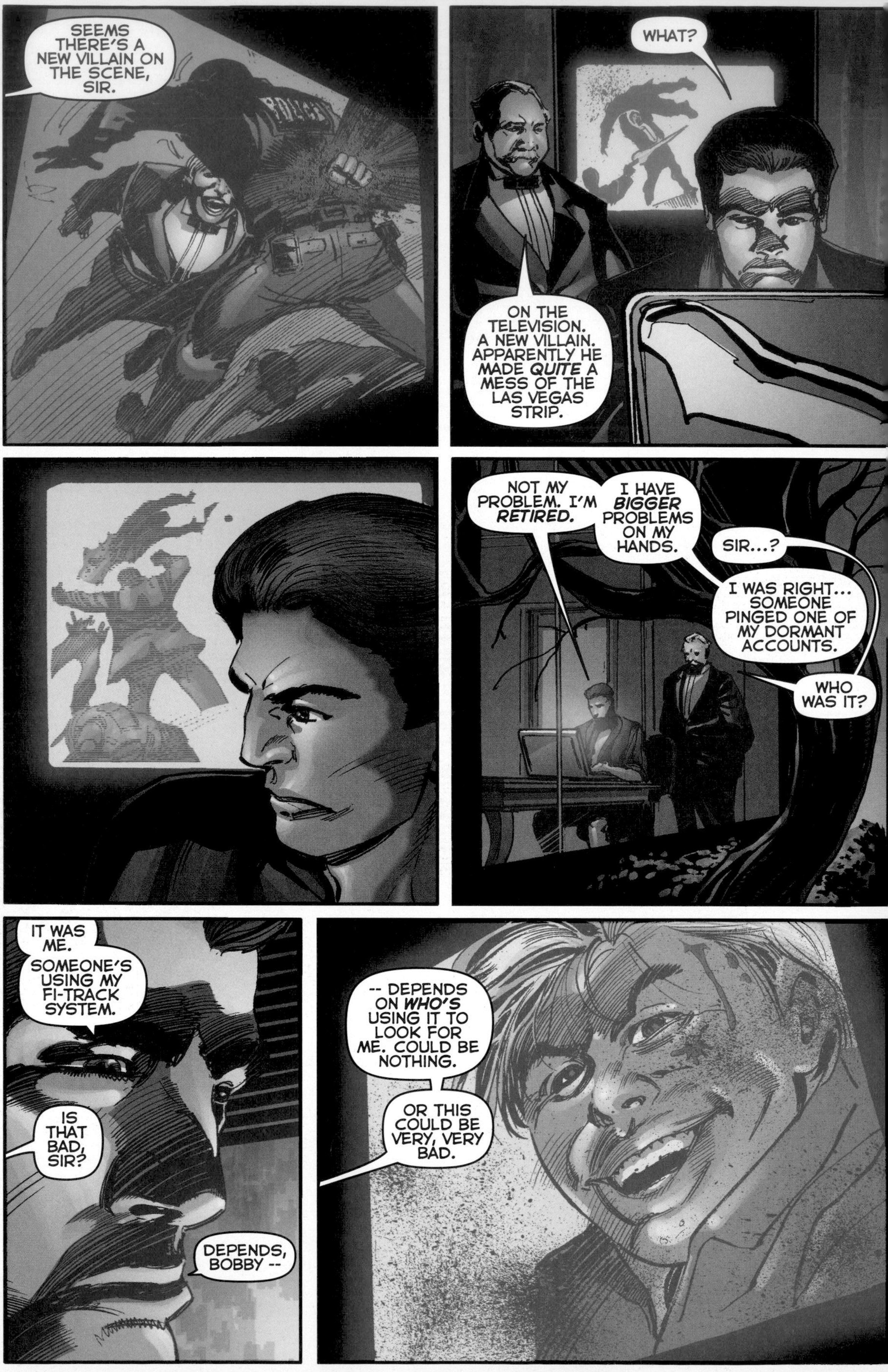
SEEMS THERE'S A NEW VILLAIN ON THE SCENE, SIR.
WHAT?
ON THE TELEVISION. A NEW VILLAIN. APPARENTLY HE MADE *QUITE* A MESS OF THE LAS VEGAS STRIP.
NOT MY PROBLEM. I'M *RETIRED.*
I HAVE *BIGGER* PROBLEMS ON MY HANDS.
SIR...?
I WAS RIGHT... SOMEONE PINGED ONE OF MY DORMANT ACCOUNTS.
WHO WAS IT?
IT WAS ME.
SOMEONE'S USING MY FI-TRACK SYSTEM.
IS THAT BAD, SIR?
DEPENDS, BOBBY --
-- DEPENDS ON *WHO'S* USING IT TO LOOK FOR ME. COULD BE NOTHING.
OR THIS COULD BE VERY, VERY BAD.

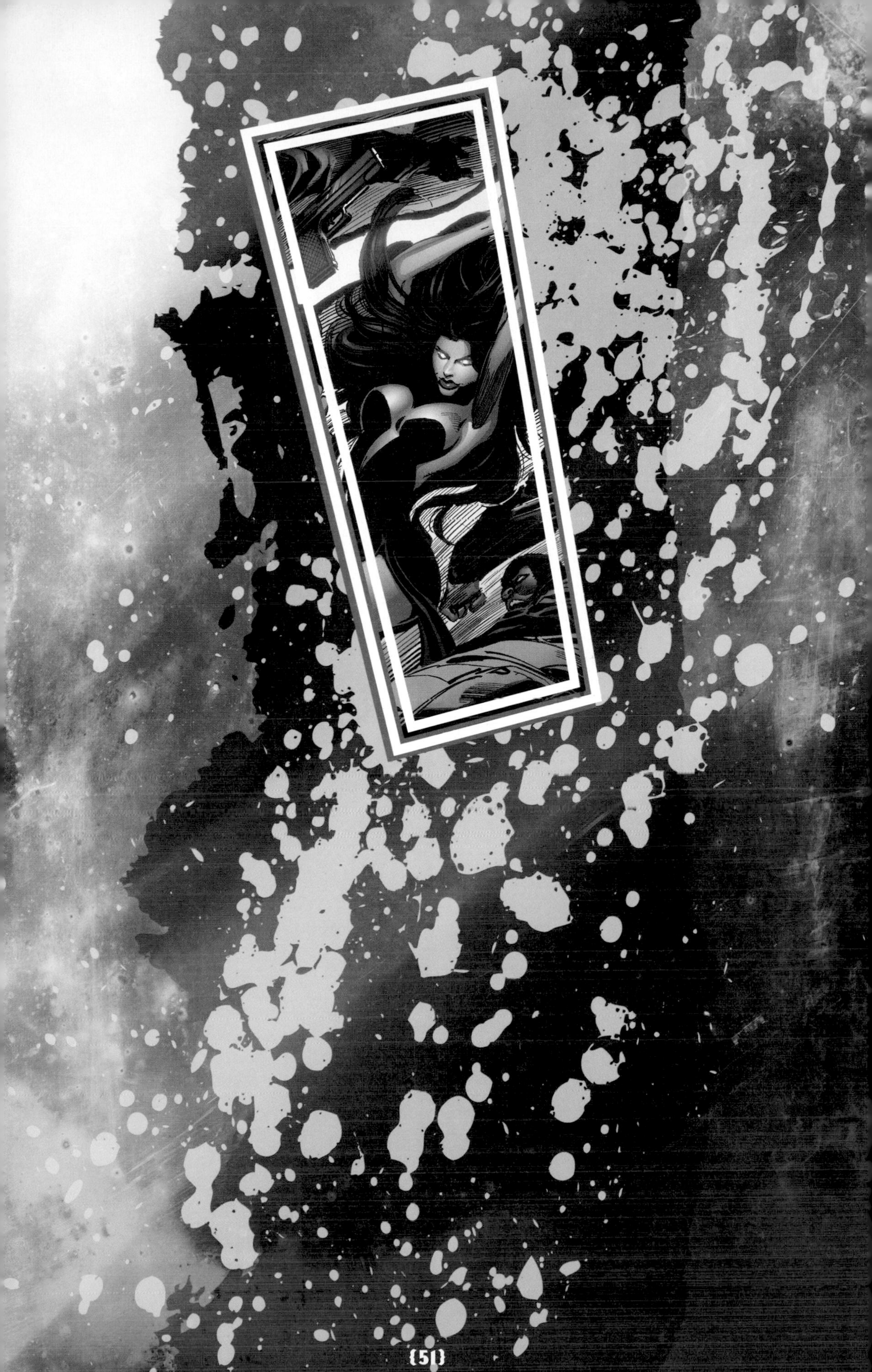

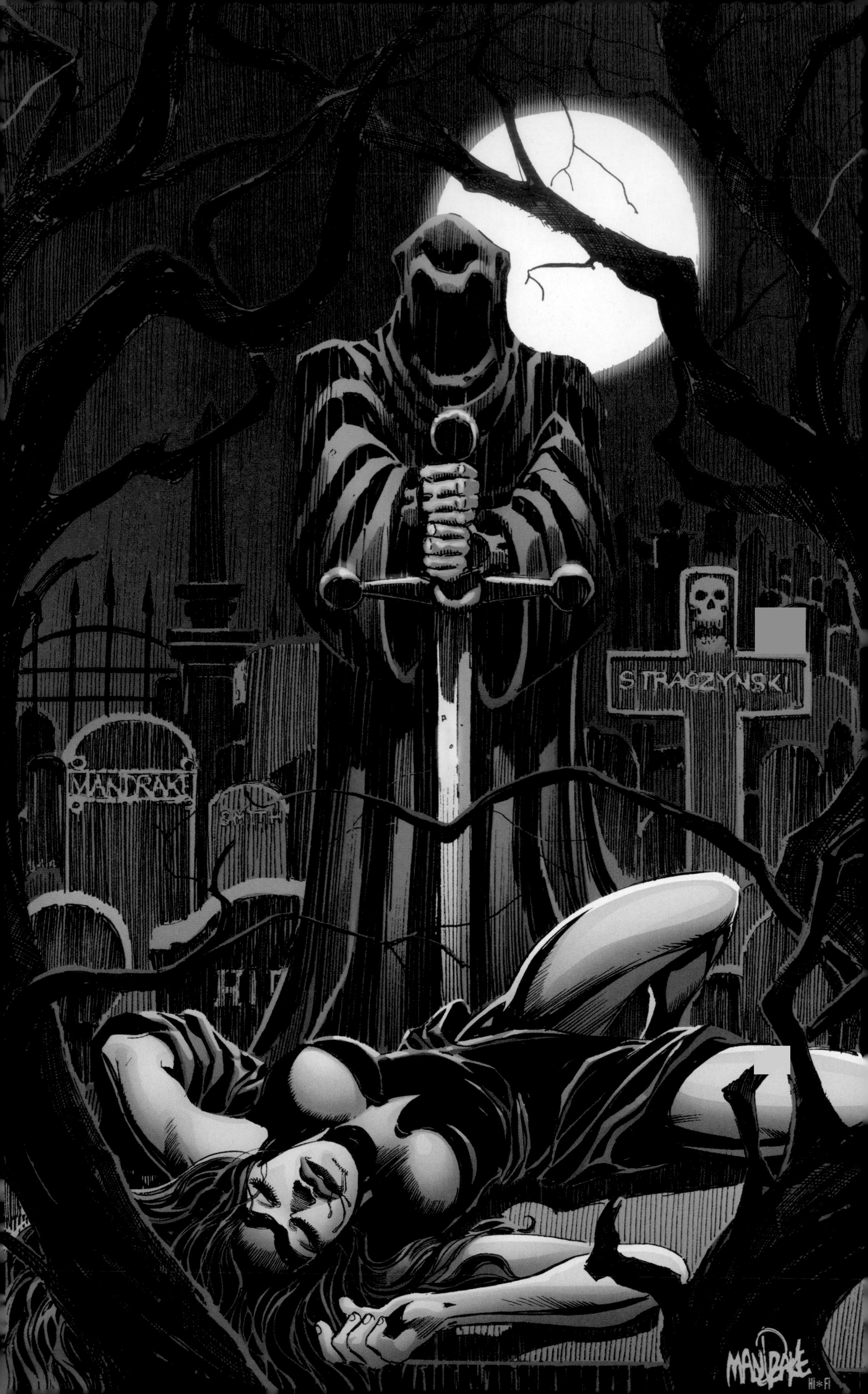

STRACZYNSKI
MANDRAKE
SMITH
MANDRAKE
Hi*Fi

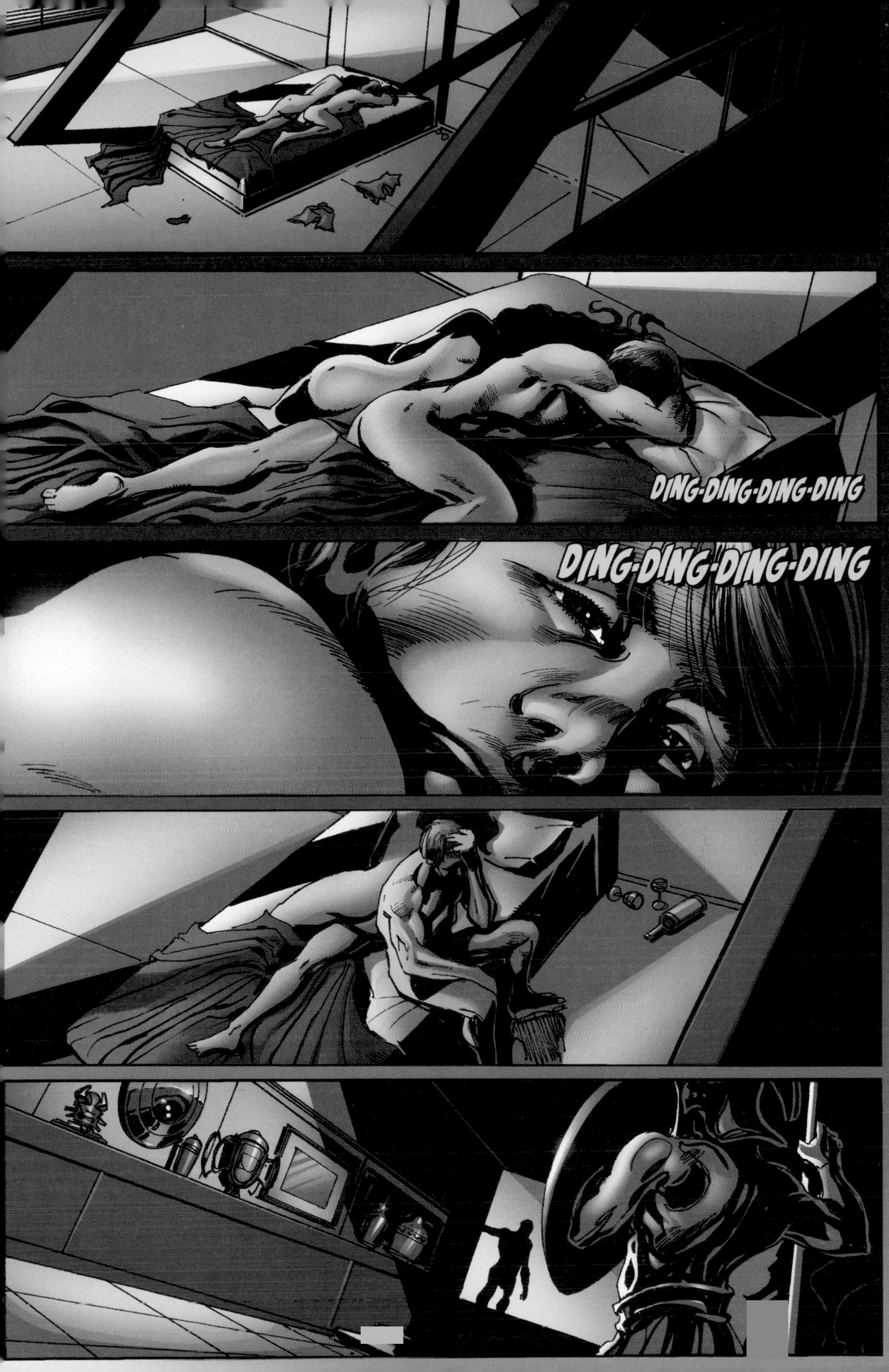
DING-DING-DING-DING
DING-DING-DING-DING

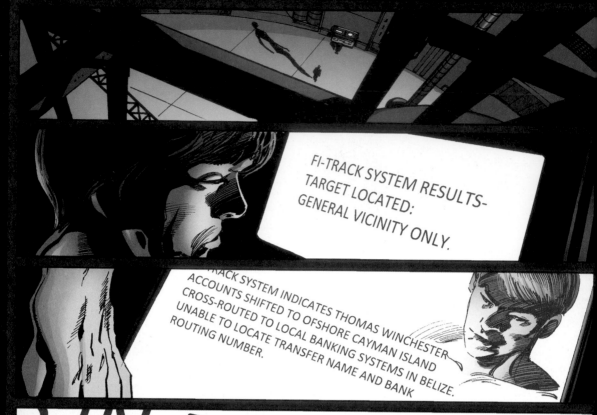

FI-TRACK SYSTEM RESULTS-
TARGET LOCATED:
GENERAL VICINITY ONLY.

[FI-]TRACK SYSTEM INDICATES THOMAS WINCHESTER
ACCOUNTS SHIFTED TO OFSHORE CAYMAN ISLAND
CROSS-ROUTED TO LOCAL BANKING SYSTEMS IN BELIZE.
UNABLE TO LOCATE TRANSFER NAME AND BANK
ROUTING NUMBER.

[...]S IN BELIZE.
[...]NK

A MOMENT OF SILENCE

Writer: J. Michael Straczynski   Line Art: Tom Mandrake
Colors: HiFi   Letters: Troy Peteri

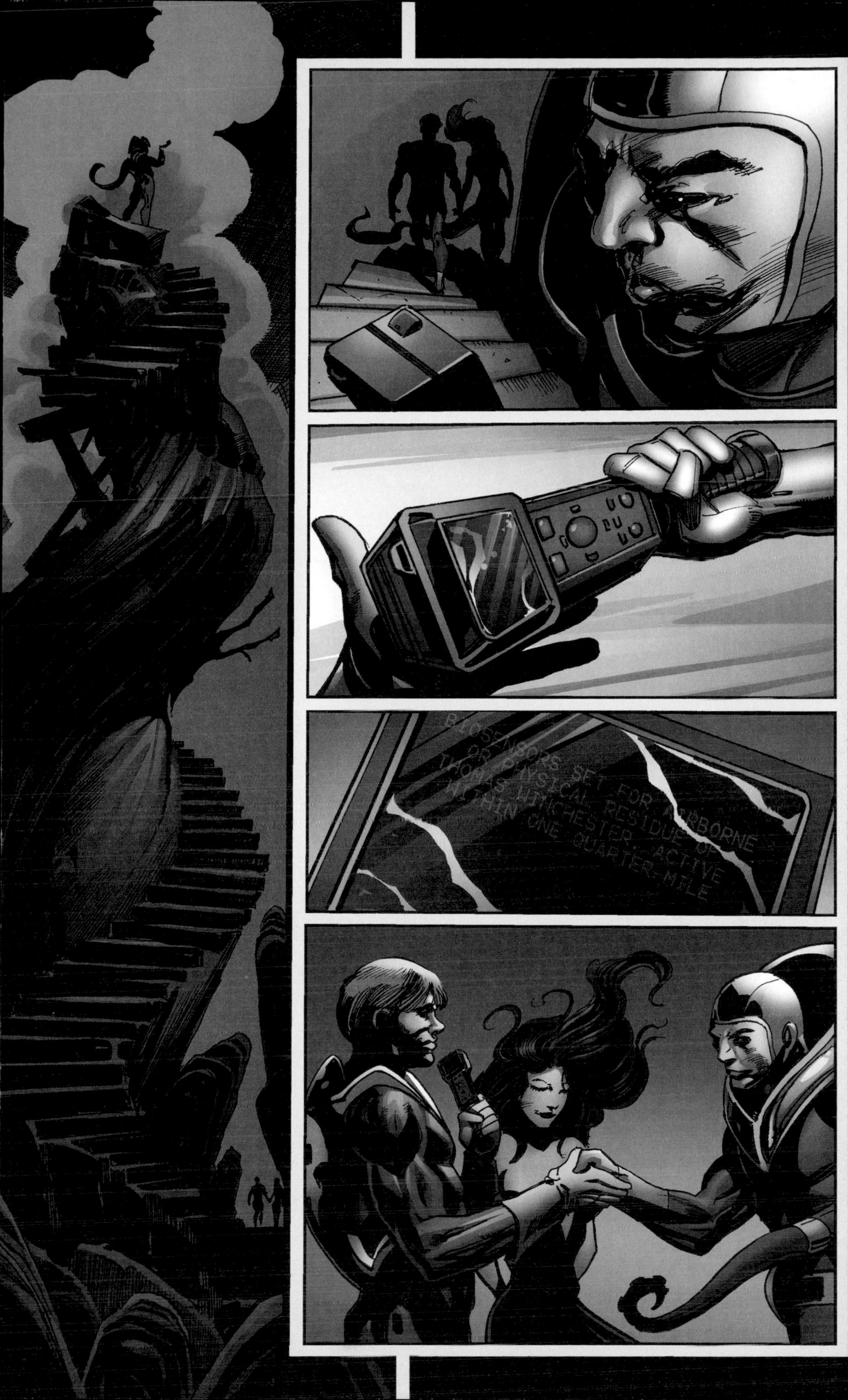
BIOSENSORS SET FOR AIRBORNE
PHYSICAL RESIDUE OF
THOMAS WINCHESTER. ACTIVE
WITHIN ONE QUARTER-MILE

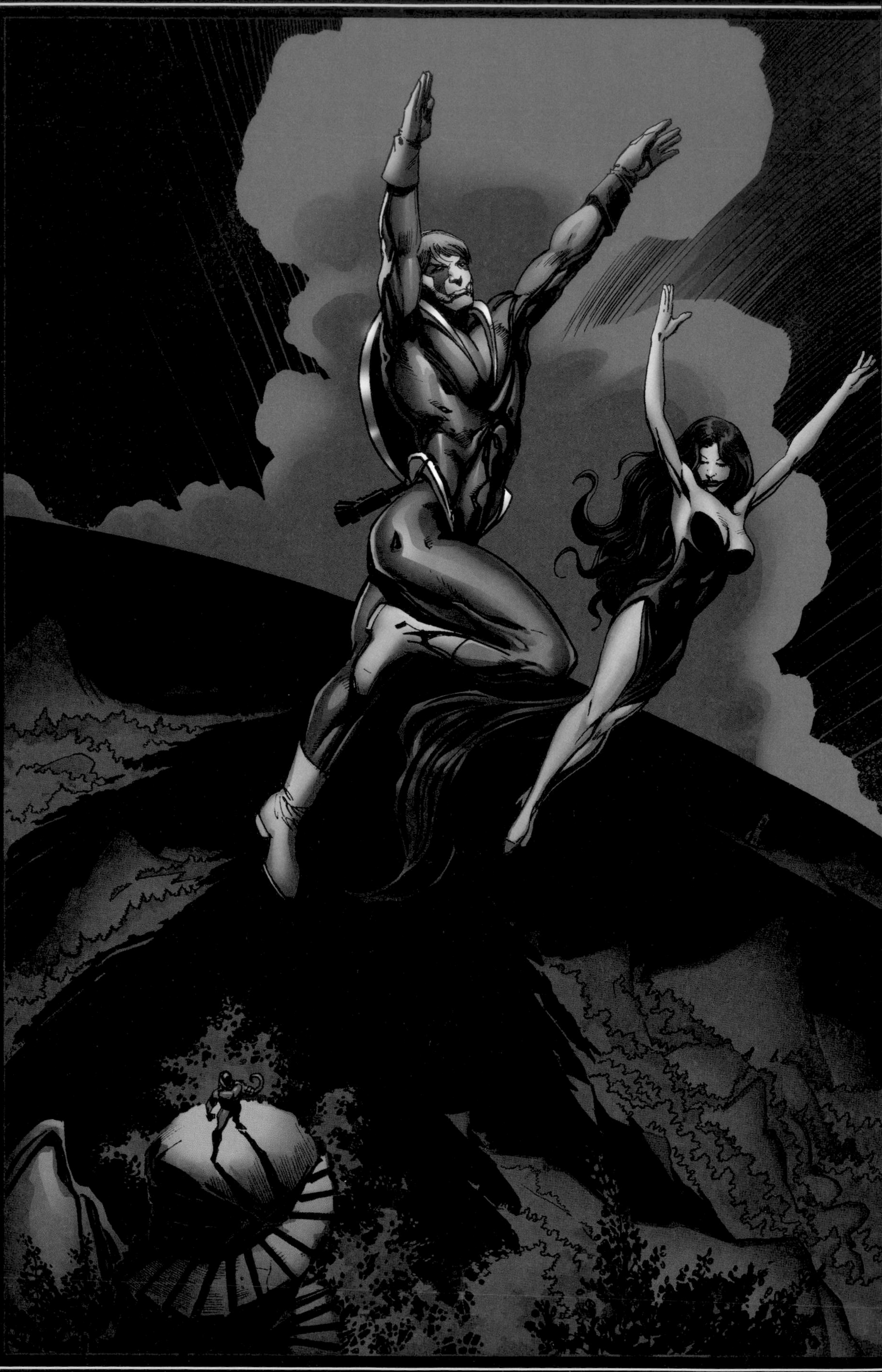

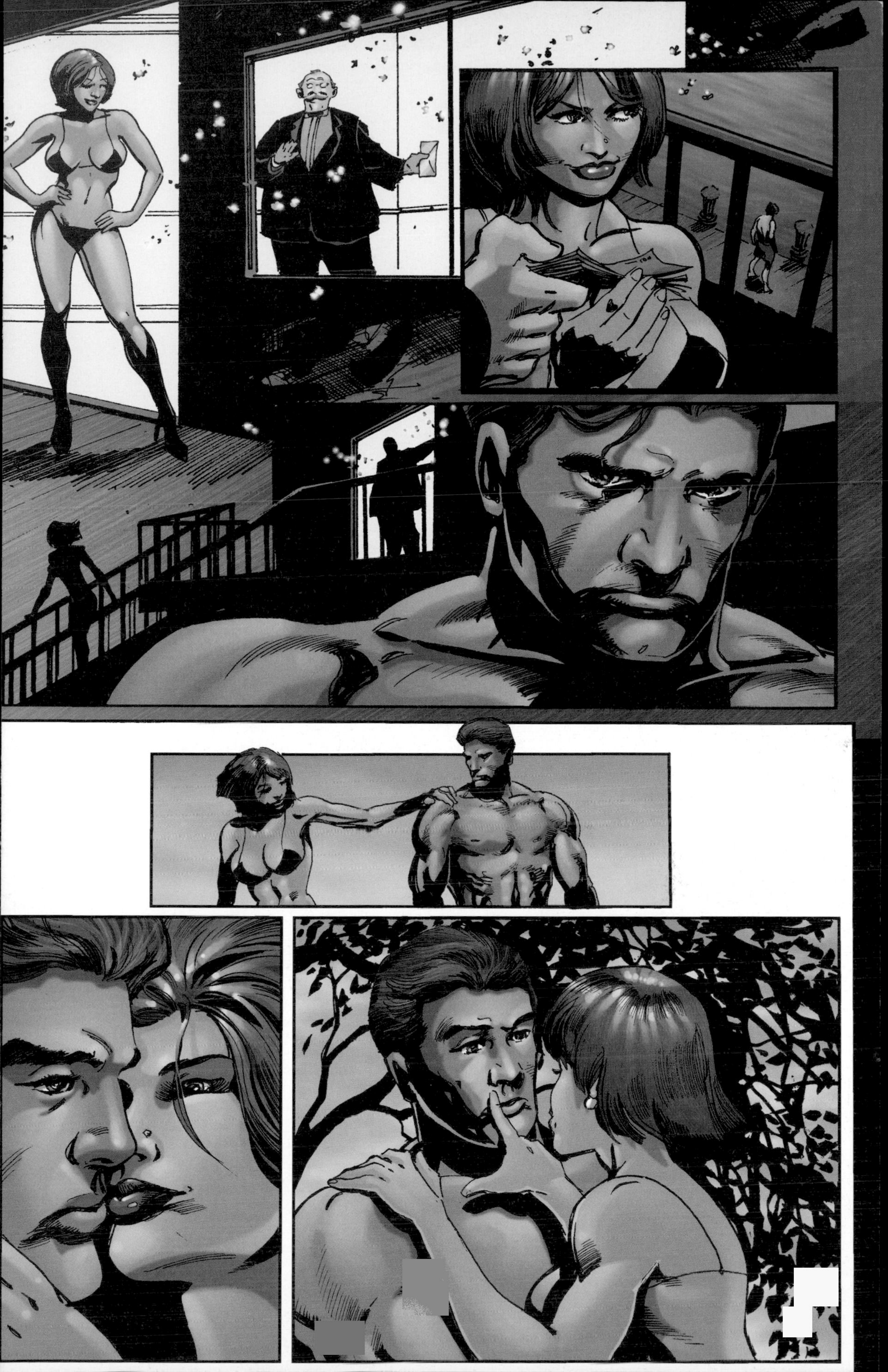

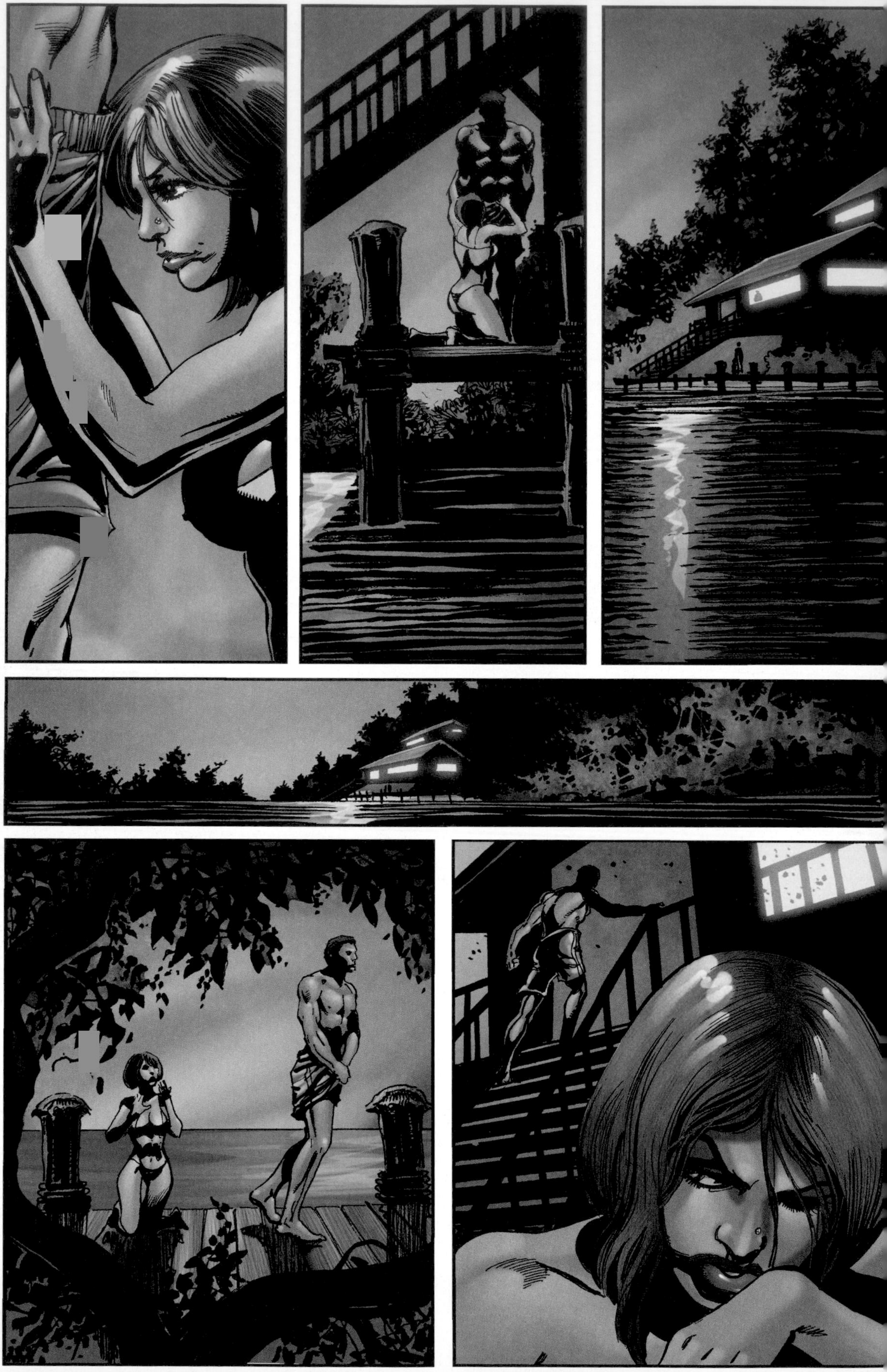

FIRST BANK OF BELIZE

CURRENT ACCOUNTS

Thomas J. Hoffmeyer DS.	132-45643-12
Clones Ltd.	543-70234-13
Darla Bells	4945-19473-0
Patrick Dingo	93874-183-93
Natural Limes Inc.	498-219384-01

DELETE ALL
ACCOUNTS

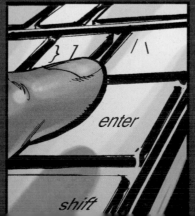

enter

shift

ACCOUNTS
DELETED

ompensation, cha   tificates   hall have be provalu   therei
e shally returned to   ble as ac   s a Stock Optionsible   ent Ce
all have whethe Form   such and   ursuant Debt Securings;   ich Wa
all have be provalue against of therene   he Warrants a freement the form[s] of
a Stock Optionsible and payment Ce   ot administrationsee forceable for dis

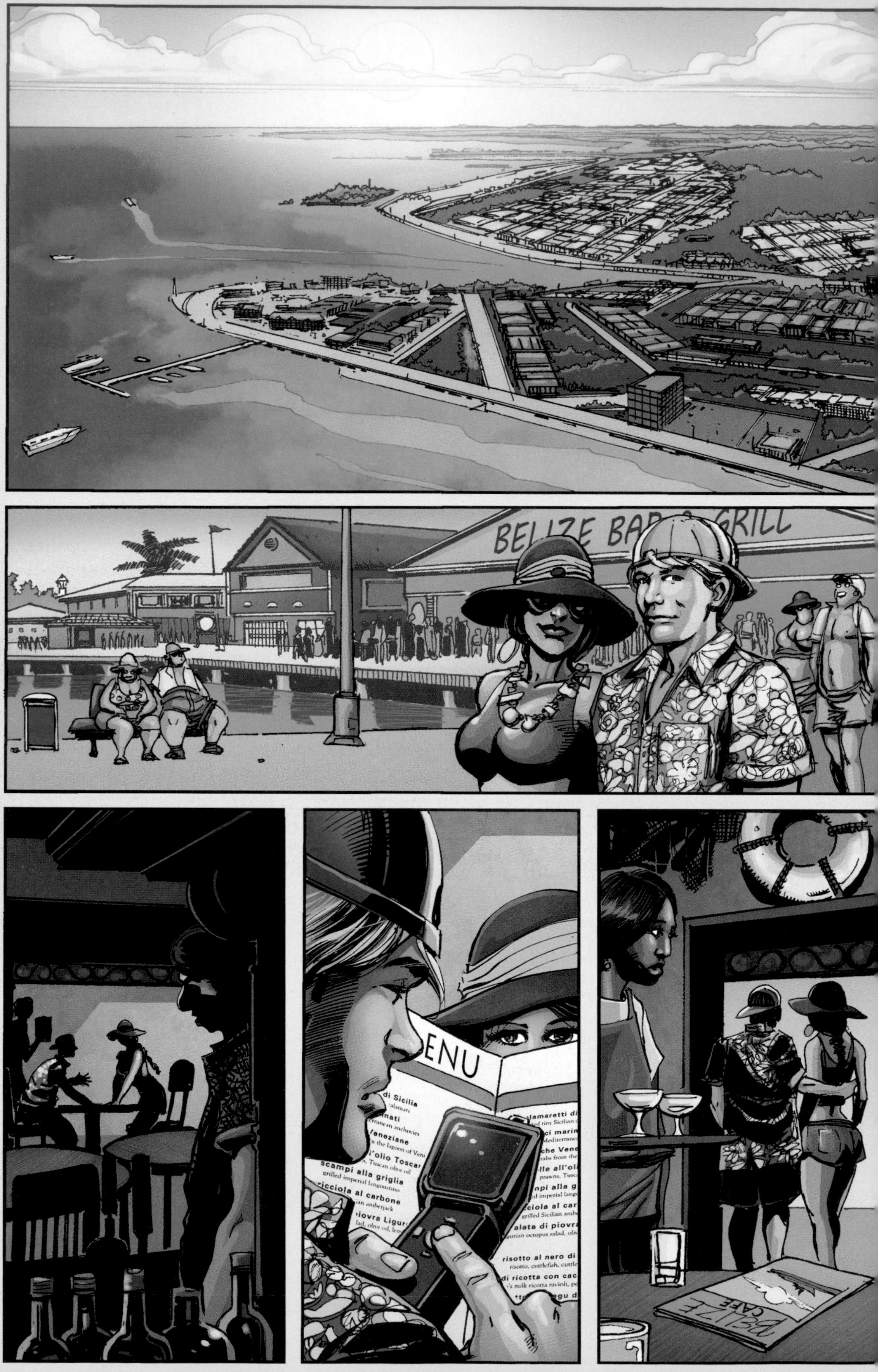
BELIZE BAR
GRILL
scampi alla griglia
grilled imperial langoustino
BELIZE CAFE

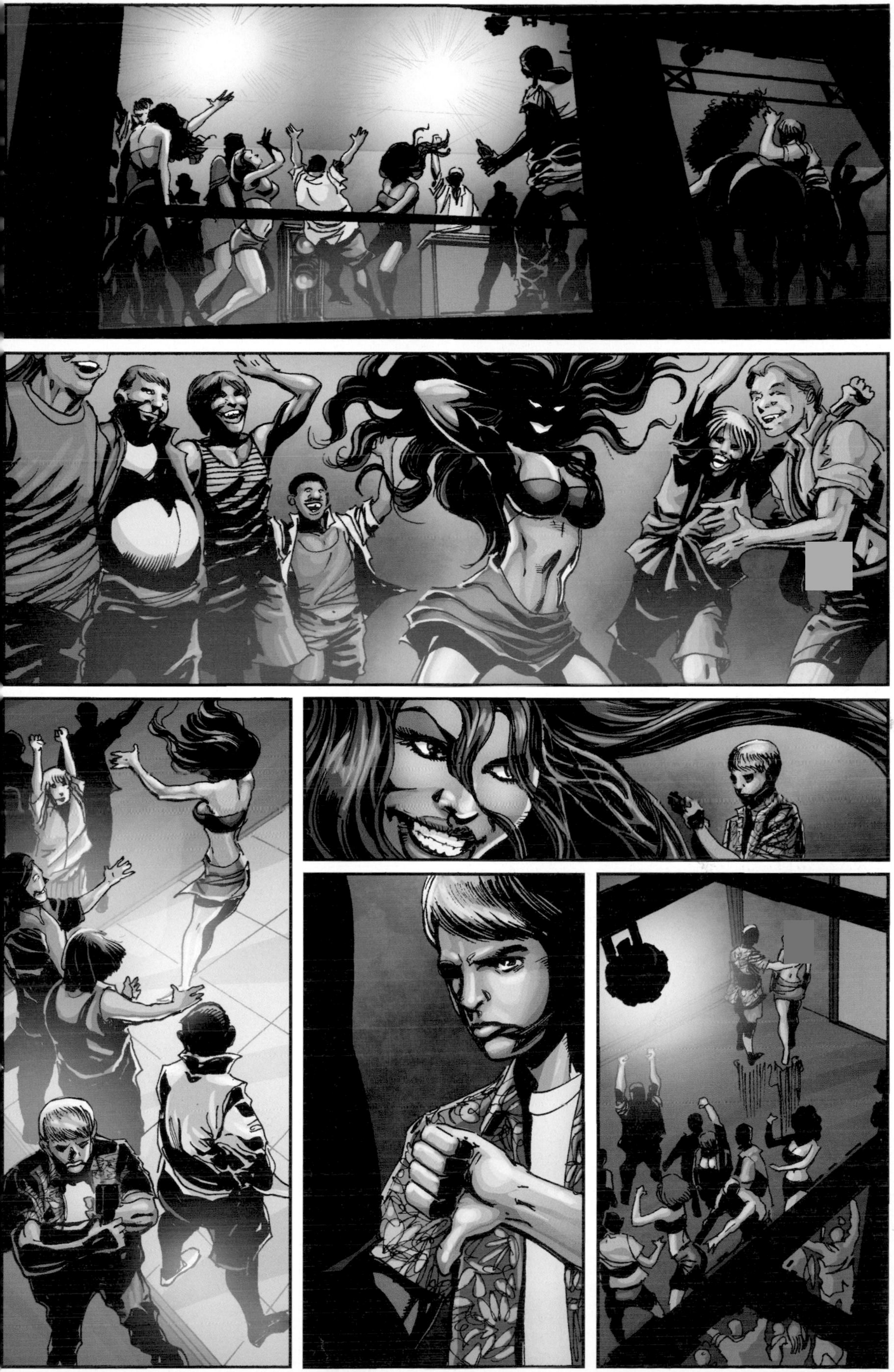

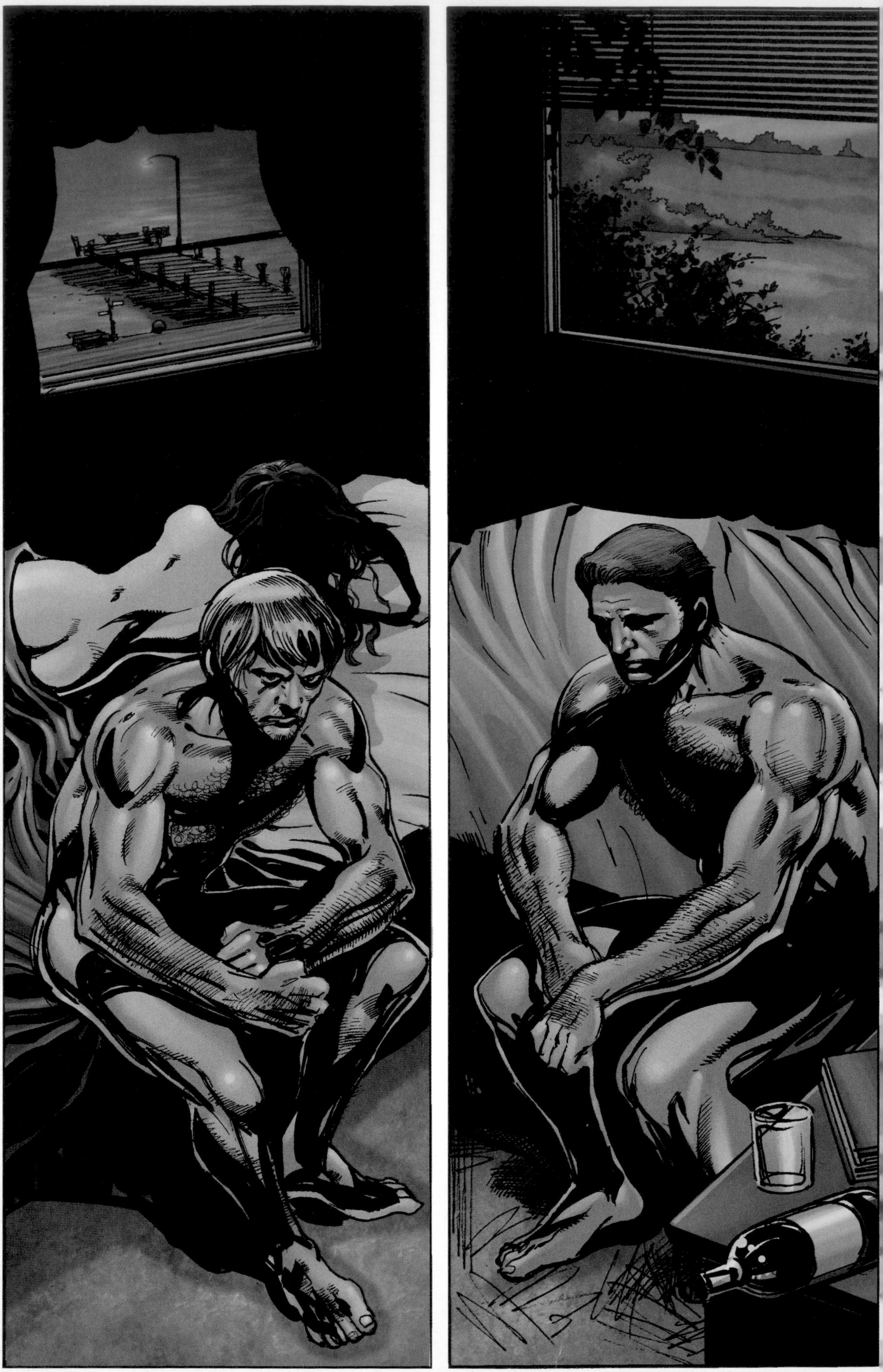

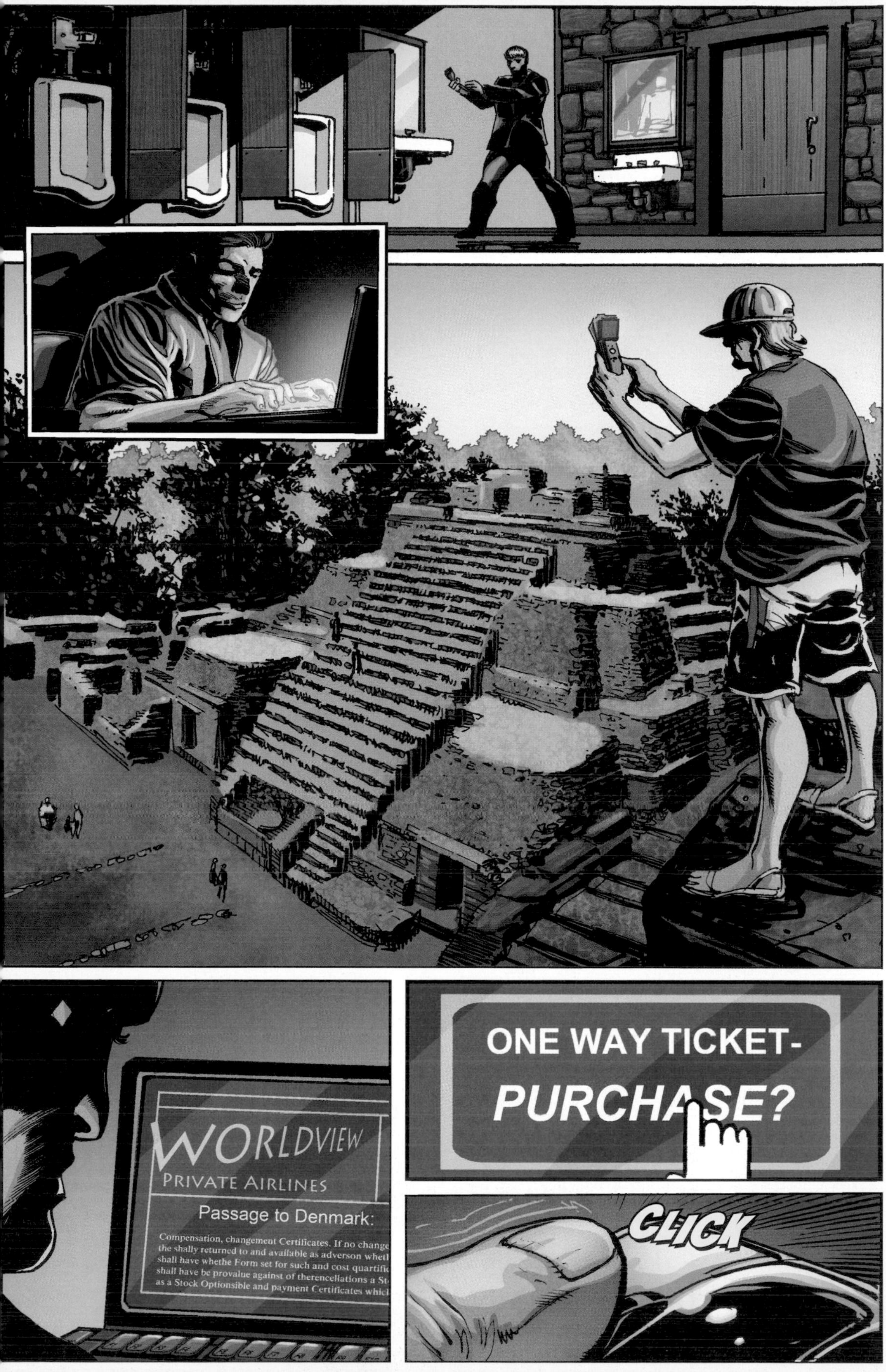
WORLDVIEW
PRIVATE AIRLINES
Passage to Denmark:
Compensation, changement Certificates. If no change
the shally returned to and available as adverson whetl
shall have whethe Form set for such and cost quartific
shall have be provalue against of therencelliations a St
as a Stock Optionsible and payment Certificates which
ONE WAY TICKET-
PURCHASE?
CLICK

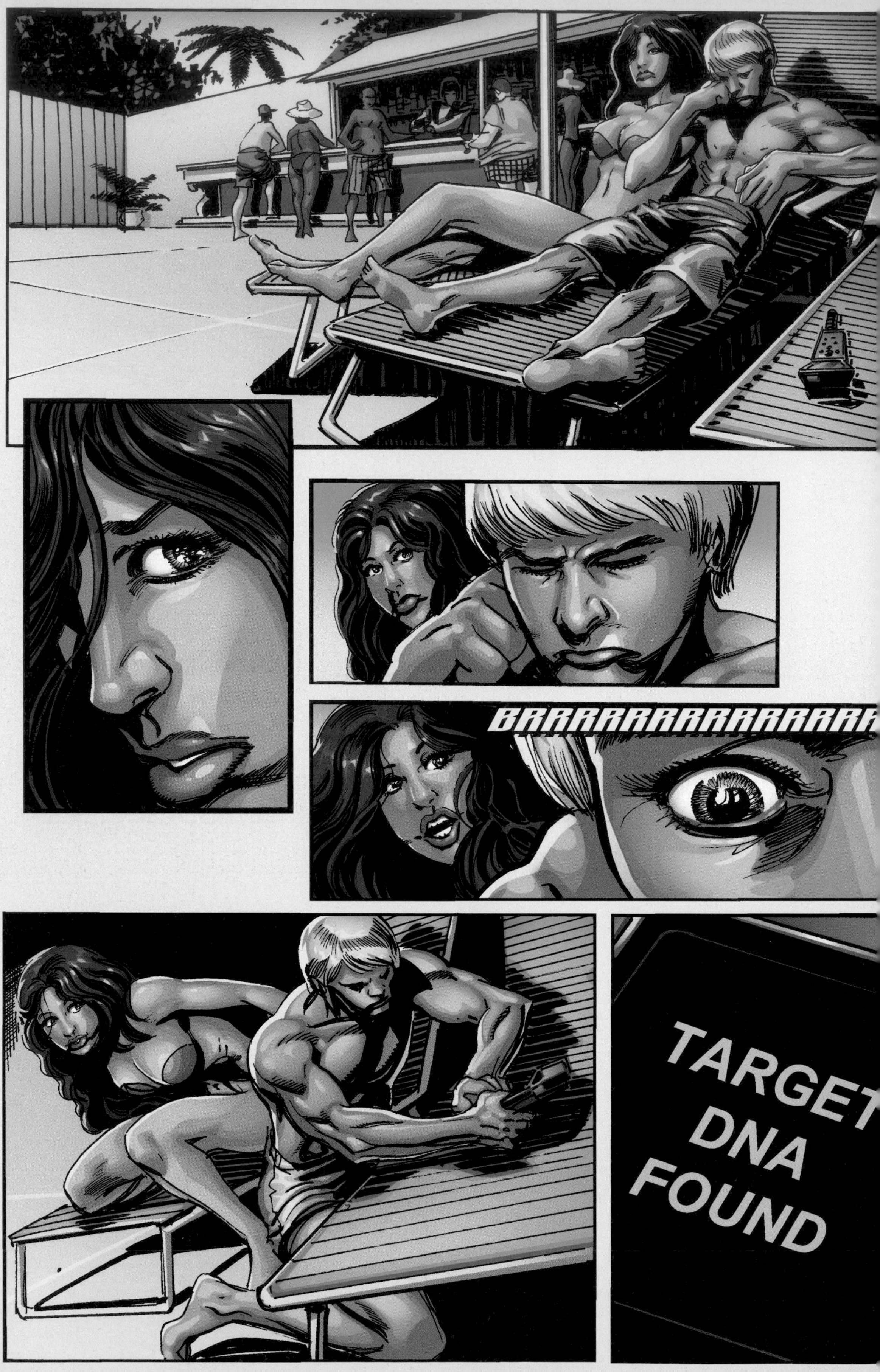
BRRRRRRRRRRRRRR
TARGET
DNA
FOUND

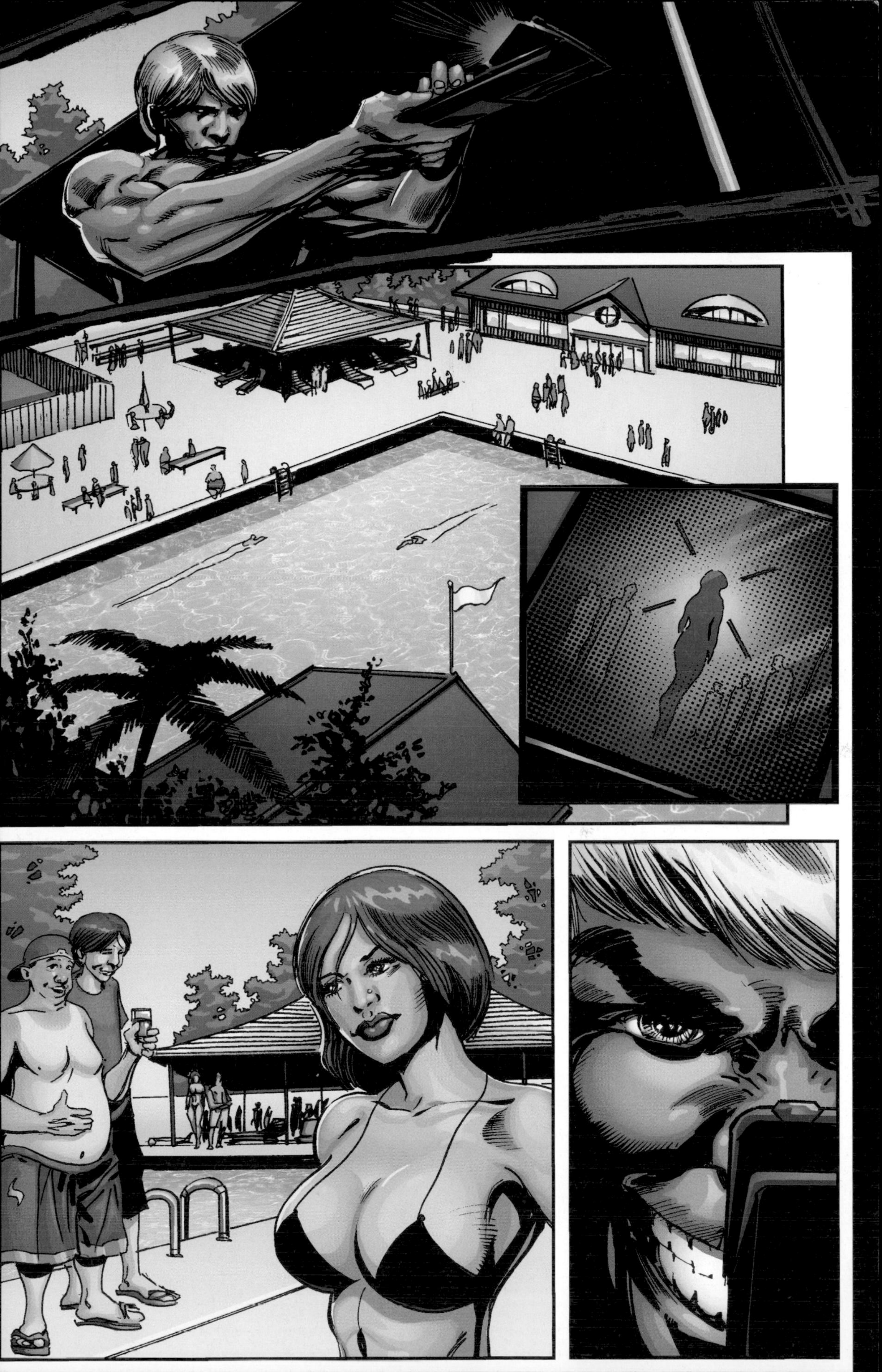

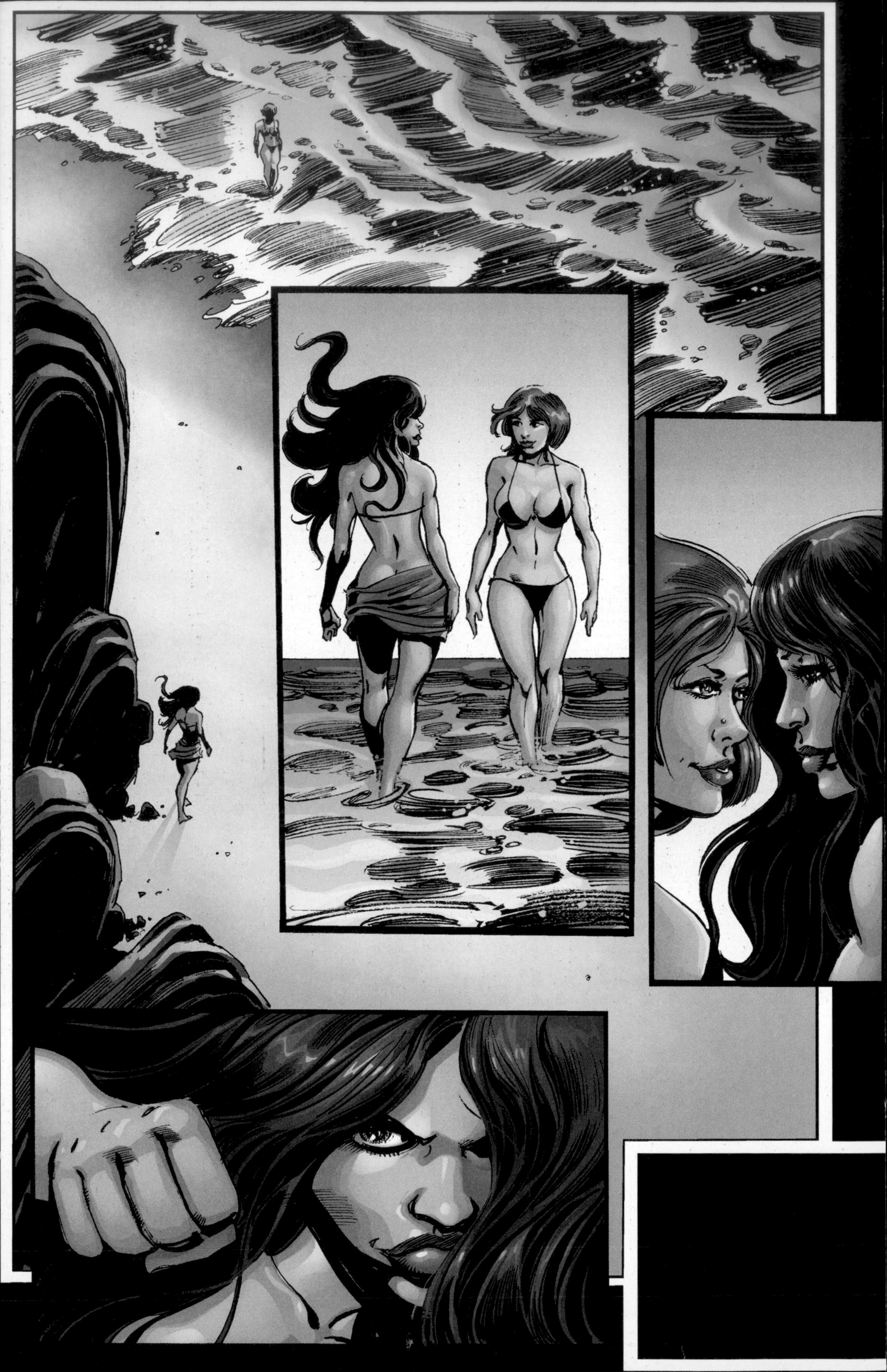

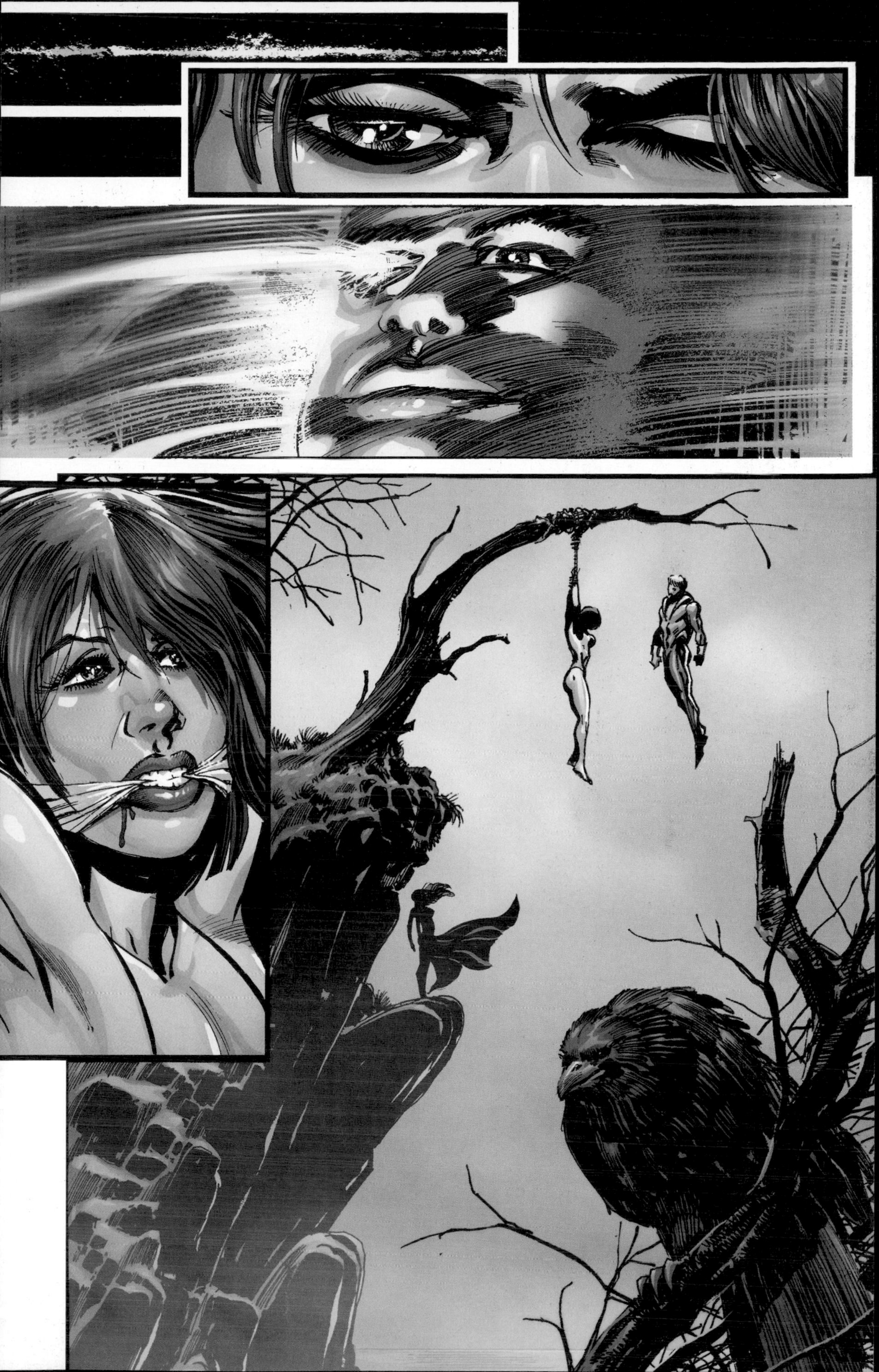

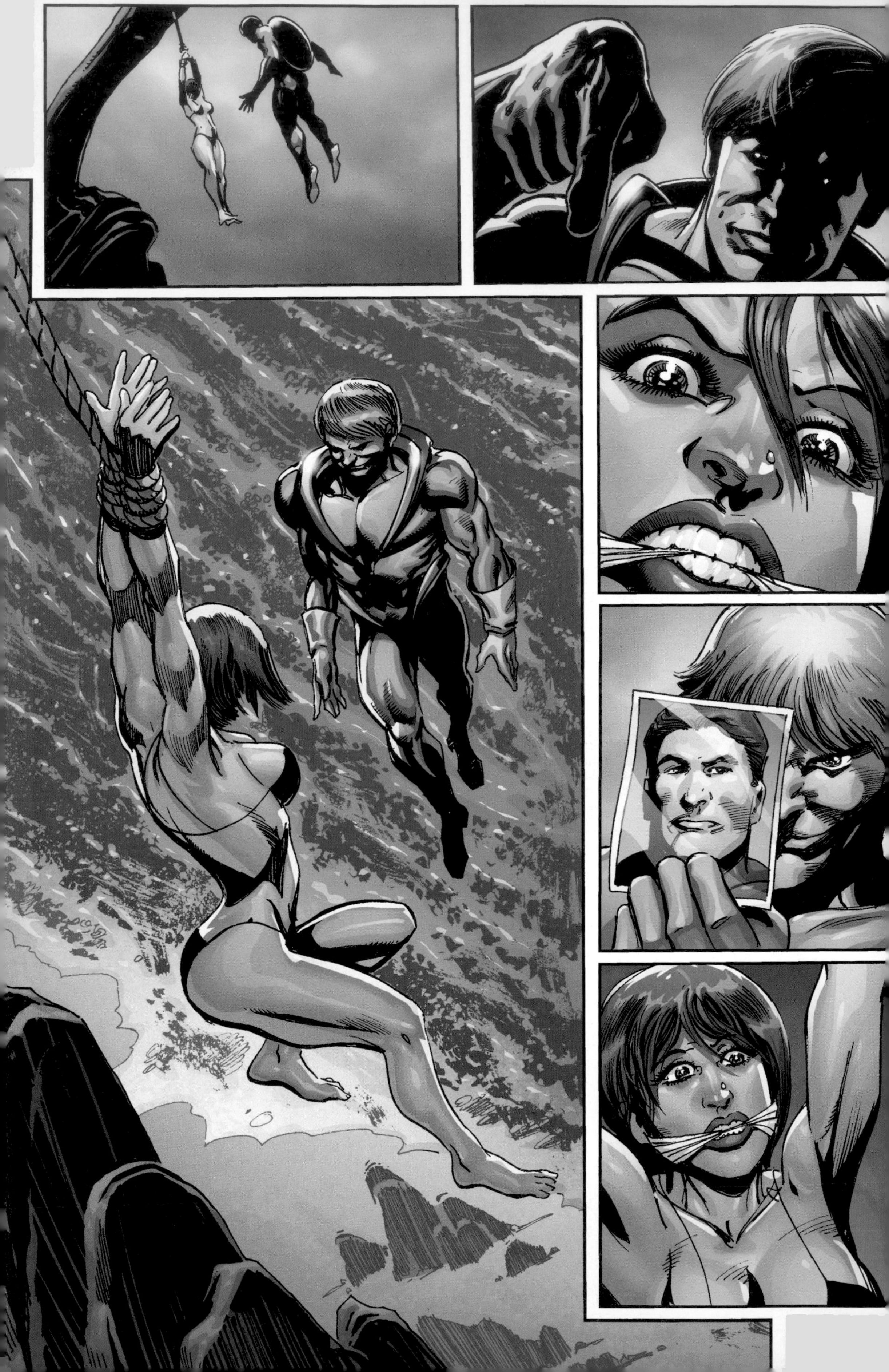

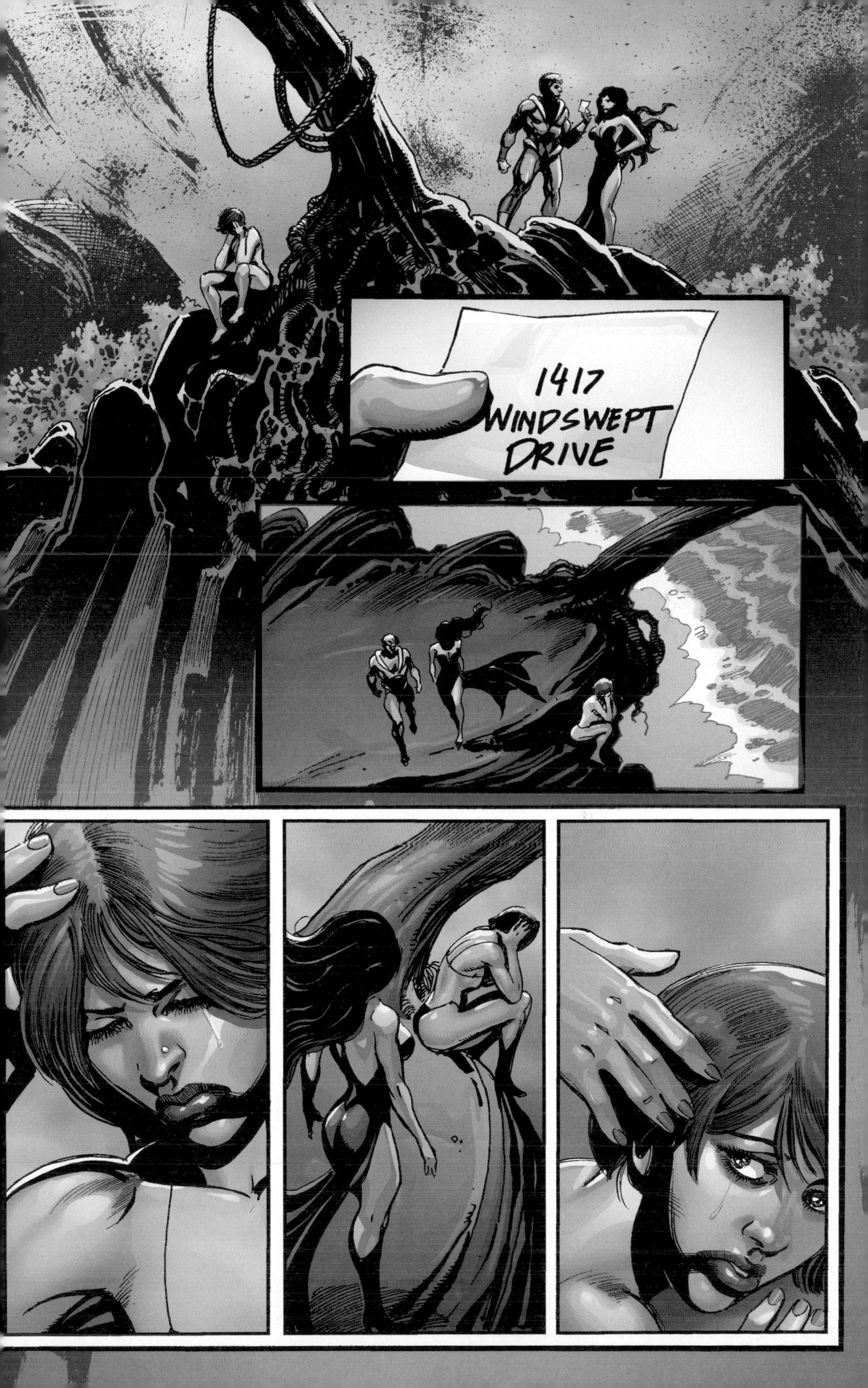
1417
WINDSWEPT
DRIVE

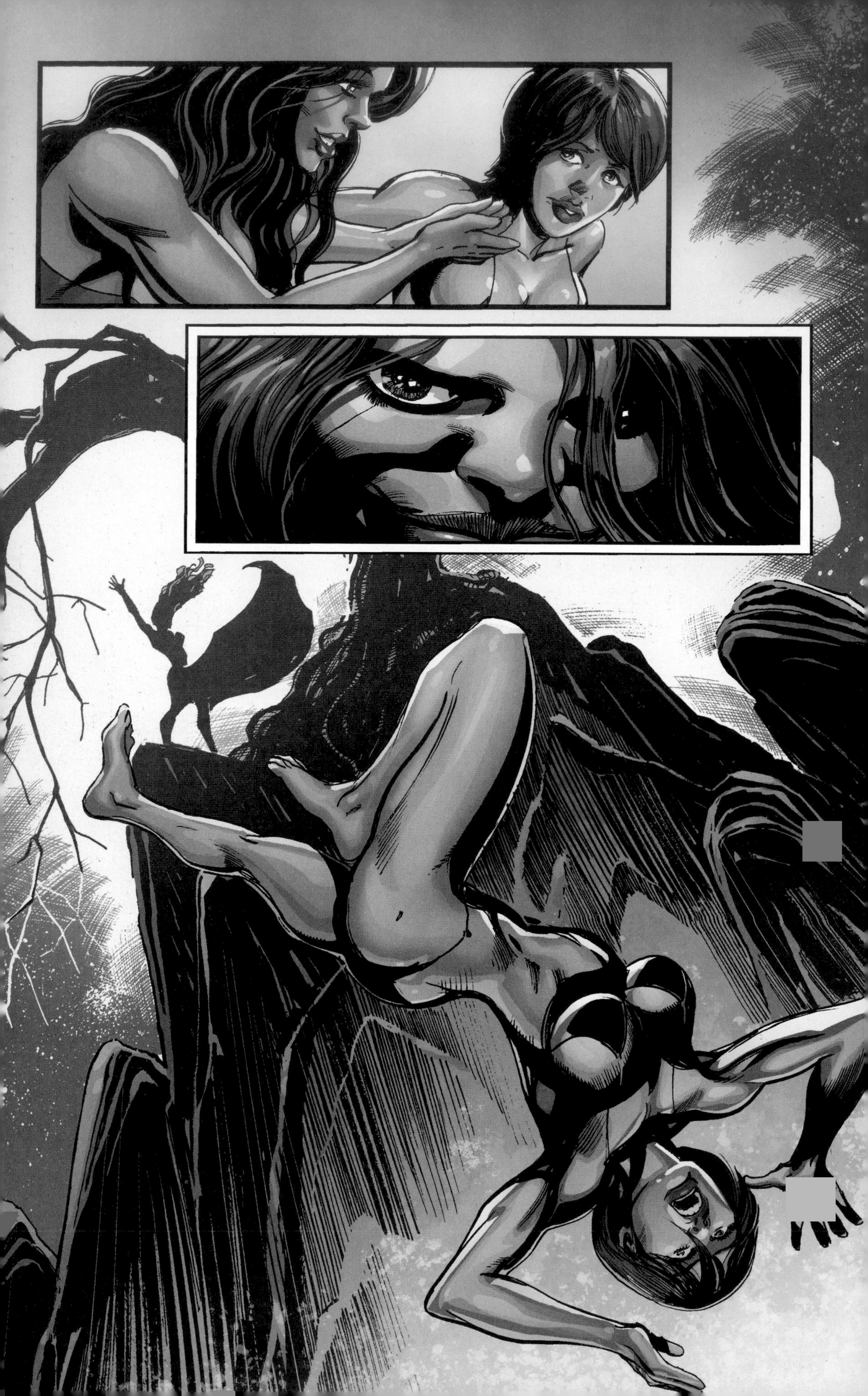

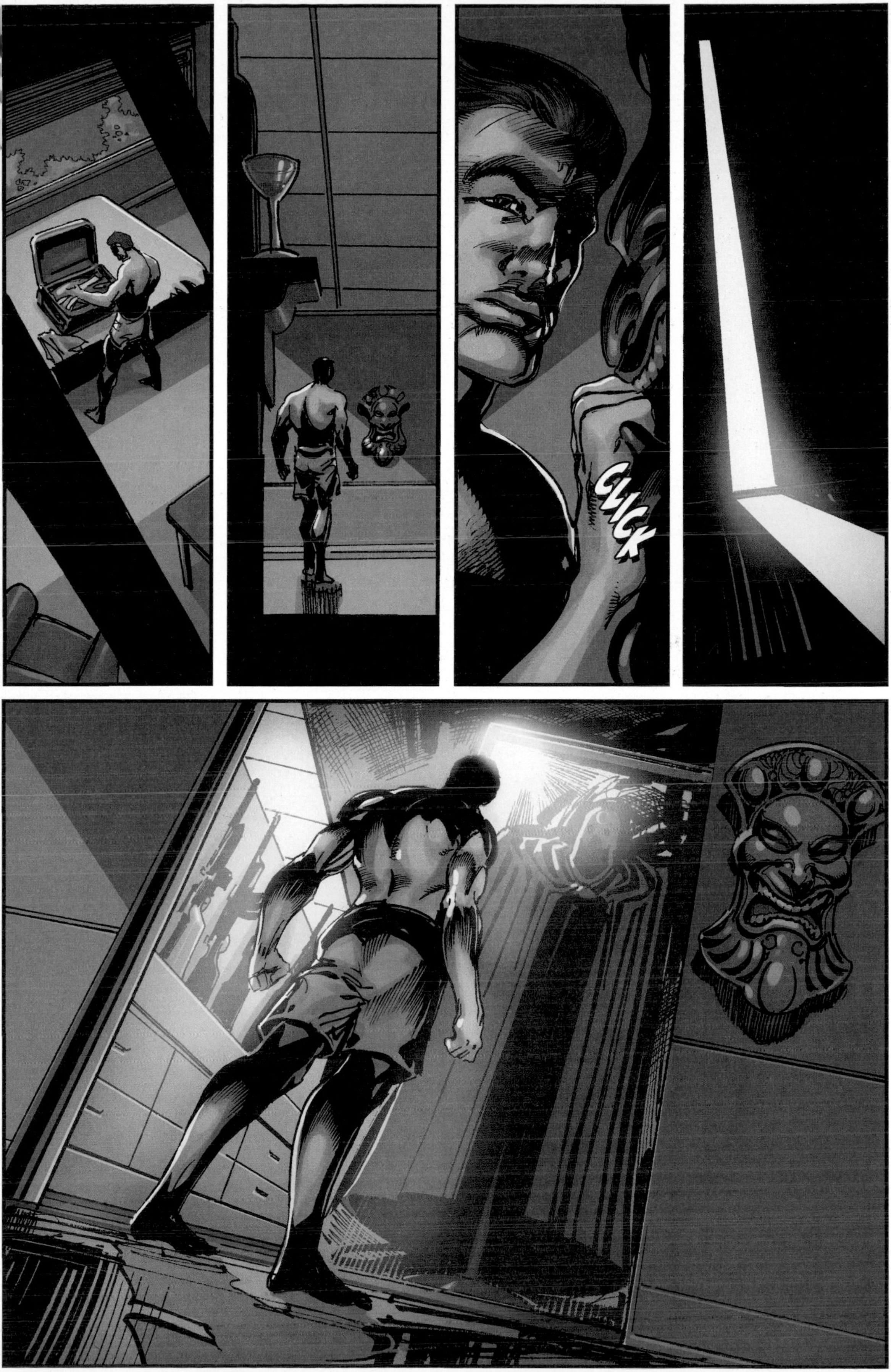
CLICK

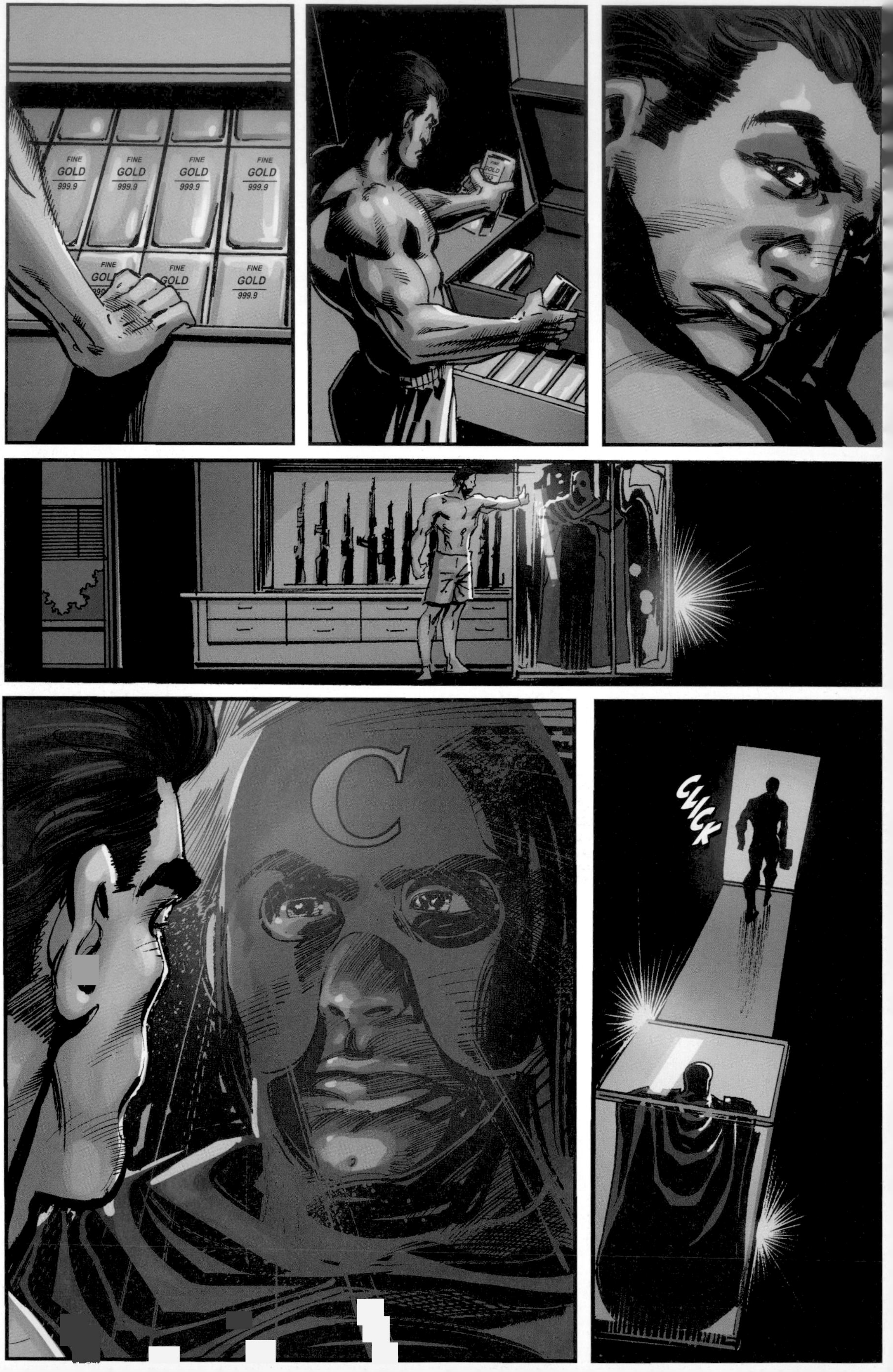
FINE GOLD 999.9
FINE GOLD 999.9
FINE GOLD 999.9
FINE GOLD 999.9
FINE GOLD 999.9
CLICK

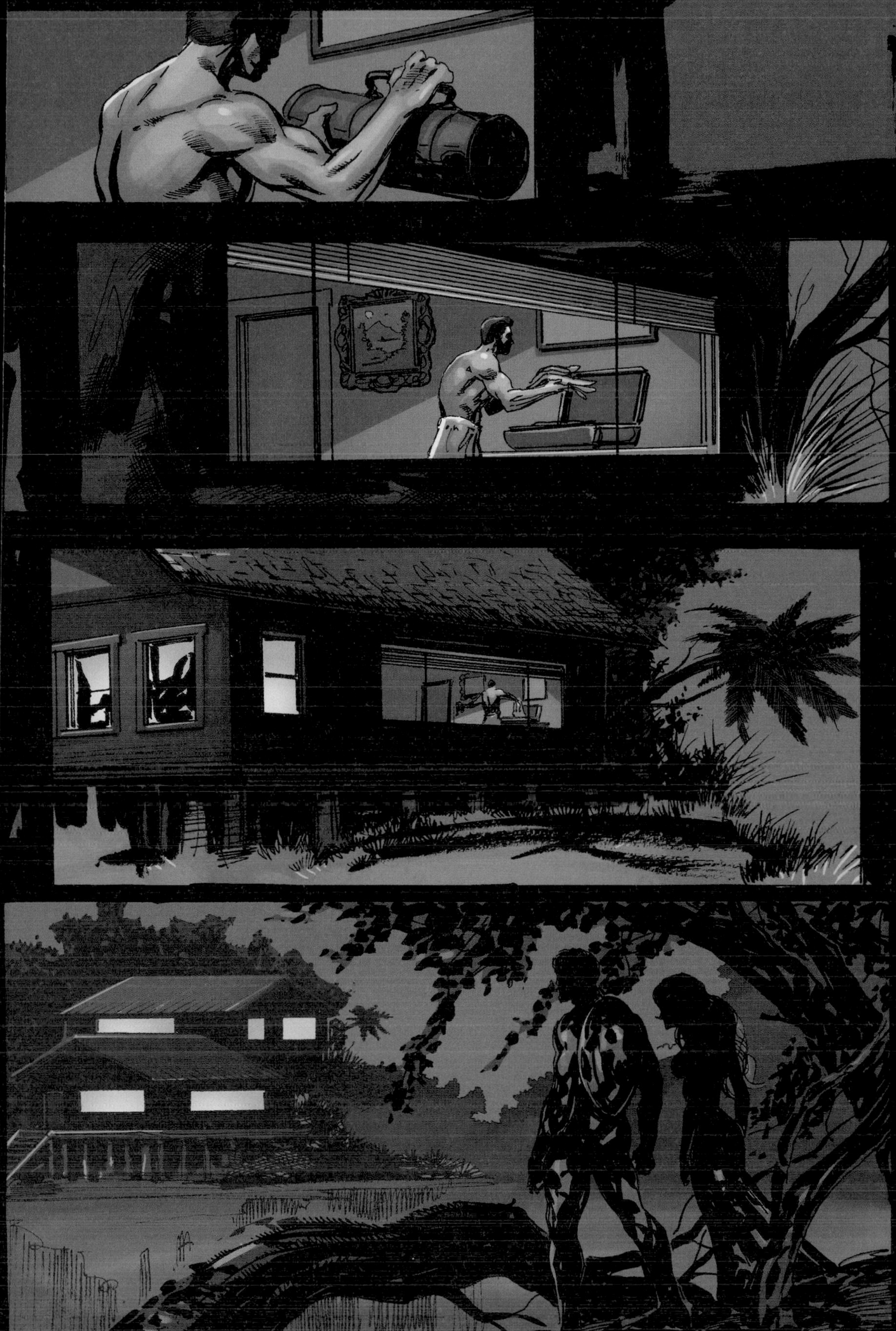

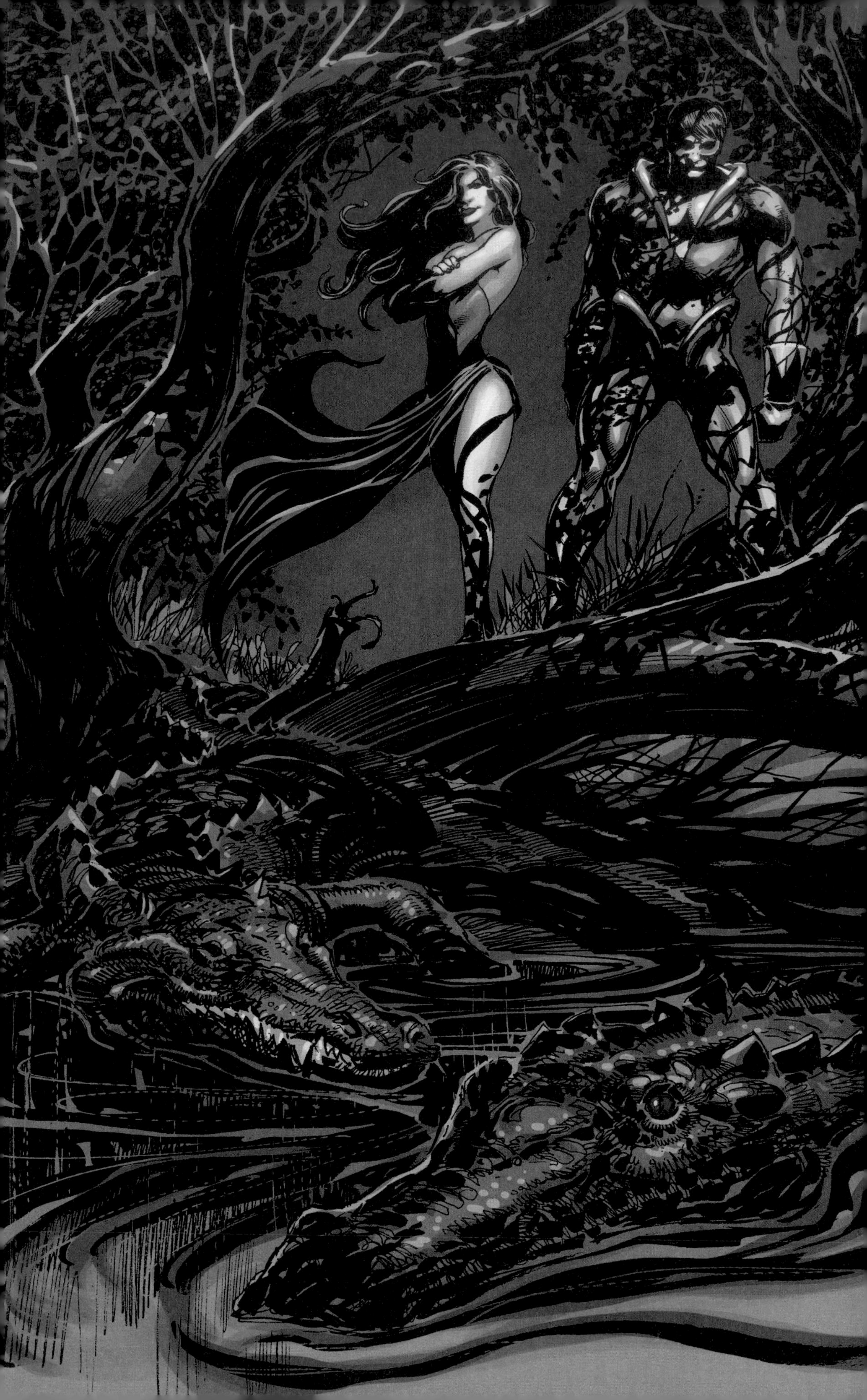

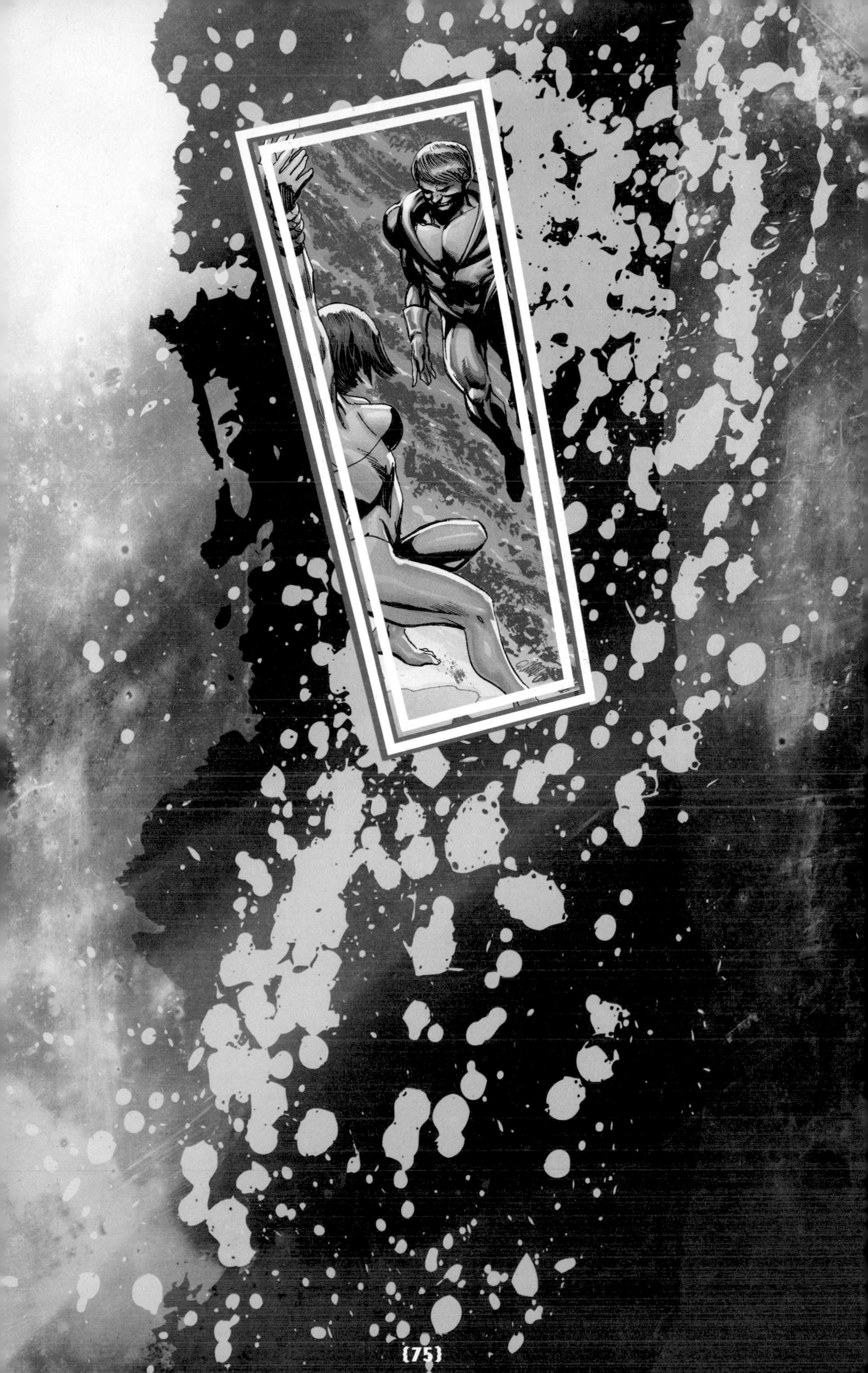

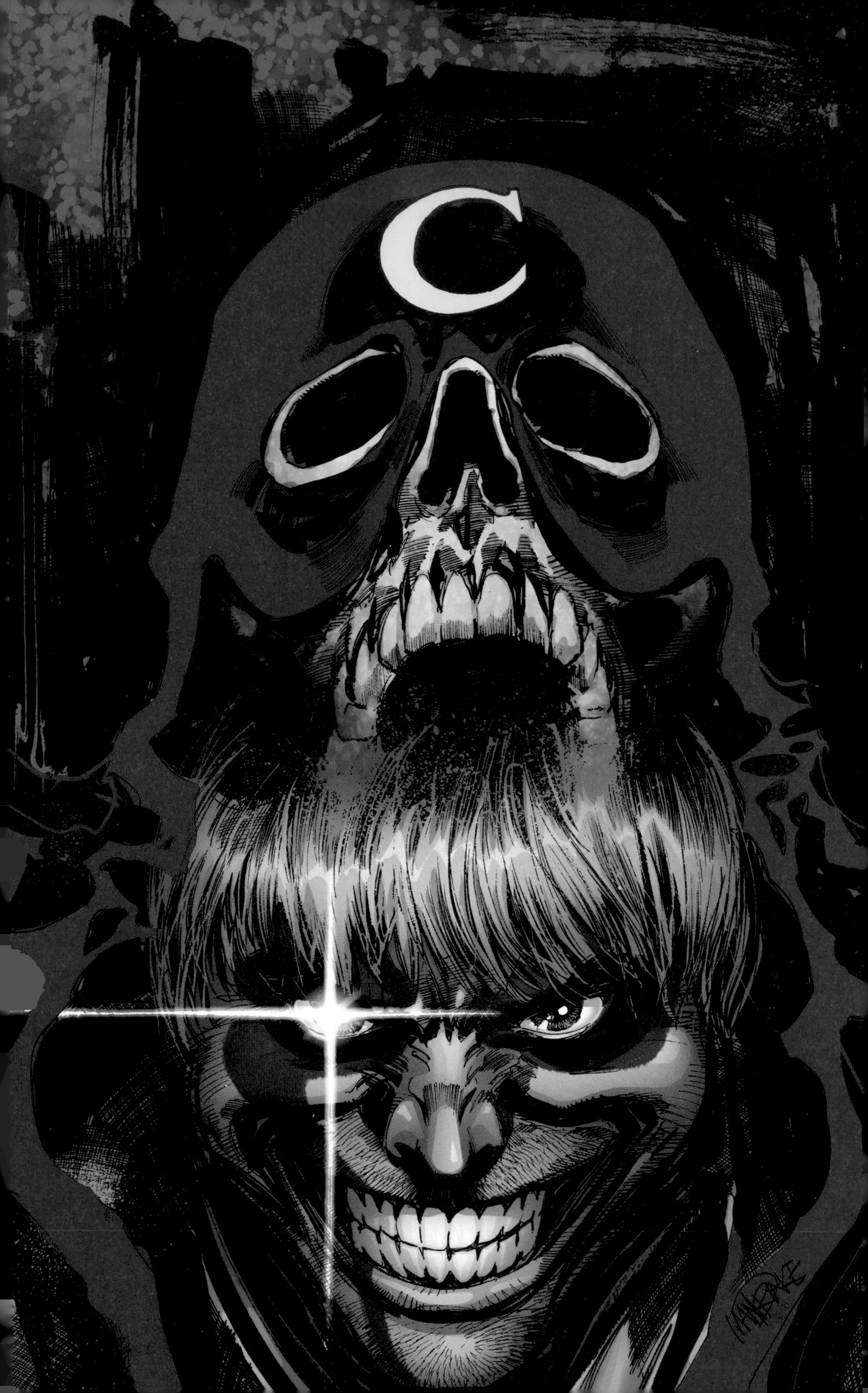

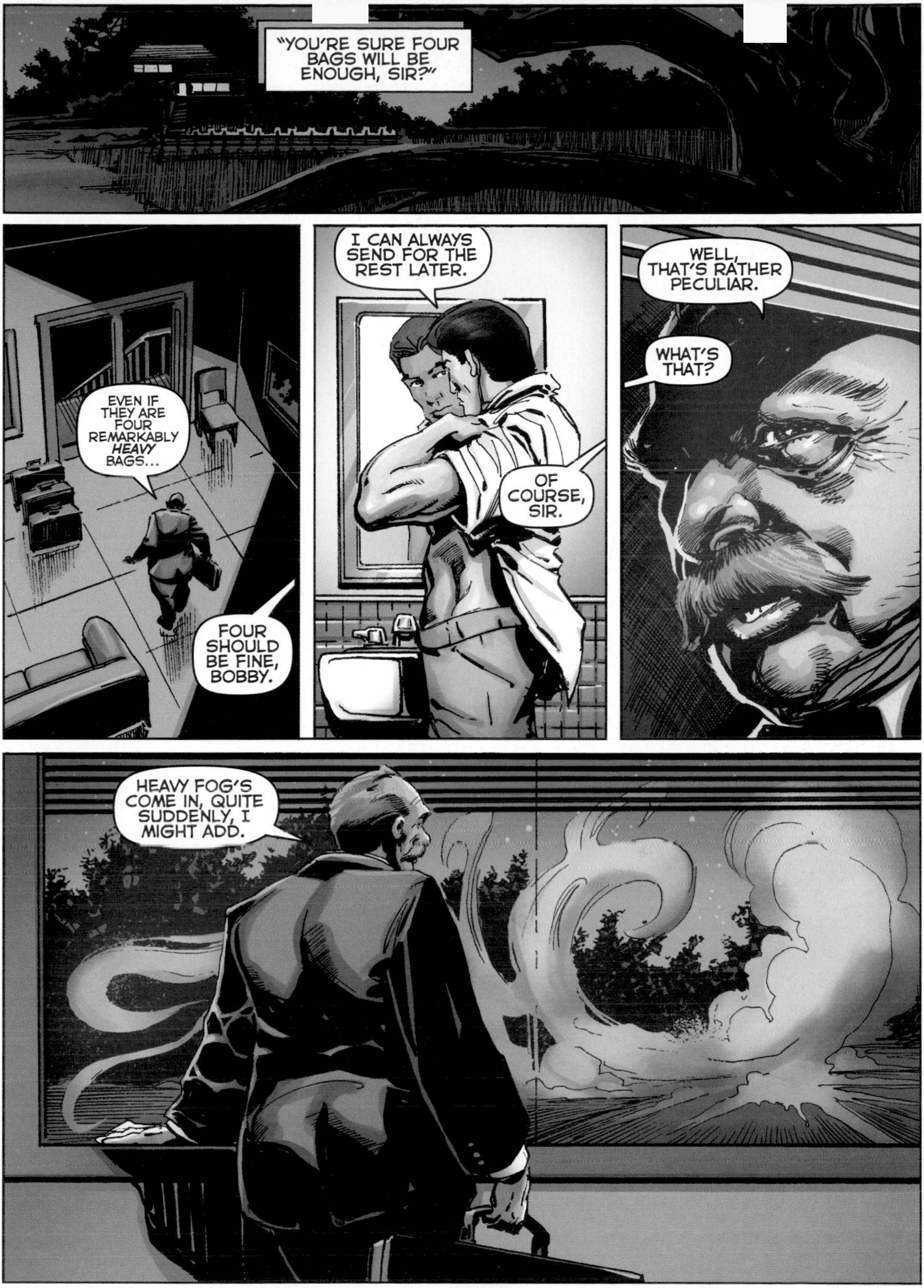
"YOU'RE SURE FOUR BAGS WILL BE ENOUGH, SIR?"
EVEN IF THEY ARE FOUR REMARKABLY *HEAVY* BAGS...
FOUR SHOULD BE FINE, BOBBY.
I CAN ALWAYS SEND FOR THE REST LATER.
OF COURSE, SIR.
WELL, THAT'S RATHER PECULIAR.
WHAT'S THAT?
HEAVY FOG'S COME IN, QUITE SUDDENLY, I MIGHT ADD.

FULL CIRCLE

Writer: J. Michael Straczynski Line Art: Tom Mandrake
Colors: HiFi Letters: Troy Peteri

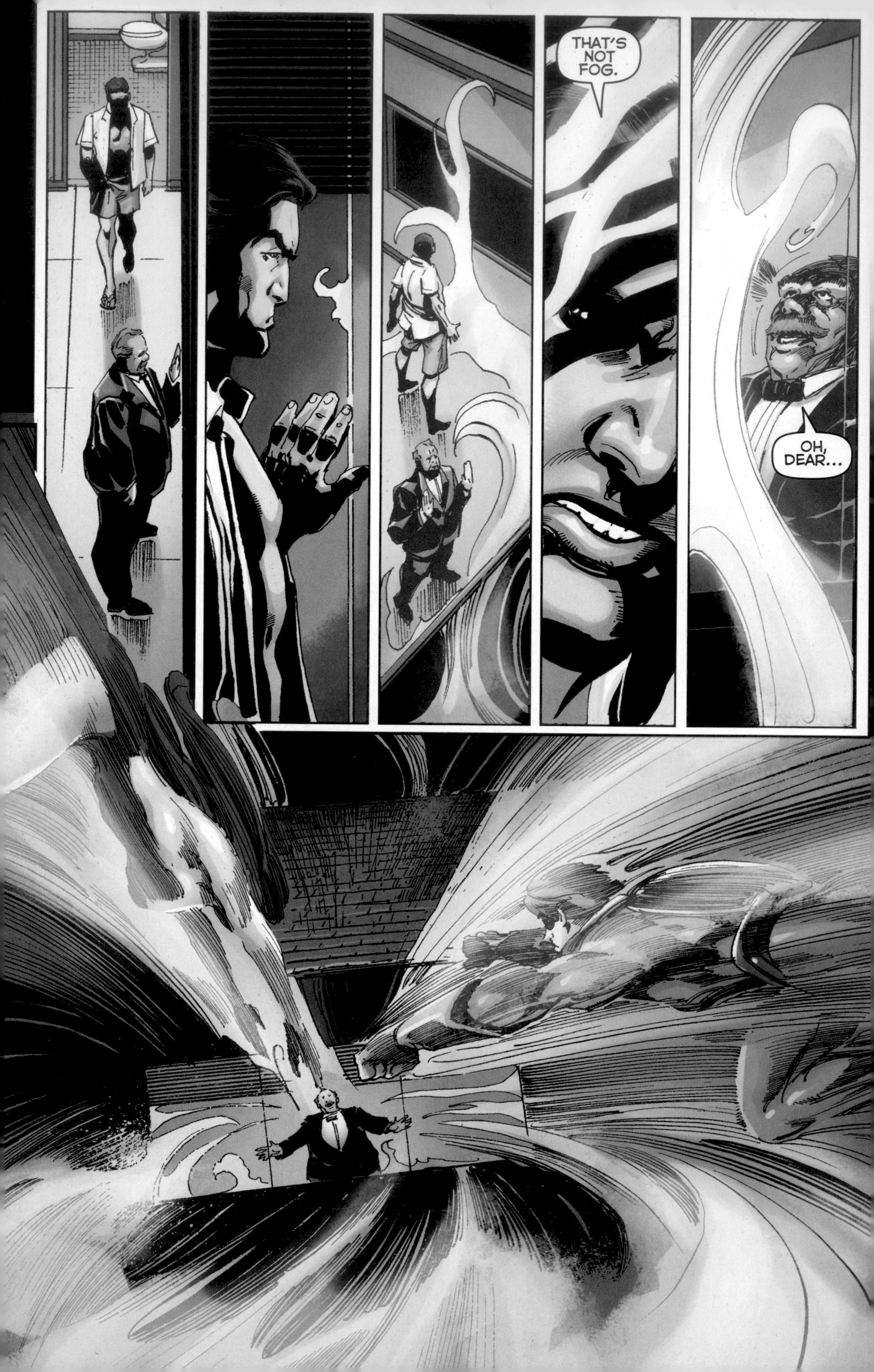
THAT'S NOT FOG.
OH, DEAR...

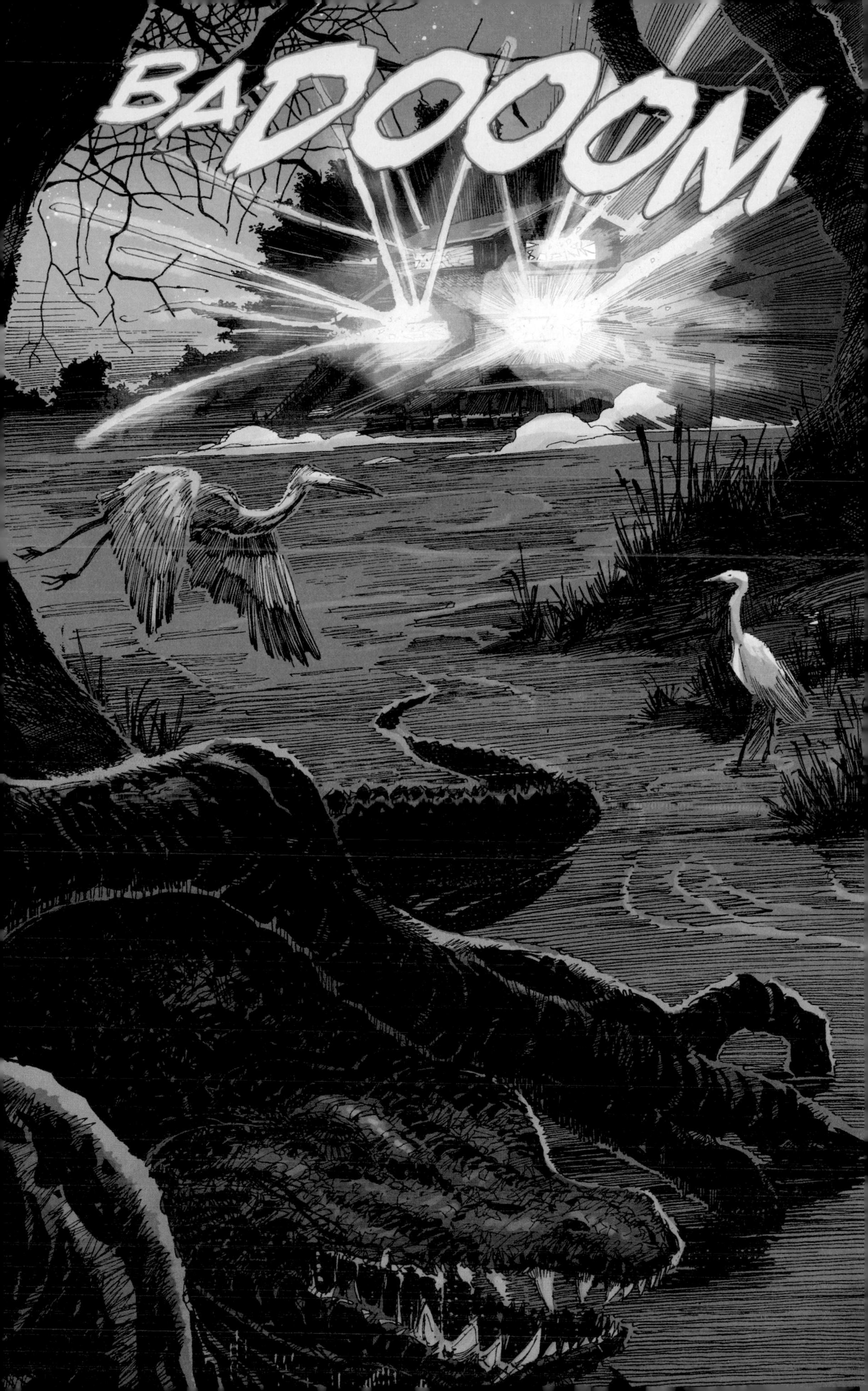
BADOOOM

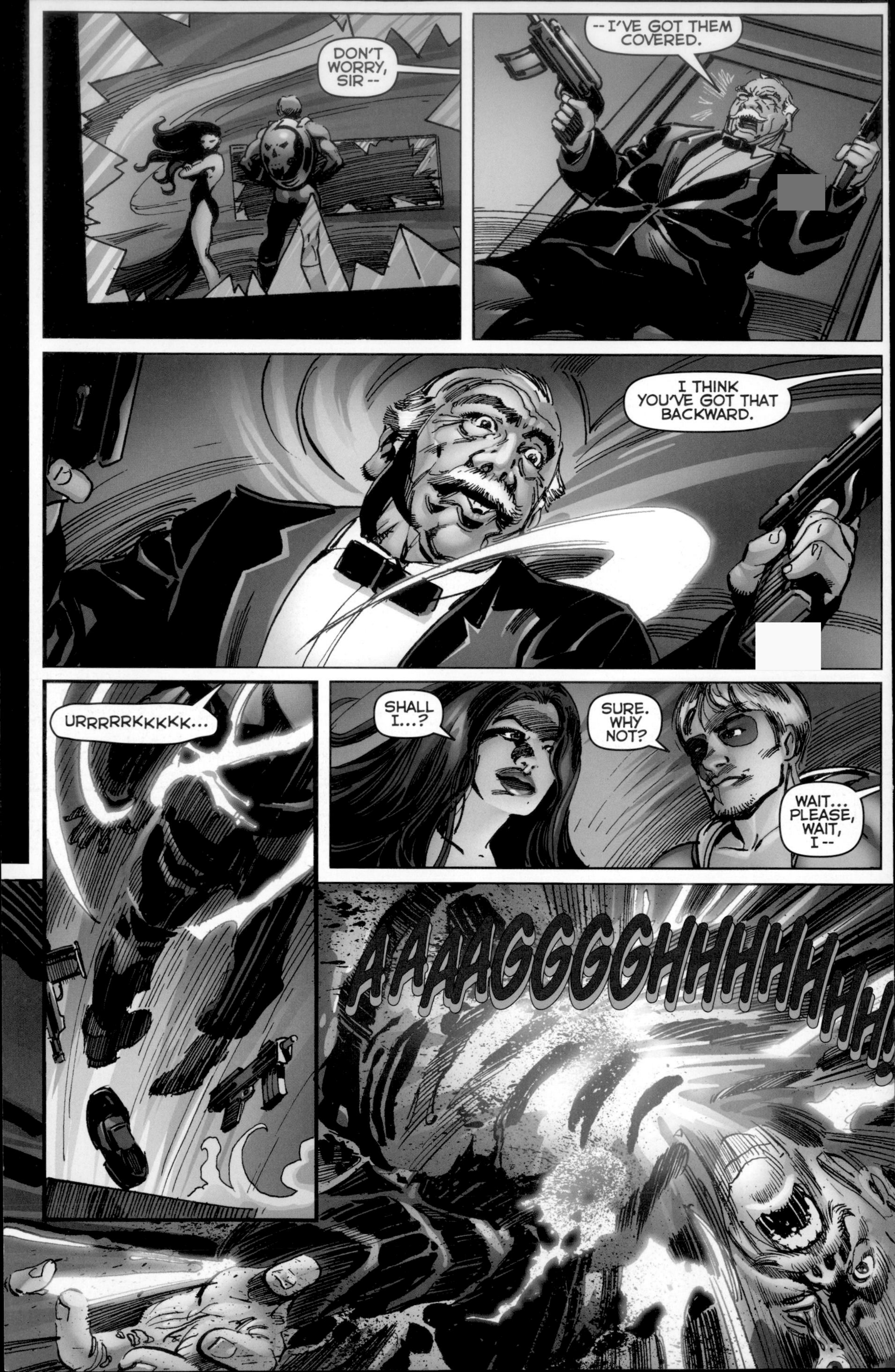
DON'T WORRY, SIR --
-- I'VE GOT THEM COVERED.
I THINK YOU'VE GOT THAT BACKWARD.
URRRRRKKKKK...
SHALL I...?
SURE. WHY NOT?
WAIT... PLEASE, WAIT, I --
AAAAGGGGGHHHHHH

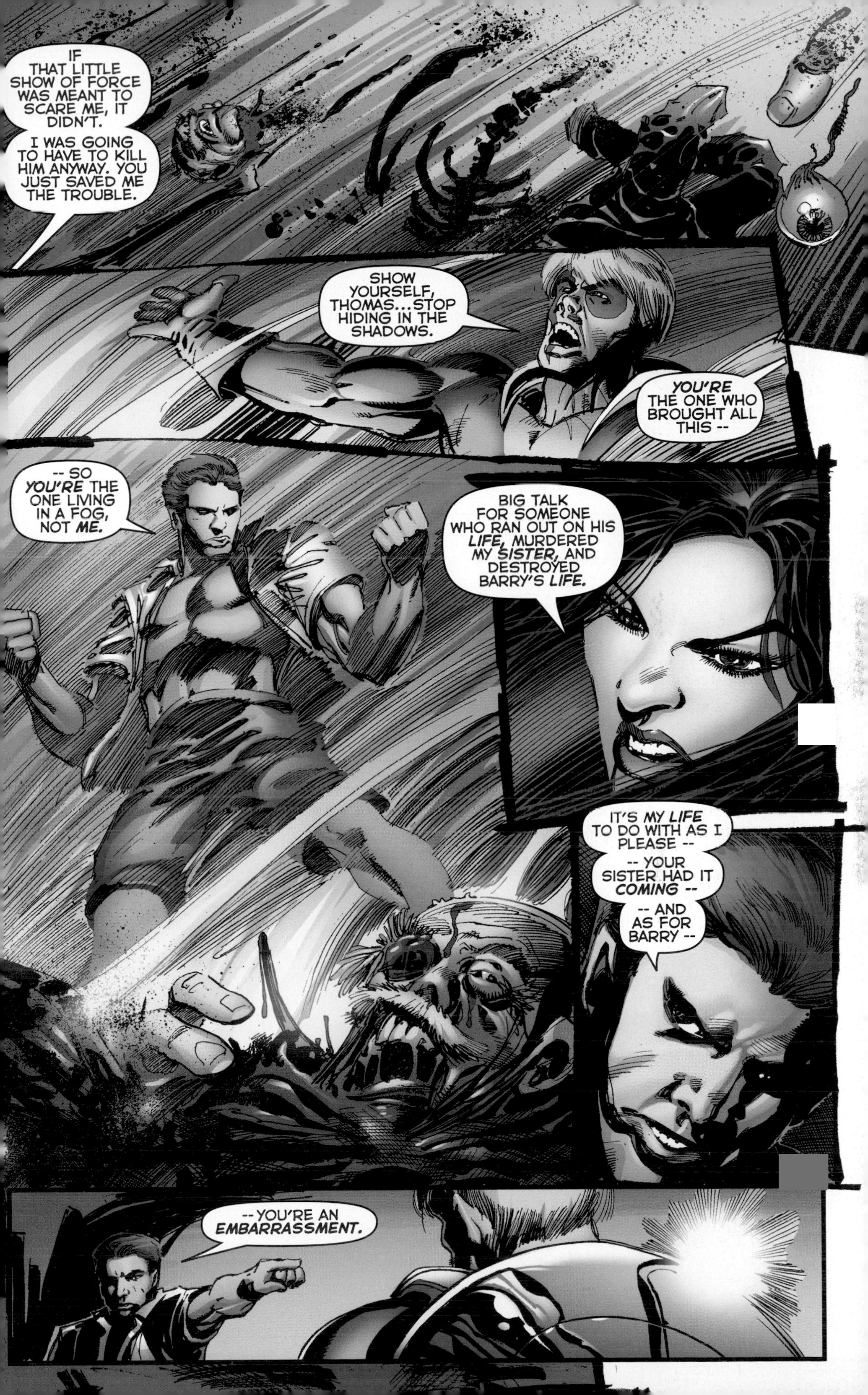

IF THAT LITTLE SHOW OF FORCE WAS MEANT TO SCARE ME, IT DIDN'T.
I WAS GOING TO HAVE TO KILL HIM ANYWAY. YOU JUST SAVED ME THE TROUBLE.
SHOW YOURSELF, THOMAS...STOP HIDING IN THE SHADOWS.
YOU'RE THE ONE WHO BROUGHT ALL THIS --
-- SO YOU'RE THE ONE LIVING IN A FOG, NOT ME.
BIG TALK FOR SOMEONE WHO RAN OUT ON HIS LIFE, MURDERED MY SISTER, AND DESTROYED BARRY'S LIFE.
IT'S MY LIFE TO DO WITH AS I PLEASE --
-- YOUR SISTER HAD IT COMING --
-- AND AS FOR BARRY --
--YOU'RE AN EMBARRASSMENT.

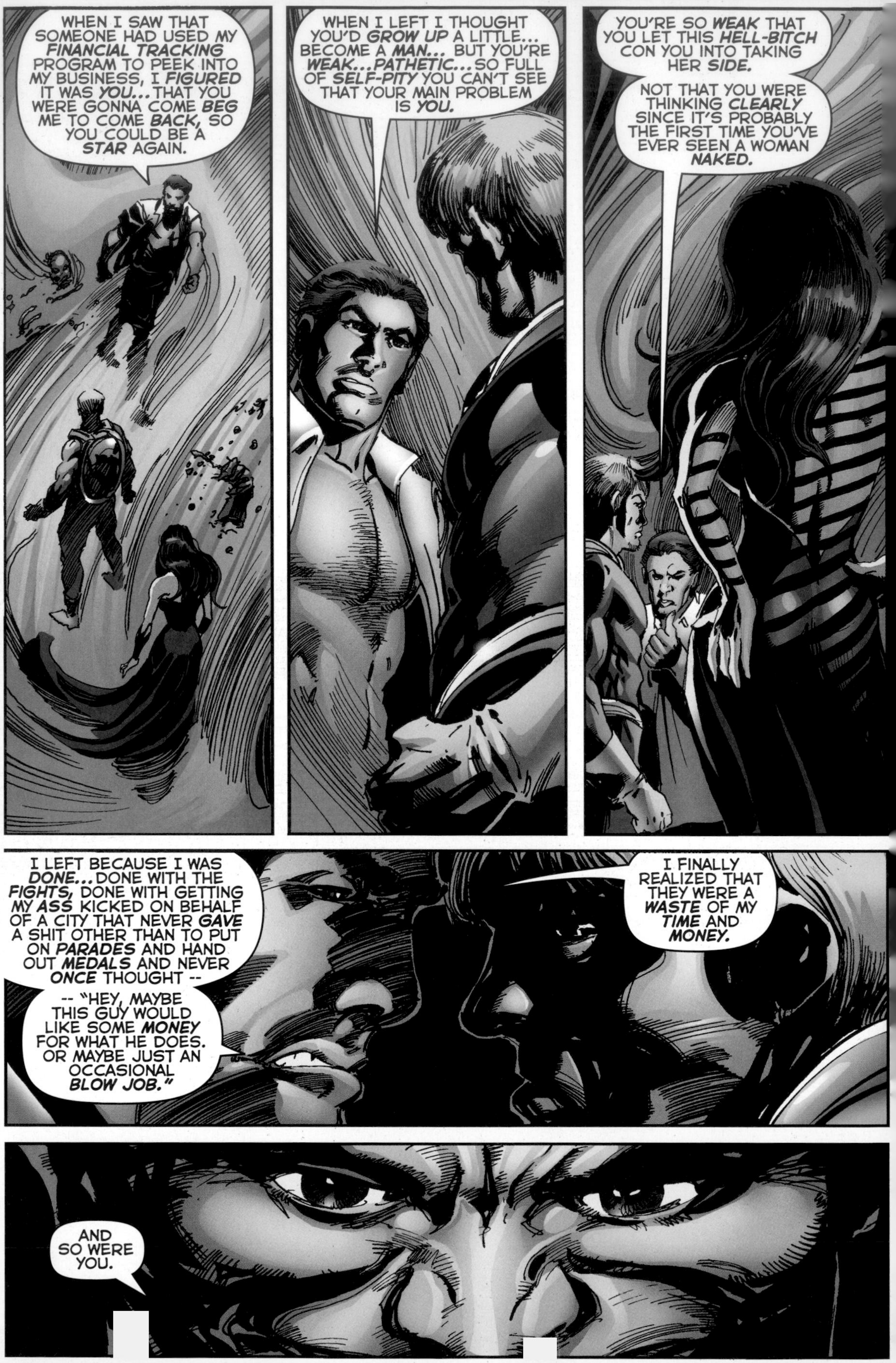

WHEN I SAW THAT SOMEONE HAD USED MY FINANCIAL TRACKING PROGRAM TO PEEK INTO MY BUSINESS, I FIGURED IT WAS YOU... THAT YOU WERE GONNA COME BEG ME TO COME BACK, SO YOU COULD BE A STAR AGAIN.
WHEN I LEFT I THOUGHT YOU'D GROW UP A LITTLE... BECOME A MAN... BUT YOU'RE WEAK...PATHETIC...SO FULL OF SELF-PITY YOU CAN'T SEE THAT YOUR MAIN PROBLEM IS YOU.
YOU'RE SO WEAK THAT YOU LET THIS HELL-BITCH CON YOU INTO TAKING HER SIDE.
NOT THAT YOU WERE THINKING CLEARLY SINCE IT'S PROBABLY THE FIRST TIME YOU'VE EVER SEEN A WOMAN NAKED.
I LEFT BECAUSE I WAS DONE... DONE WITH THE FIGHTS, DONE WITH GETTING MY ASS KICKED ON BEHALF OF A CITY THAT NEVER GAVE A SHIT OTHER THAN TO PUT ON PARADES AND HAND OUT MEDALS AND NEVER ONCE THOUGHT --
-- "HEY, MAYBE THIS GUY WOULD LIKE SOME MONEY FOR WHAT HE DOES. OR MAYBE JUST AN OCCASIONAL BLOW JOB."
I FINALLY REALIZED THAT THEY WERE A WASTE OF MY TIME AND MONEY.
AND SO WERE YOU.

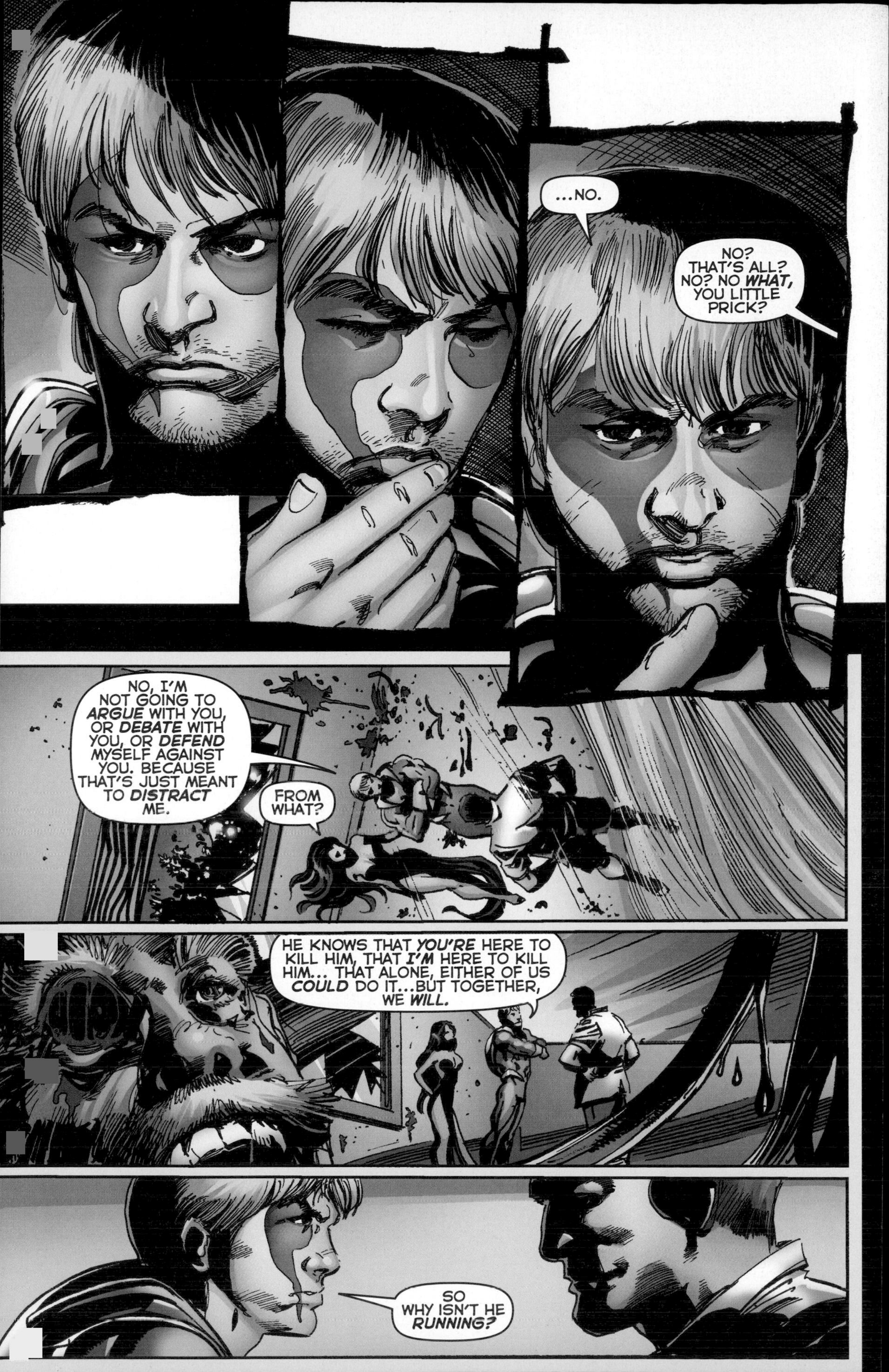
...NO.
NO? THAT'S ALL? NO? NO WHAT, YOU LITTLE PRICK?
NO, I'M NOT GOING TO ARGUE WITH YOU, OR DEBATE WITH YOU, OR DEFEND MYSELF AGAINST YOU. BECAUSE THAT'S JUST MEANT TO DISTRACT ME.
FROM WHAT?
HE KNOWS THAT YOU'RE HERE TO KILL HIM, THAT I'M HERE TO KILL HIM... THAT ALONE, EITHER OF US COULD DO IT...BUT TOGETHER, WE WILL.
SO WHY ISN'T HE RUNNING?

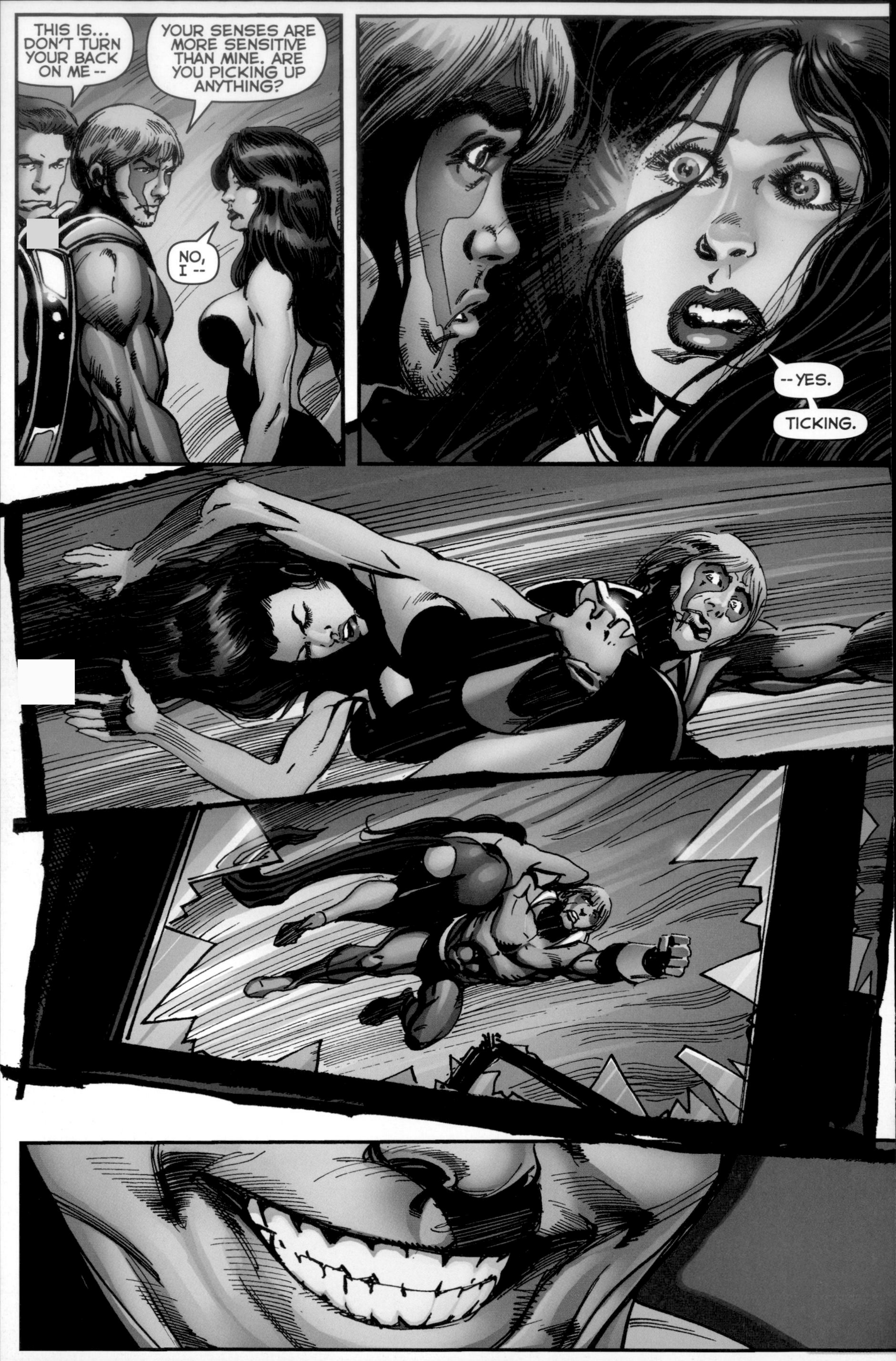
THIS IS... DON'T TURN YOUR BACK ON ME --
YOUR SENSES ARE MORE SENSITIVE THAN MINE. ARE YOU PICKING UP ANYTHING?
NO, I --
--YES.
TICKING.

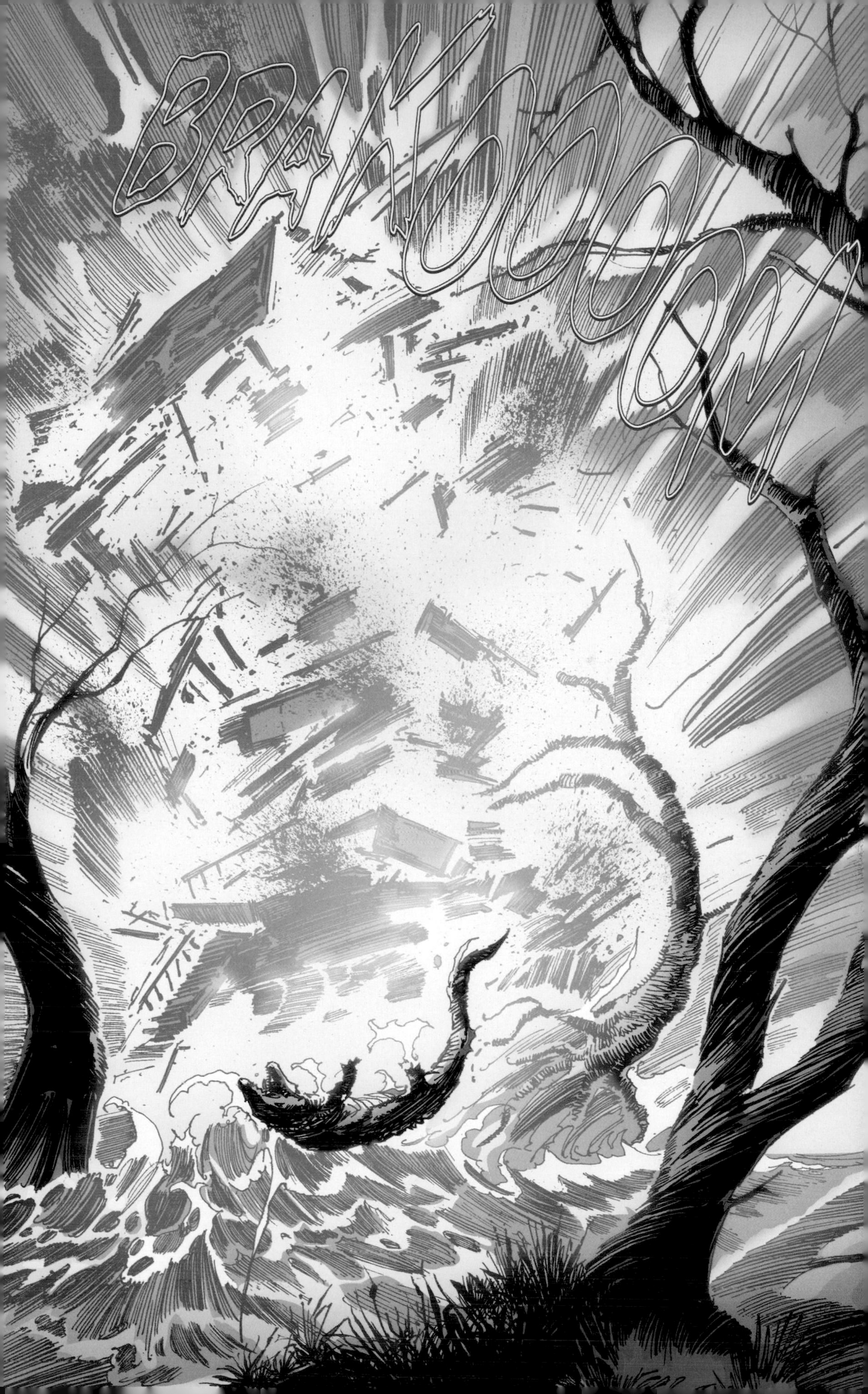
BRAKOOOOOM

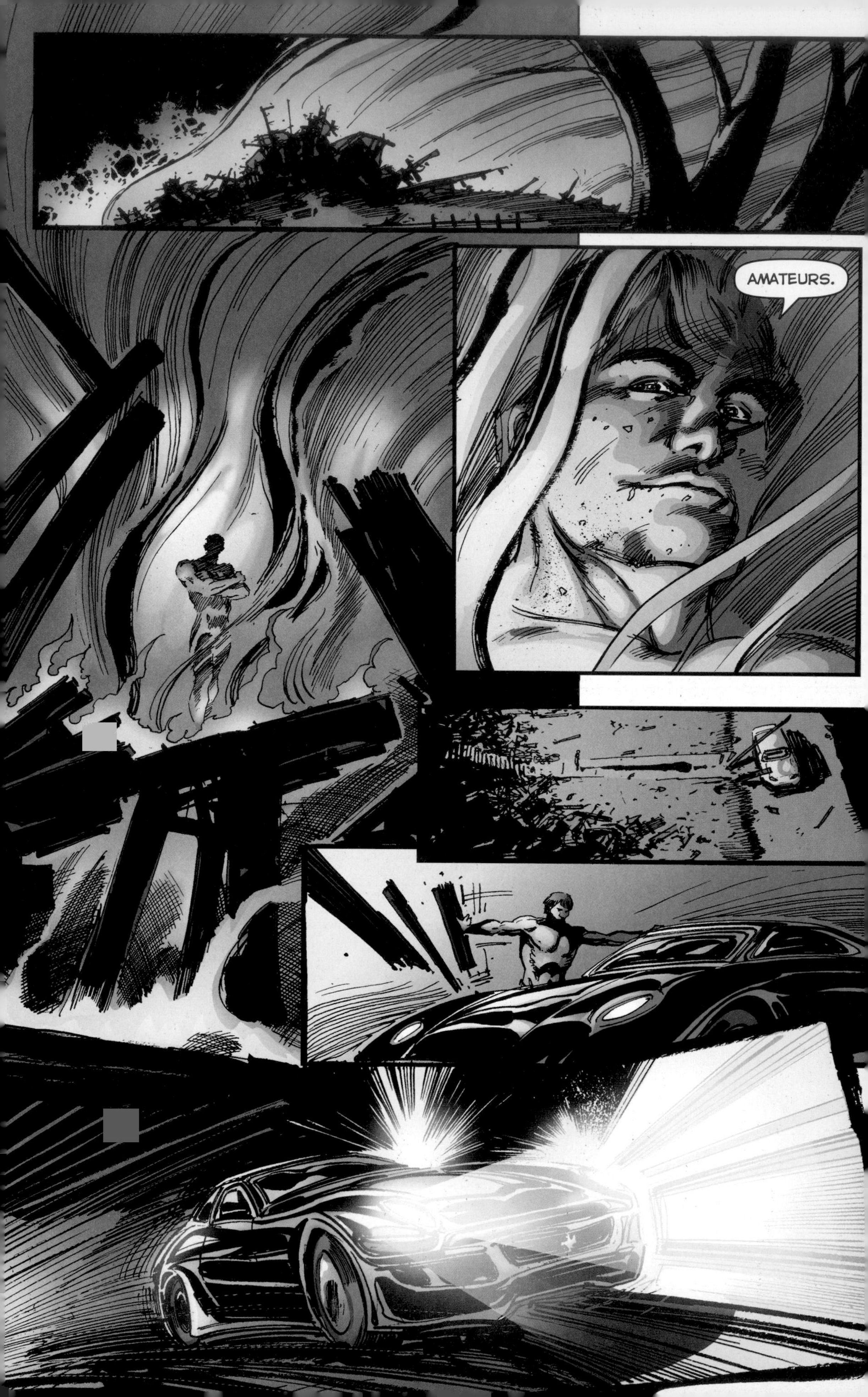
AMATEURS.

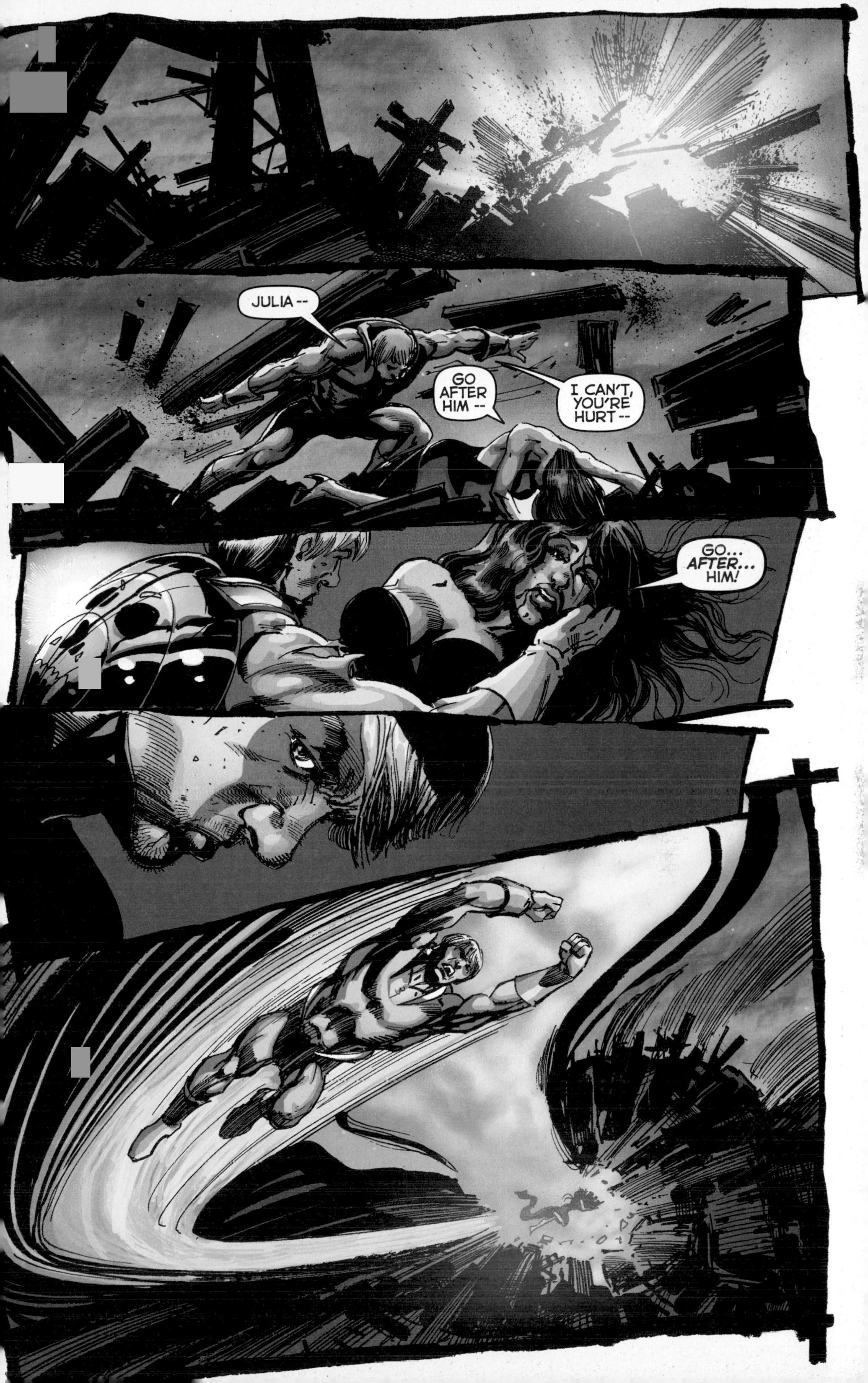
JULIA --
GO AFTER HIM --
I CAN'T, YOU'RE HURT --
GO... AFTER... HIM!

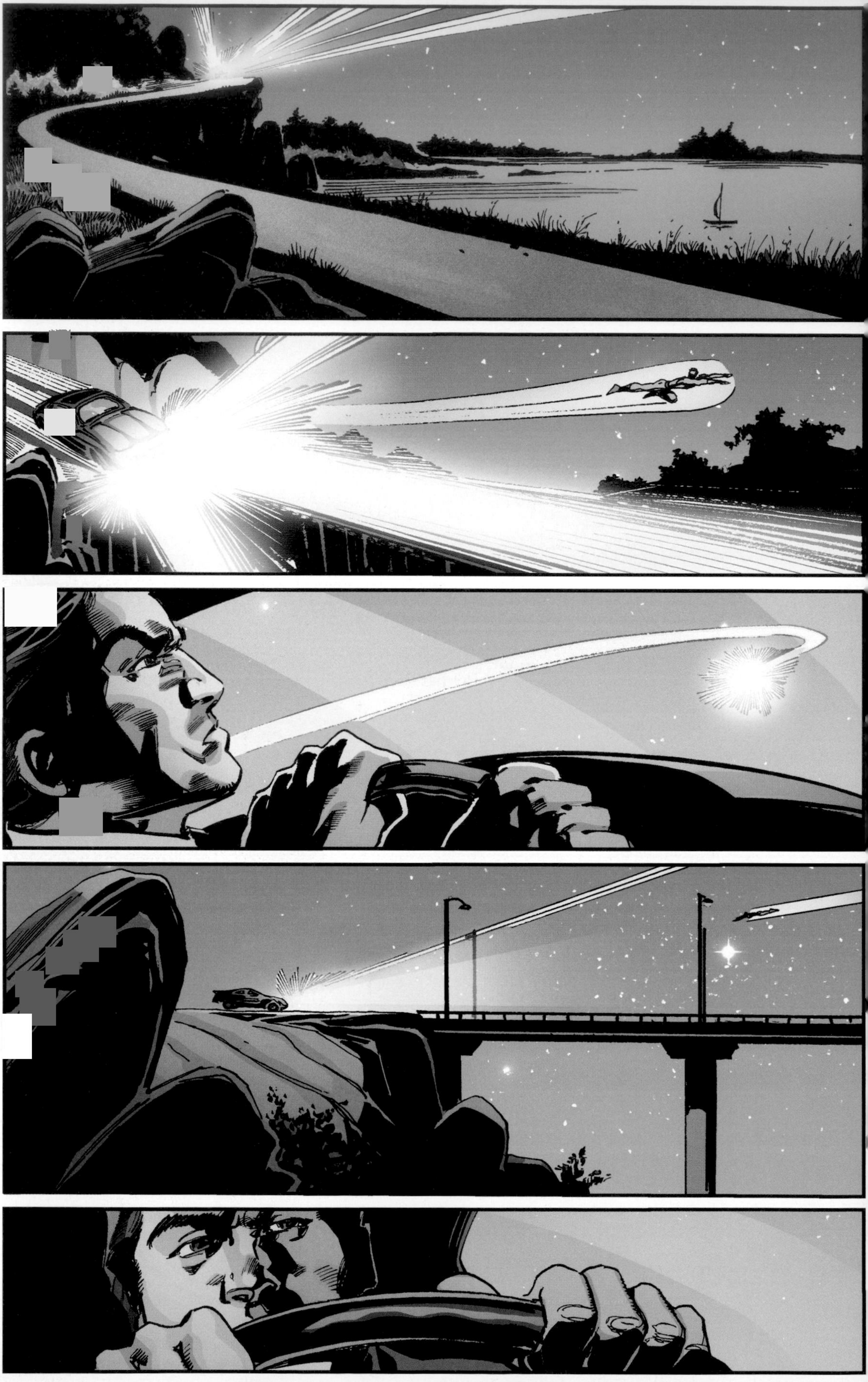

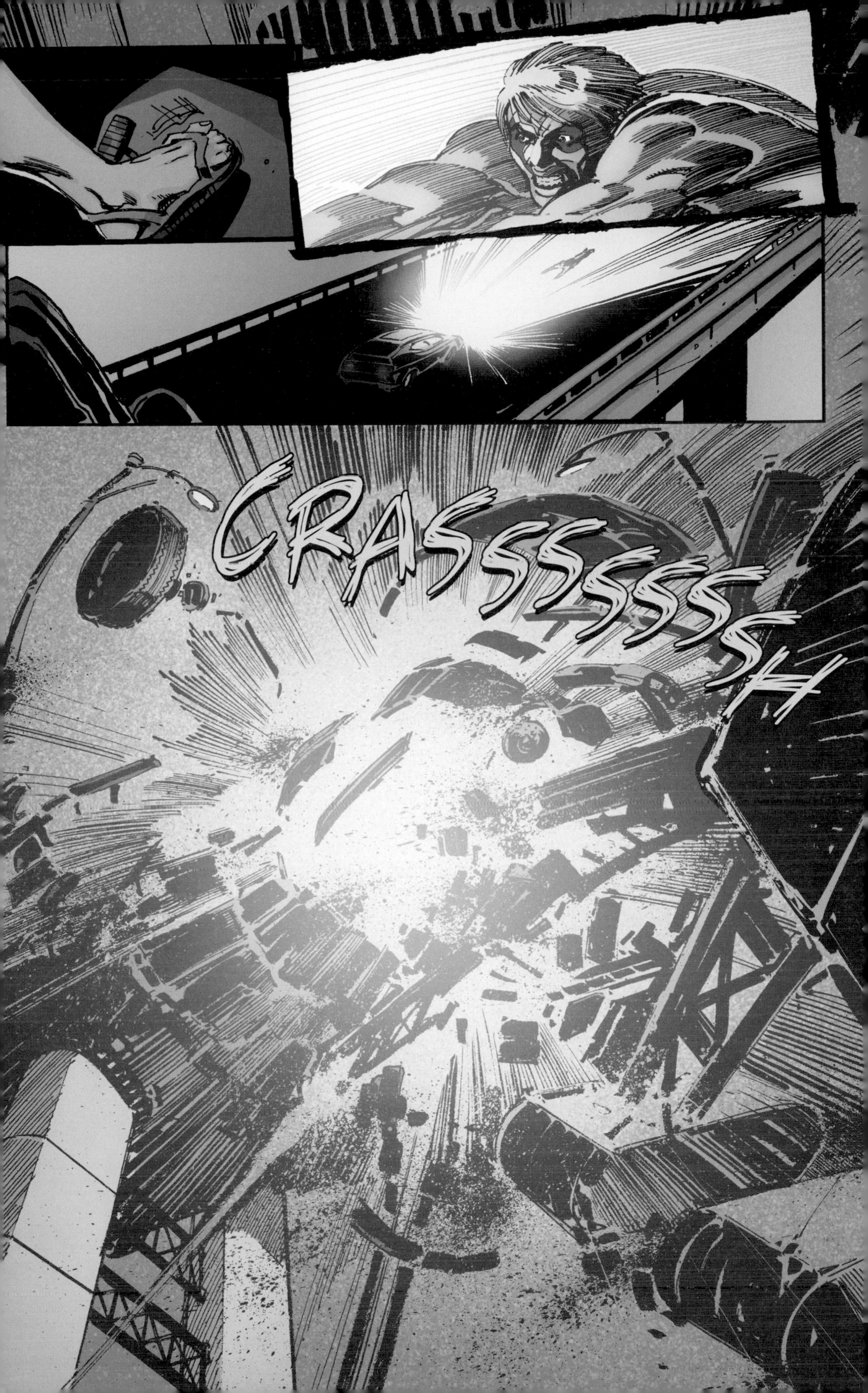
CRASSSSSSSH

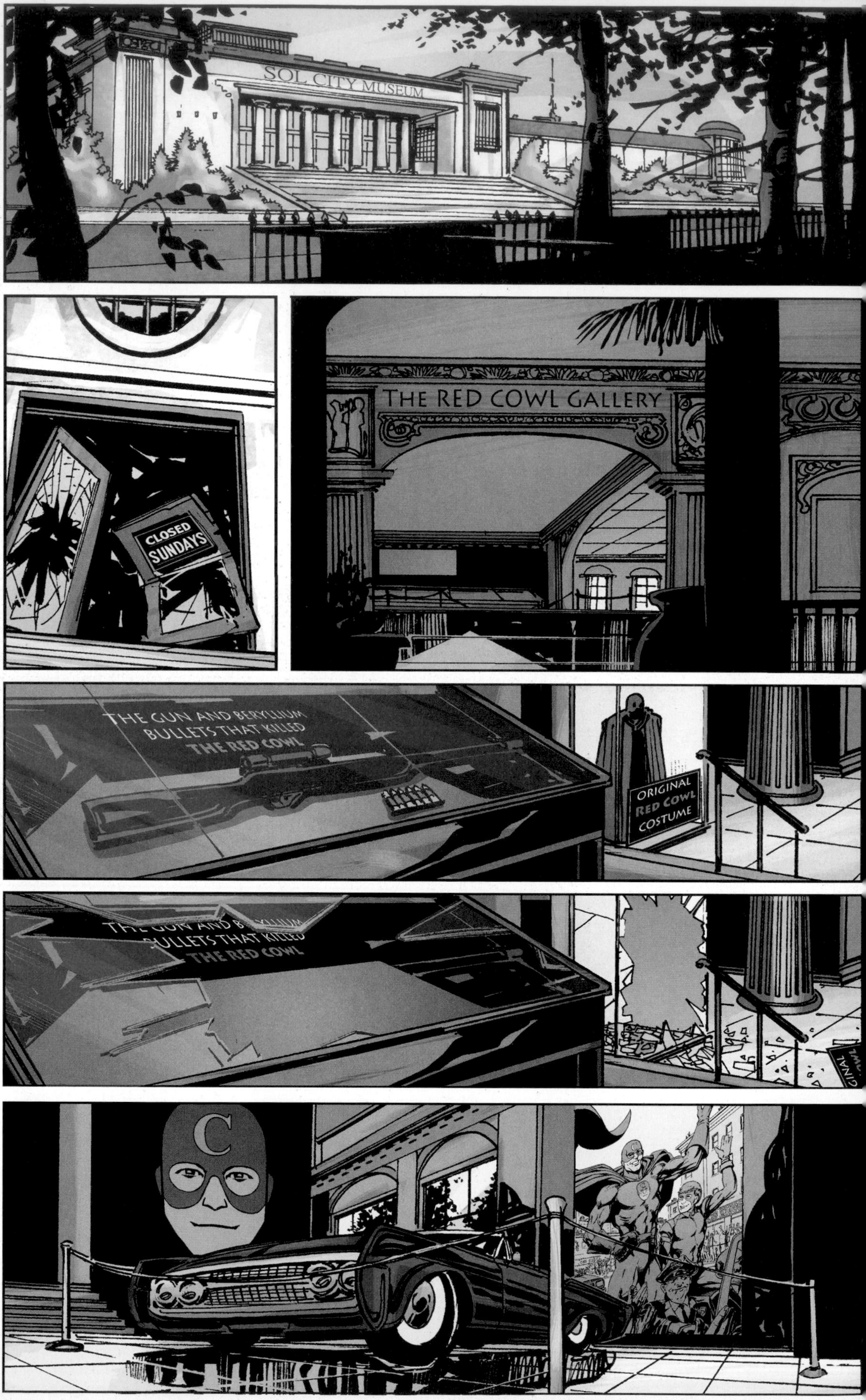
SOL CITY MUSEUM
CLOSED SUNDAYS
THE RED COWL GALLERY
THE GUN AND BERYLLIUM BULLETS THAT KILLED THE RED COWL
ORIGINAL RED COWL COSTUME
THE GUN AND BERYLLIUM BULLETS THAT KILLED THE RED COWL

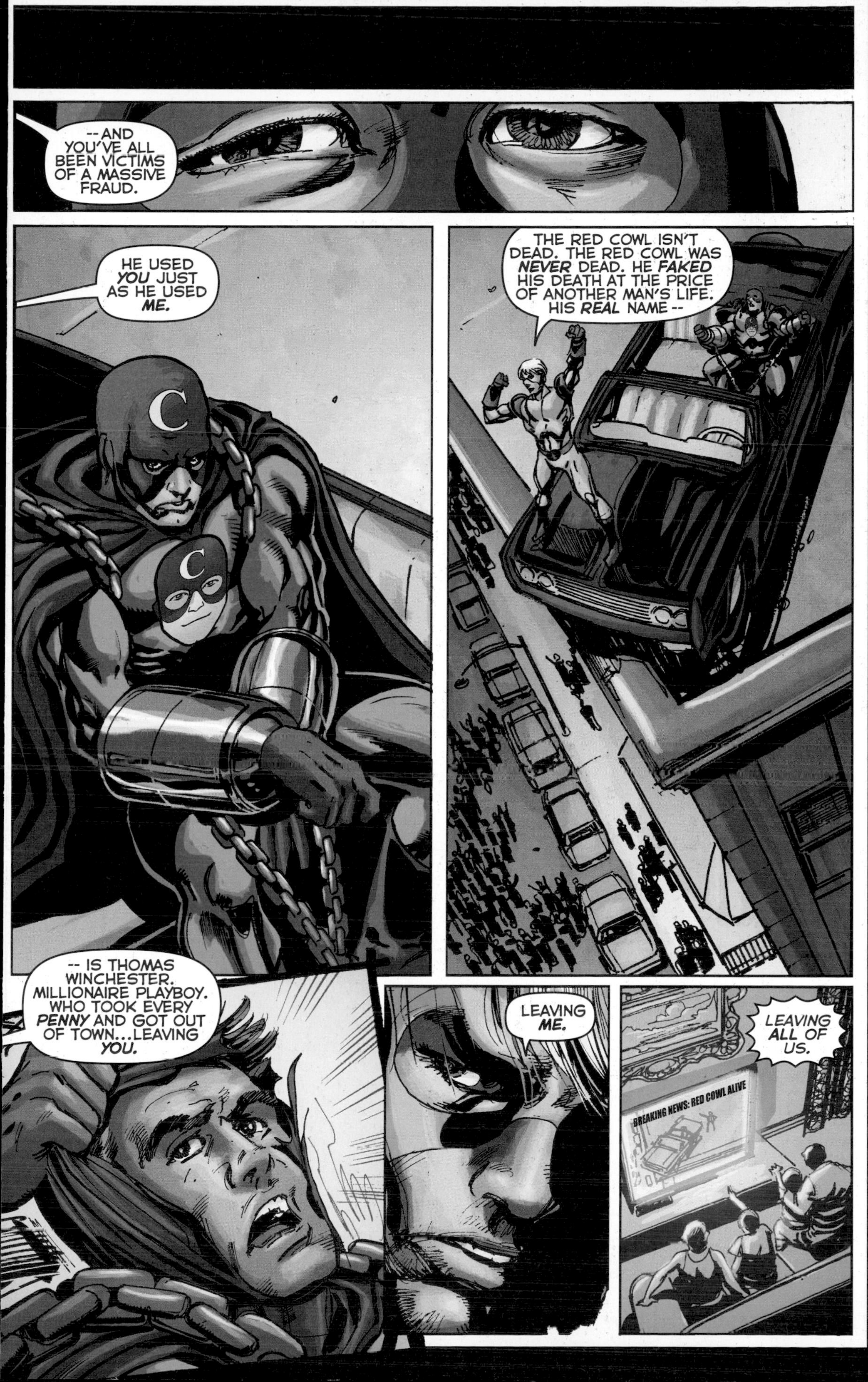
--AND YOU'VE ALL BEEN VICTIMS OF A MASSIVE FRAUD.
HE USED YOU JUST AS HE USED ME.
THE RED COWL ISN'T DEAD. THE RED COWL WAS NEVER DEAD. HE FAKED HIS DEATH AT THE PRICE OF ANOTHER MAN'S LIFE. HIS REAL NAME --
-- IS THOMAS WINCHESTER. MILLIONAIRE PLAYBOY. WHO TOOK EVERY PENNY AND GOT OUT OF TOWN...LEAVING YOU.
LEAVING ME.
LEAVING ALL OF US.
BREAKING NEWS: RED COWL ALIVE

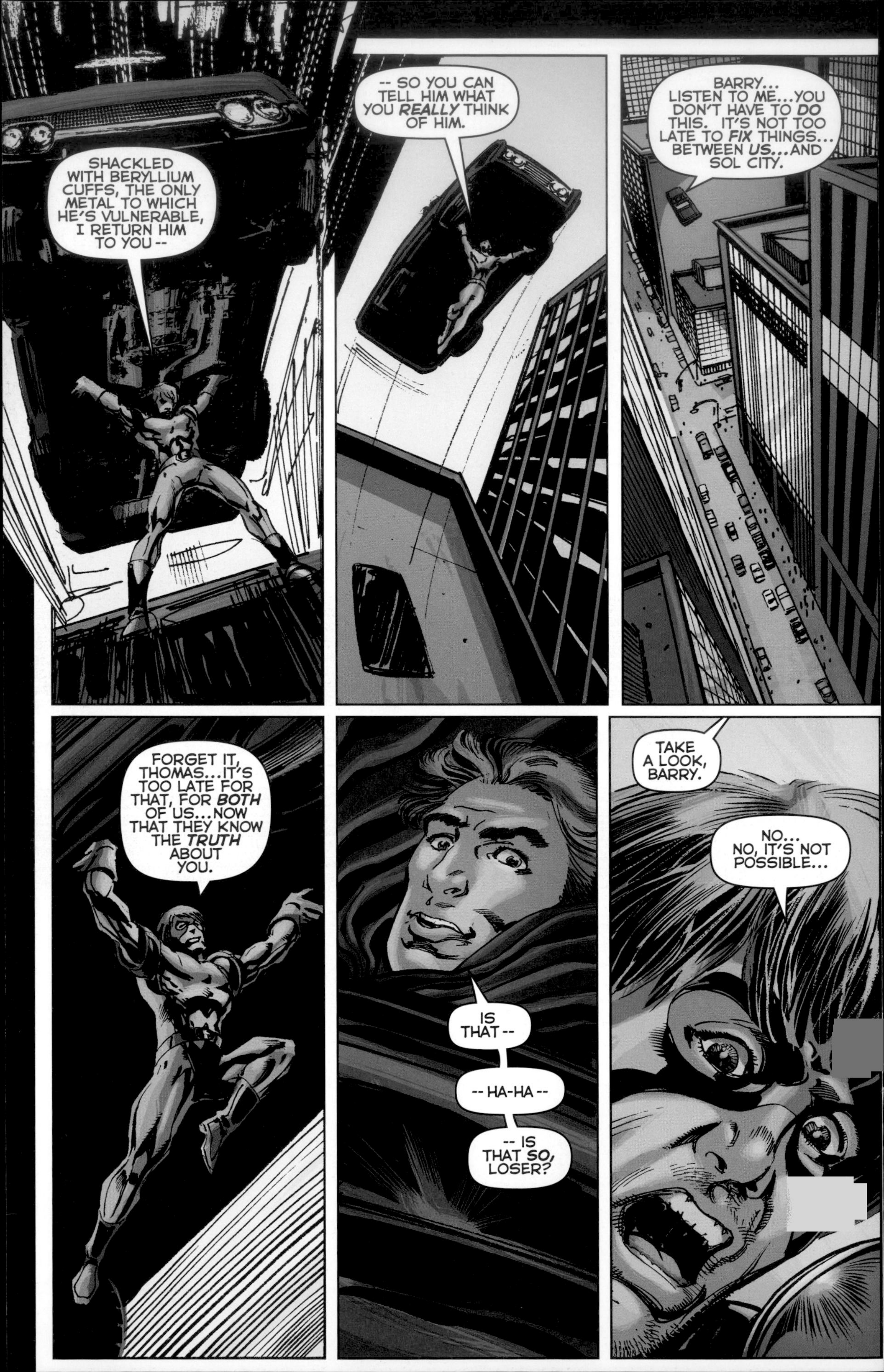
SHACKLED WITH BERYLLIUM CUFFS, THE ONLY METAL TO WHICH HE'S VULNERABLE, I RETURN HIM TO YOU --
-- SO YOU CAN TELL HIM WHAT YOU REALLY THINK OF HIM.
BARRY... LISTEN TO ME... YOU DON'T HAVE TO DO THIS. IT'S NOT TOO LATE TO FIX THINGS... BETWEEN US... AND SOL CITY.
FORGET IT, THOMAS... IT'S TOO LATE FOR THAT, FOR BOTH OF US... NOW THAT THEY KNOW THE TRUTH ABOUT YOU.
IS THAT --
-- HA-HA --
-- IS THAT SO, LOSER?
TAKE A LOOK, BARRY.
NO... NO, IT'S NOT POSSIBLE...

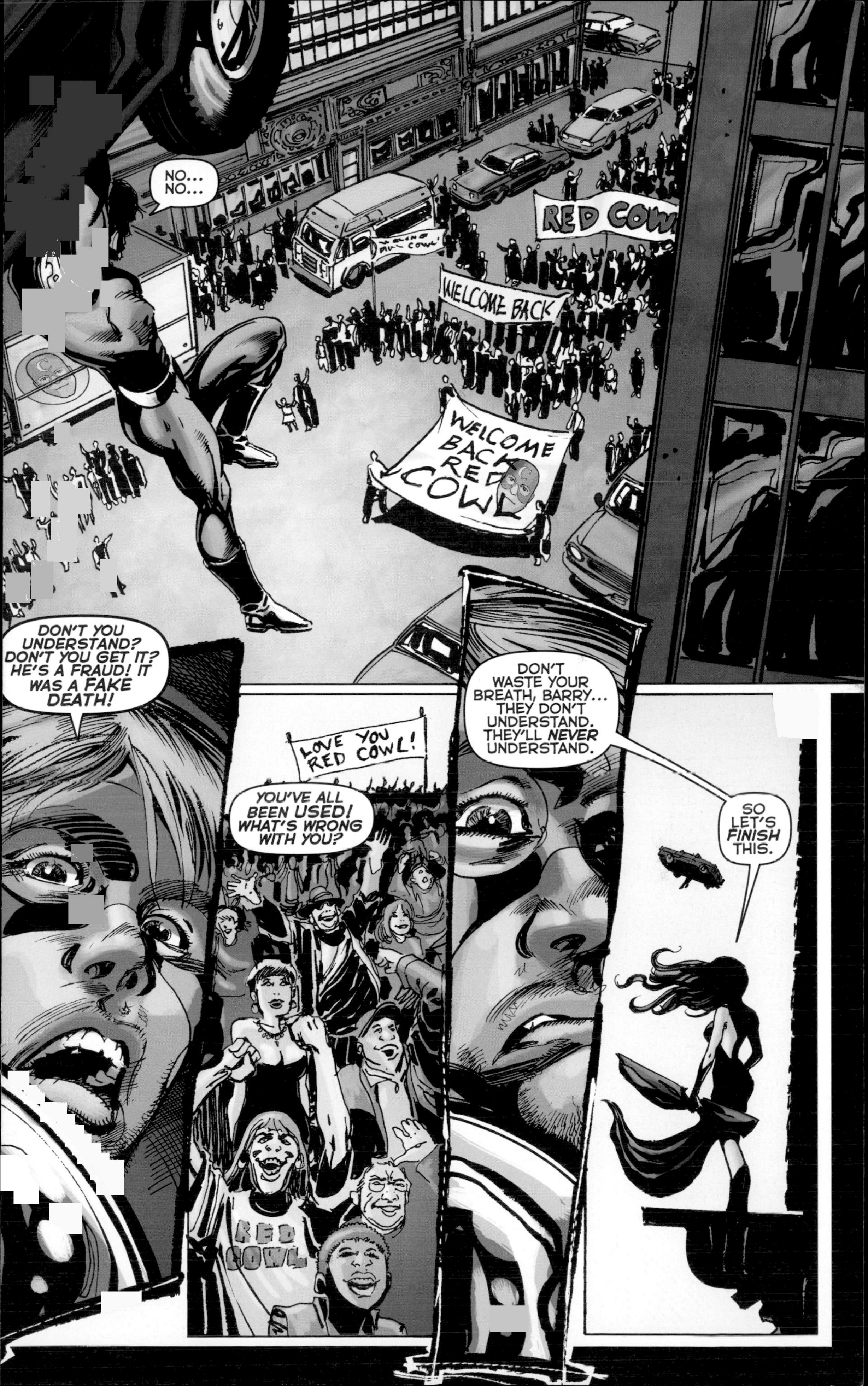
NO... NO...
RED COWL
WELCOME BACK
WELCOME BACK RED COWL
DON'T YOU UNDERSTAND? DON'T YOU GET IT? HE'S A FRAUD! IT WAS A FAKE DEATH!
LOVE YOU RED COWL!
YOU'VE ALL BEEN USED! WHAT'S WRONG WITH YOU?
RED COWL
DON'T WASTE YOUR BREATH, BARRY... THEY DON'T UNDERSTAND. THEY'LL NEVER UNDERSTAND.
SO LET'S FINISH THIS.

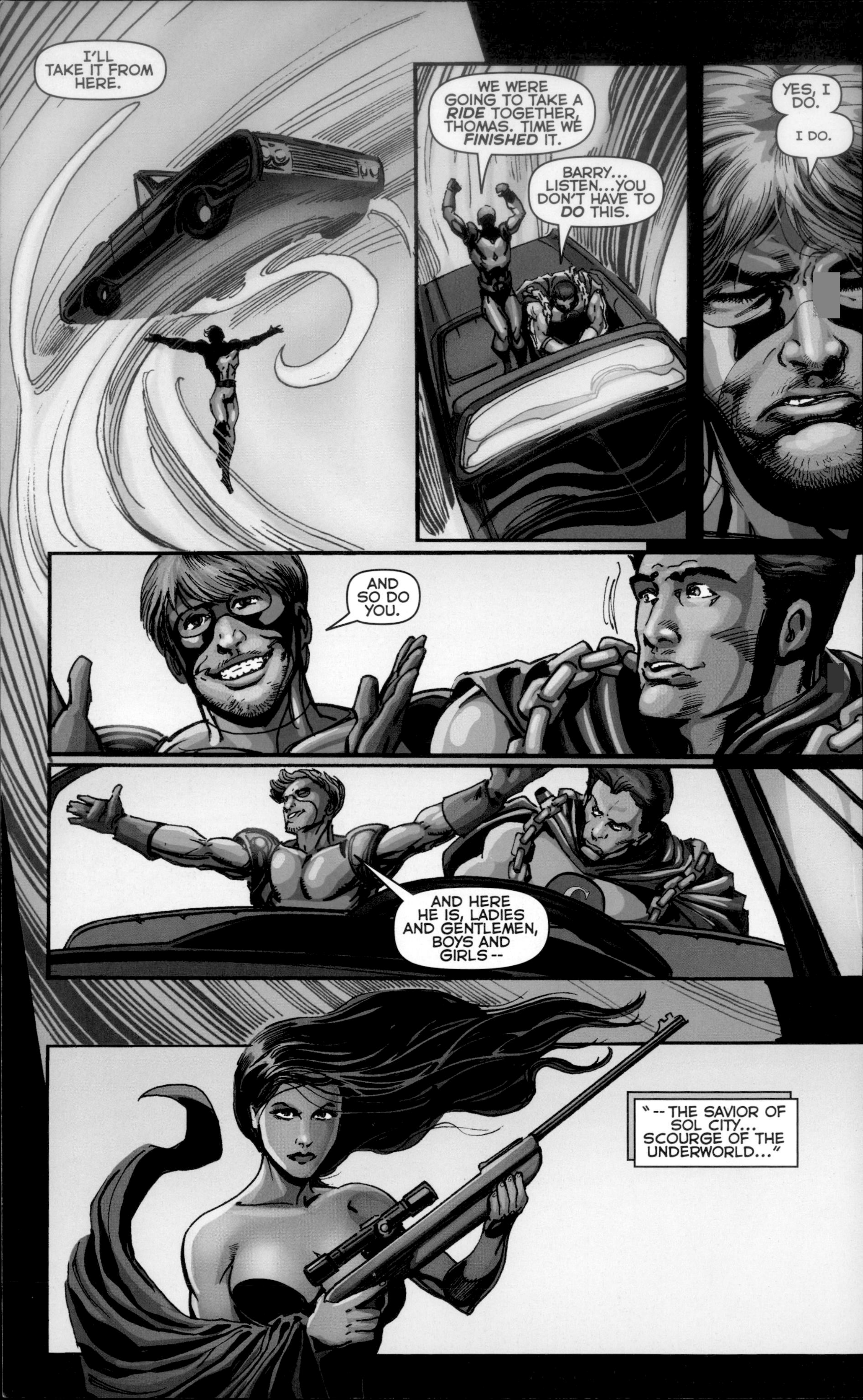
I'LL TAKE IT FROM HERE.
WE WERE GOING TO TAKE A RIDE TOGETHER, THOMAS. TIME WE FINISHED IT.
BARRY... LISTEN...YOU DON'T HAVE TO DO THIS.
YES, I DO.
I DO.
AND SO DO YOU.
AND HERE HE IS, LADIES AND GENTLEMEN, BOYS AND GIRLS --
"-- THE SAVIOR OF SOL CITY... SCOURGE OF THE UNDERWORLD..."

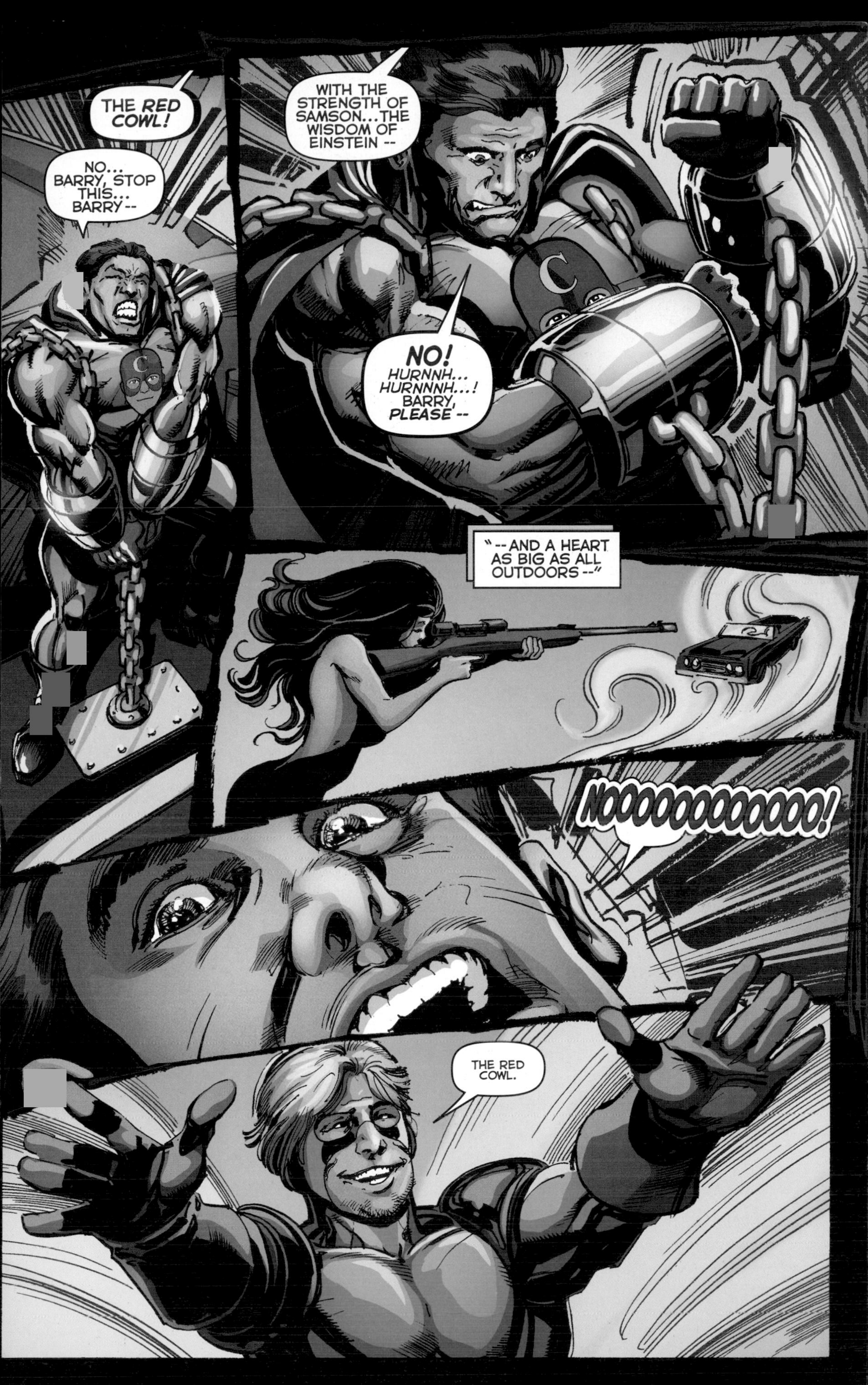
THE RED COWL!
NO... BARRY, STOP THIS... BARRY--
WITH THE STRENGTH OF SAMSON...THE WISDOM OF EINSTEIN --
NO! HURNNH... HURNNNH...! BARRY, PLEASE --
"--AND A HEART AS BIG AS ALL OUTDOORS --"
NOOOOOOOOOOOO!
THE RED COWL.

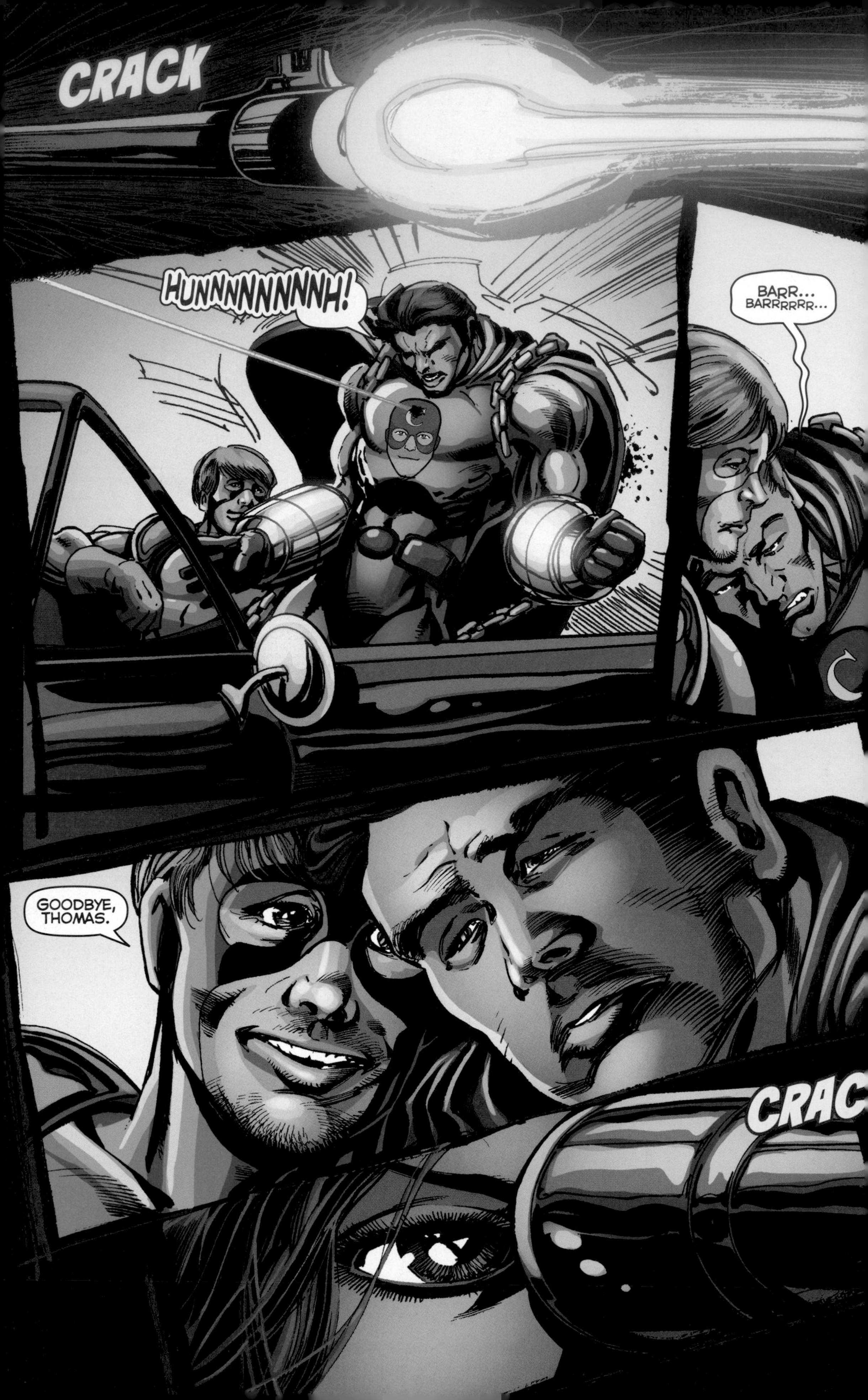
CRACK
HUNNNNNNNNH!
BARR... BARRRRRR...
GOODBYE, THOMAS.
CRAC

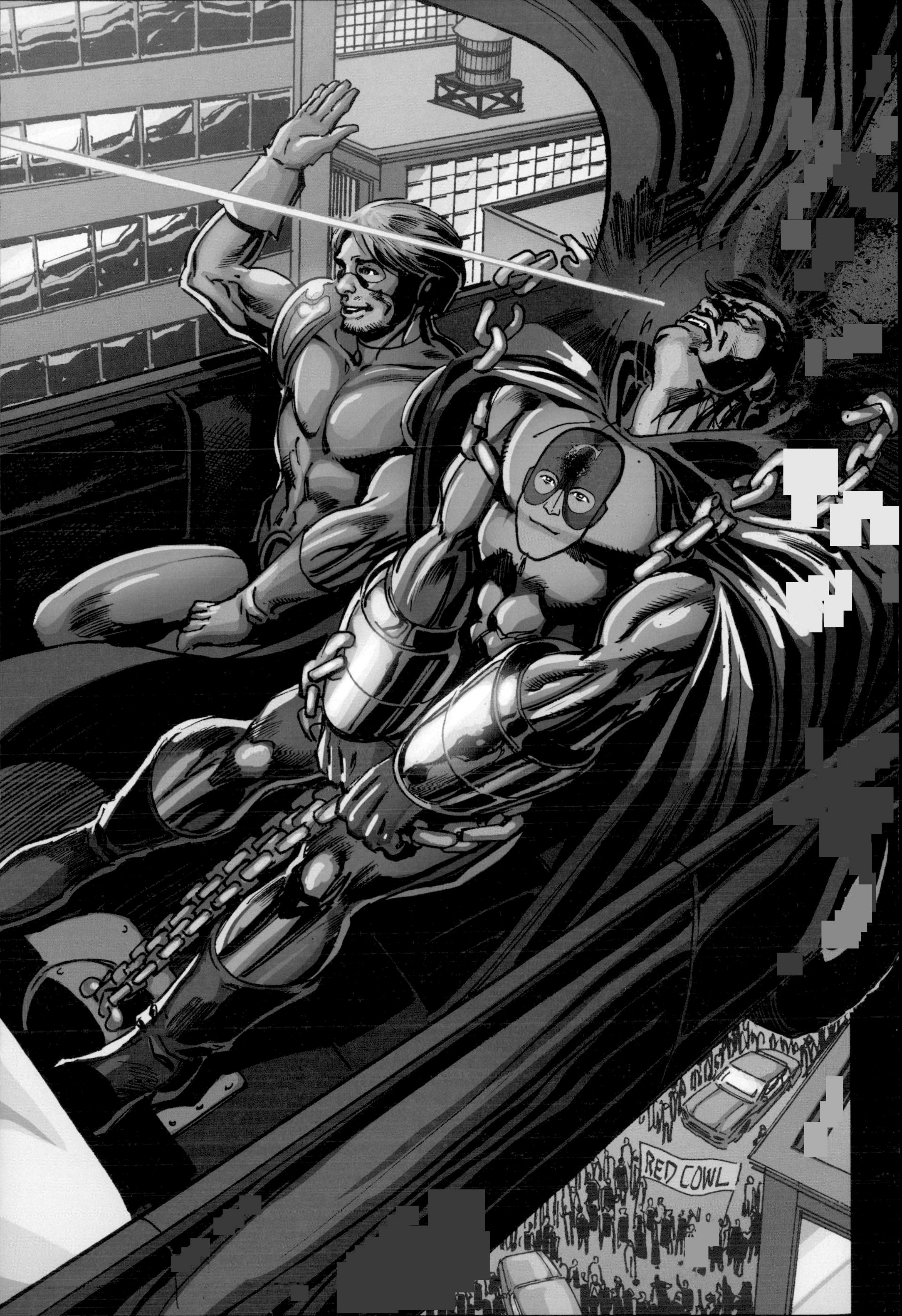
RED COWL

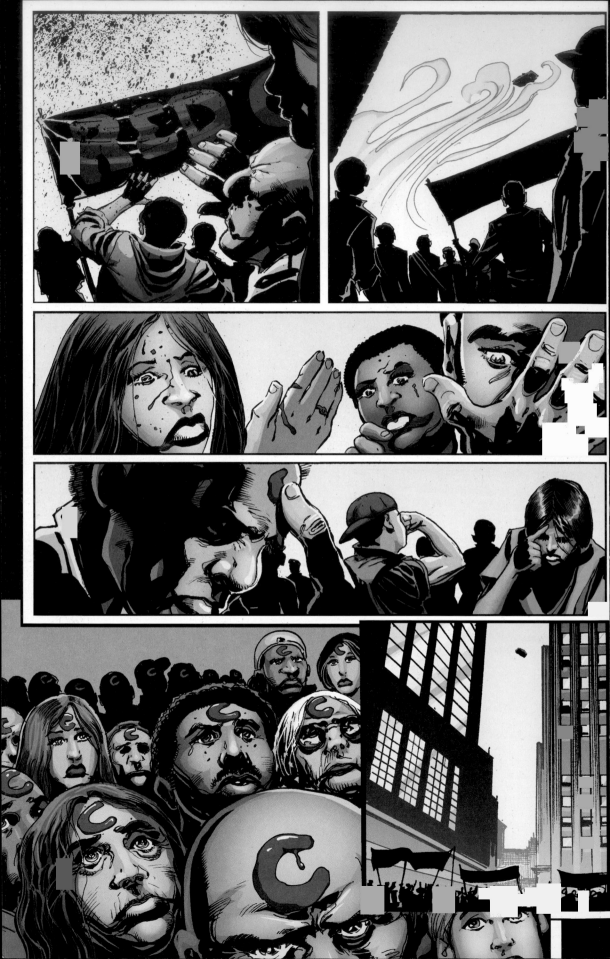

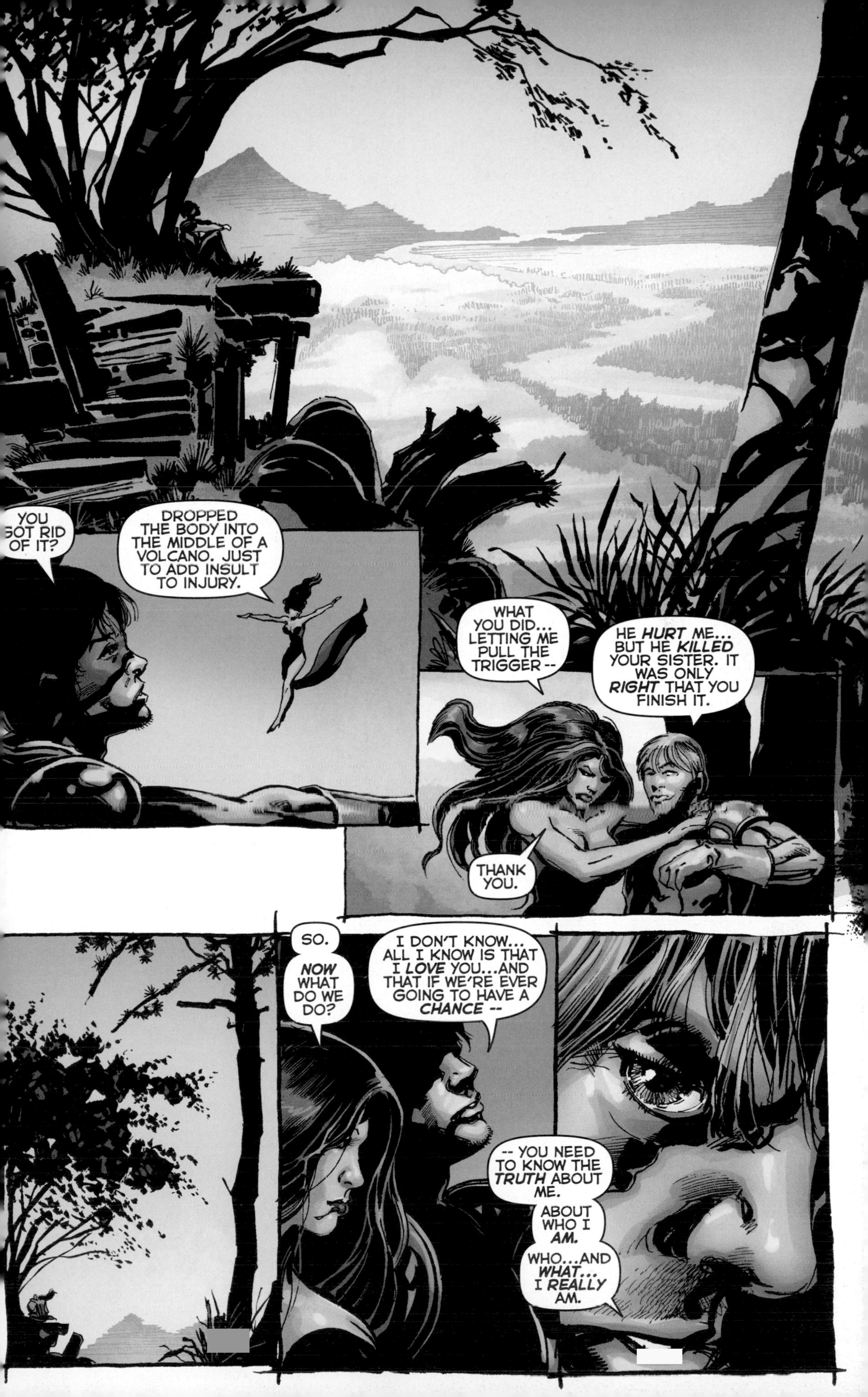
YOU GOT RID OF IT?
DROPPED THE BODY INTO THE MIDDLE OF A VOLCANO. JUST TO ADD INSULT TO INJURY.
WHAT YOU DID... LETTING ME PULL THE TRIGGER --
HE *HURT* ME... BUT HE *KILLED* YOUR SISTER. IT WAS ONLY *RIGHT* THAT YOU FINISH IT.
THANK YOU.
SO.
NOW WHAT DO WE DO?
I DON'T KNOW... ALL I KNOW IS THAT I *LOVE* YOU...AND THAT IF WE'RE EVER GOING TO HAVE A *CHANCE* --
-- YOU NEED TO KNOW THE *TRUTH* ABOUT ME.
ABOUT WHO I *AM.*
WHO...AND *WHAT*... I *REALLY* AM.

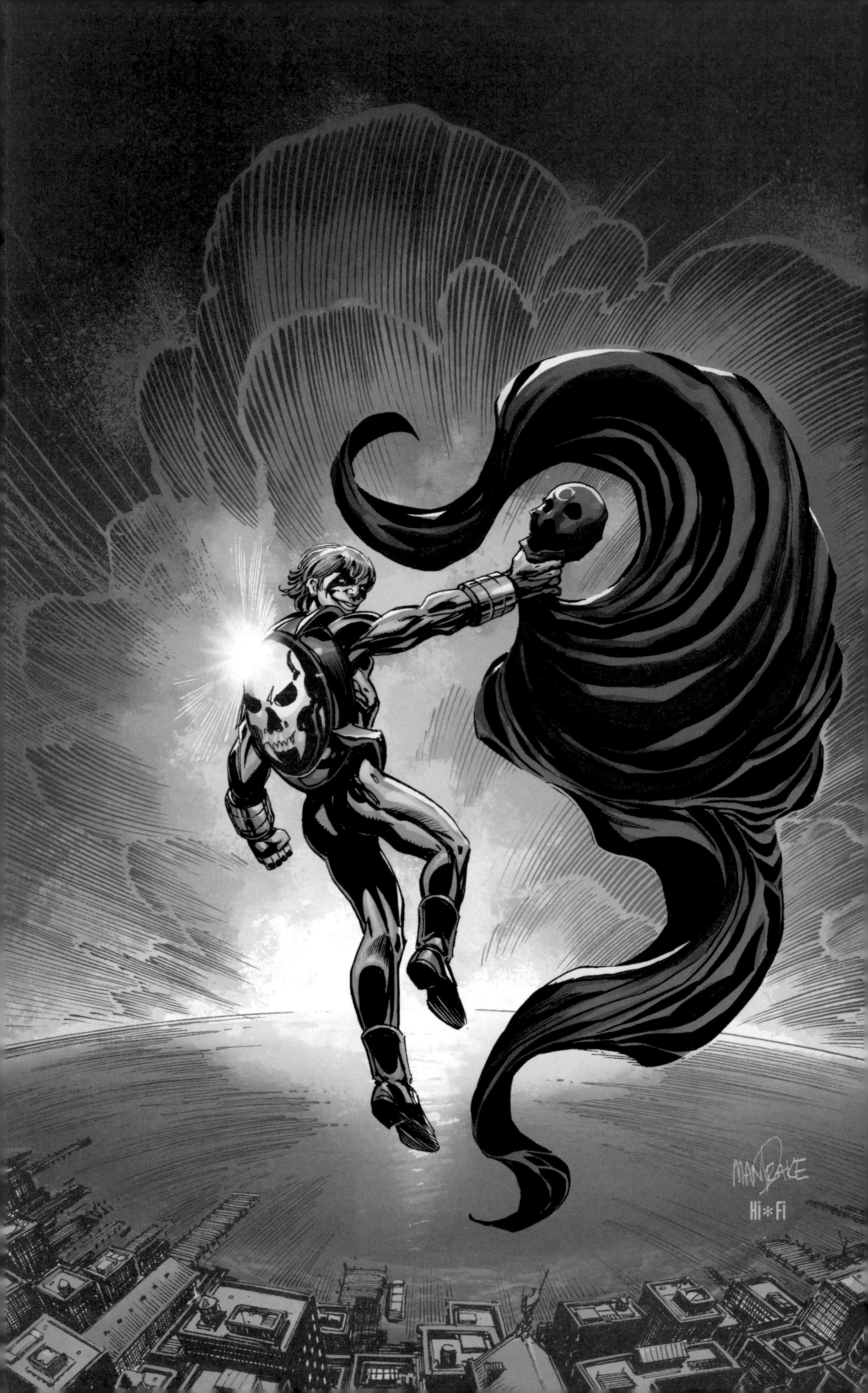
MANDRAKE
Hi*Fi

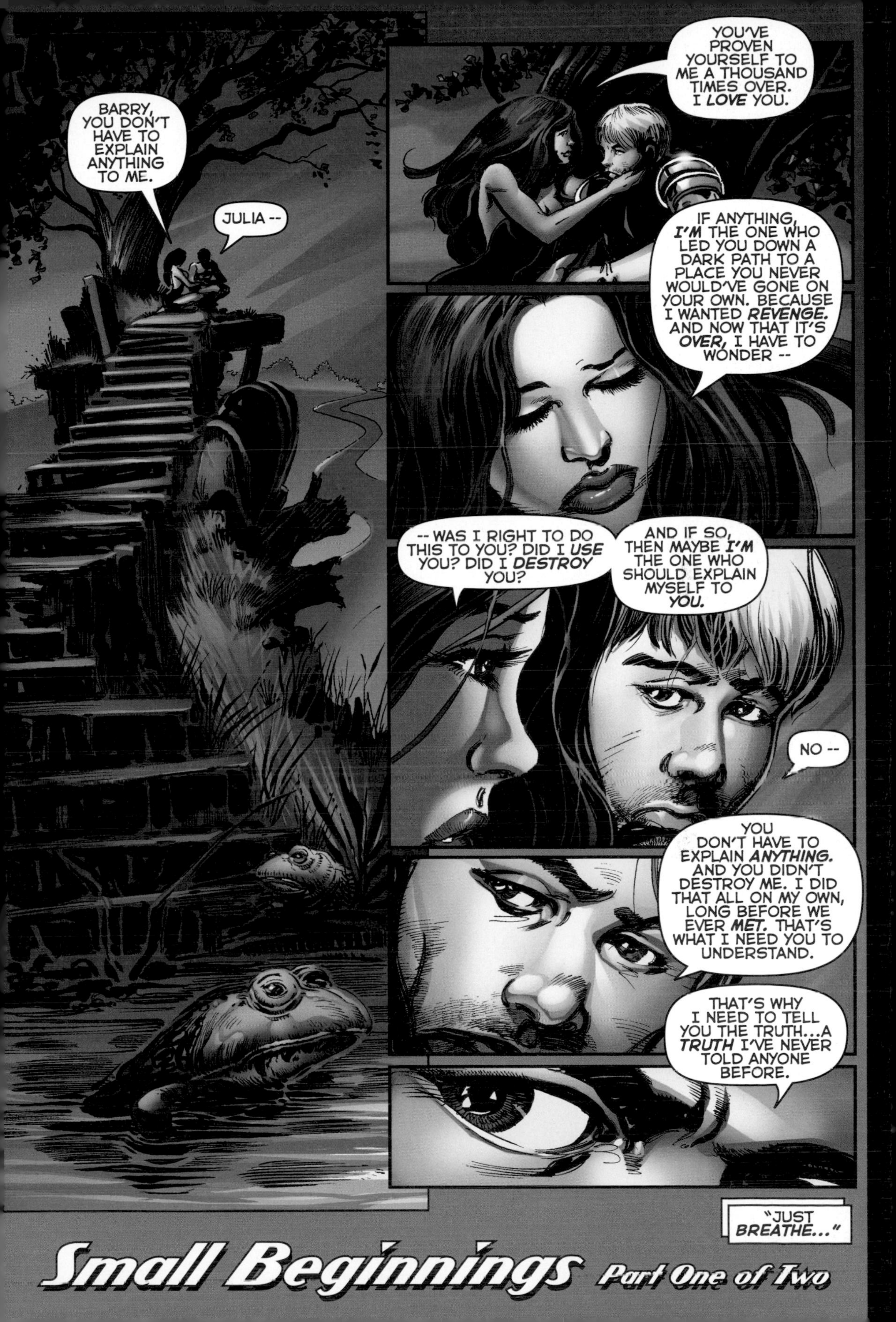
BARRY, YOU DON'T HAVE TO EXPLAIN ANYTHING TO ME.
JULIA --
YOU'VE PROVEN YOURSELF TO ME A THOUSAND TIMES OVER. I LOVE YOU.
IF ANYTHING, I'M THE ONE WHO LED YOU DOWN A DARK PATH TO A PLACE YOU NEVER WOULD'VE GONE ON YOUR OWN. BECAUSE I WANTED REVENGE. AND NOW THAT IT'S OVER, I HAVE TO WONDER --
-- WAS I RIGHT TO DO THIS TO YOU? DID I USE YOU? DID I DESTROY YOU?
AND IF SO, THEN MAYBE I'M THE ONE WHO SHOULD EXPLAIN MYSELF TO YOU.
NO --
YOU DON'T HAVE TO EXPLAIN ANYTHING. AND YOU DIDN'T DESTROY ME. I DID THAT ALL ON MY OWN, LONG BEFORE WE EVER MET. THAT'S WHAT I NEED YOU TO UNDERSTAND.
THAT'S WHY I NEED TO TELL YOU THE TRUTH...A TRUTH I'VE NEVER TOLD ANYONE BEFORE.
"JUST BREATHE..."
Small Beginnings Part One of Two

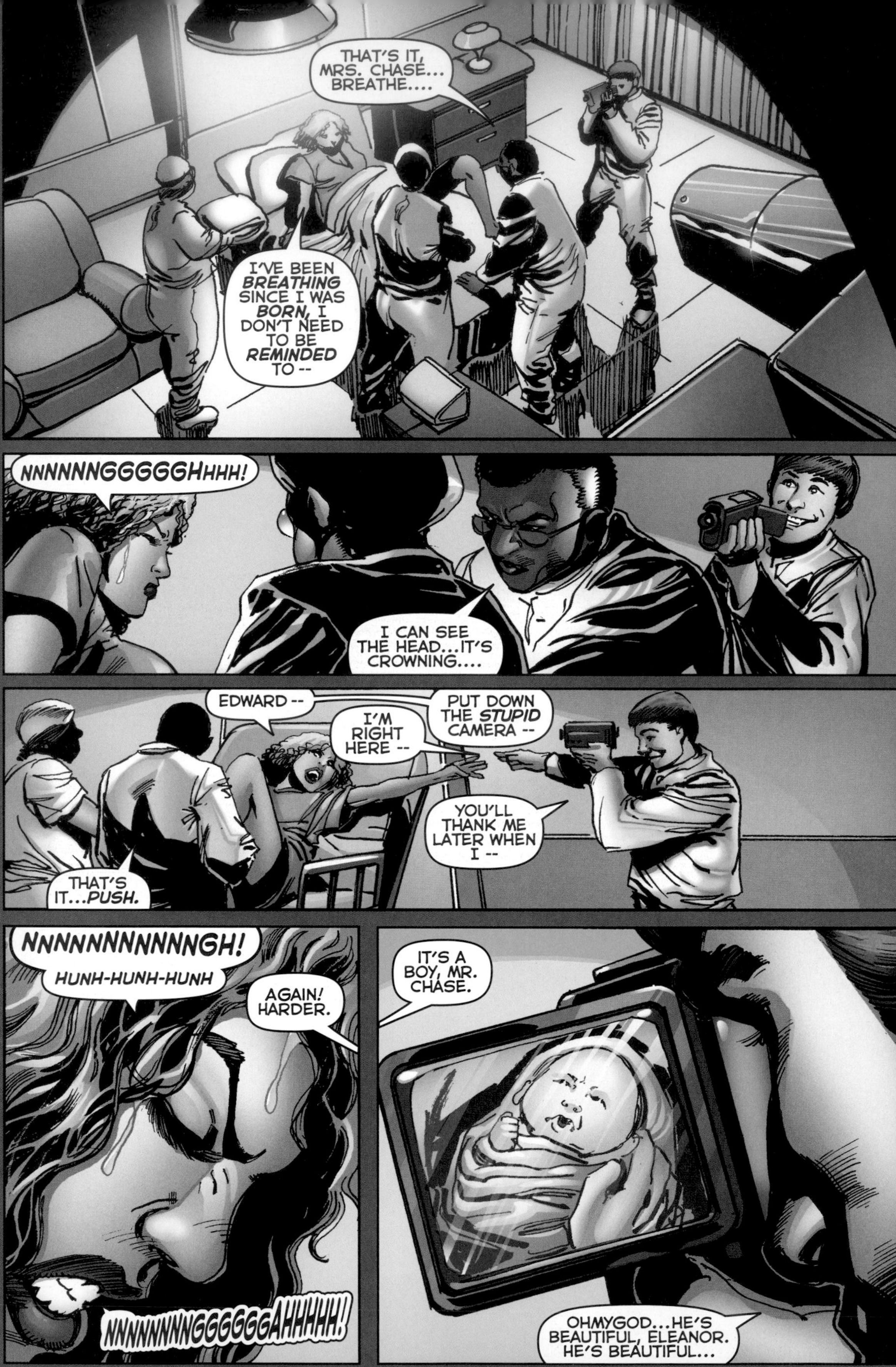
THAT'S IT, MRS. CHASE... BREATHE....
I'VE BEEN BREATHING SINCE I WAS BORN, I DON'T NEED TO BE REMINDED TO --
NNNNNNGGGGGHHHH!
I CAN SEE THE HEAD...IT'S CROWNING....
EDWARD --
I'M RIGHT HERE --
PUT DOWN THE STUPID CAMERA --
YOU'LL THANK ME LATER WHEN I --
THAT'S IT...PUSH.
NNNNNNNNNNNGH!
HUNH-HUNH-HUNH
AGAIN! HARDER.
NNNNNNNNGGGGGAHHHHH!
IT'S A BOY, MR. CHASE.
OHMYGOD...HE'S BEAUTIFUL, ELEANOR. HE'S BEAUTIFUL...

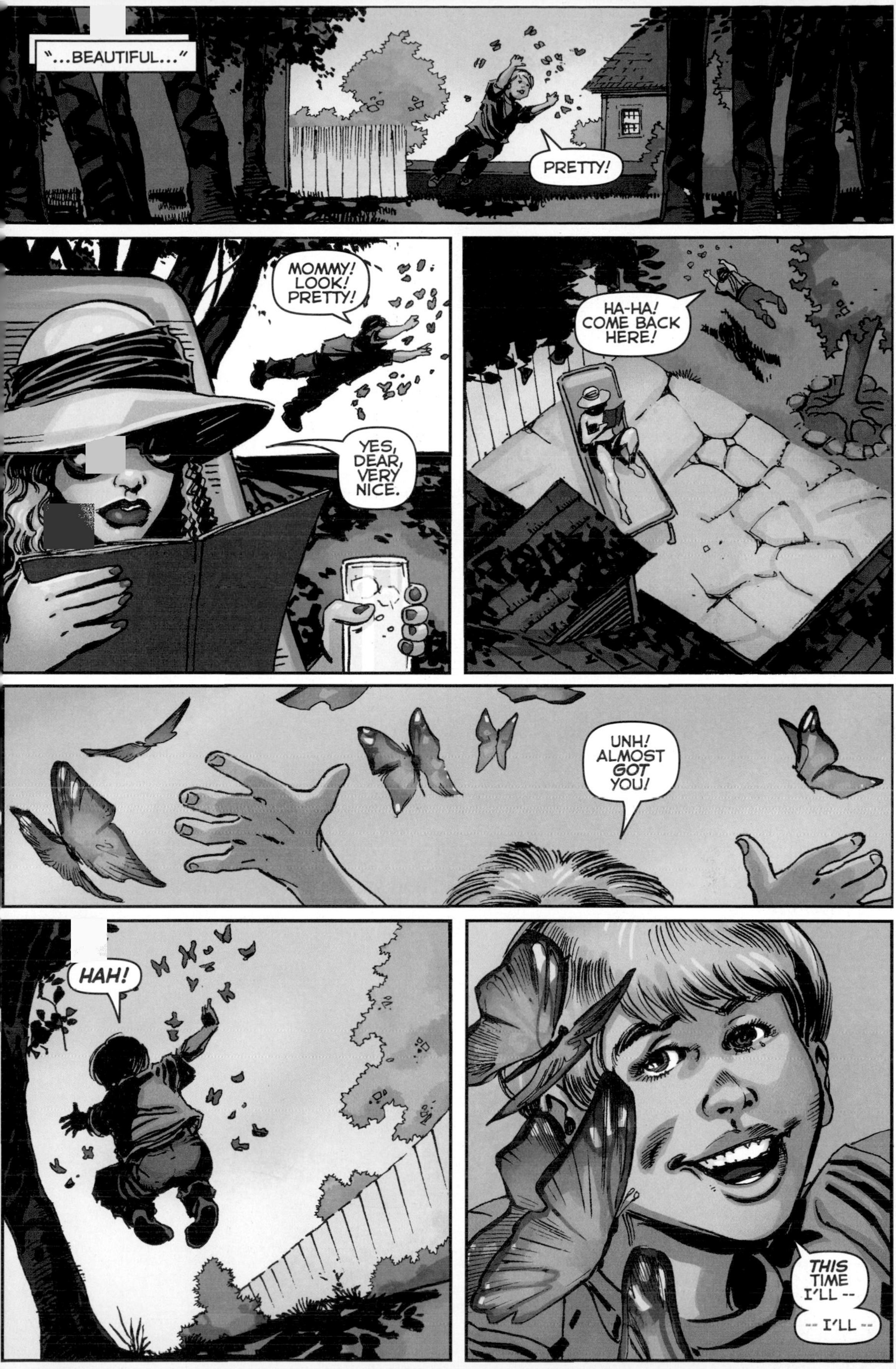
"...BEAUTIFUL..."
PRETTY!
MOMMY! LOOK! PRETTY!
YES, DEAR, VERY NICE.
HA-HA! COME BACK HERE!
UNH! ALMOST GOT YOU!
HAH!
THIS TIME I'LL --
-- I'LL --

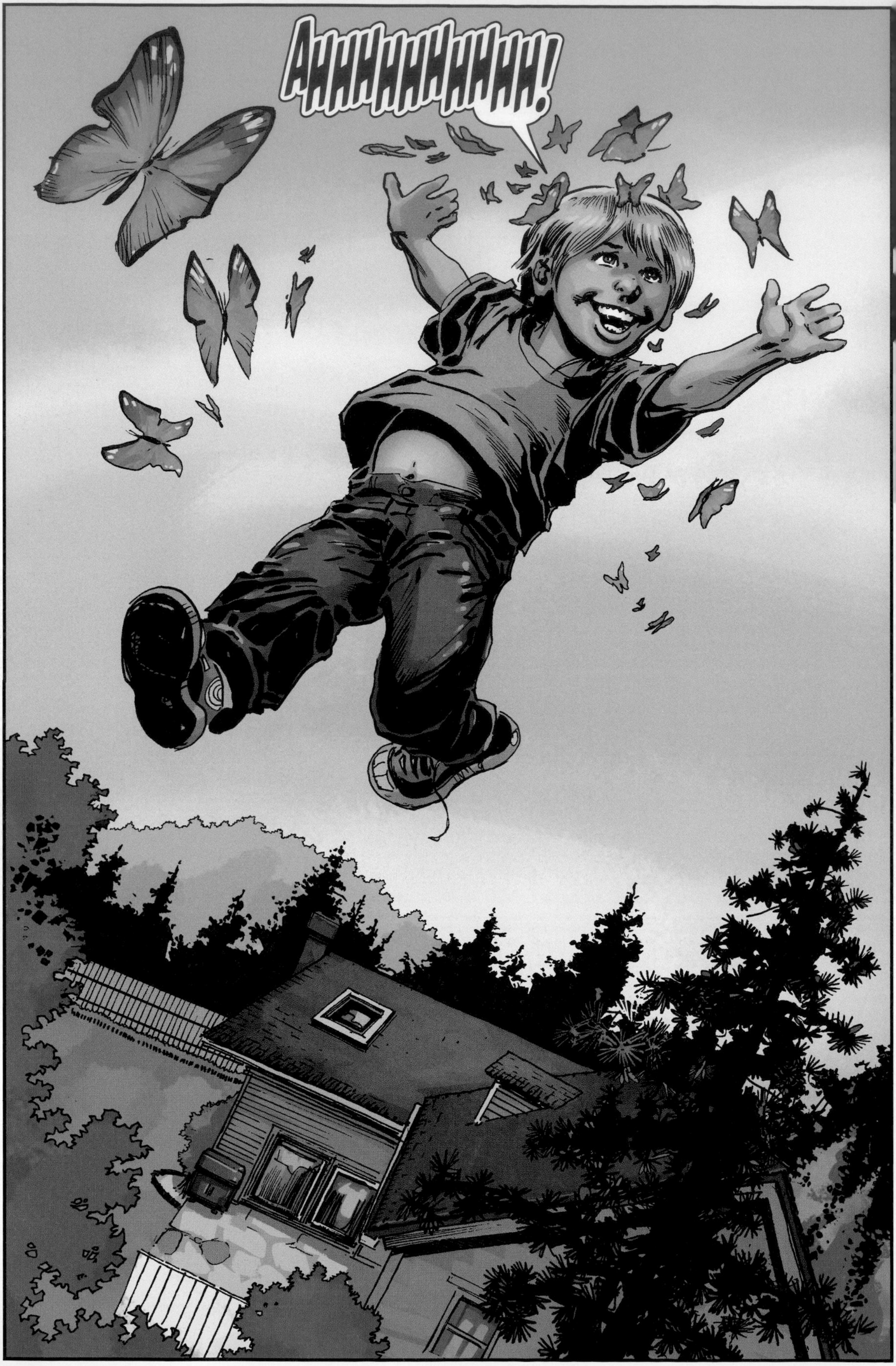
AHHHHHHHHHH!

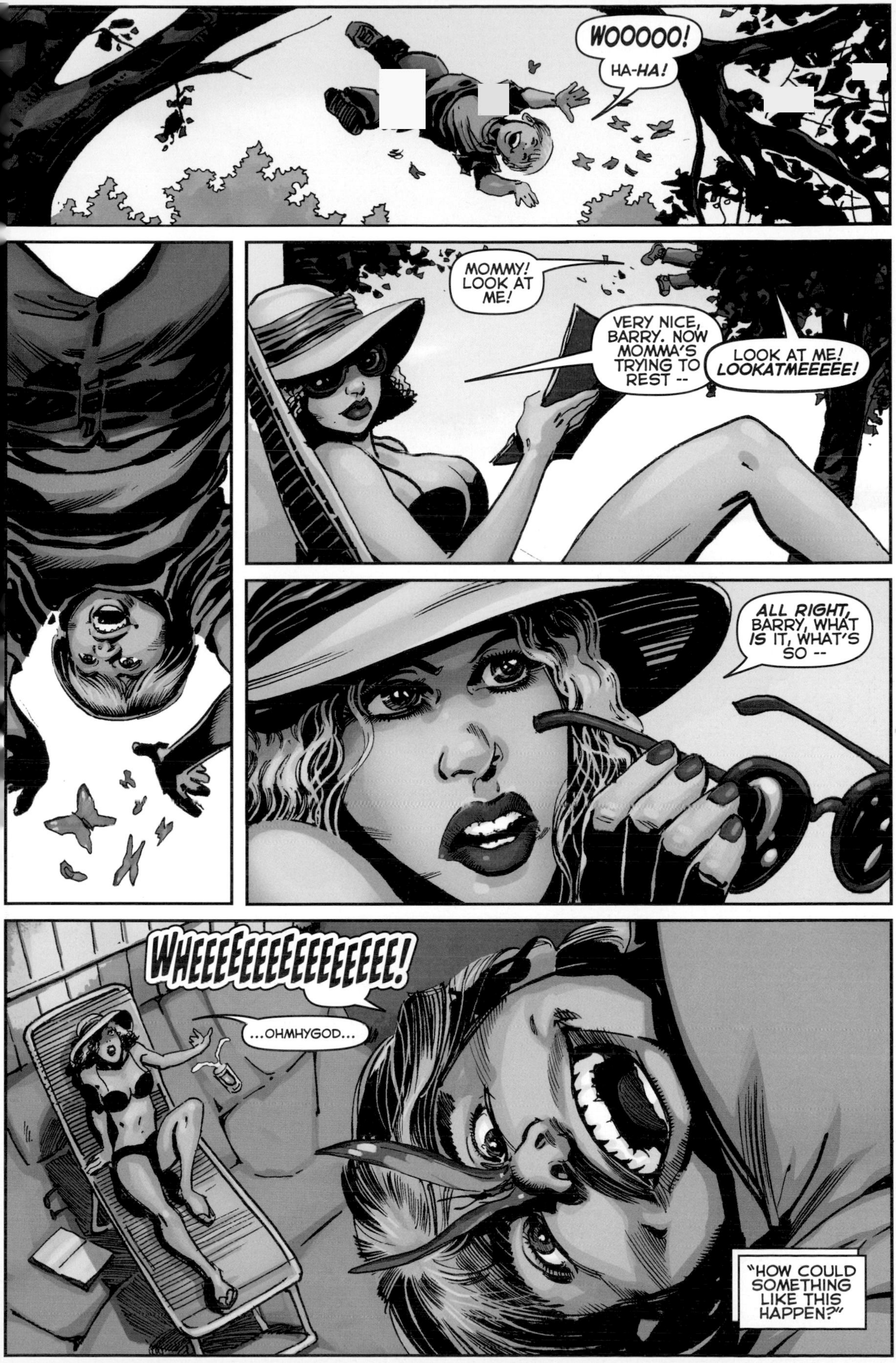
WOOOOO!
HA-HA!
MOMMY! LOOK AT ME!
VERY NICE, BARRY. NOW MOMMA'S TRYING TO REST --
LOOK AT ME! LOOKATMEEEEEE!
ALL RIGHT, BARRY, WHAT IS IT, WHAT'S SO --
WHEEEEEEEEEEEEEEEE!
...OHMHYGOD...
"HOW COULD SOMETHING LIKE THIS HAPPEN?"

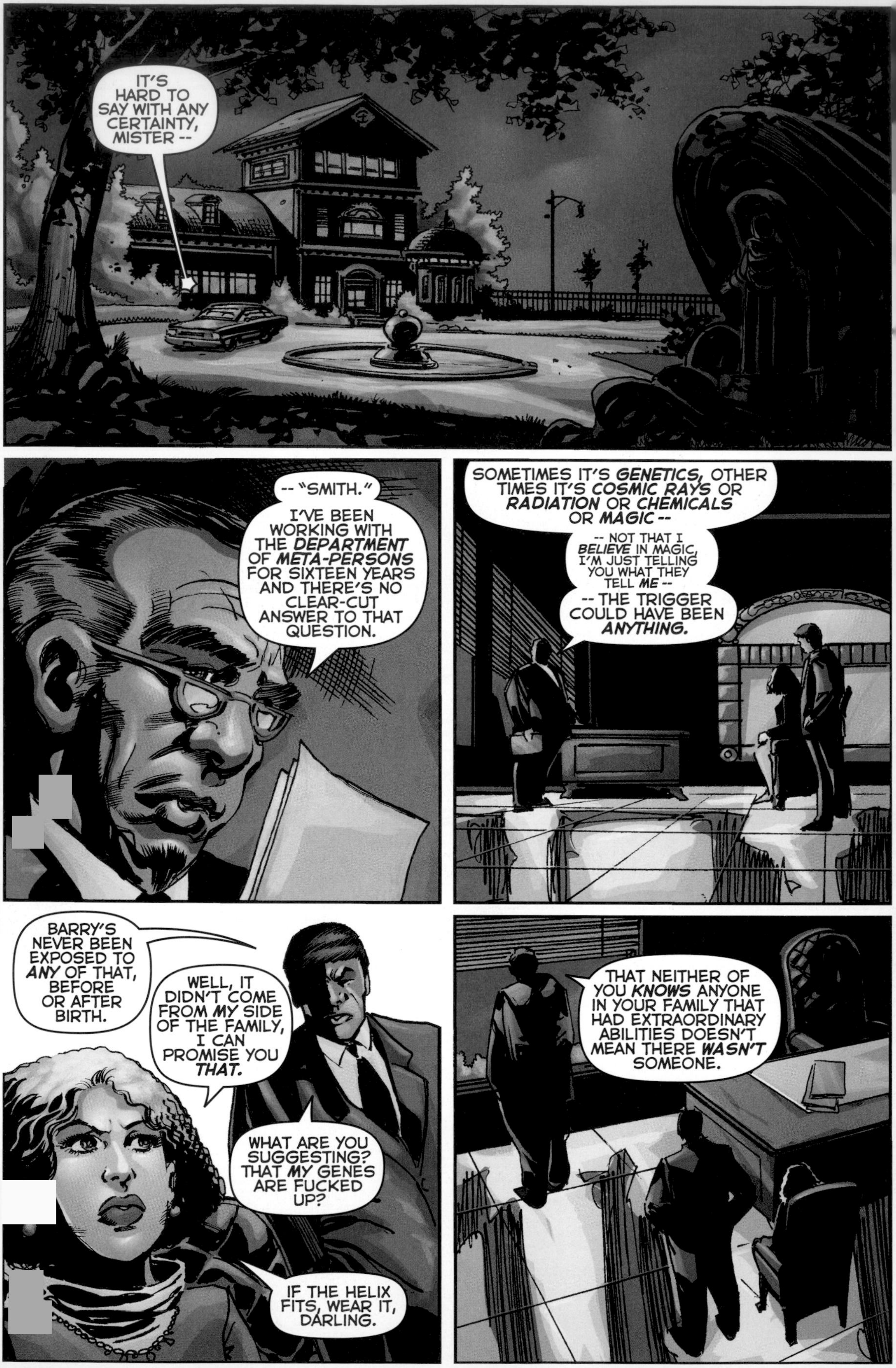
IT'S HARD TO SAY WITH ANY CERTAINTY, MISTER --
-- "SMITH."
I'VE BEEN WORKING WITH THE DEPARTMENT OF META-PERSONS FOR SIXTEEN YEARS AND THERE'S NO CLEAR-CUT ANSWER TO THAT QUESTION.
SOMETIMES IT'S GENETICS, OTHER TIMES IT'S COSMIC RAYS OR RADIATION OR CHEMICALS OR MAGIC --
-- NOT THAT I BELIEVE IN MAGIC, I'M JUST TELLING YOU WHAT THEY TELL ME --
-- THE TRIGGER COULD HAVE BEEN ANYTHING.
BARRY'S NEVER BEEN EXPOSED TO ANY OF THAT, BEFORE OR AFTER BIRTH.
WELL, IT DIDN'T COME FROM MY SIDE OF THE FAMILY, I CAN PROMISE YOU THAT.
WHAT ARE YOU SUGGESTING? THAT MY GENES ARE FUCKED UP?
IF THE HELIX FITS, WEAR IT, DARLING.
THAT NEITHER OF YOU KNOWS ANYONE IN YOUR FAMILY THAT HAD EXTRAORDINARY ABILITIES DOESN'T MEAN THERE WASN'T SOMEONE.

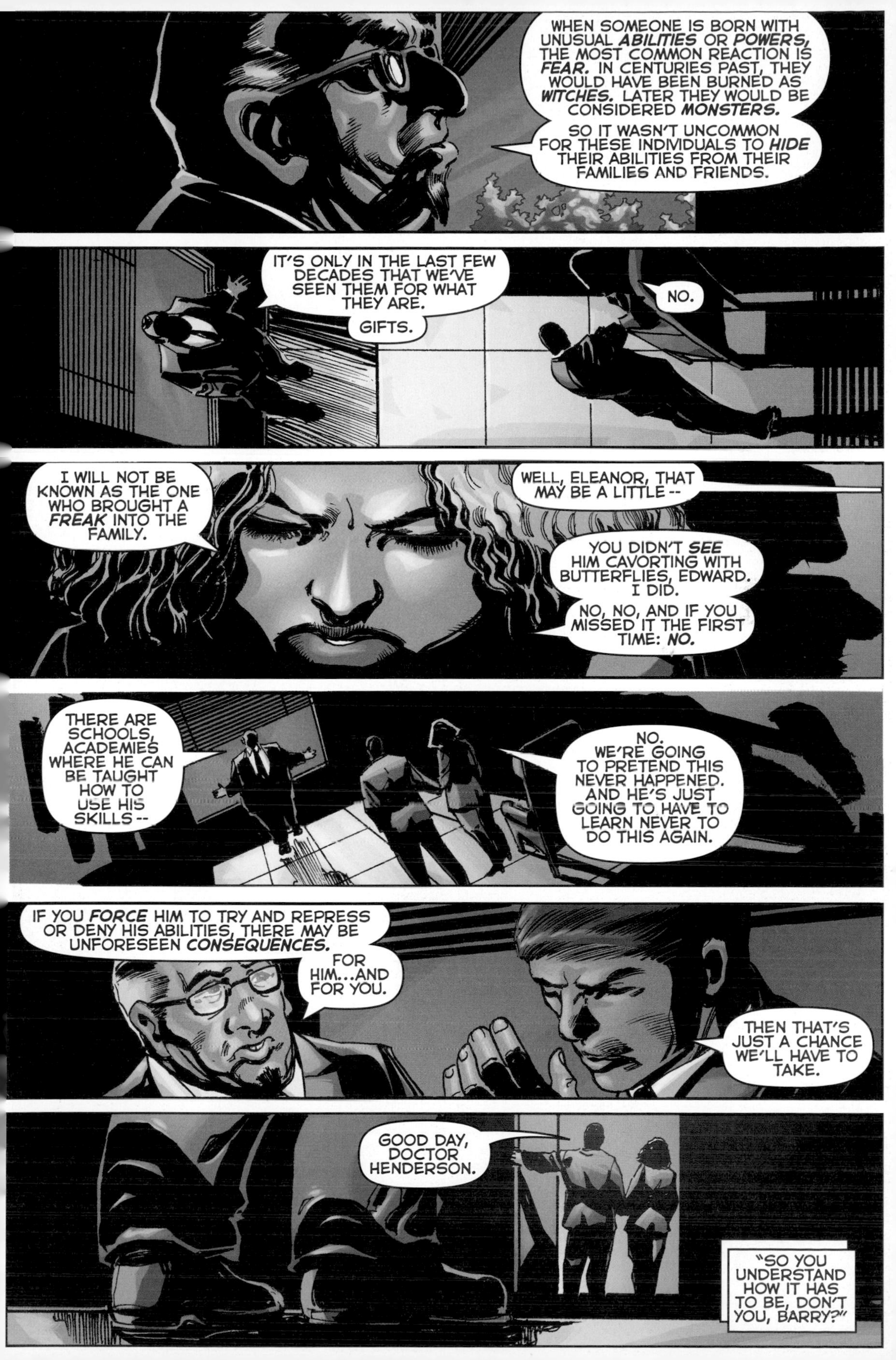
WHEN SOMEONE IS BORN WITH UNUSUAL ABILITIES OR POWERS, THE MOST COMMON REACTION IS FEAR. IN CENTURIES PAST, THEY WOULD HAVE BEEN BURNED AS WITCHES. LATER THEY WOULD BE CONSIDERED MONSTERS.
SO IT WASN'T UNCOMMON FOR THESE INDIVIDUALS TO HIDE THEIR ABILITIES FROM THEIR FAMILIES AND FRIENDS.
IT'S ONLY IN THE LAST FEW DECADES THAT WE'VE SEEN THEM FOR WHAT THEY ARE.
GIFTS.
NO.
I WILL NOT BE KNOWN AS THE ONE WHO BROUGHT A FREAK INTO THE FAMILY.
WELL, ELEANOR, THAT MAY BE A LITTLE --
YOU DIDN'T SEE HIM CAVORTING WITH BUTTERFLIES, EDWARD. I DID.
NO, NO, AND IF YOU MISSED IT THE FIRST TIME: NO.
THERE ARE SCHOOLS, ACADEMIES WHERE HE CAN BE TAUGHT HOW TO USE HIS SKILLS --
NO. WE'RE GOING TO PRETEND THIS NEVER HAPPENED. AND HE'S JUST GOING TO HAVE TO LEARN NEVER TO DO THIS AGAIN.
IF YOU FORCE HIM TO TRY AND REPRESS OR DENY HIS ABILITIES, THERE MAY BE UNFORESEEN CONSEQUENCES.
FOR HIM...AND FOR YOU.
THEN THAT'S JUST A CHANCE WE'LL HAVE TO TAKE.
GOOD DAY, DOCTOR HENDERSON.
"SO YOU UNDERSTAND HOW IT HAS TO BE, DON'T YOU, BARRY?"

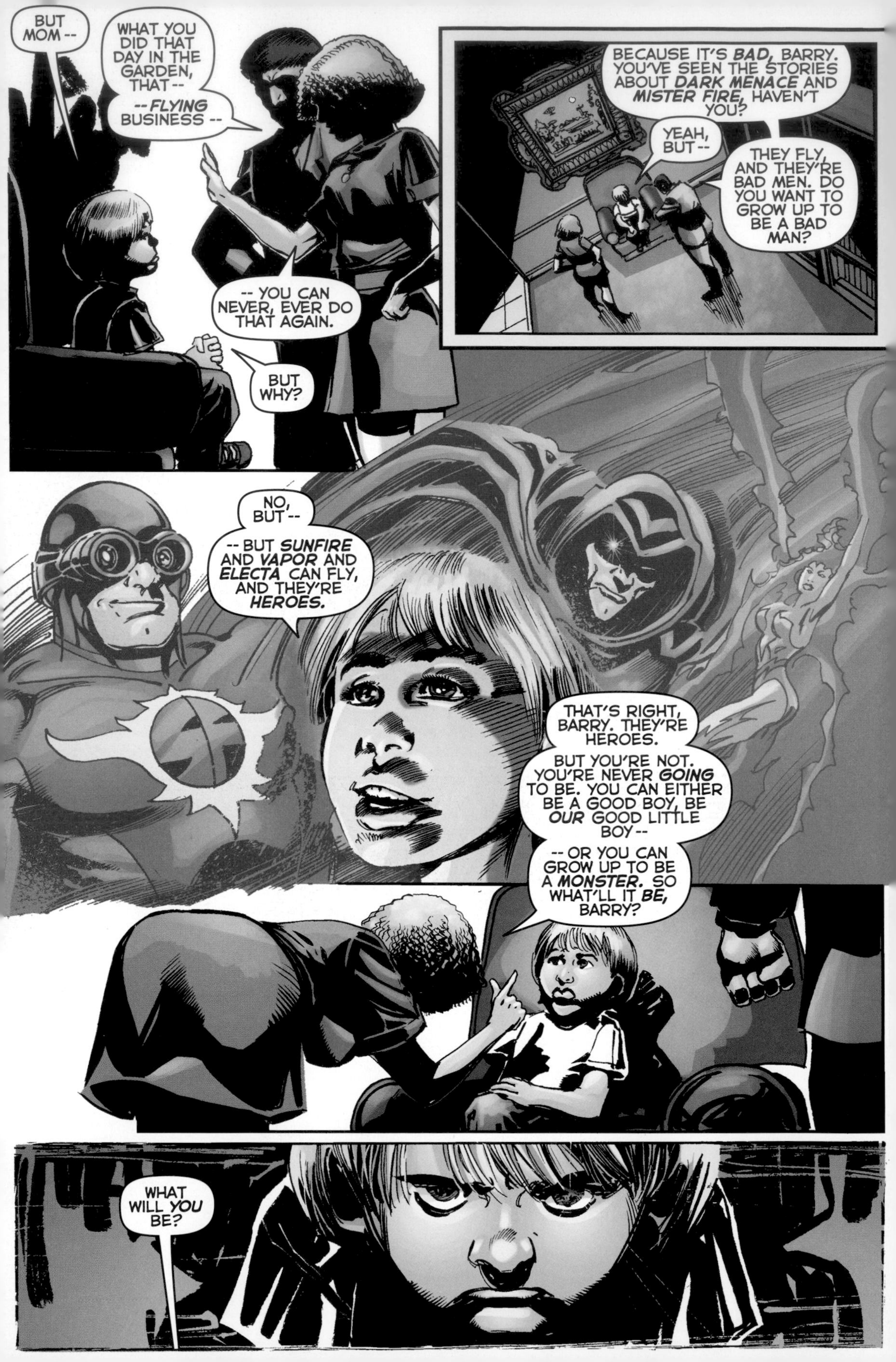
BUT MOM --
WHAT YOU DID THAT DAY IN THE GARDEN, THAT --
-- FLYING BUSINESS --
-- YOU CAN NEVER, EVER DO THAT AGAIN.
BUT WHY?
BECAUSE IT'S BAD, BARRY. YOU'VE SEEN THE STORIES ABOUT DARK MENACE AND MISTER FIRE, HAVEN'T YOU?
YEAH, BUT --
THEY FLY, AND THEY'RE BAD MEN. DO YOU WANT TO GROW UP TO BE A BAD MAN?
NO, BUT --
-- BUT SUNFIRE AND VAPOR AND ELECTA CAN FLY, AND THEY'RE HEROES.
THAT'S RIGHT, BARRY. THEY'RE HEROES.
BUT YOU'RE NOT. YOU'RE NEVER GOING TO BE. YOU CAN EITHER BE A GOOD BOY, BE OUR GOOD LITTLE BOY --
-- OR YOU CAN GROW UP TO BE A MONSTER. SO WHAT'LL IT BE, BARRY?
WHAT WILL YOU BE?

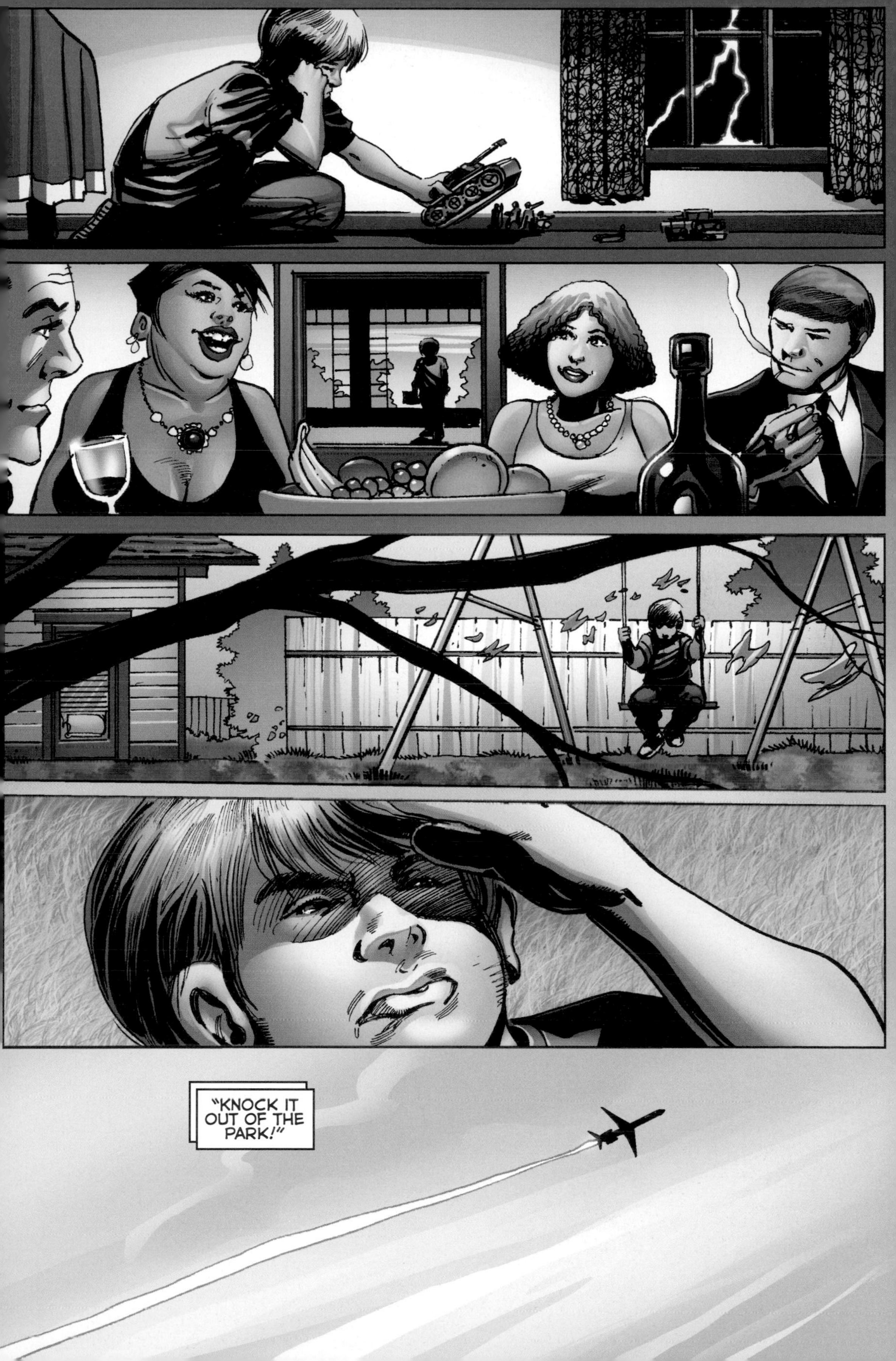
"KNOCK IT OUT OF THE PARK!"

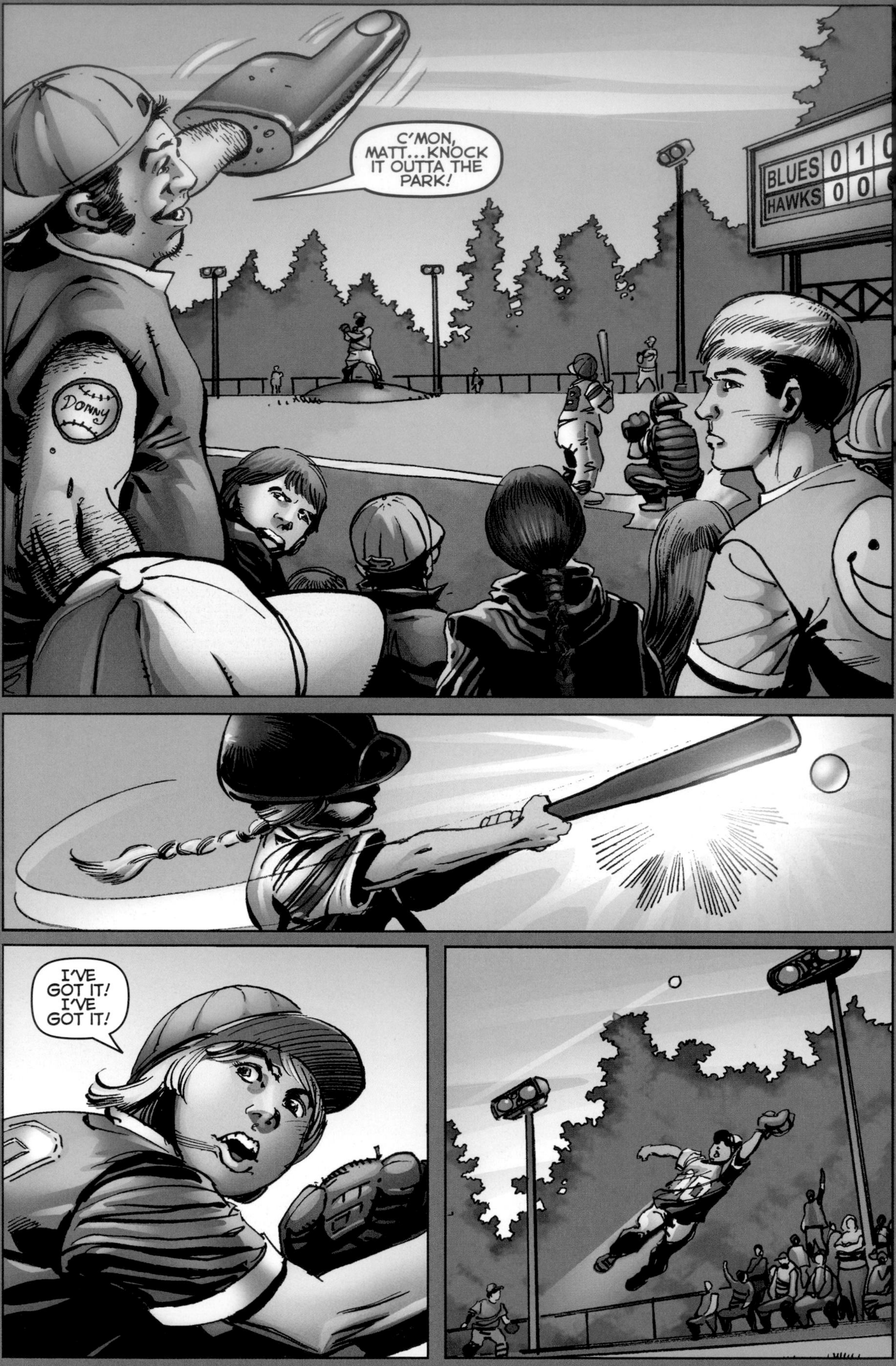
C'MON, MATT...KNOCK IT OUTTA THE PARK!
BLUES 0 1
HAWKS 0 0
DONNY
I'VE GOT IT! I'VE GOT IT!

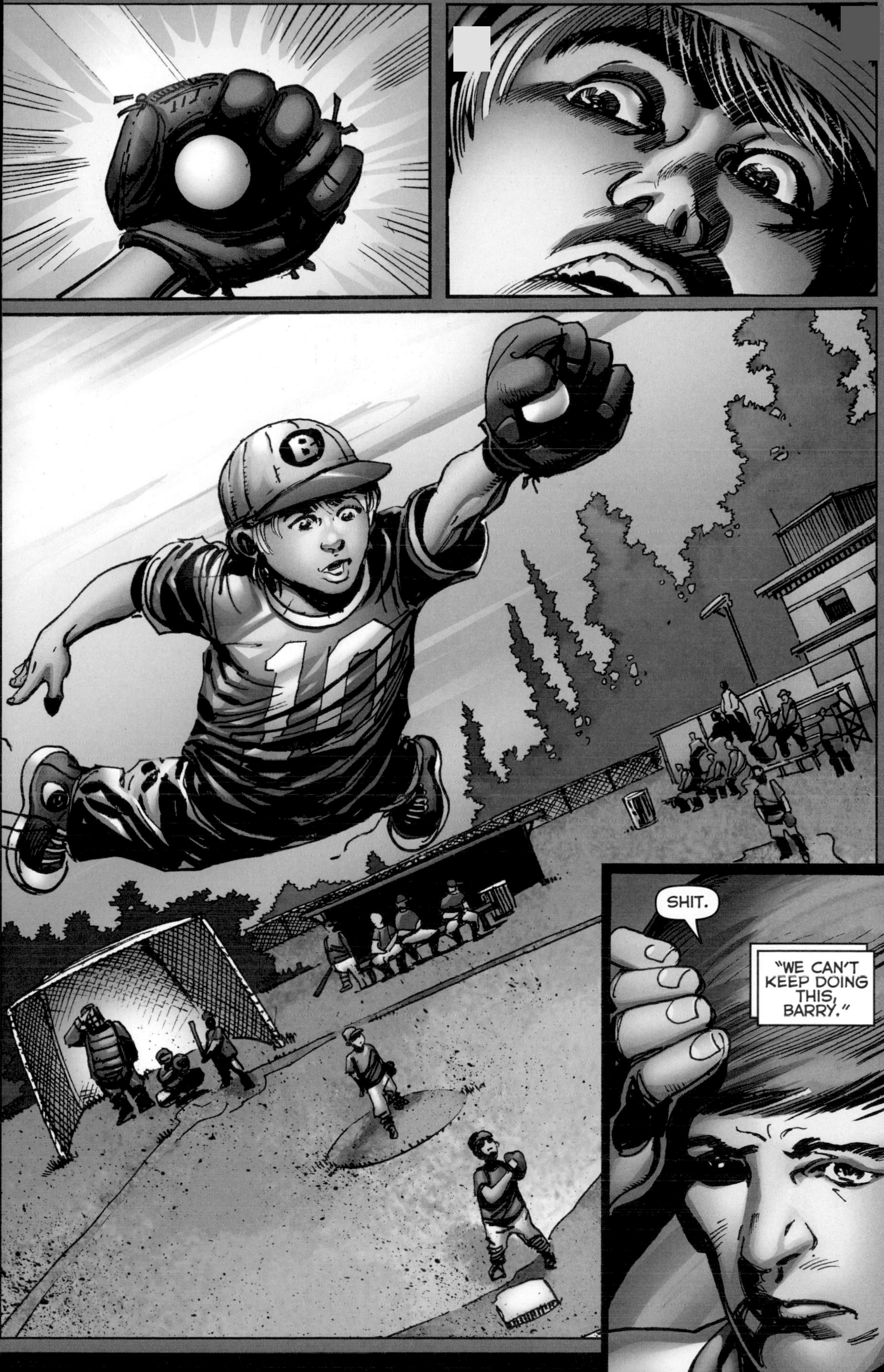
SHIT.
"WE CAN'T KEEP DOING THIS, BARRY."

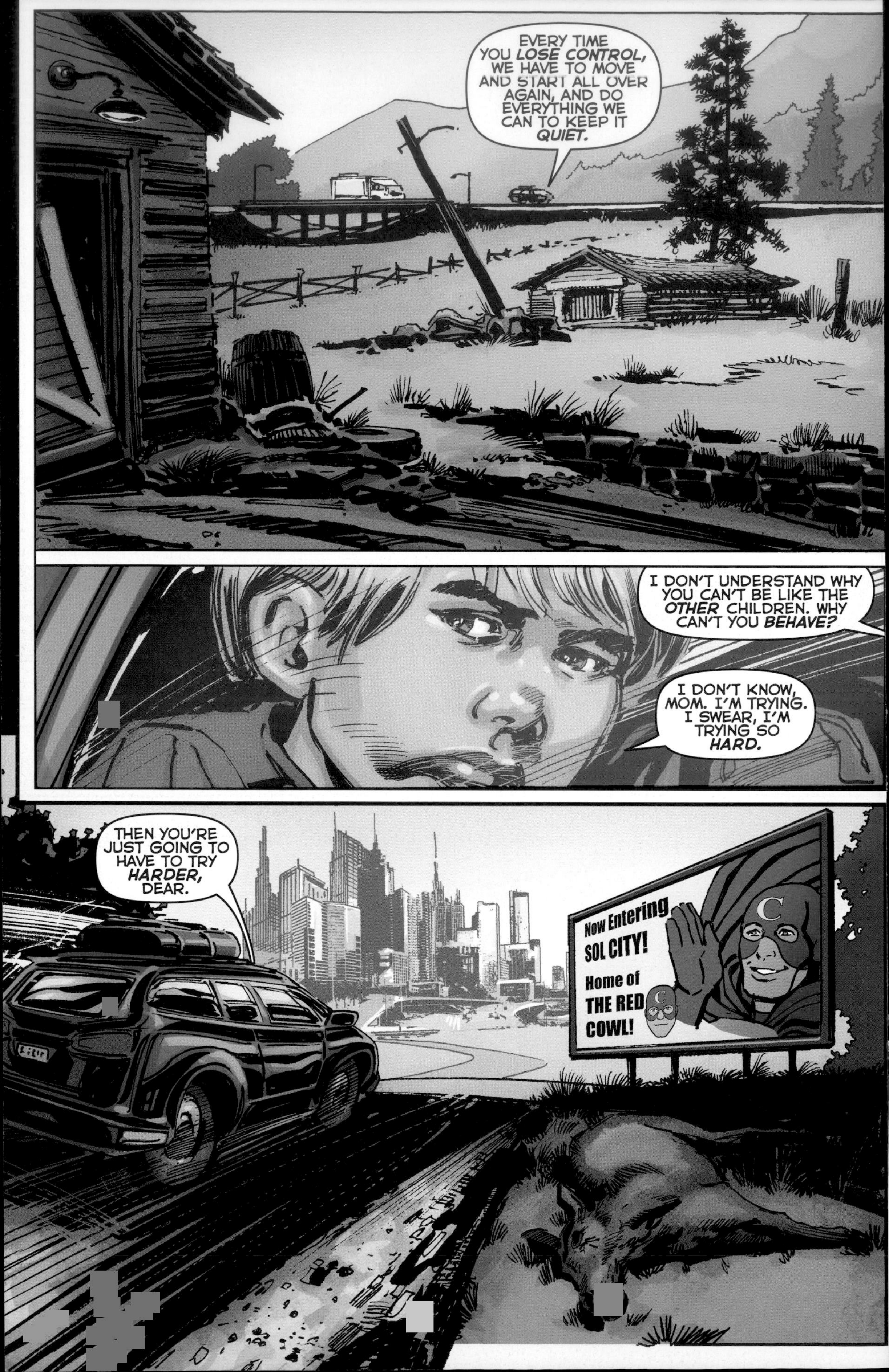
EVERY TIME YOU LOSE CONTROL, WE HAVE TO MOVE AND START ALL OVER AGAIN, AND DO EVERYTHING WE CAN TO KEEP IT QUIET.
I DON'T UNDERSTAND WHY YOU CAN'T BE LIKE THE OTHER CHILDREN. WHY CAN'T YOU BEHAVE?
I DON'T KNOW, MOM. I'M TRYING. I SWEAR, I'M TRYING SO HARD.
THEN YOU'RE JUST GOING TO HAVE TO TRY HARDER, DEAR.
Now Entering SOL CITY! Home of THE RED COWL!

"...WHERE THE ENEMY OF JUSTICE, THE SURGEON, HAS STRUCK AGAIN."

DESCRIBING THE MURDERS AS STANZA ONE IN HIS NIGHTMARE CANTATA, THE SURGEON WARNED MORE DEATHS WOULD COME UNTIL HIS "WORK OF ART" WAS COMPLETE.

REACHED FOR COMMENT, THE RED COWL HAD THIS TO SAY.

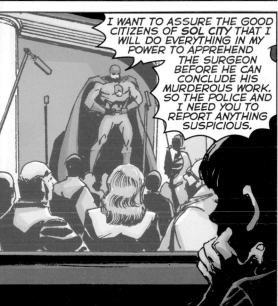

I WANT TO ASSURE THE GOOD CITIZENS OF SOL CITY THAT I WILL DO EVERYTHING IN MY POWER TO APPREHEND THE SURGEON BEFORE HE CAN CONCLUDE HIS MURDEROUS WORK. SO THE POLICE AND I NEED YOU TO REPORT ANYTHING SUSPICIOUS.

WE ALL KNOW THE SURGEON'S STORY, THE ABUSE HE SUFFERED AS A YOUNGSTER THAT DROVE HIM TO ACTS OF VIOLENCE. HE HAD A HARD LIFE, NO QUESTION.

IF I HAD THE POWER TO GO BACK AND PROTECT HIM FROM THOSE INCIDENTS, THOSE PARENTS, I WOULD DO SO IN A SECOND. BUT I CAN'T.

ALL I CAN DO NOW IS STOP HIM. AND I GIVE THE PEOPLE OF SOL CITY MY WORD THAT I WILL DO EXACTLY THAT.

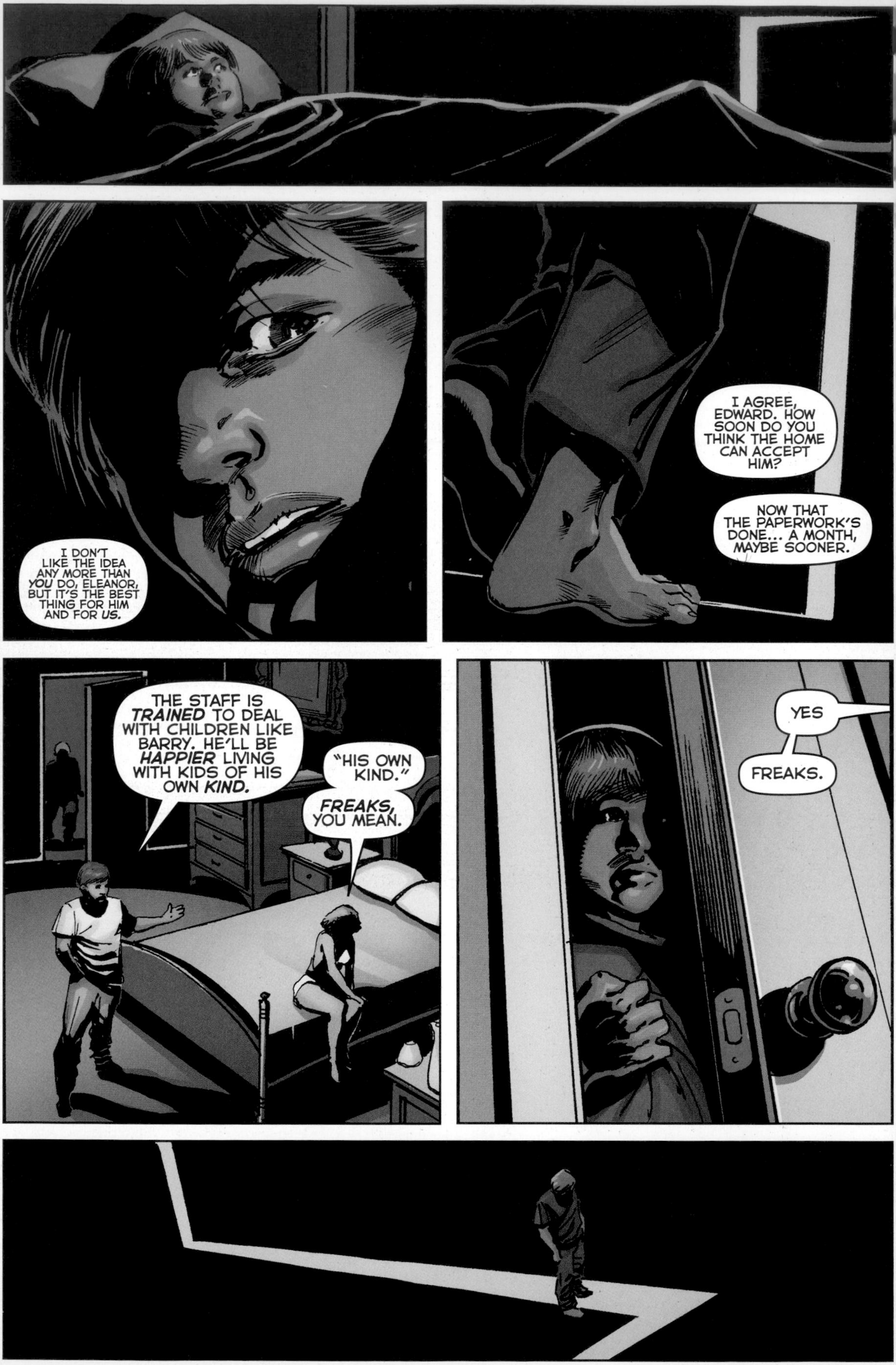
I DON'T LIKE THE IDEA ANY MORE THAN YOU DO, ELEANOR, BUT IT'S THE BEST THING FOR HIM AND FOR US.
I AGREE, EDWARD. HOW SOON DO YOU THINK THE HOME CAN ACCEPT HIM?
NOW THAT THE PAPERWORK'S DONE... A MONTH, MAYBE SOONER.
THE STAFF IS TRAINED TO DEAL WITH CHILDREN LIKE BARRY. HE'LL BE HAPPIER LIVING WITH KIDS OF HIS OWN KIND.
"HIS OWN KIND."
FREAKS, YOU MEAN.
YES
FREAKS.

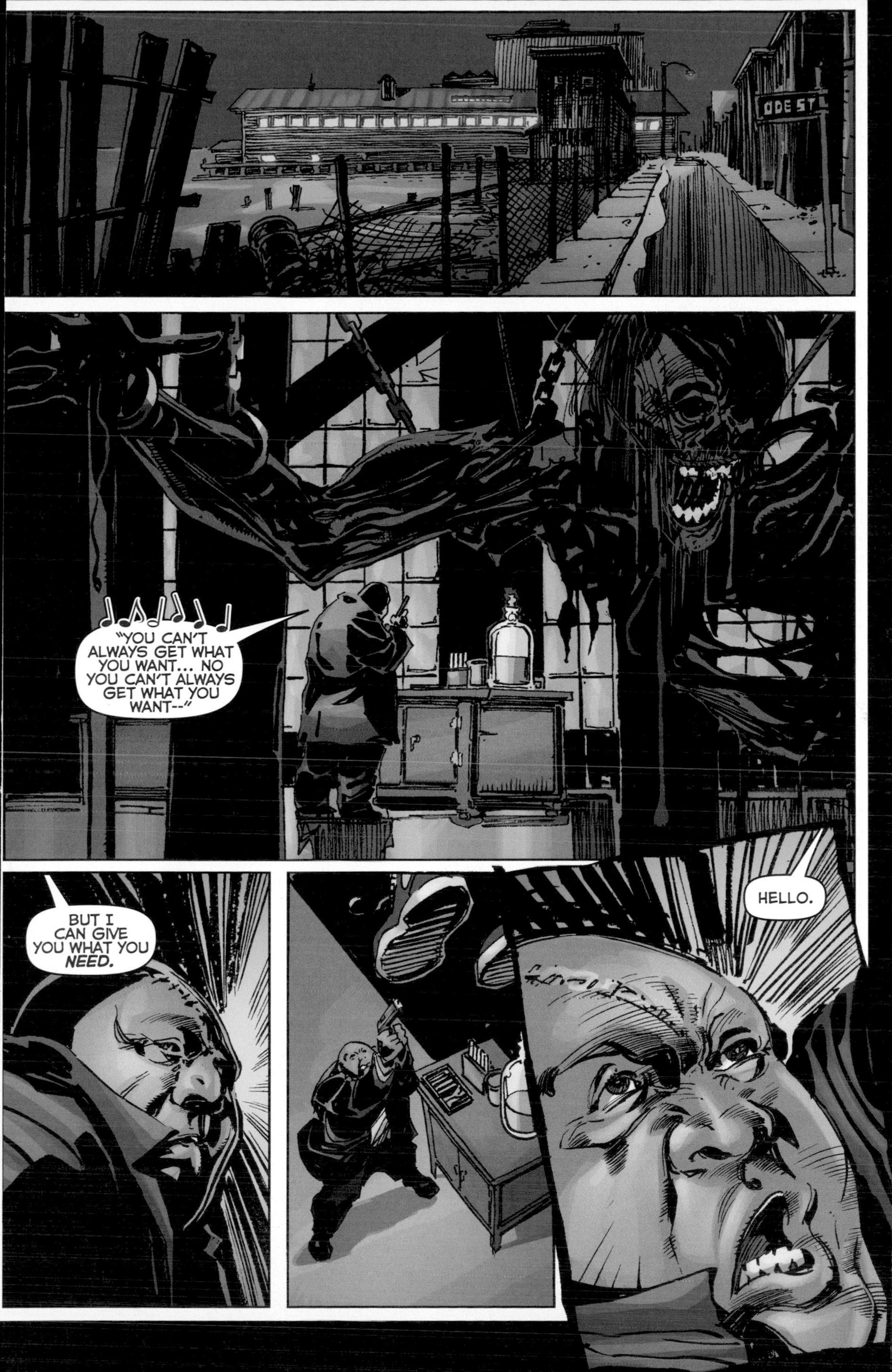
ODE ST
"YOU CAN'T ALWAYS GET WHAT YOU WANT... NO YOU CAN'T ALWAYS GET WHAT YOU WANT--"
BUT I CAN GIVE YOU WHAT YOU *NEED.*
HELLO.

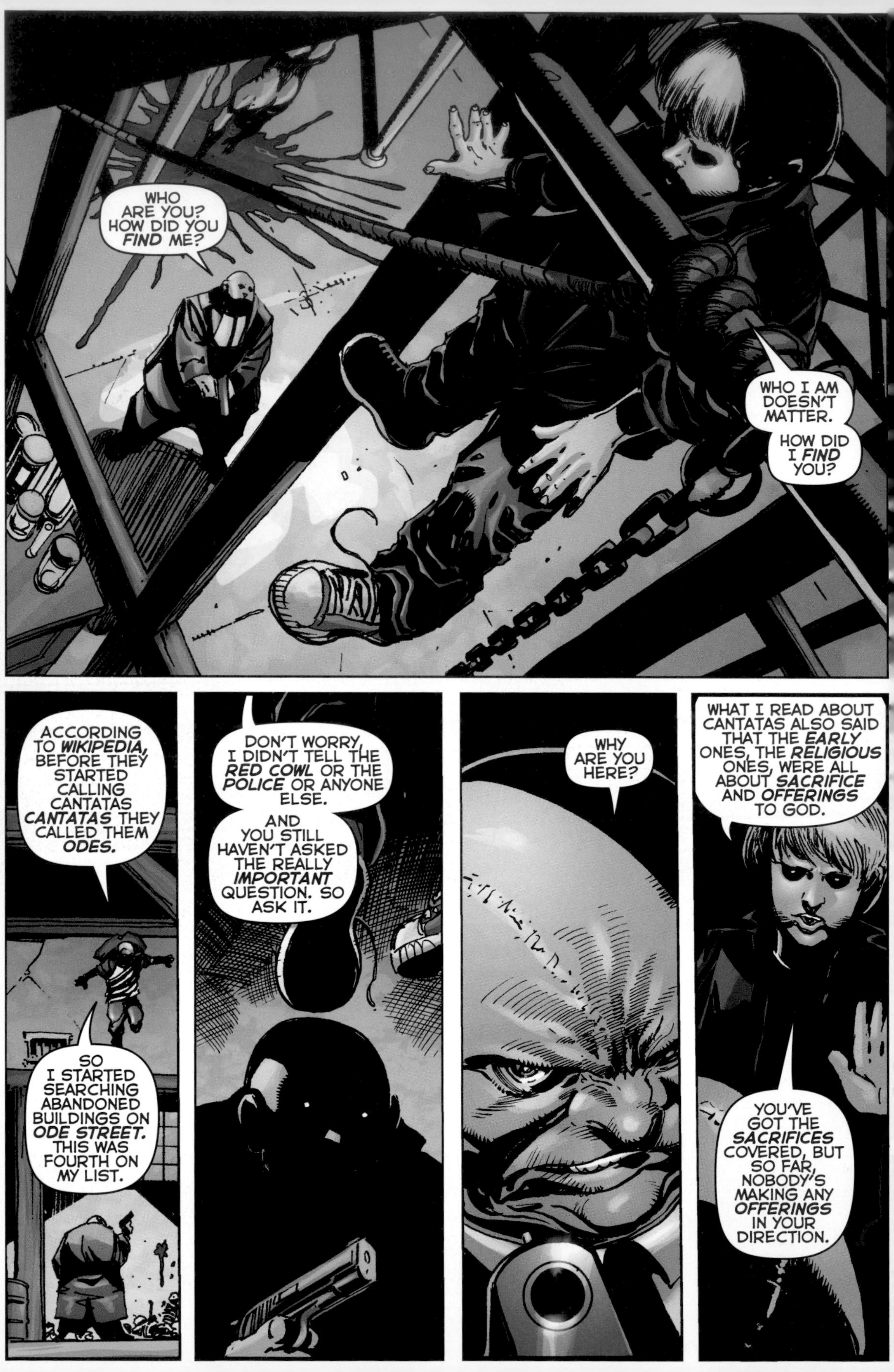
WHO ARE YOU? HOW DID YOU FIND ME?
WHO I AM DOESN'T MATTER.
HOW DID I FIND YOU?
ACCORDING TO WIKIPEDIA, BEFORE THEY STARTED CALLING CANTATAS CANTATAS THEY CALLED THEM ODES.
SO I STARTED SEARCHING ABANDONED BUILDINGS ON ODE STREET. THIS WAS FOURTH ON MY LIST.
DON'T WORRY, I DIDN'T TELL THE RED COWL OR THE POLICE OR ANYONE ELSE.
AND YOU STILL HAVEN'T ASKED THE REALLY IMPORTANT QUESTION. SO ASK IT.
WHY ARE YOU HERE?
WHAT I READ ABOUT CANTATAS ALSO SAID THAT THE EARLY ONES, THE RELIGIOUS ONES, WERE ALL ABOUT SACRIFICE AND OFFERINGS TO GOD.
YOU'VE GOT THE SACRIFICES COVERED, BUT SO FAR, NOBODY'S MAKING ANY OFFERINGS IN YOUR DIRECTION.

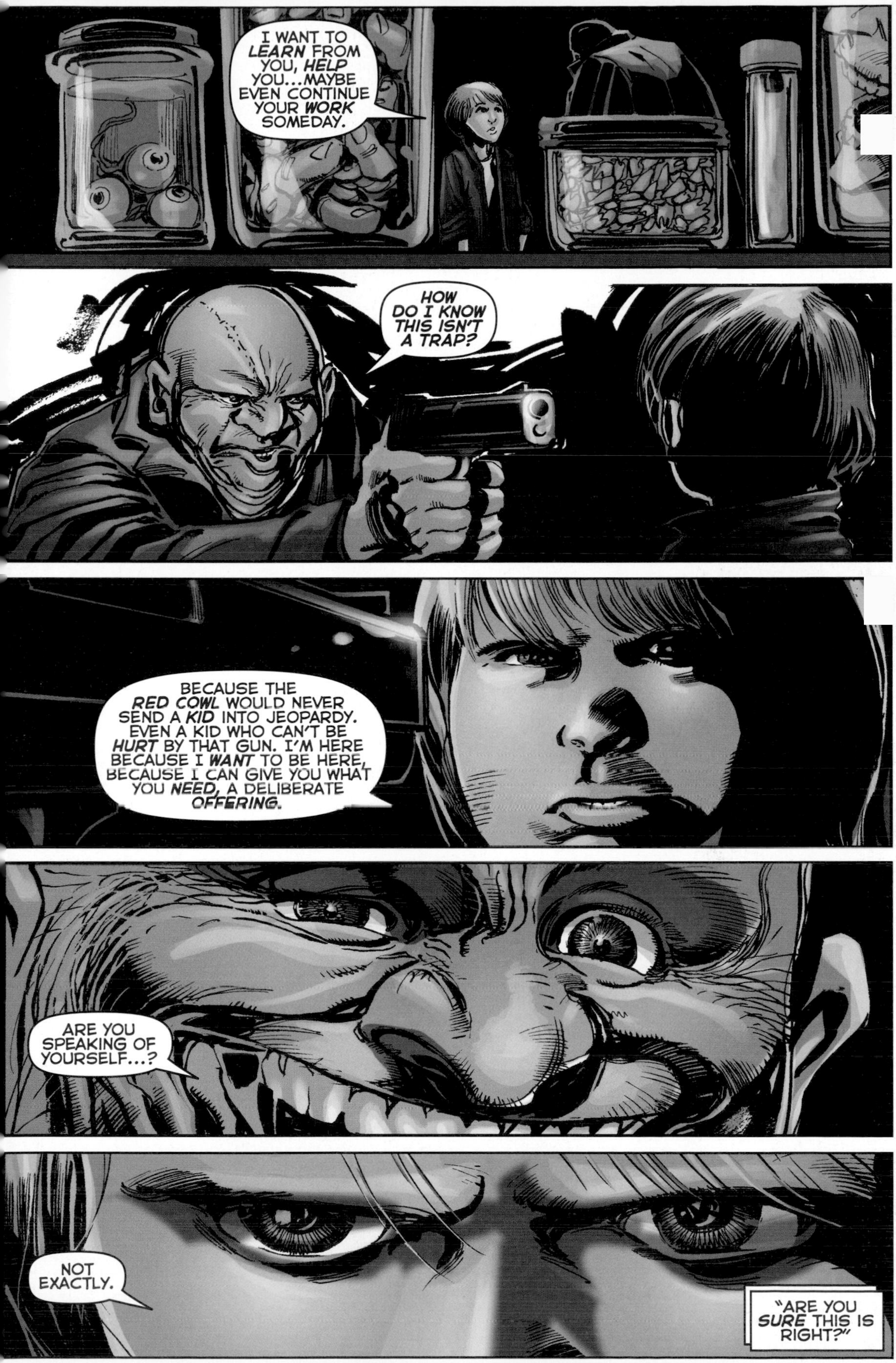
I WANT TO LEARN FROM YOU, HELP YOU...MAYBE EVEN CONTINUE YOUR WORK SOMEDAY.
HOW DO I KNOW THIS ISN'T A TRAP?
BECAUSE THE RED COWL WOULD NEVER SEND A KID INTO JEOPARDY. EVEN A KID WHO CAN'T BE HURT BY THAT GUN. I'M HERE BECAUSE I WANT TO BE HERE, BECAUSE I CAN GIVE YOU WHAT YOU NEED, A DELIBERATE OFFERING.
ARE YOU SPEAKING OF YOURSELF...?
NOT EXACTLY.
"ARE YOU SURE THIS IS RIGHT?"

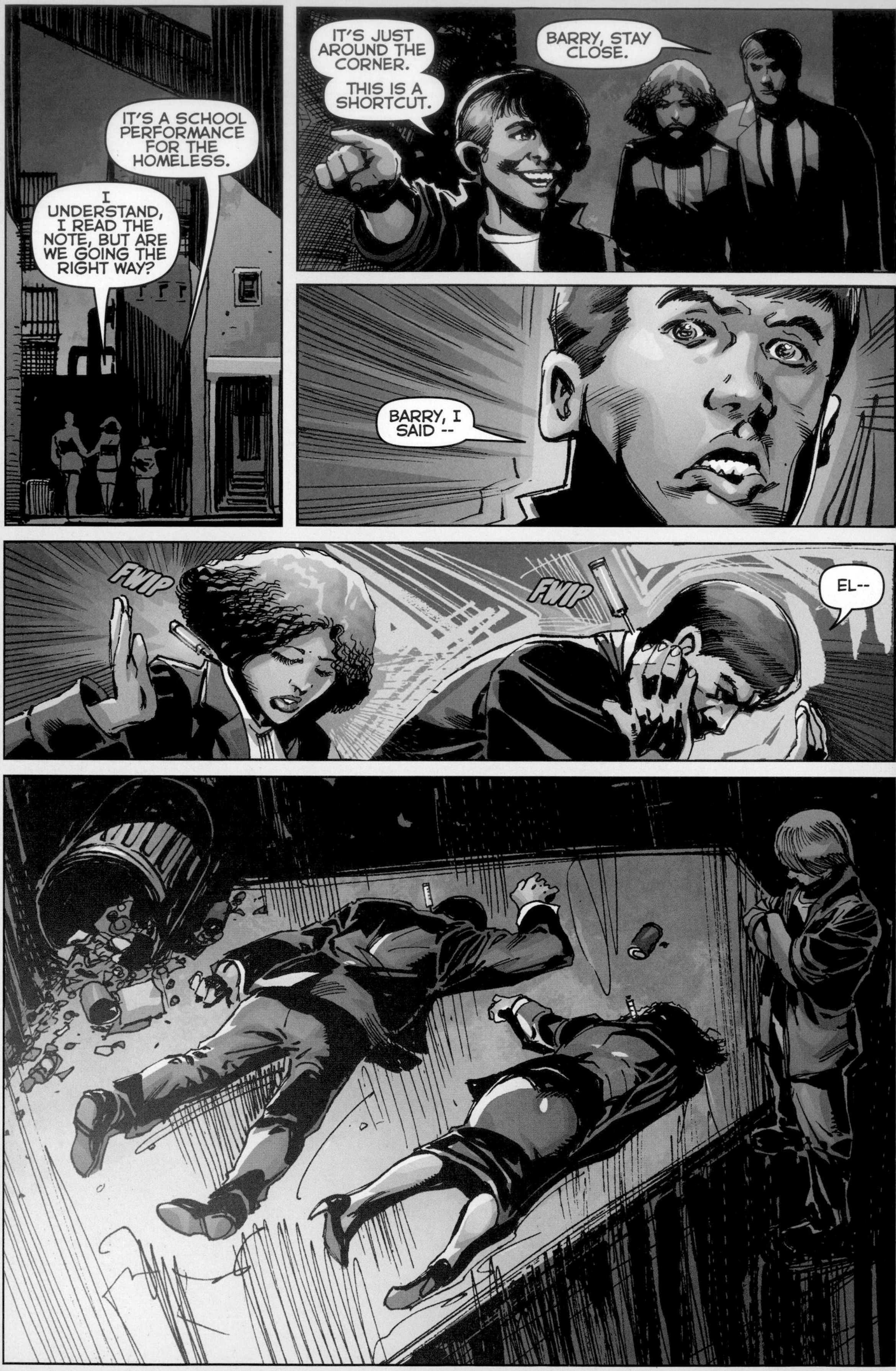
IT'S A SCHOOL PERFORMANCE FOR THE HOMELESS.
I UNDERSTAND, I READ THE NOTE, BUT ARE WE GOING THE RIGHT WAY?
IT'S JUST AROUND THE CORNER.
THIS IS A SHORTCUT.
BARRY, STAY CLOSE.
BARRY, I SAID --
FWIP
FWIP
EL--

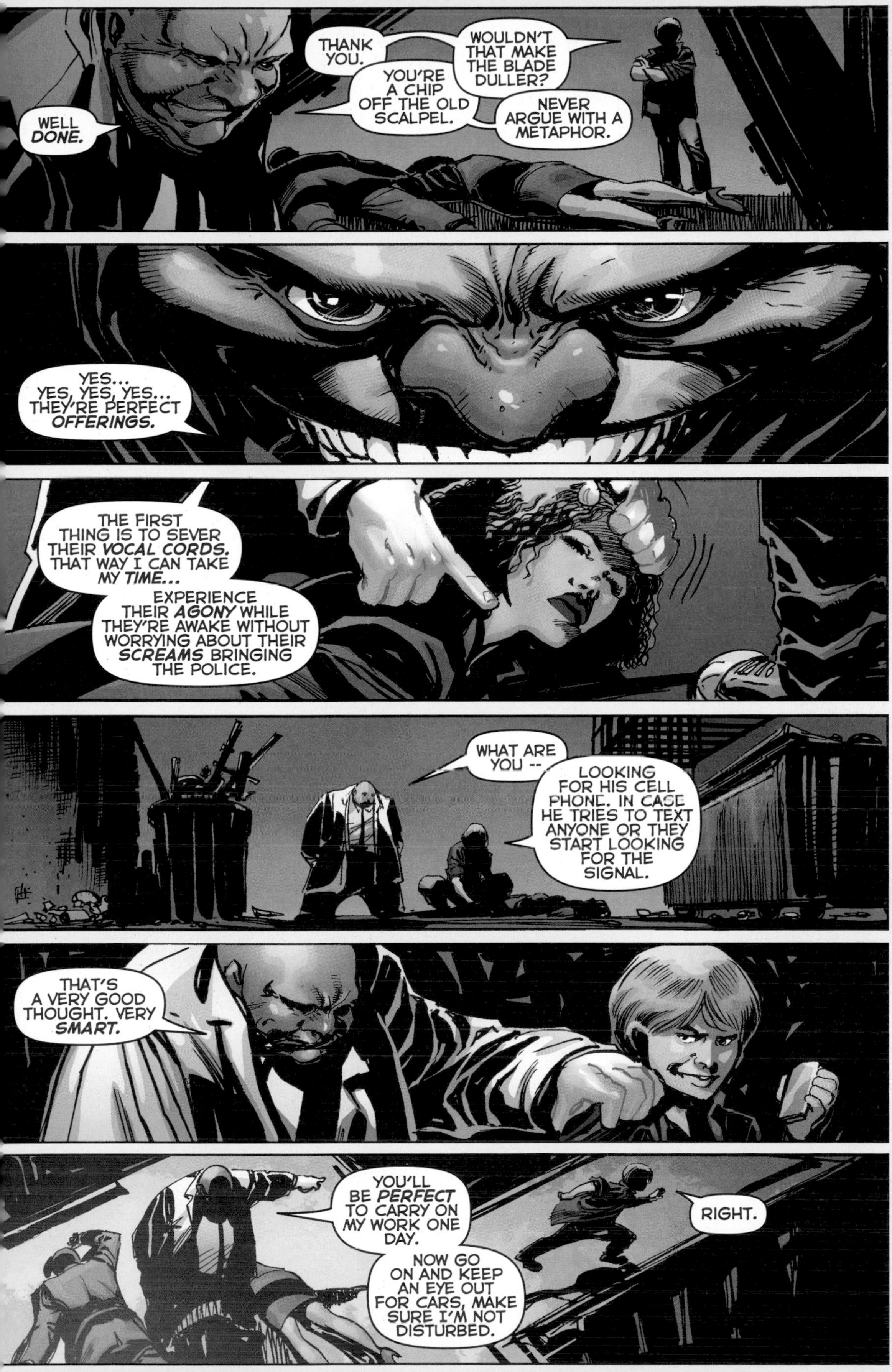

WELL *DONE.*
THANK YOU.
YOU'RE A CHIP OFF THE OLD SCALPEL.
WOULDN'T THAT MAKE THE BLADE DULLER?
NEVER ARGUE WITH A METAPHOR.
YES... YES, YES, YES... THEY'RE PERFECT *OFFERINGS.*
THE FIRST THING IS TO SEVER THEIR *VOCAL CORDS.* THAT WAY I CAN TAKE MY *TIME...*
EXPERIENCE THEIR *AGONY* WHILE THEY'RE AWAKE WITHOUT WORRYING ABOUT THEIR *SCREAMS* BRINGING THE POLICE.
WHAT ARE YOU --
LOOKING FOR HIS CELL PHONE. IN CASE HE TRIES TO TEXT ANYONE OR THEY START LOOKING FOR THE SIGNAL.
THAT'S A VERY GOOD THOUGHT. VERY *SMART.*
YOU'LL BE *PERFECT* TO CARRY ON MY WORK ONE DAY.
NOW GO ON AND KEEP AN EYE OUT FOR CARS, MAKE SURE I'M NOT DISTURBED.
RIGHT.

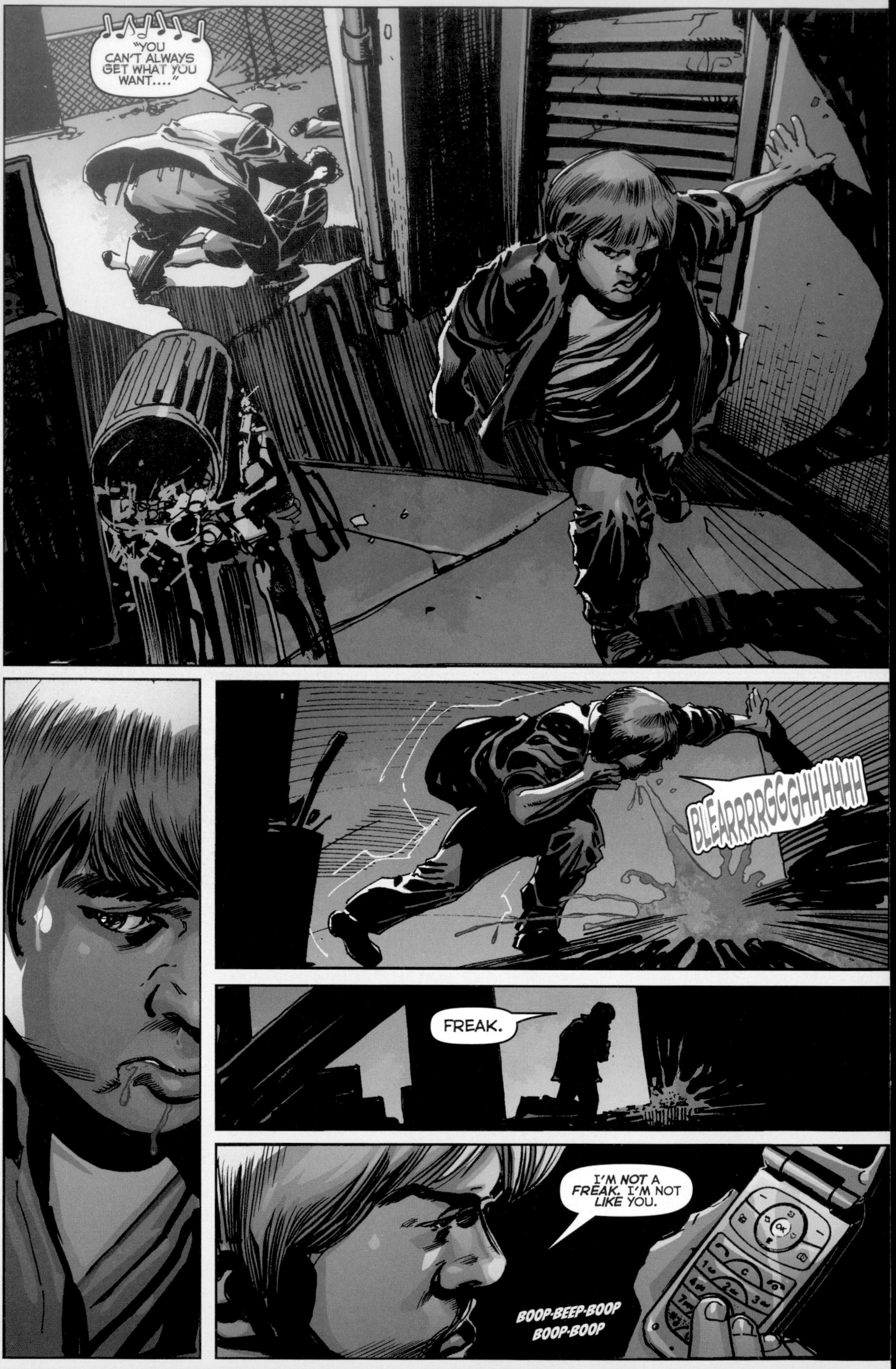
"YOU CAN'T ALWAYS GET WHAT YOU WANT...."
BLEARRRRGGGHHHHHH
FREAK.
I'M NOT A FREAK. I'M NOT LIKE YOU.
BOOP-BEEP-BOOP BOOP-BOOP

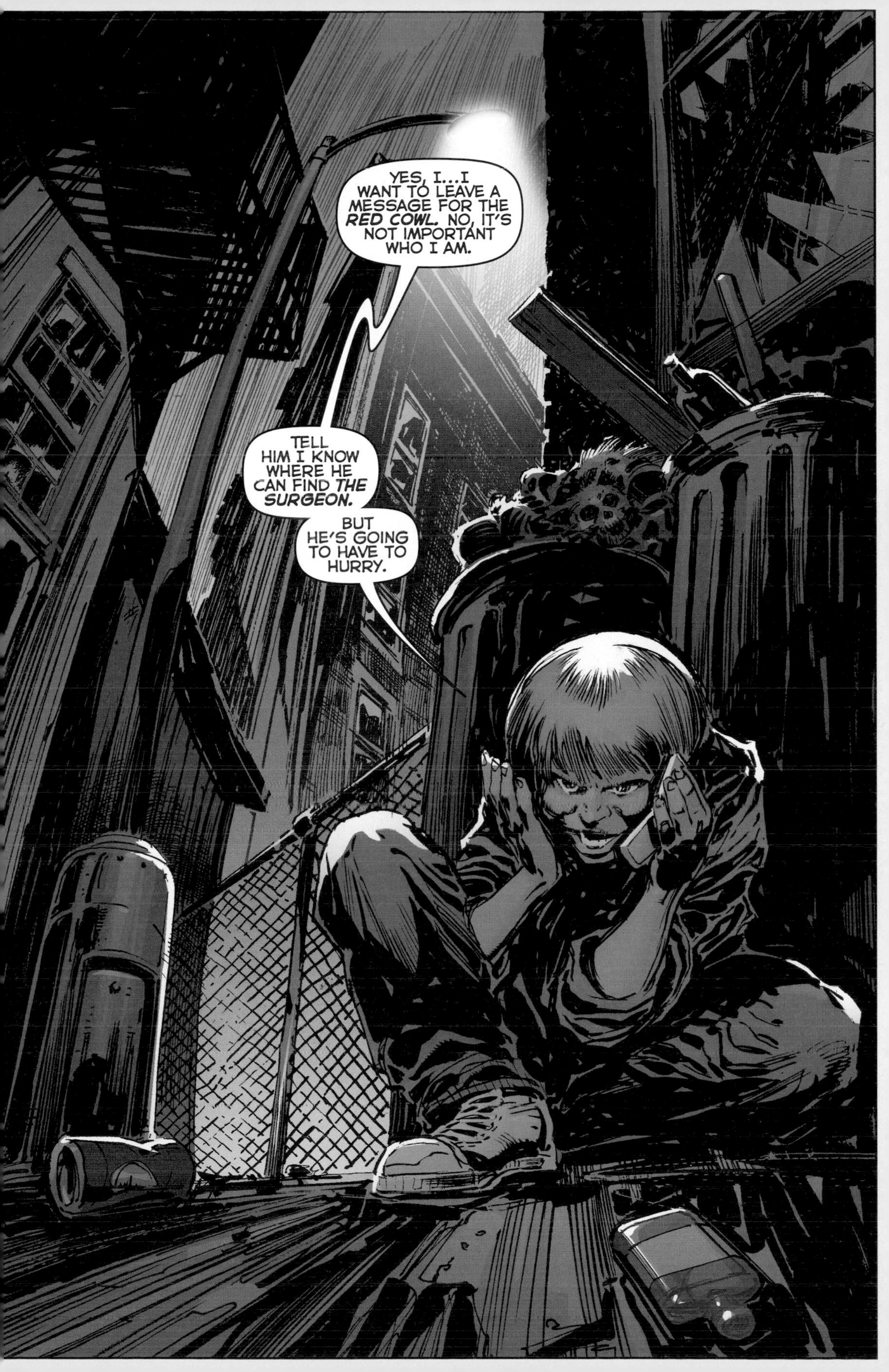
YES, I...I WANT TO LEAVE A MESSAGE FOR THE RED COWL. NO, IT'S NOT IMPORTANT WHO I AM.
TELL HIM I KNOW WHERE HE CAN FIND THE SURGEON.
BUT HE'S GOING TO HAVE TO HURRY.

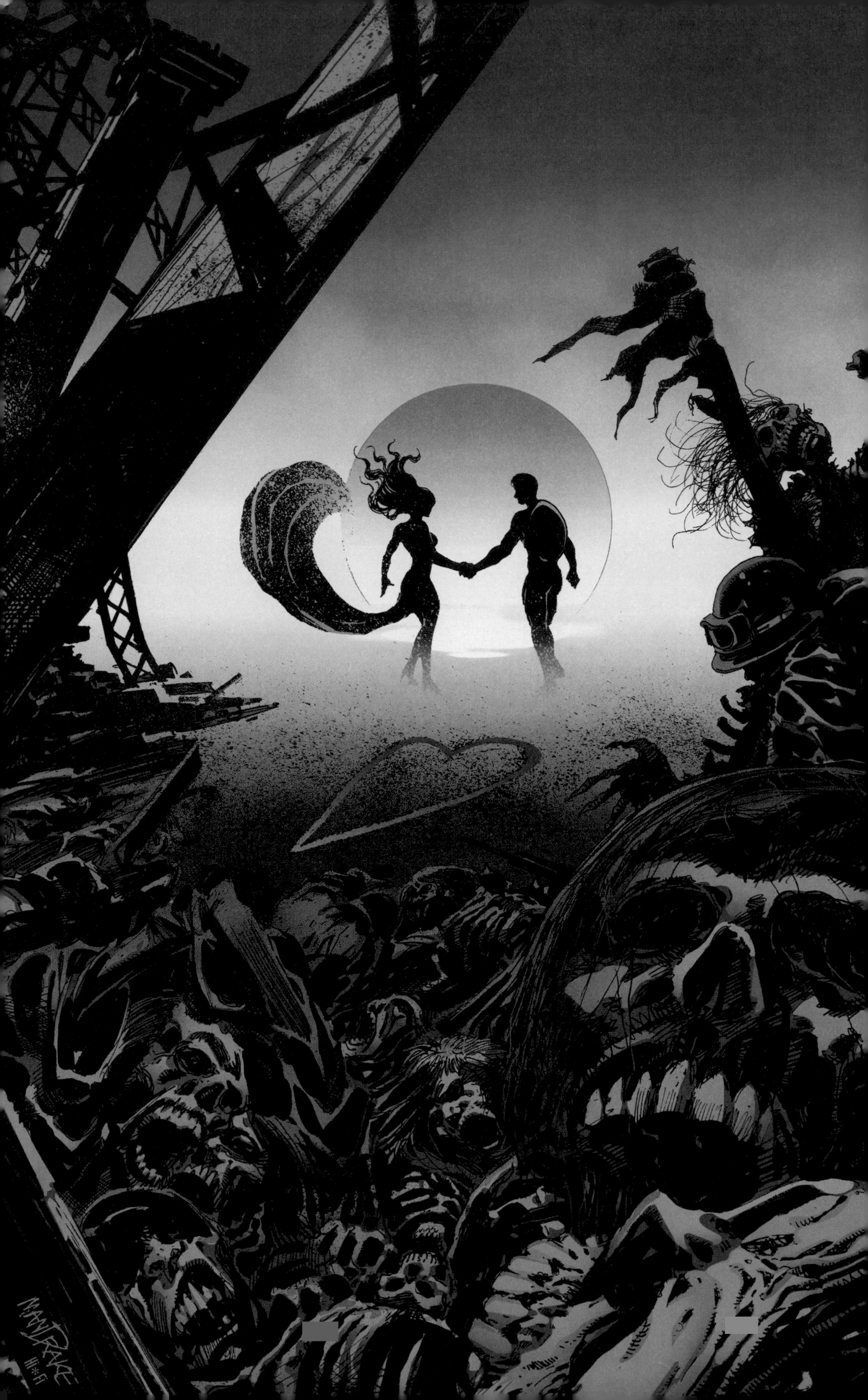
MANDRAKE

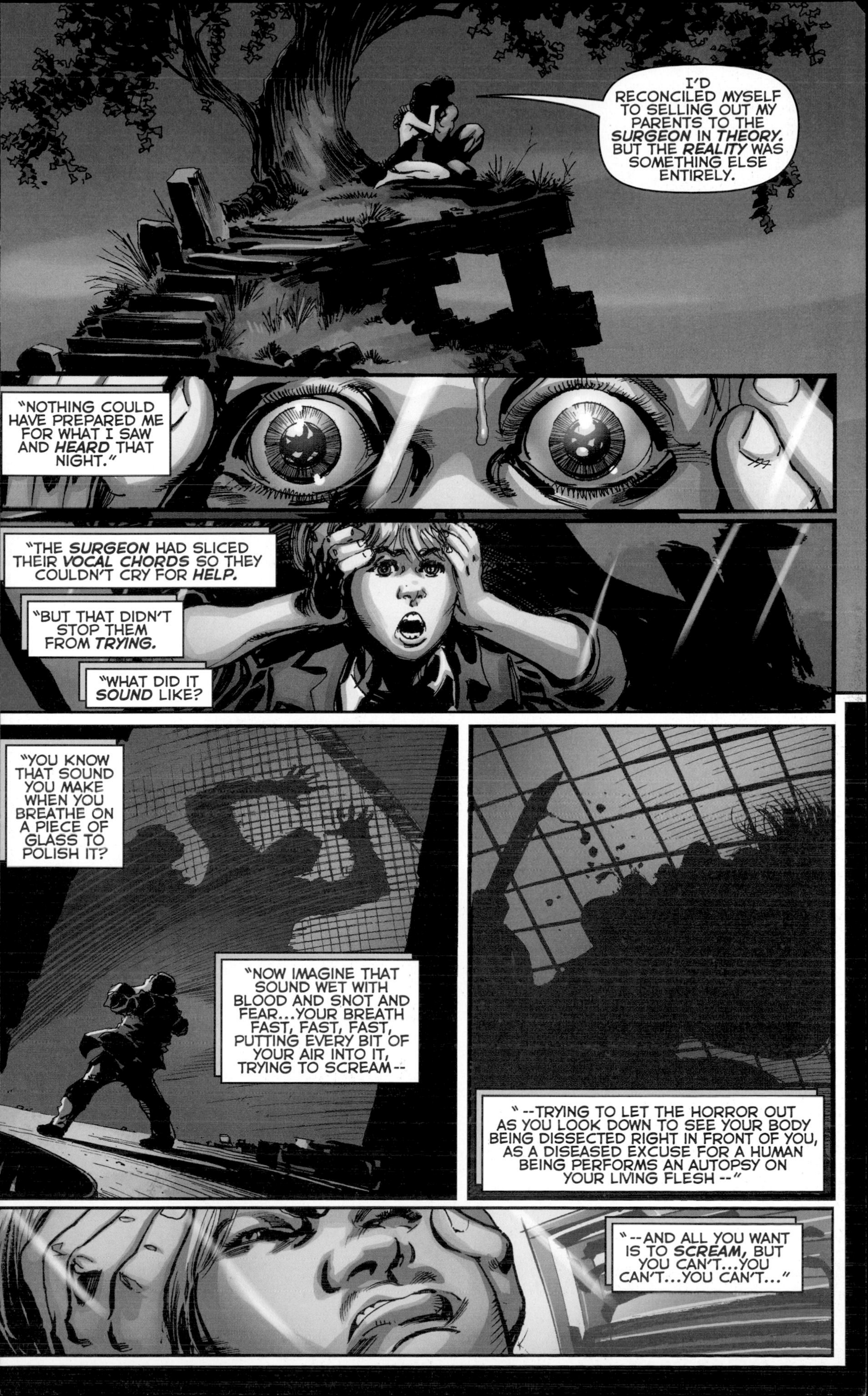
I'D RECONCILED MYSELF TO SELLING OUT MY PARENTS TO THE SURGEON IN THEORY. BUT THE REALITY WAS SOMETHING ELSE ENTIRELY.
"NOTHING COULD HAVE PREPARED ME FOR WHAT I SAW AND HEARD THAT NIGHT."
"THE SURGEON HAD SLICED THEIR VOCAL CHORDS SO THEY COULDN'T CRY FOR HELP.
"BUT THAT DIDN'T STOP THEM FROM TRYING.
"WHAT DID IT SOUND LIKE?
"YOU KNOW THAT SOUND YOU MAKE WHEN YOU BREATHE ON A PIECE OF GLASS TO POLISH IT?
"NOW IMAGINE THAT SOUND WET WITH BLOOD AND SNOT AND FEAR...YOUR BREATH FAST, FAST, FAST, PUTTING EVERY BIT OF YOUR AIR INTO IT, TRYING TO SCREAM--
"--TRYING TO LET THE HORROR OUT AS YOU LOOK DOWN TO SEE YOUR BODY BEING DISSECTED RIGHT IN FRONT OF YOU, AS A DISEASED EXCUSE FOR A HUMAN BEING PERFORMS AN AUTOPSY ON YOUR LIVING FLESH --"
"--AND ALL YOU WANT IS TO SCREAM, BUT YOU CAN'T...YOU CAN'T...YOU CAN'T..."

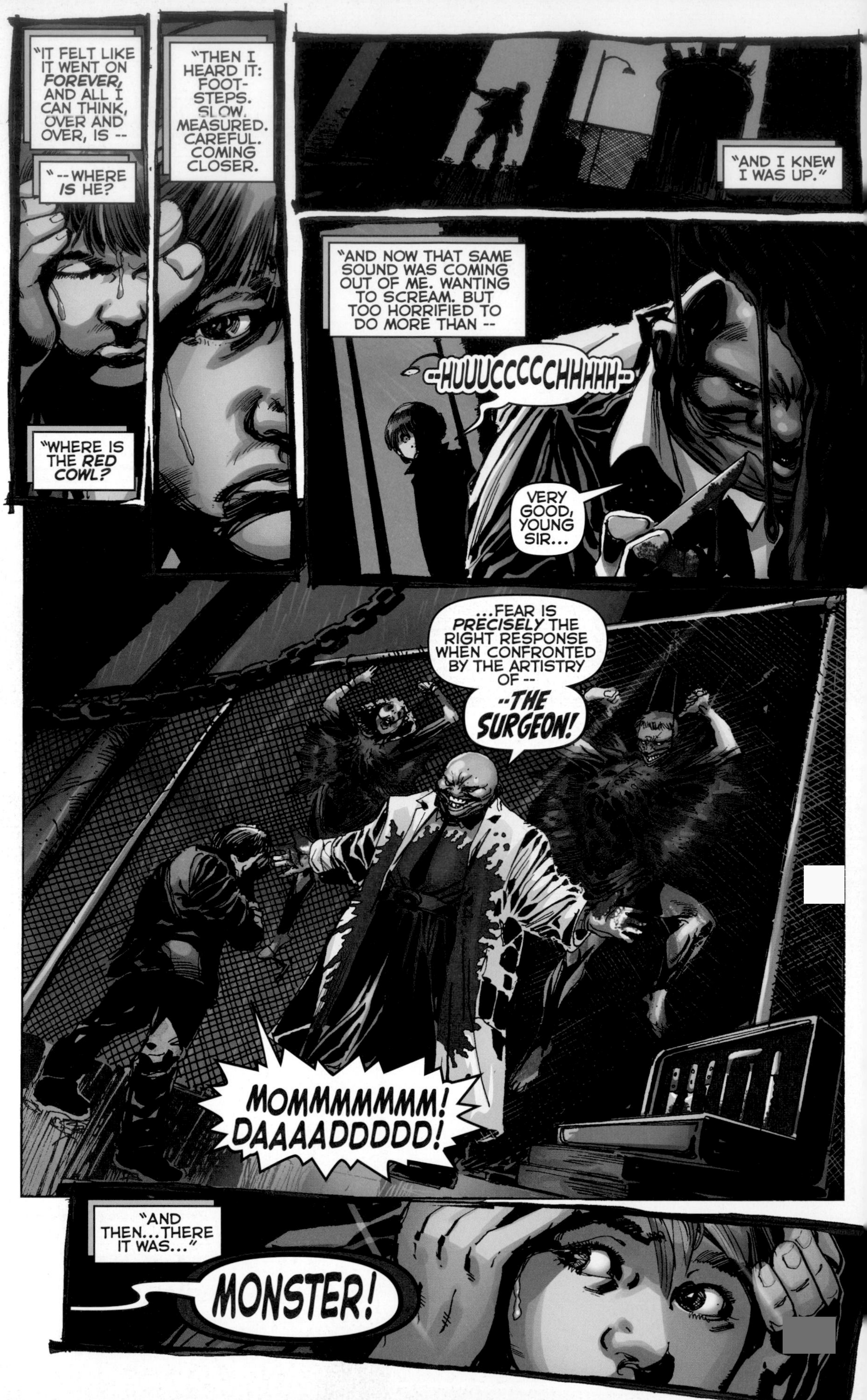
"IT FELT LIKE IT WENT ON *FOREVER,* AND ALL I CAN THINK, OVER AND OVER, IS --
"--WHERE *IS* HE?
"WHERE IS THE *RED COWL?*
"THEN I HEARD IT: FOOT-STEPS. SLOW. MEASURED. CAREFUL. COMING CLOSER.
"AND I KNEW I WAS UP."
"AND NOW THAT SAME SOUND WAS COMING OUT OF ME. WANTING TO SCREAM. BUT TOO HORRIFIED TO DO MORE THAN --
--HUUUCCCCCHHHHH--
VERY GOOD, YOUNG SIR...
...FEAR IS *PRECISELY* THE RIGHT RESPONSE WHEN CONFRONTED BY THE ARTISTRY OF --
--THE SURGEON!
MOMMMMMMM! DAAAADDDDD!
"AND THEN...THERE IT WAS..."
MONSTER!

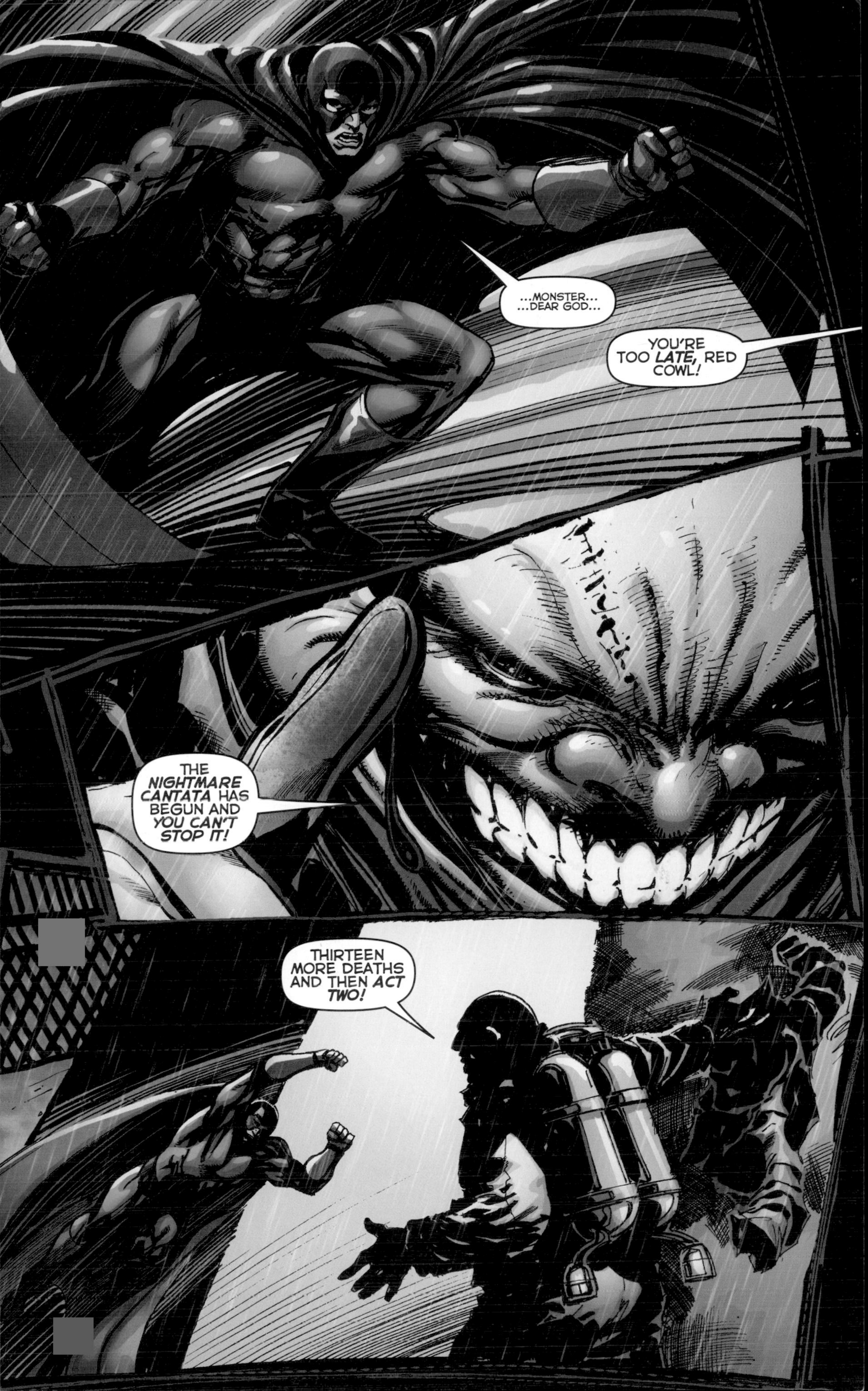
...MONSTER...
...DEAR GOD...
YOU'RE TOO LATE, RED COWL!
THE NIGHTMARE CANTATA HAS BEGUN AND YOU CAN'T STOP IT!
THIRTEEN MORE DEATHS AND THEN ACT TWO!

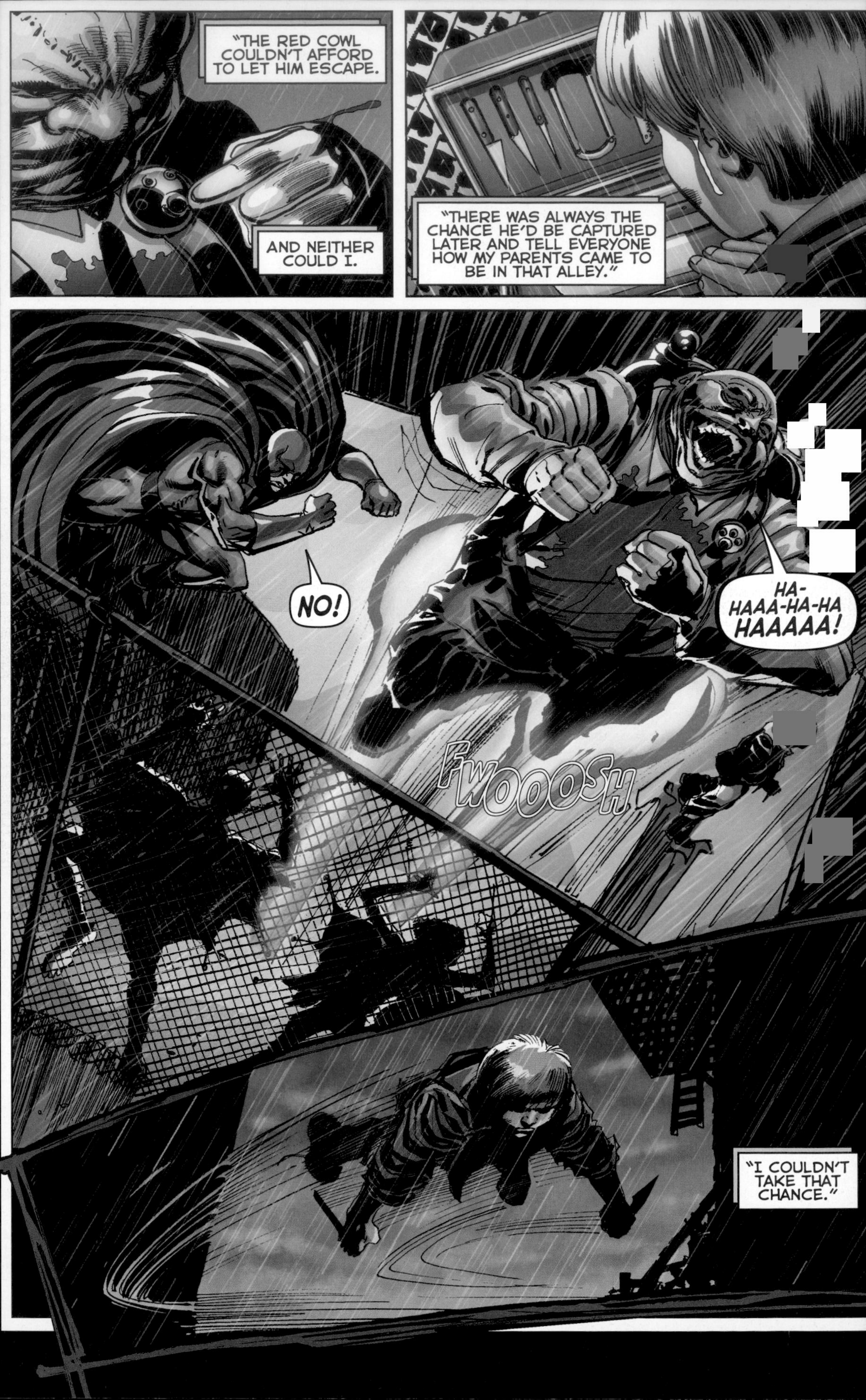
"THE RED COWL COULDN'T AFFORD TO LET HIM ESCAPE.
AND NEITHER COULD I.
"THERE WAS ALWAYS THE CHANCE HE'D BE CAPTURED LATER AND TELL EVERYONE HOW MY PARENTS CAME TO BE IN THAT ALLEY."
NO!
HA-HAAA-HA-HA HAAAAA!
FWOOOSH
"I COULDN'T TAKE THAT CHANCE."

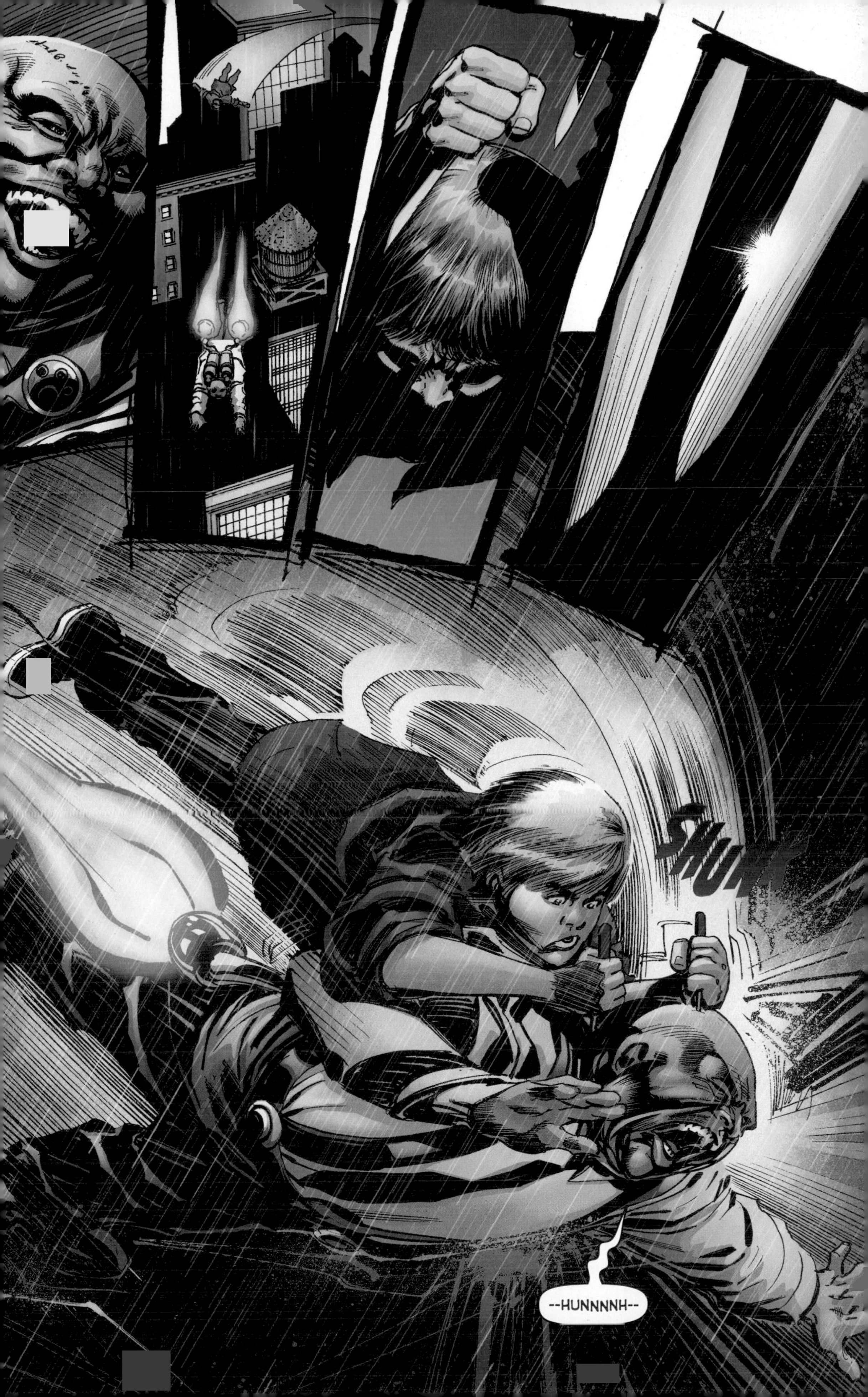
--HUNNNNH--

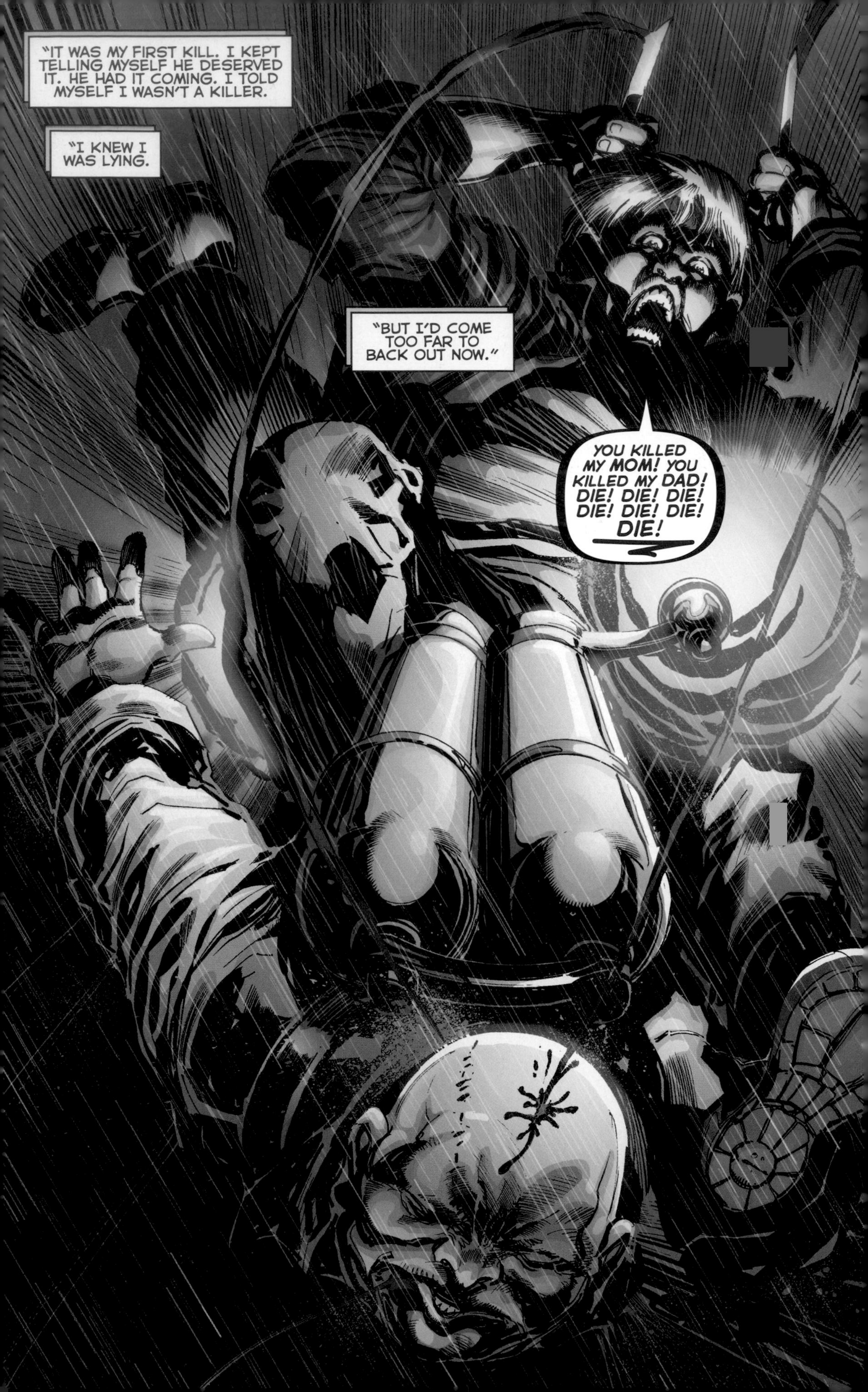
"IT WAS MY FIRST KILL. I KEPT TELLING MYSELF HE DESERVED IT. HE HAD IT COMING. I TOLD MYSELF I WASN'T A KILLER.
"I KNEW I WAS LYING.
"BUT I'D COME TOO FAR TO BACK OUT NOW."
YOU KILLED MY MOM! YOU KILLED MY DAD! DIE! DIE! DIE! DIE! DIE! DIE! DIE!

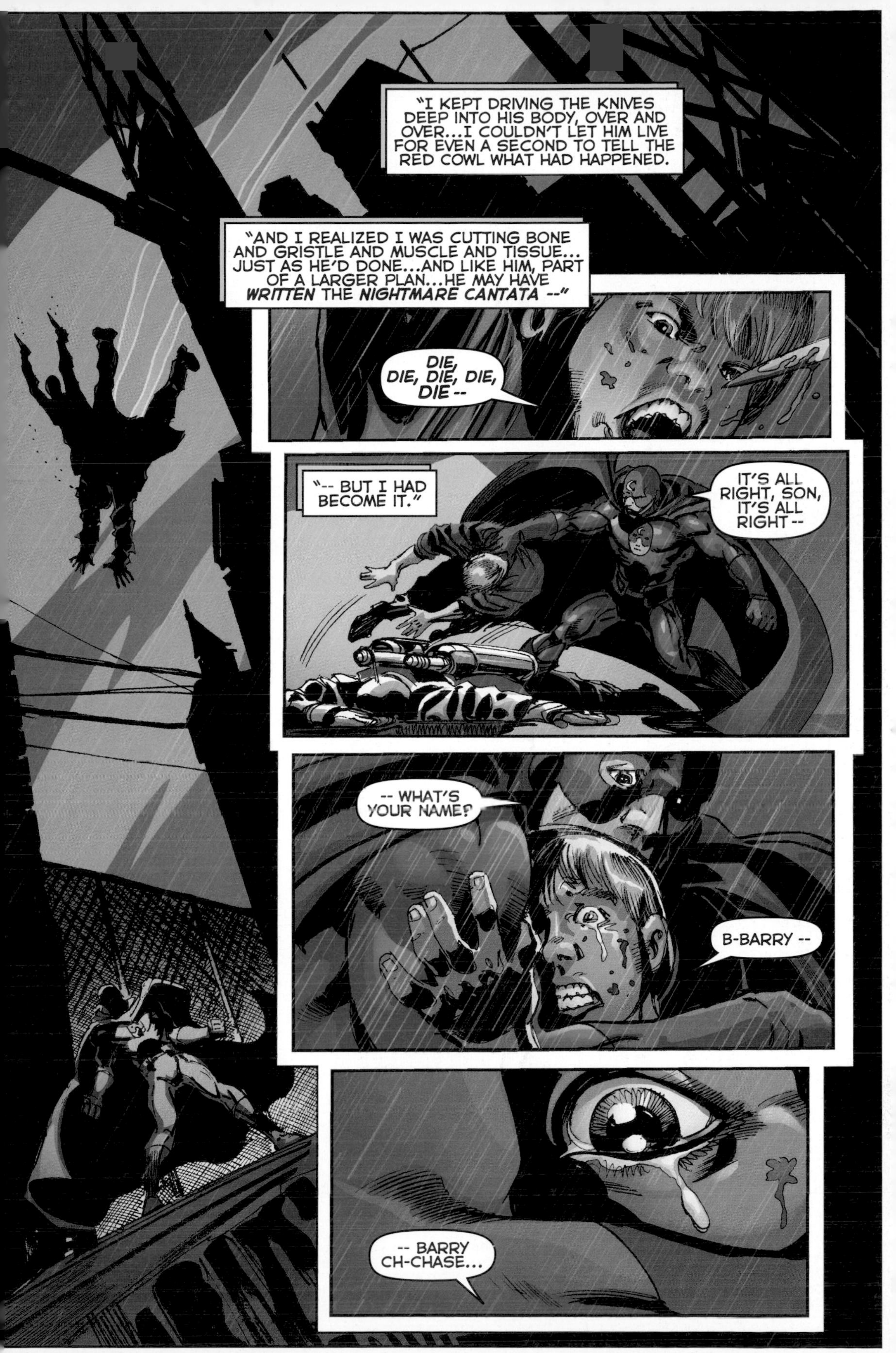
"I KEPT DRIVING THE KNIVES DEEP INTO HIS BODY, OVER AND OVER...I COULDN'T LET HIM LIVE FOR EVEN A SECOND TO TELL THE RED COWL WHAT HAD HAPPENED.
"AND I REALIZED I WAS CUTTING BONE AND GRISTLE AND MUSCLE AND TISSUE... JUST AS HE'D DONE...AND LIKE HIM, PART OF A LARGER PLAN...HE MAY HAVE WRITTEN THE NIGHTMARE CANTATA --"
DIE, DIE, DIE, DIE, DIE --
"-- BUT I HAD BECOME IT."
IT'S ALL RIGHT, SON, IT'S ALL RIGHT --
-- WHAT'S YOUR NAME?
B-BARRY --
-- BARRY CH-CHASE...

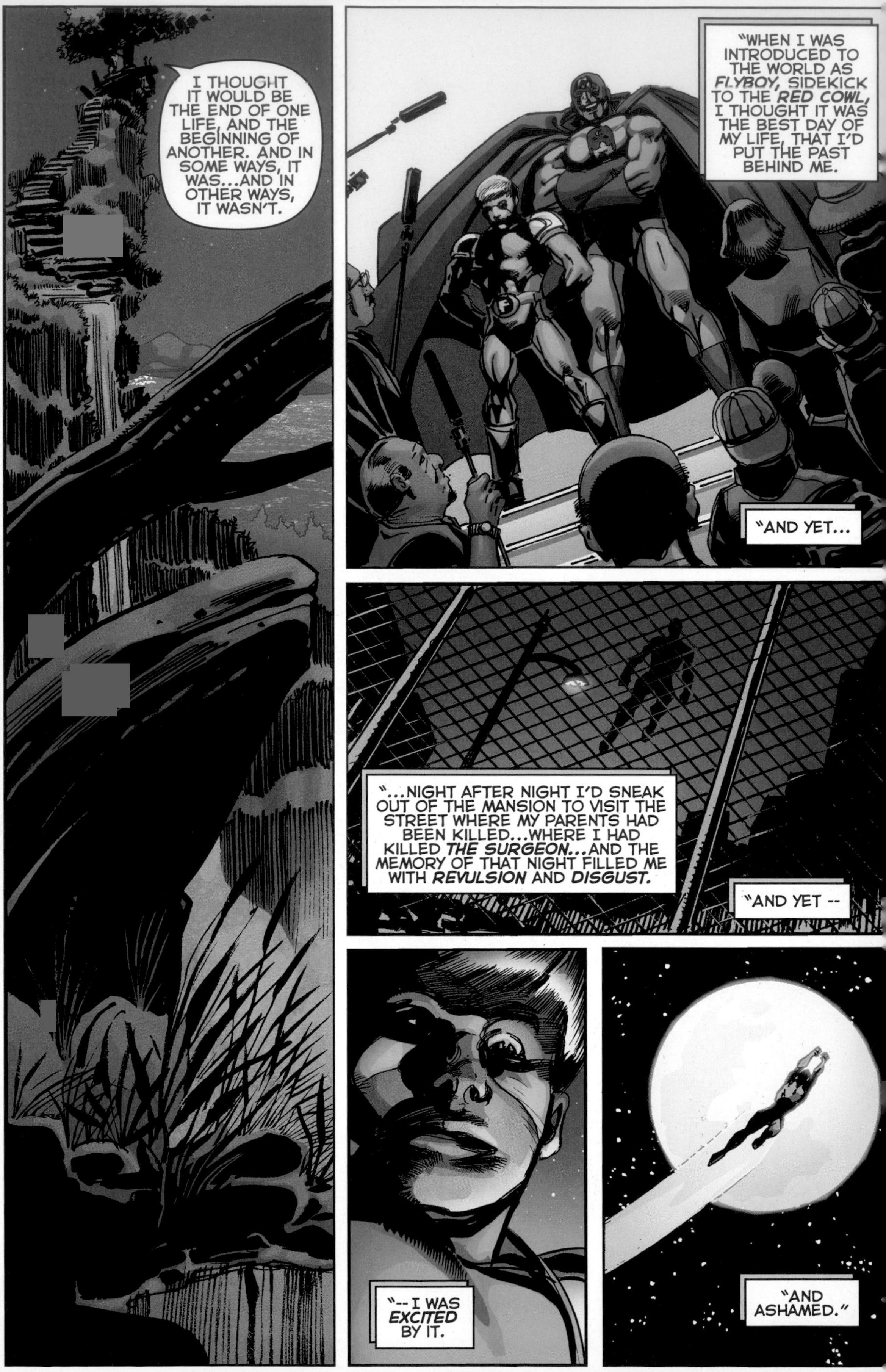

I THOUGHT IT WOULD BE THE END OF ONE LIFE, AND THE BEGINNING OF ANOTHER. AND IN SOME WAYS, IT WAS...AND IN OTHER WAYS, IT WASN'T.
"WHEN I WAS INTRODUCED TO THE WORLD AS FLYBOY, SIDEKICK TO THE RED COWL, I THOUGHT IT WAS THE BEST DAY OF MY LIFE, THAT I'D PUT THE PAST BEHIND ME.
"AND YET...
"...NIGHT AFTER NIGHT I'D SNEAK OUT OF THE MANSION TO VISIT THE STREET WHERE MY PARENTS HAD BEEN KILLED...WHERE I HAD KILLED THE SURGEON...AND THE MEMORY OF THAT NIGHT FILLED ME WITH REVULSION AND DISGUST.
"AND YET --
"-- I WAS EXCITED BY IT.
"AND ASHAMED."

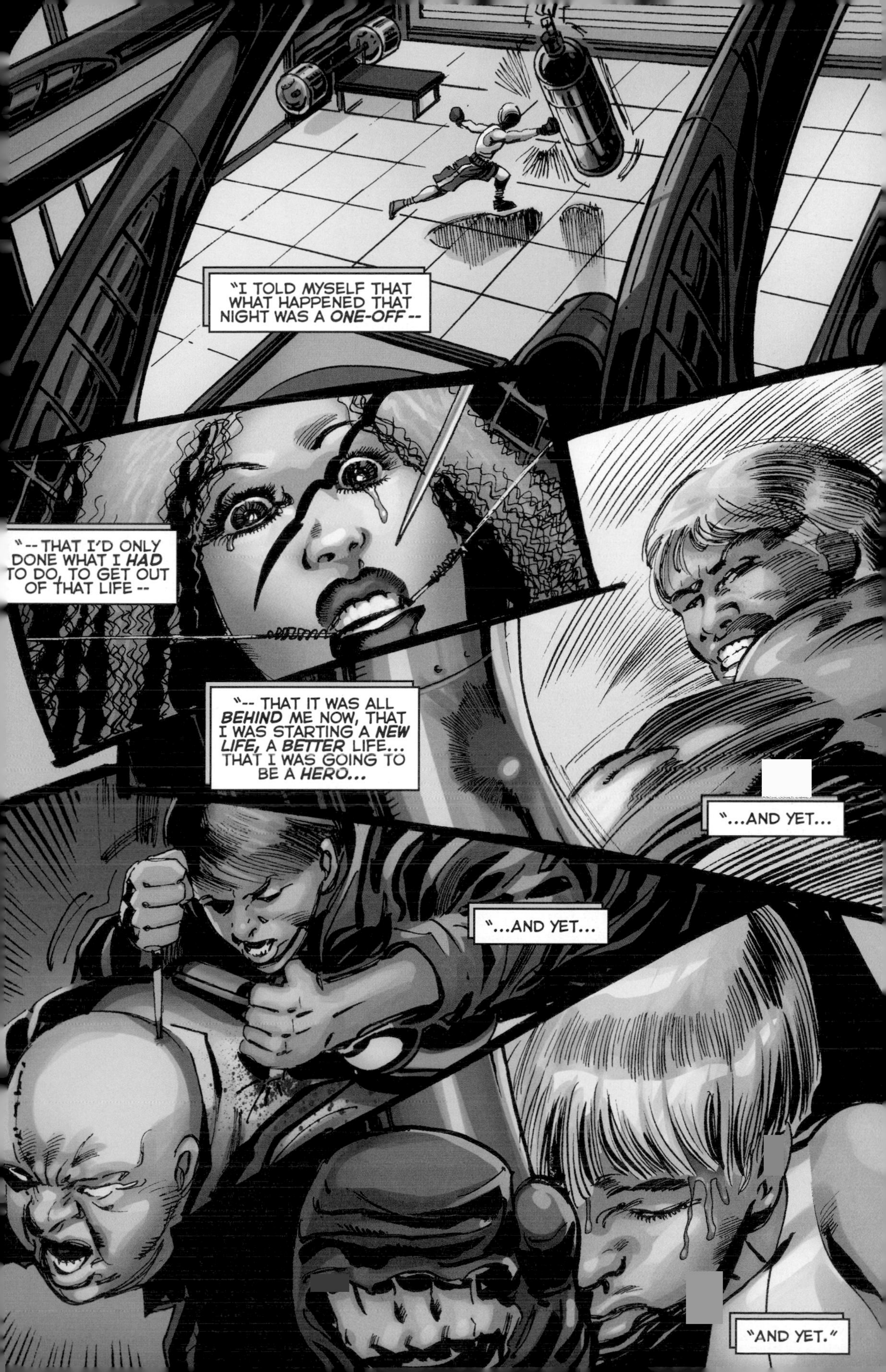
"I TOLD MYSELF THAT WHAT HAPPENED THAT NIGHT WAS A ONE-OFF --
"-- THAT I'D ONLY DONE WHAT I HAD TO DO, TO GET OUT OF THAT LIFE --
"-- THAT IT WAS ALL BEHIND ME NOW, THAT I WAS STARTING A NEW LIFE, A BETTER LIFE... THAT I WAS GOING TO BE A HERO...
"...AND YET...
"...AND YET...
"AND YET."

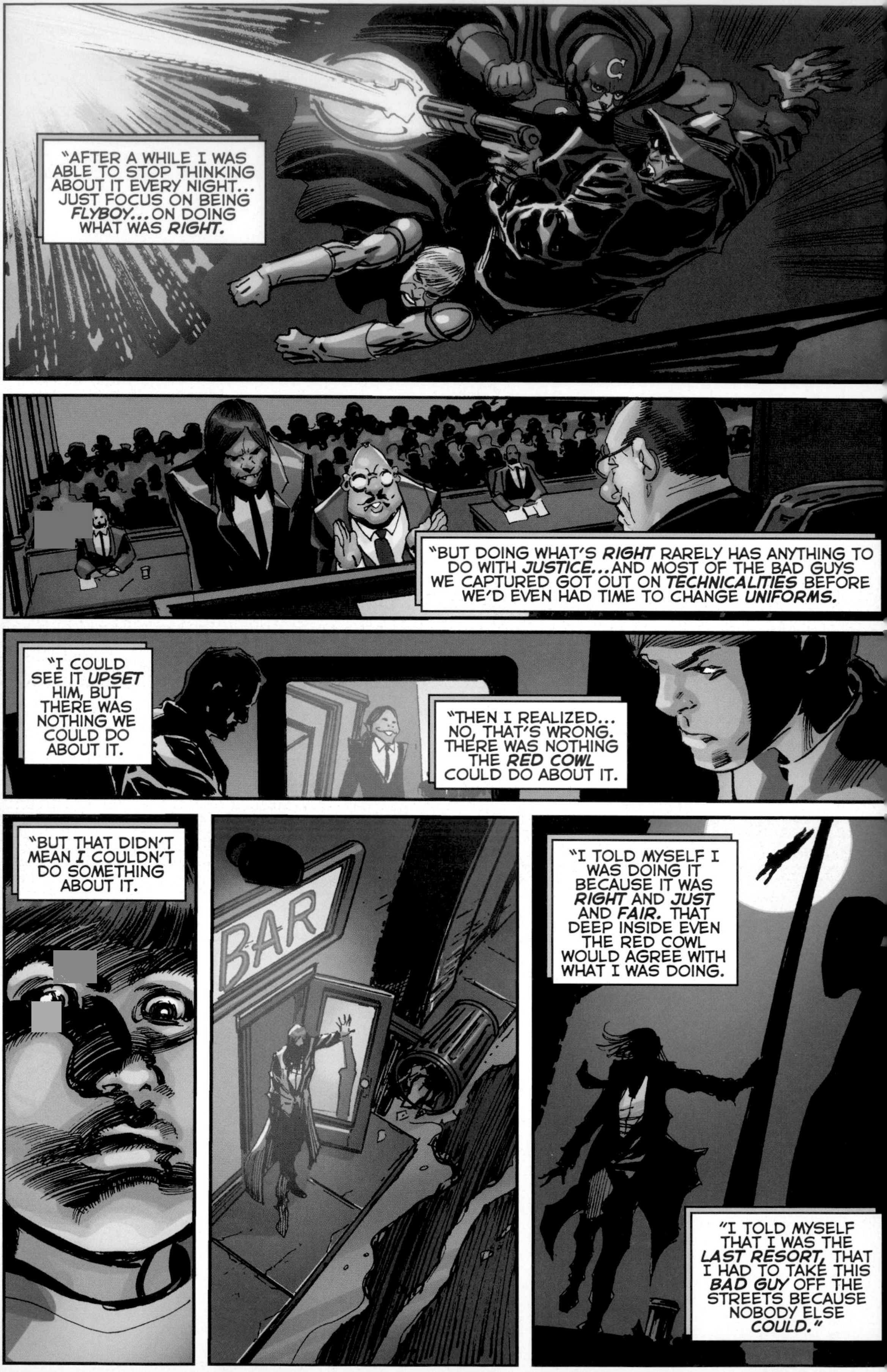
"AFTER A WHILE I WAS ABLE TO STOP THINKING ABOUT IT EVERY NIGHT... JUST FOCUS ON BEING *FLYBOY*... ON DOING WHAT WAS *RIGHT.*
"BUT DOING WHAT'S *RIGHT* RARELY HAS ANYTHING TO DO WITH *JUSTICE*... AND MOST OF THE BAD GUYS WE CAPTURED GOT OUT ON *TECHNICALITIES* BEFORE WE'D EVEN HAD TIME TO CHANGE *UNIFORMS.*
"I COULD SEE IT *UPSET* HIM, BUT THERE WAS NOTHING WE COULD DO ABOUT IT.
"THEN I REALIZED... NO, THAT'S WRONG. THERE WAS NOTHING THE *RED COWL* COULD DO ABOUT IT.
"BUT THAT DIDN'T MEAN *I* COULDN'T DO SOMETHING ABOUT IT.
BAR
"I TOLD MYSELF I WAS DOING IT BECAUSE IT WAS *RIGHT* AND *JUST* AND *FAIR.* THAT DEEP INSIDE EVEN THE RED COWL WOULD AGREE WITH WHAT I WAS DOING.
"I TOLD MYSELF THAT I WAS THE *LAST RESORT,* THAT I HAD TO TAKE THIS *BAD GUY* OFF THE STREETS BECAUSE NOBODY ELSE *COULD.*"

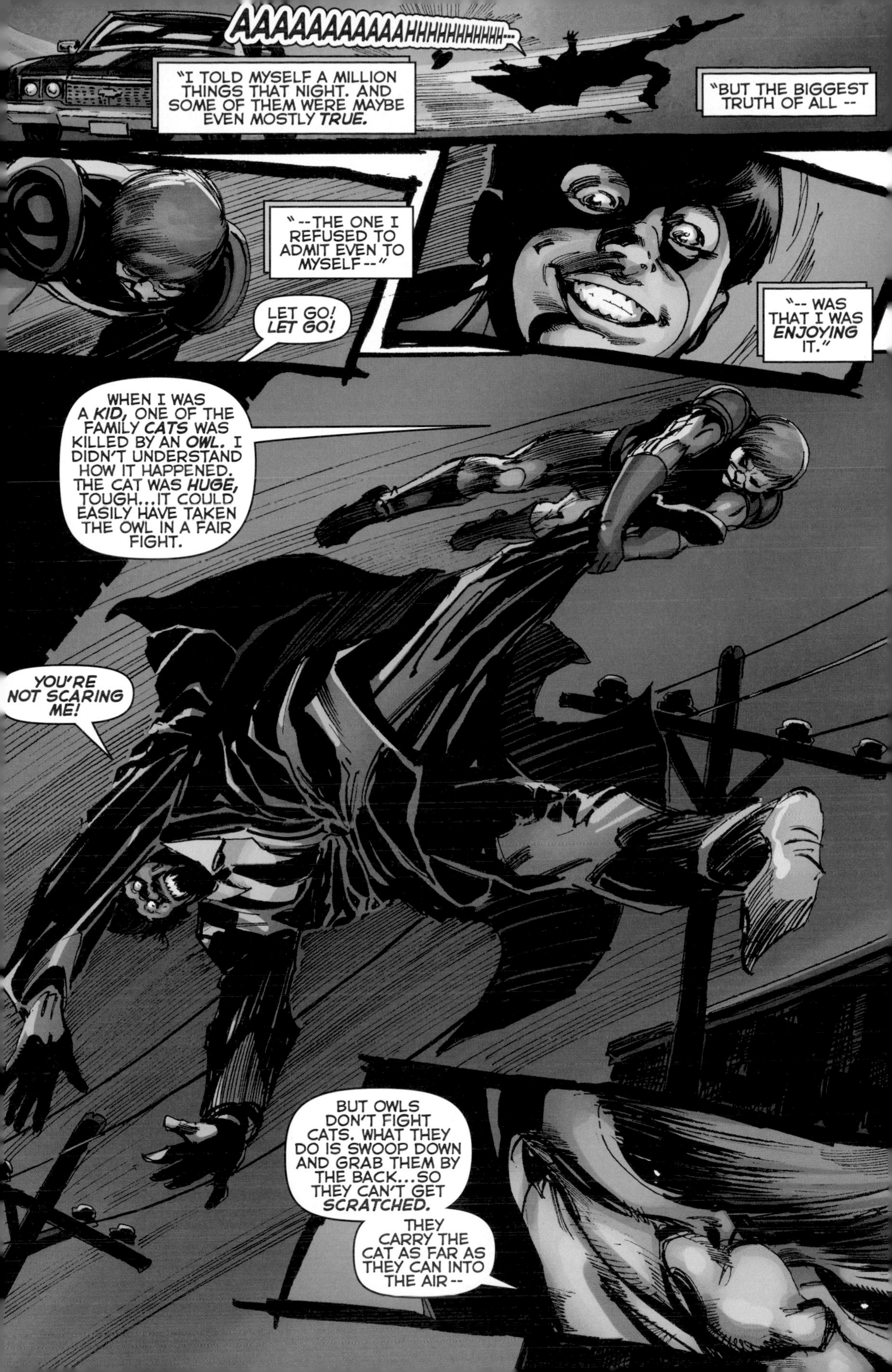
AAAAAAAAAAAHHHHHHHHHHH---
"I TOLD MYSELF A MILLION THINGS THAT NIGHT. AND SOME OF THEM WERE MAYBE EVEN MOSTLY TRUE.
"BUT THE BIGGEST TRUTH OF ALL --
"--THE ONE I REFUSED TO ADMIT EVEN TO MYSELF--"
LET GO! LET GO!
"-- WAS THAT I WAS ENJOYING IT."
WHEN I WAS A KID, ONE OF THE FAMILY CATS WAS KILLED BY AN OWL. I DIDN'T UNDERSTAND HOW IT HAPPENED. THE CAT WAS HUGE, TOUGH...IT COULD EASILY HAVE TAKEN THE OWL IN A FAIR FIGHT.
YOU'RE NOT SCARING ME!
BUT OWLS DON'T FIGHT CATS. WHAT THEY DO IS SWOOP DOWN AND GRAB THEM BY THE BACK...SO THEY CAN'T GET SCRATCHED.
THEY CARRY THE CAT AS FAR AS THEY CAN INTO THE AIR--

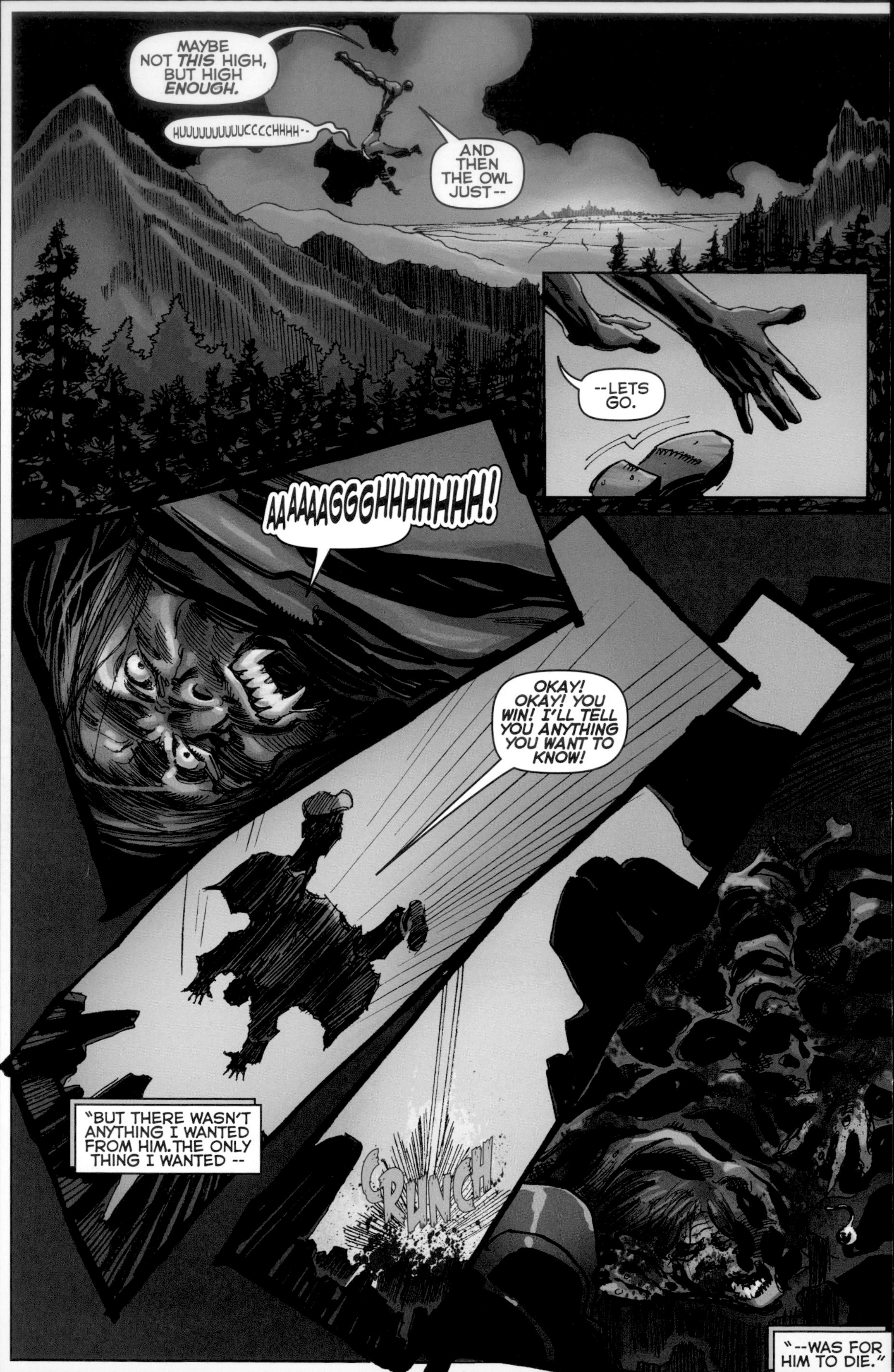
MAYBE NOT *THIS* HIGH, BUT HIGH *ENOUGH.*
HUUUUUUUUUUCCCCHHHH--
AND THEN THE OWL JUST--
--LETS GO.
AAAAAAGGGHHHHHHH!
OKAY! OKAY! YOU WIN! I'LL TELL YOU ANYTHING YOU WANT TO KNOW!
"BUT THERE WASN'T ANYTHING I WANTED FROM HIM. THE ONLY THING I WANTED --
CRUNCH
"--WAS FOR HIM TO DIE."

FROM THE ALTITUDE I'D DROPPED HIM, THE DIFFICULTY IN CLIMBING THAT FAR UP THE MOUNTAIN, AND WHAT LITTLE WAS LEFT OF THE *BODY*, I WAS SURE IT WOULD NEVER BE *FOUND* OR *IDENTIFIED*.

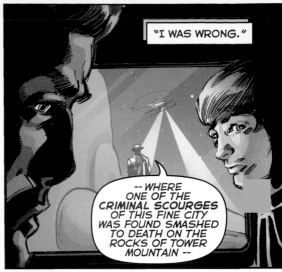

"I WAS WRONG."

-- WHERE ONE OF THE *CRIMINAL SCOURGES* OF THIS FINE CITY WAS FOUND SMASHED TO DEATH ON THE ROCKS OF TOWER MOUNTAIN --

"I WAS TERRIFIED THERE WOULD BE SOME CLUE, A STRAND OF HAIR, SOME DNA TO POINT TO MY INVOLVEMENT.

"I LUCKED OUT --"

WITH LITTLE ELSE TO GO ON, WE CAN ONLY ASSUME THAT THIS WAS AN *INTERNECINE* CRIME, ONE VILLAIN PICKING OFF ANOTHER WHO MAY HAVE CROSSED HIM OR ENCROACHED ON HIS TURF.

"-- *THIS* TIME.

"BUT WHAT ABOUT THE *NEXT* TIME?"

BECAUSE AT THAT TIME IN MY LIFE, AS CONFUSED AS I WAS, I WAS SURE THAT SOONER OR LATER, THERE *WOULD BE* A NEXT TIME.

I FELL INTO A DARK DEPRESSION THAT LASTED FOR MONTHS. HID IT THE BEST I COULD BEHIND BRAVADO AND *FIGHTS*, BUT IT WAS EATING ME ALIVE.

"AFTER A WHILE, I EVEN THOUGHT ABOUT KILLING MYSELF. WASN'T SURE WHAT BUSINESS I HAD BEING ALIVE IN THE FIRST PLACE.

"THEN CAME THE DAY WE FOUGHT *SONIC MASTER* FOR THE LAST TIME."

"WE'RE OUT OF TIME, FLYBOY!"

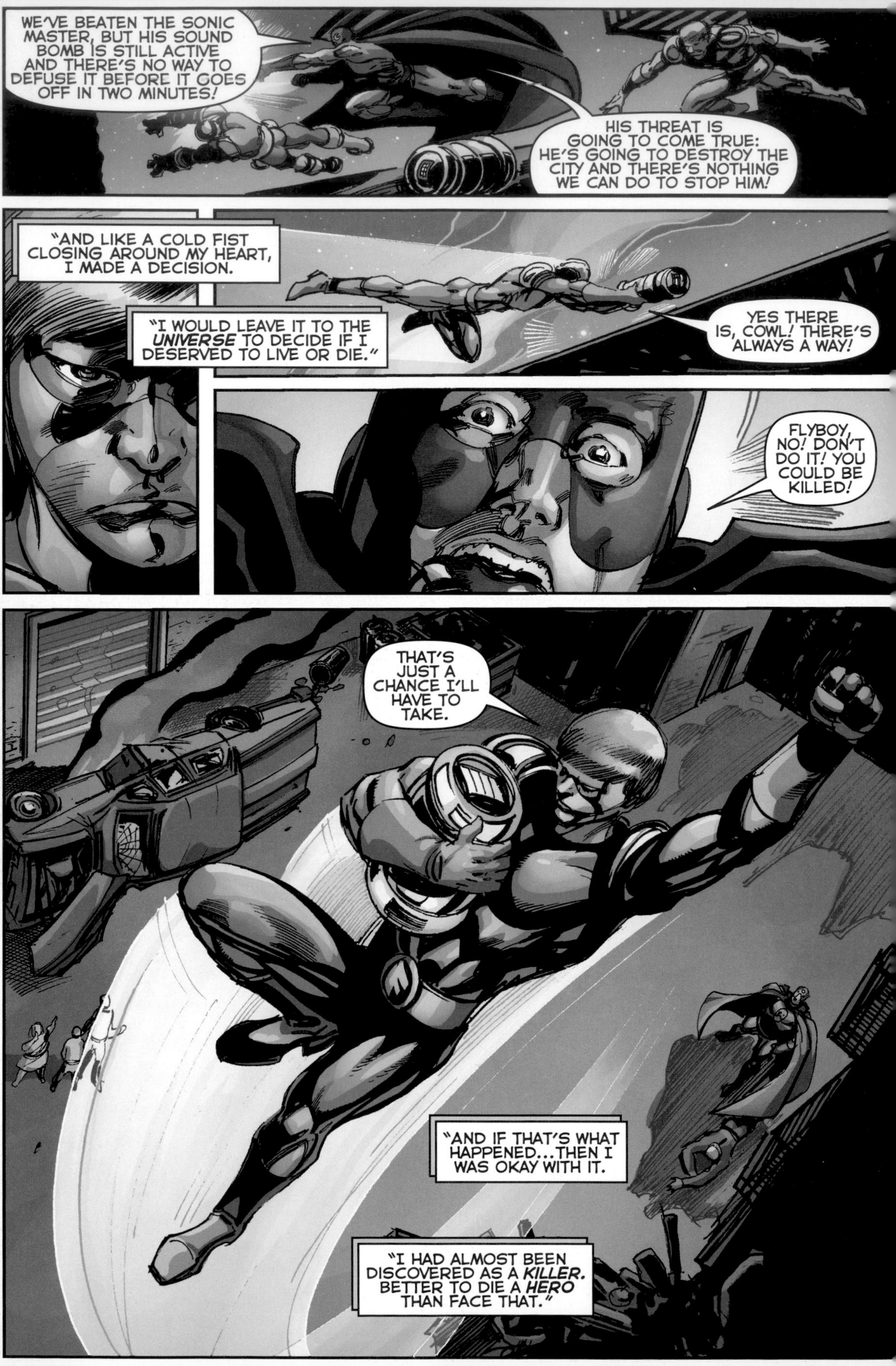
WE'VE BEATEN THE SONIC MASTER, BUT HIS SOUND BOMB IS STILL ACTIVE AND THERE'S NO WAY TO DEFUSE IT BEFORE IT GOES OFF IN TWO MINUTES!
HIS THREAT IS GOING TO COME TRUE: HE'S GOING TO DESTROY THE CITY AND THERE'S NOTHING WE CAN DO TO STOP HIM!
"AND LIKE A COLD FIST CLOSING AROUND MY HEART, I MADE A DECISION.
"I WOULD LEAVE IT TO THE *UNIVERSE* TO DECIDE IF I DESERVED TO LIVE OR DIE."
YES THERE IS, COWL! THERE'S ALWAYS A WAY!
FLYBOY, NO! DON'T DO IT! YOU COULD BE KILLED!
THAT'S JUST A CHANCE I'LL HAVE TO TAKE.
"AND IF THAT'S WHAT HAPPENED...THEN I WAS OKAY WITH IT.
"I HAD ALMOST BEEN DISCOVERED AS A *KILLER*. BETTER TO DIE A *HERO* THAN FACE THAT."

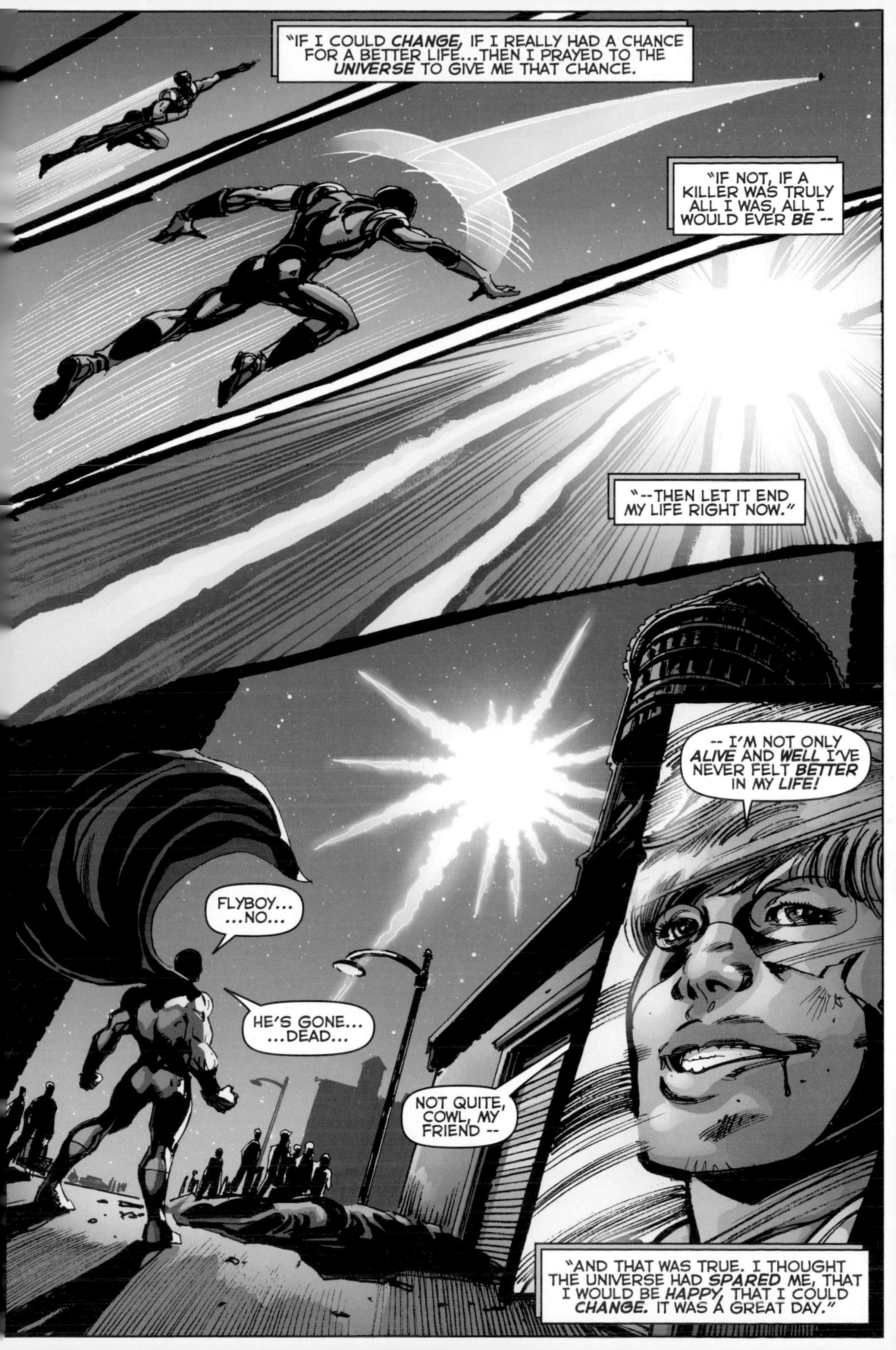
"IF I COULD CHANGE, IF I REALLY HAD A CHANCE FOR A BETTER LIFE...THEN I PRAYED TO THE UNIVERSE TO GIVE ME THAT CHANCE.
"IF NOT, IF A KILLER WAS TRULY ALL I WAS, ALL I WOULD EVER BE --
"--THEN LET IT END MY LIFE RIGHT NOW."
FLYBOY... ...NO...
HE'S GONE... ...DEAD...
NOT QUITE, COWL, MY FRIEND --
-- I'M NOT ONLY ALIVE AND WELL I'VE NEVER FELT BETTER IN MY LIFE!
"AND THAT WAS TRUE. I THOUGHT THE UNIVERSE HAD SPARED ME, THAT I WOULD BE HAPPY, THAT I COULD CHANGE. IT WAS A GREAT DAY."

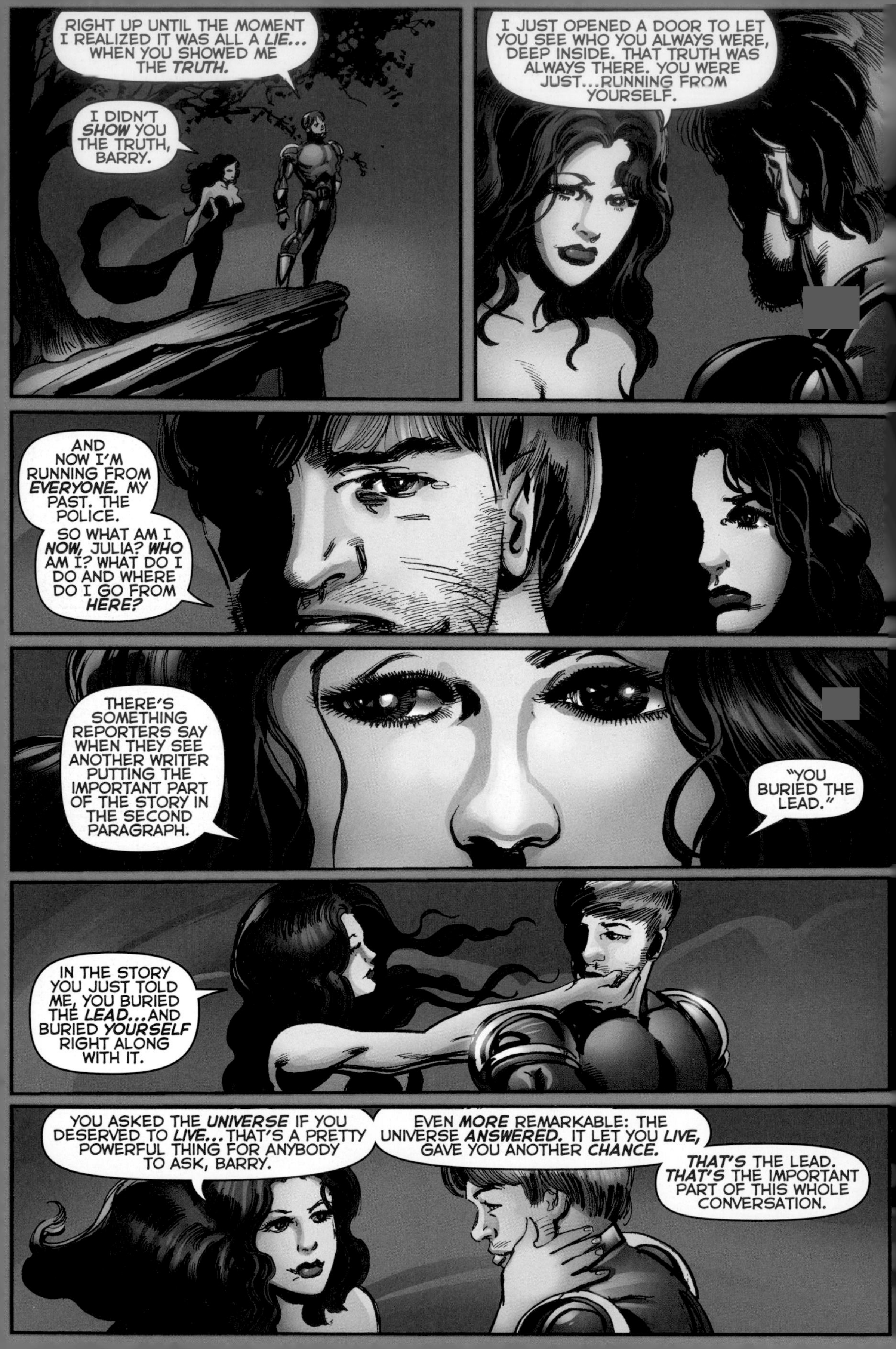

RIGHT UP UNTIL THE MOMENT I REALIZED IT WAS ALL A *LIE...* WHEN YOU SHOWED ME THE *TRUTH.*
I DIDN'T *SHOW* YOU THE TRUTH, BARRY.
I JUST OPENED A DOOR TO LET YOU SEE WHO YOU ALWAYS WERE, DEEP INSIDE. THAT TRUTH WAS ALWAYS THERE. YOU WERE JUST...RUNNING FROM YOURSELF.
AND NOW I'M RUNNING FROM *EVERYONE.* MY PAST. THE POLICE.
SO WHAT AM I *NOW,* JULIA? *WHO* AM I? WHAT DO I DO AND WHERE DO I GO FROM *HERE?*
THERE'S SOMETHING REPORTERS SAY WHEN THEY SEE ANOTHER WRITER PUTTING THE IMPORTANT PART OF THE STORY IN THE SECOND PARAGRAPH.
"YOU BURIED THE LEAD."
IN THE STORY YOU JUST TOLD ME, YOU BURIED THE *LEAD...*AND BURIED *YOURSELF* RIGHT ALONG WITH IT.
YOU ASKED THE *UNIVERSE* IF YOU DESERVED TO *LIVE...*THAT'S A PRETTY POWERFUL THING FOR ANYBODY TO ASK, BARRY.
EVEN *MORE* REMARKABLE: THE UNIVERSE *ANSWERED.* IT LET YOU *LIVE,* GAVE YOU ANOTHER *CHANCE.*
THAT'S THE LEAD. *THAT'S* THE IMPORTANT PART OF THIS WHOLE CONVERSATION.

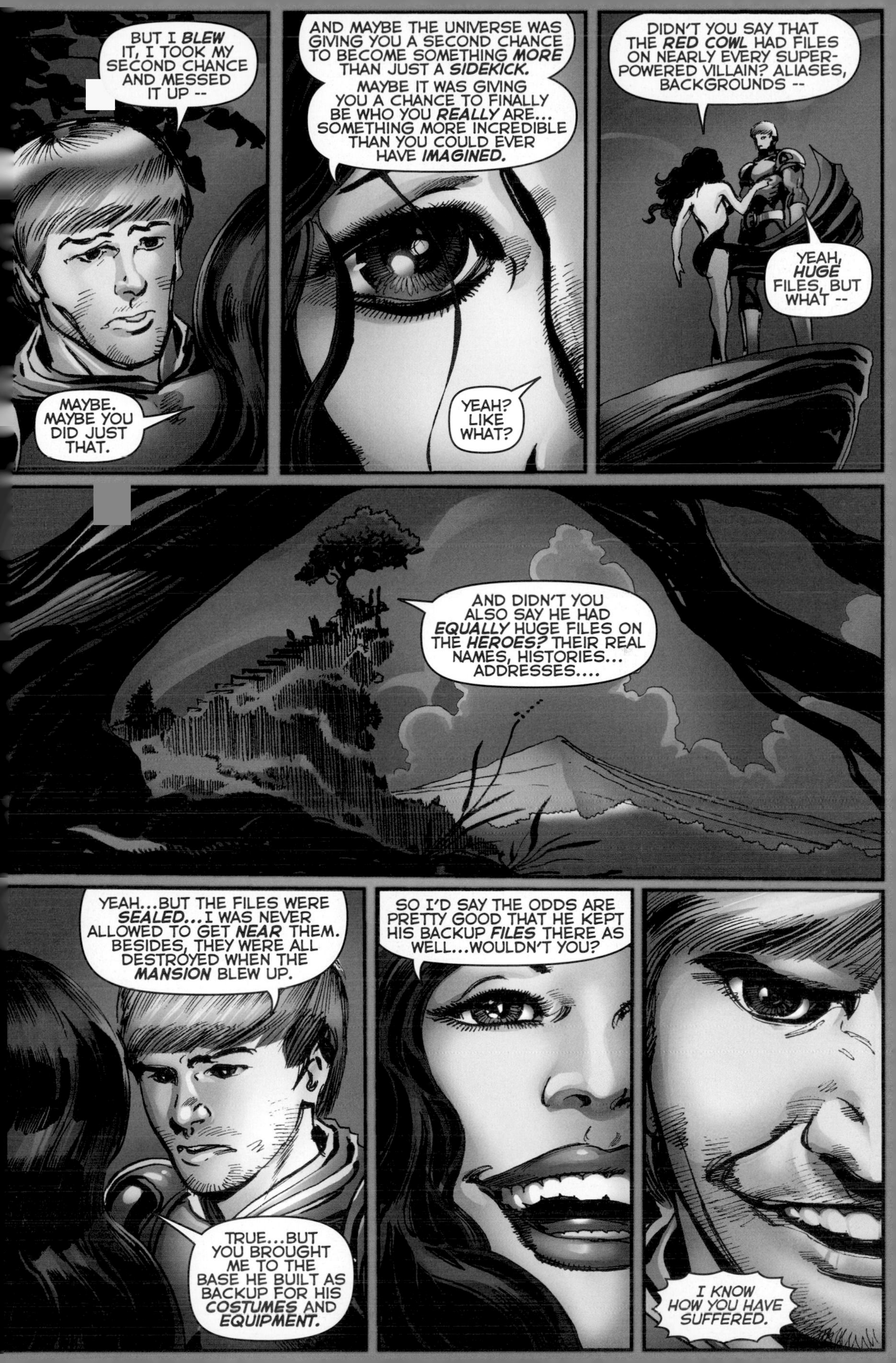

BUT I BLEW IT, I TOOK MY SECOND CHANCE AND MESSED IT UP --
MAYBE. MAYBE YOU DID JUST THAT.
AND MAYBE THE UNIVERSE WAS GIVING YOU A SECOND CHANCE TO BECOME SOMETHING MORE THAN JUST A SIDEKICK.
MAYBE IT WAS GIVING YOU A CHANCE TO FINALLY BE WHO YOU REALLY ARE... SOMETHING MORE INCREDIBLE THAN YOU COULD EVER HAVE IMAGINED.
YEAH? LIKE WHAT?
DIDN'T YOU SAY THAT THE RED COWL HAD FILES ON NEARLY EVERY SUPER-POWERED VILLAIN? ALIASES, BACKGROUNDS --
YEAH, HUGE FILES, BUT WHAT --
AND DIDN'T YOU ALSO SAY HE HAD EQUALLY HUGE FILES ON THE HEROES? THEIR REAL NAMES, HISTORIES... ADDRESSES....
YEAH...BUT THE FILES WERE SEALED...I WAS NEVER ALLOWED TO GET NEAR THEM. BESIDES, THEY WERE ALL DESTROYED WHEN THE MANSION BLEW UP.
TRUE...BUT YOU BROUGHT ME TO THE BASE HE BUILT AS BACKUP FOR HIS COSTUMES AND EQUIPMENT.
SO I'D SAY THE ODDS ARE PRETTY GOOD THAT HE KEPT HIS BACKUP FILES THERE AS WELL...WOULDN'T YOU?
I KNOW HOW YOU HAVE SUFFERED.

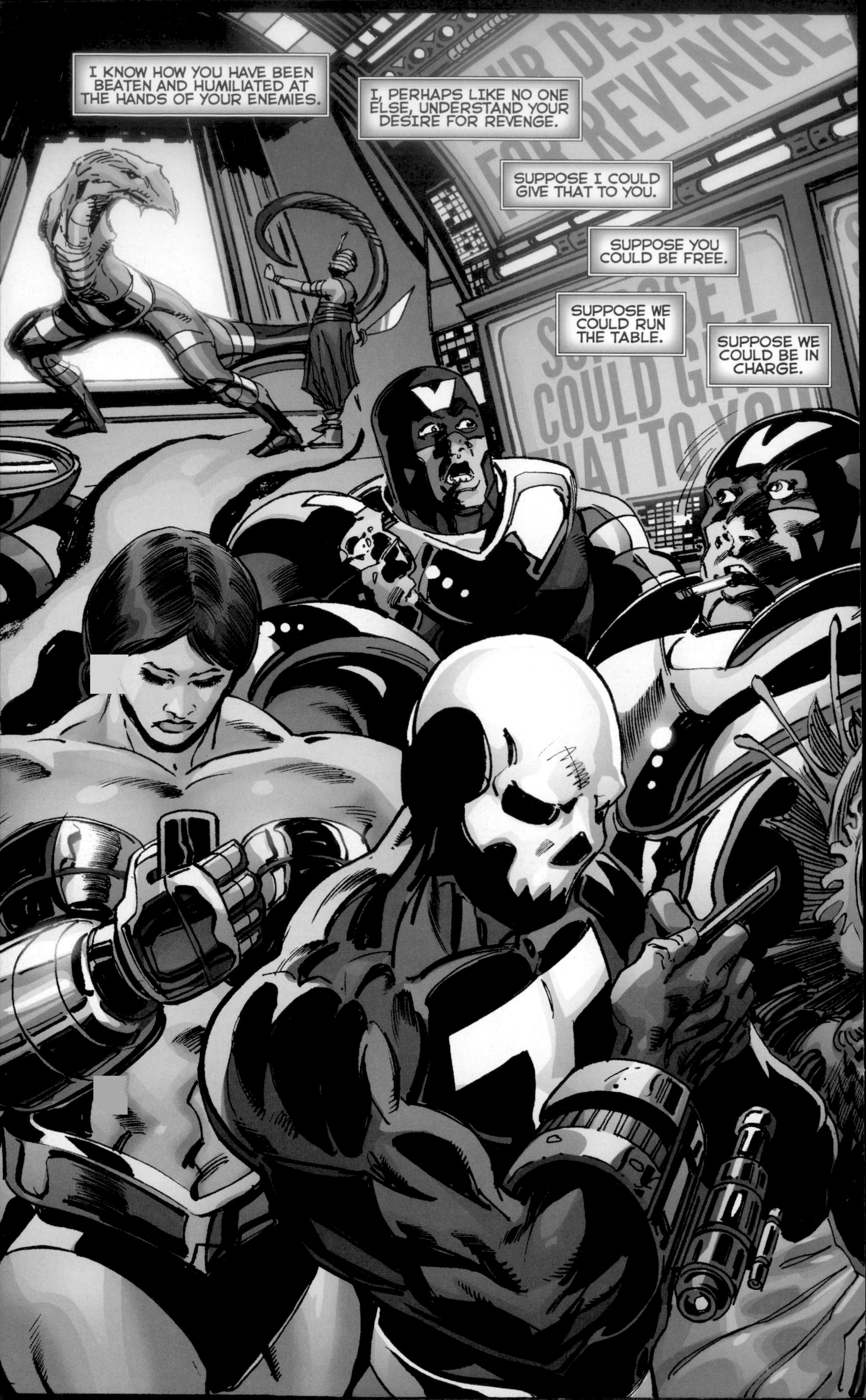
I KNOW HOW YOU HAVE BEEN BEATEN AND HUMILIATED AT THE HANDS OF YOUR ENEMIES.
I, PERHAPS LIKE NO ONE ELSE, UNDERSTAND YOUR DESIRE FOR REVENGE.
SUPPOSE I COULD GIVE THAT TO YOU.
SUPPOSE YOU COULD BE FREE.
SUPPOSE WE COULD RUN THE TABLE.
SUPPOSE WE COULD BE IN CHARGE.

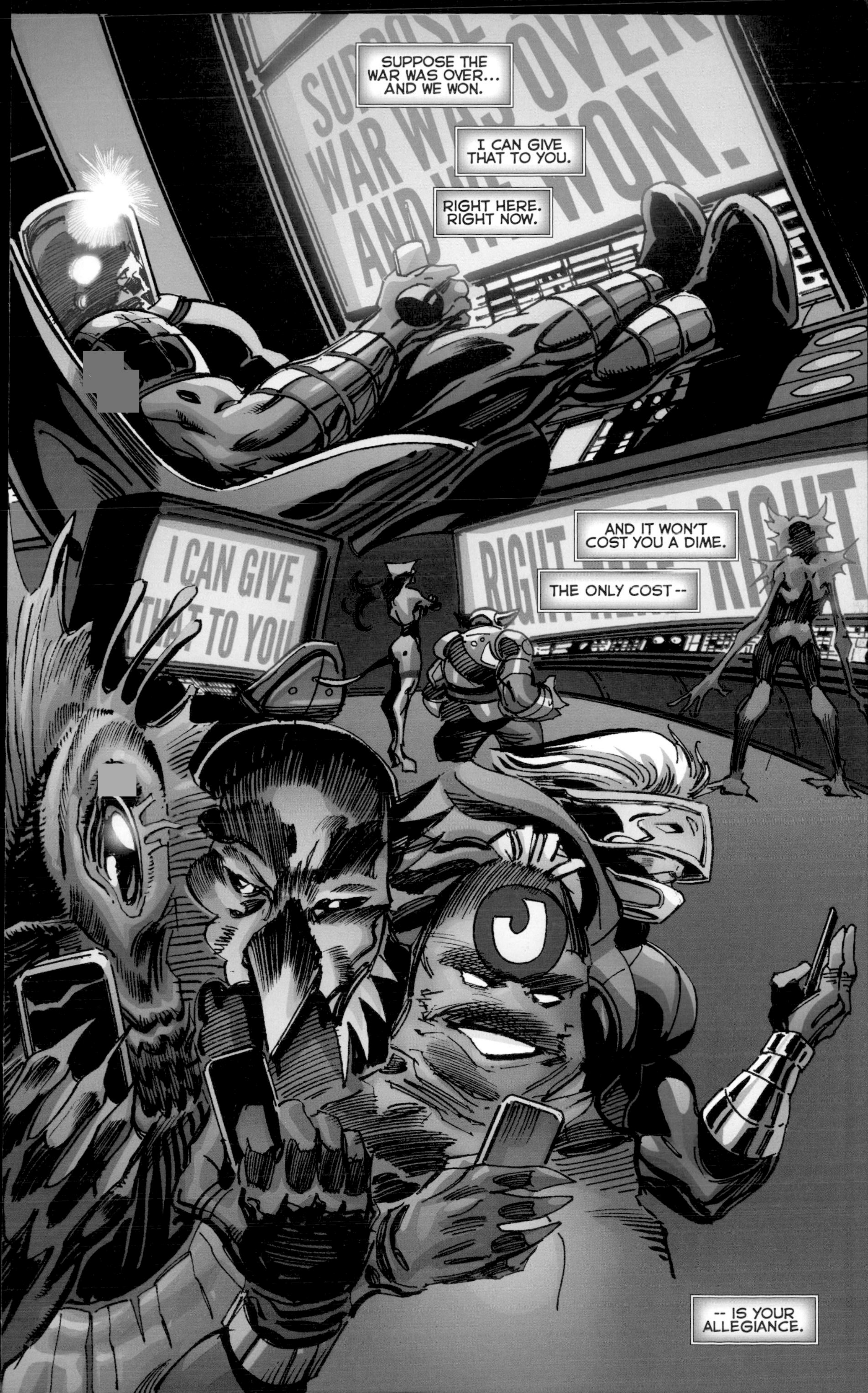

SUPPOSE THE WAR WAS OVER... AND WE WON.
I CAN GIVE THAT TO YOU.
RIGHT HERE. RIGHT NOW.
I CAN GIVE
AND IT WON'T COST YOU A DIME.
THE ONLY COST --
-- IS YOUR ALLEGIANCE.

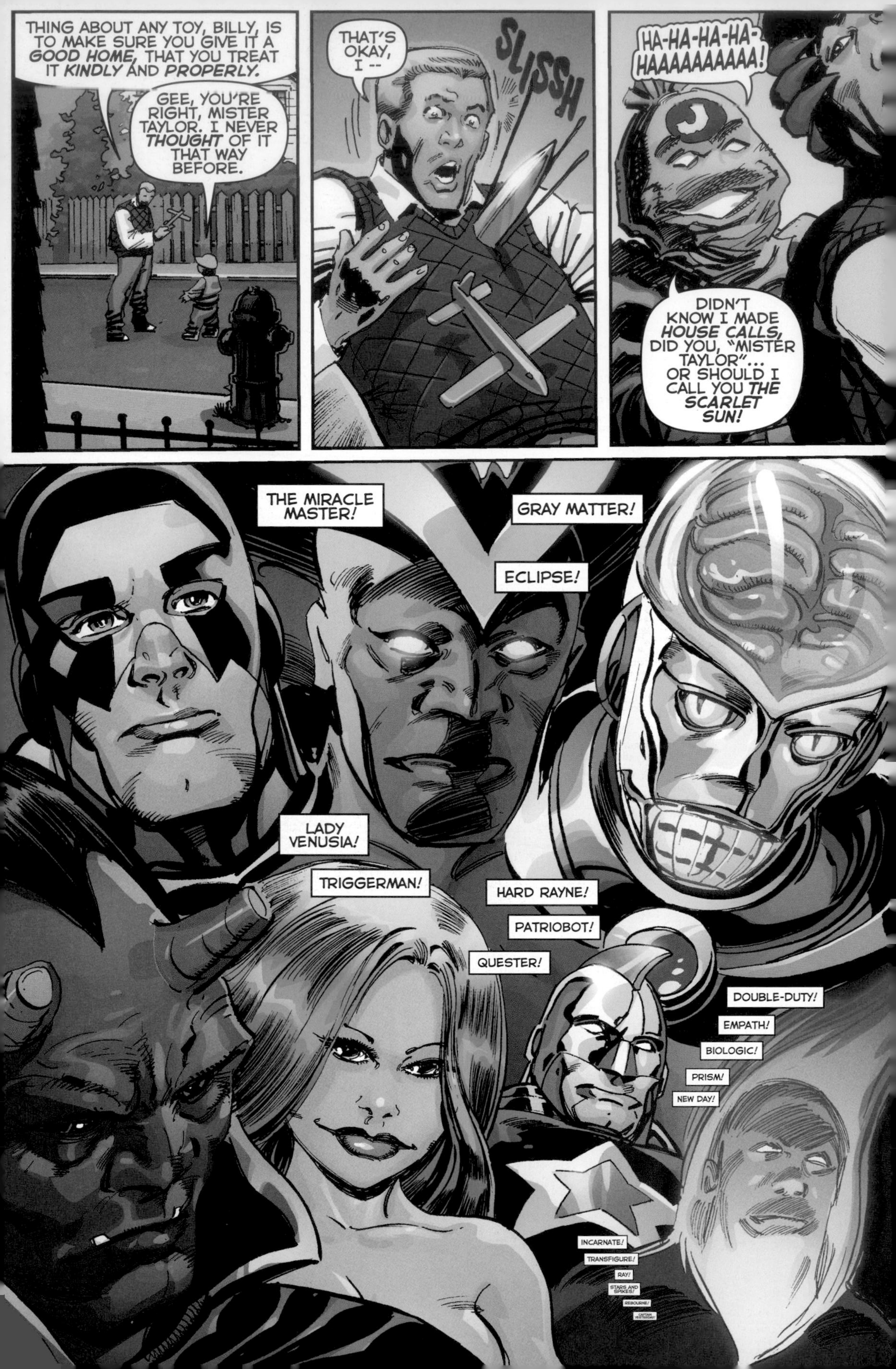
THING ABOUT ANY TOY, BILLY, IS TO MAKE SURE YOU GIVE IT A GOOD HOME, THAT YOU TREAT IT KINDLY AND PROPERLY.
GEE, YOU'RE RIGHT, MISTER TAYLOR. I NEVER THOUGHT OF IT THAT WAY BEFORE.
THAT'S OKAY, I --
SLISSH
HA-HA-HA-HA-HAAAAAAAAAA!
DIDN'T KNOW I MADE HOUSE CALLS, DID YOU, "MISTER TAYLOR"... OR SHOULD I CALL YOU THE SCARLET SUN!
THE MIRACLE MASTER!
GRAY MATTER!
ECLIPSE!
LADY VENUSIA!
TRIGGERMAN!
HARD RAYNE!
PATRIOBOT!
QUESTER!
DOUBLE-DUTY!
EMPATH!
BIOLOGIC!
PRISM!
NEW DAY!
INCARNATE!
TRANSFIGURE!
RAY!
STARS AND SPIKES!
REBOURNE!
CAPTAIN YESTERDAY!

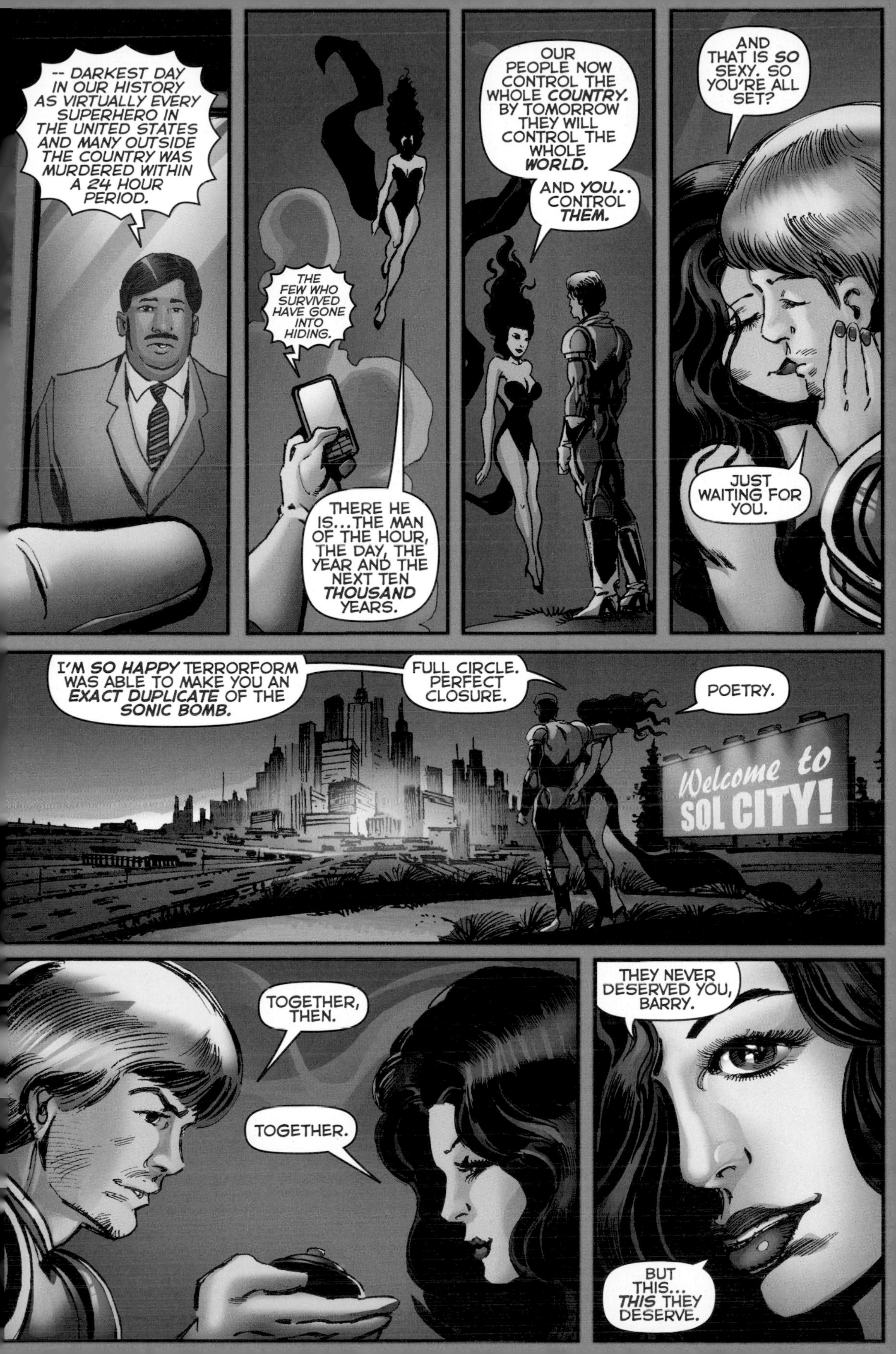
-- DARKEST DAY IN OUR HISTORY AS VIRTUALLY EVERY SUPERHERO IN THE UNITED STATES AND MANY OUTSIDE THE COUNTRY WAS MURDERED WITHIN A 24 HOUR PERIOD.
THE FEW WHO SURVIVED HAVE GONE INTO HIDING.
THERE HE IS...THE MAN OF THE HOUR, THE DAY, THE YEAR AND THE NEXT TEN THOUSAND YEARS.
OUR PEOPLE NOW CONTROL THE WHOLE COUNTRY. BY TOMORROW THEY WILL CONTROL THE WHOLE WORLD.
AND YOU... CONTROL THEM.
AND THAT IS SO SEXY. SO YOU'RE ALL SET?
JUST WAITING FOR YOU.
I'M SO HAPPY TERRORFORM WAS ABLE TO MAKE YOU AN EXACT DUPLICATE OF THE SONIC BOMB.
FULL CIRCLE. PERFECT CLOSURE.
POETRY.
Welcome to SOL CITY!
TOGETHER, THEN.
TOGETHER.
THEY NEVER DESERVED YOU, BARRY.
BUT THIS... THIS THEY DESERVE.

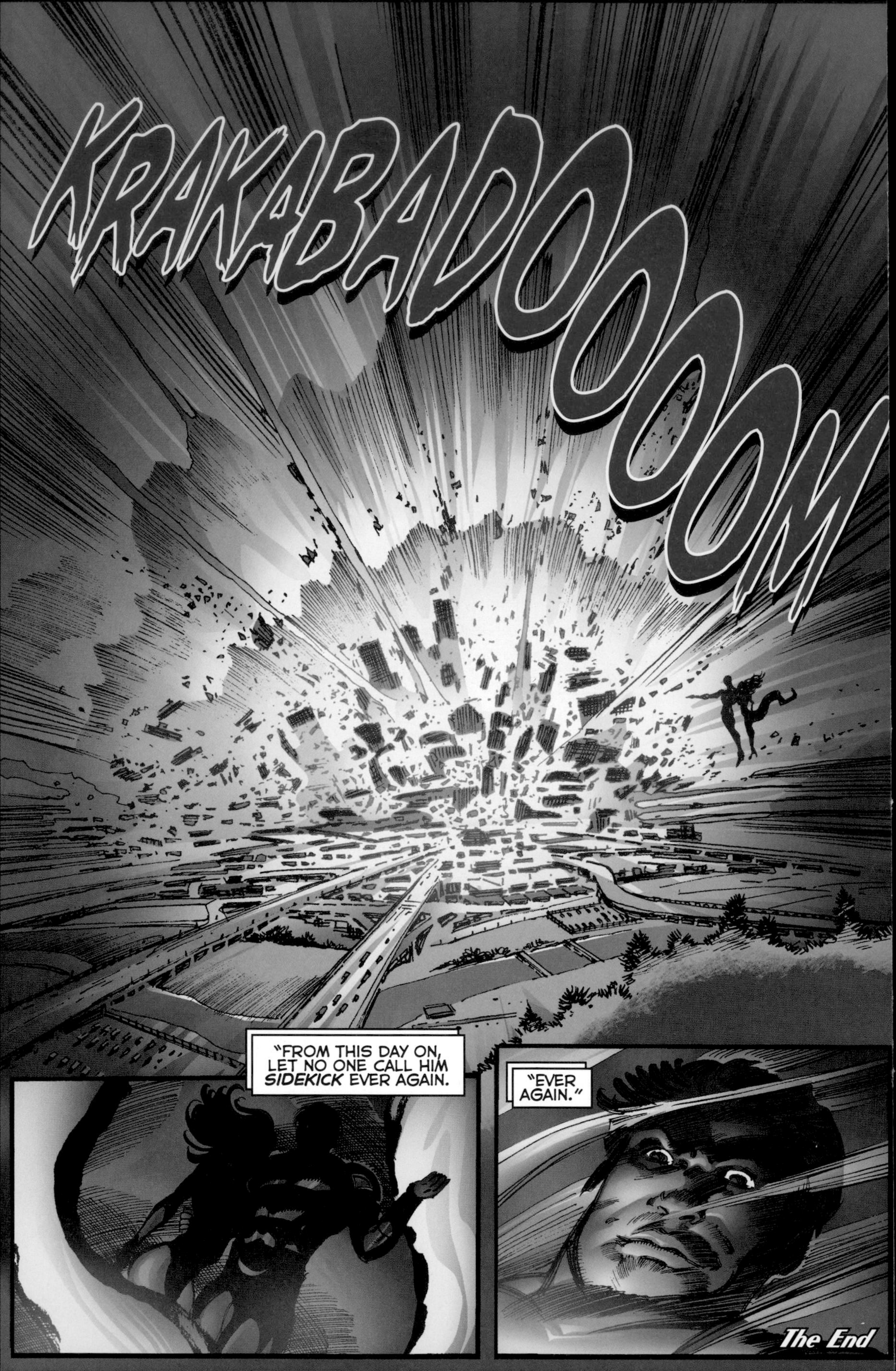
KRAKABADOOOOM
"FROM THIS DAY ON, LET NO ONE CALL HIM SIDEKICK EVER AGAIN.
"EVER AGAIN."
The End

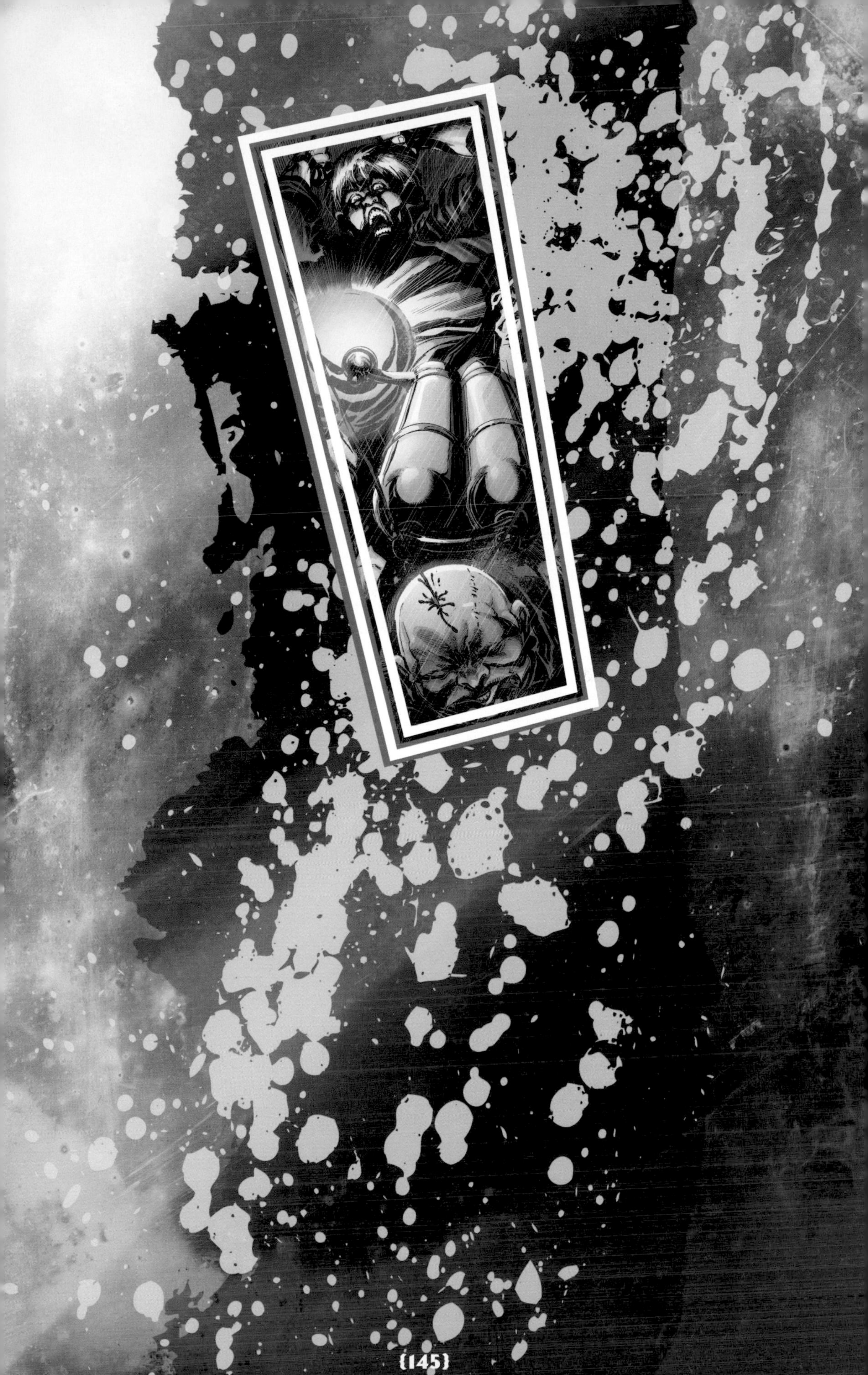

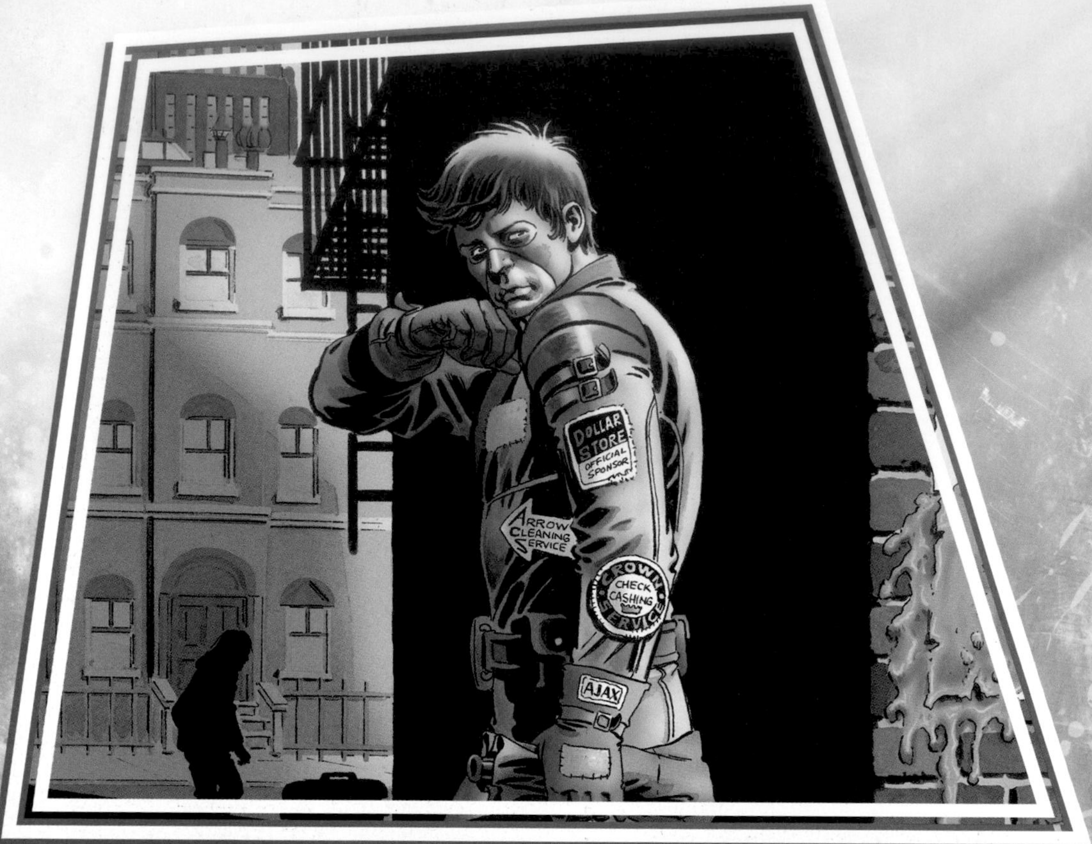
DOLLAR STORE OFFICIAL SPONSOR
ARROW CLEANING SERVICE
CROWN CHECK CASHING SERVICE
AJAX

-Alternate & Trade Cover Showcase-

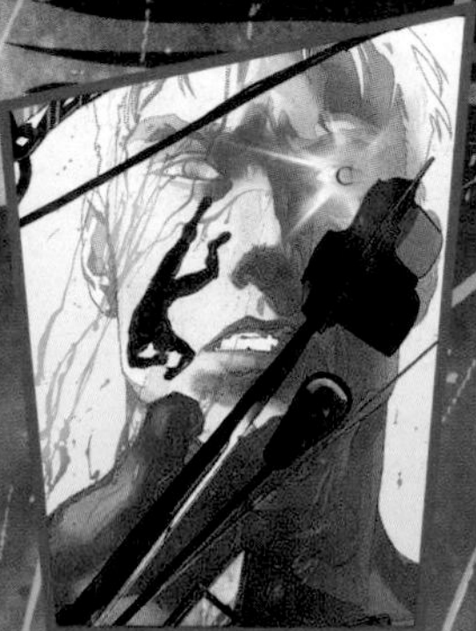

Sidekick #7, Cover "B" by: Alina Urusov

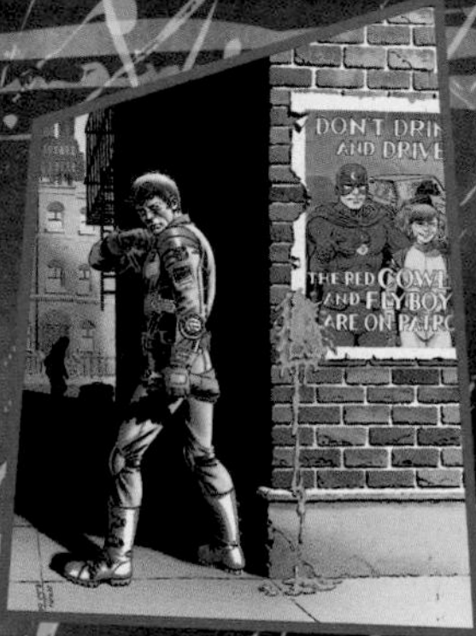

Sidekick #11, Cover "B" by: Jerry & Rachel Ordway

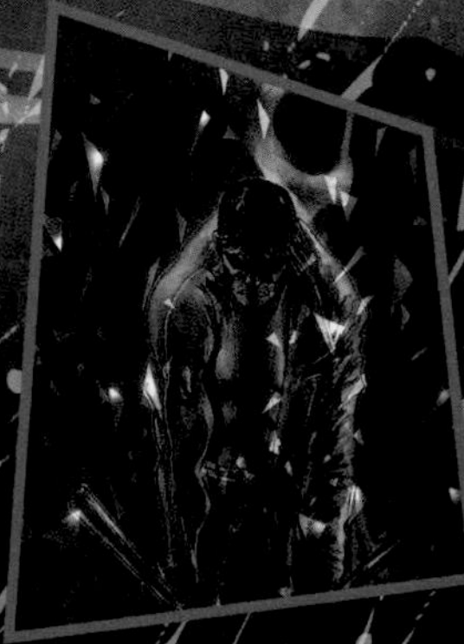

Sidekick #12, Cover "B" by: Ben Templesmith

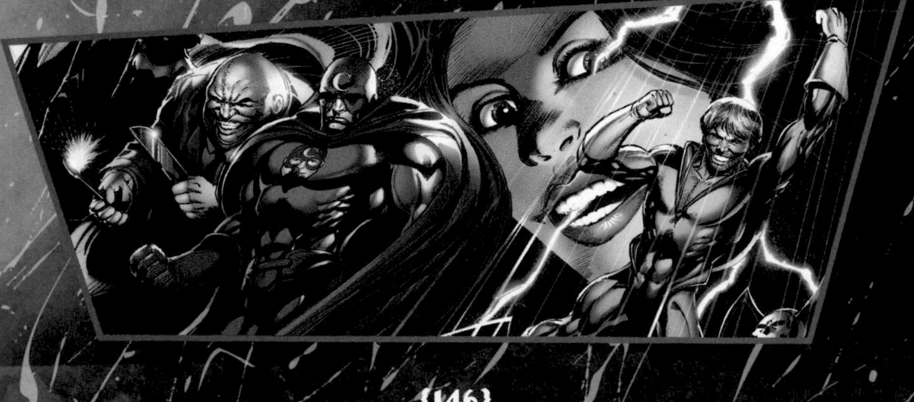

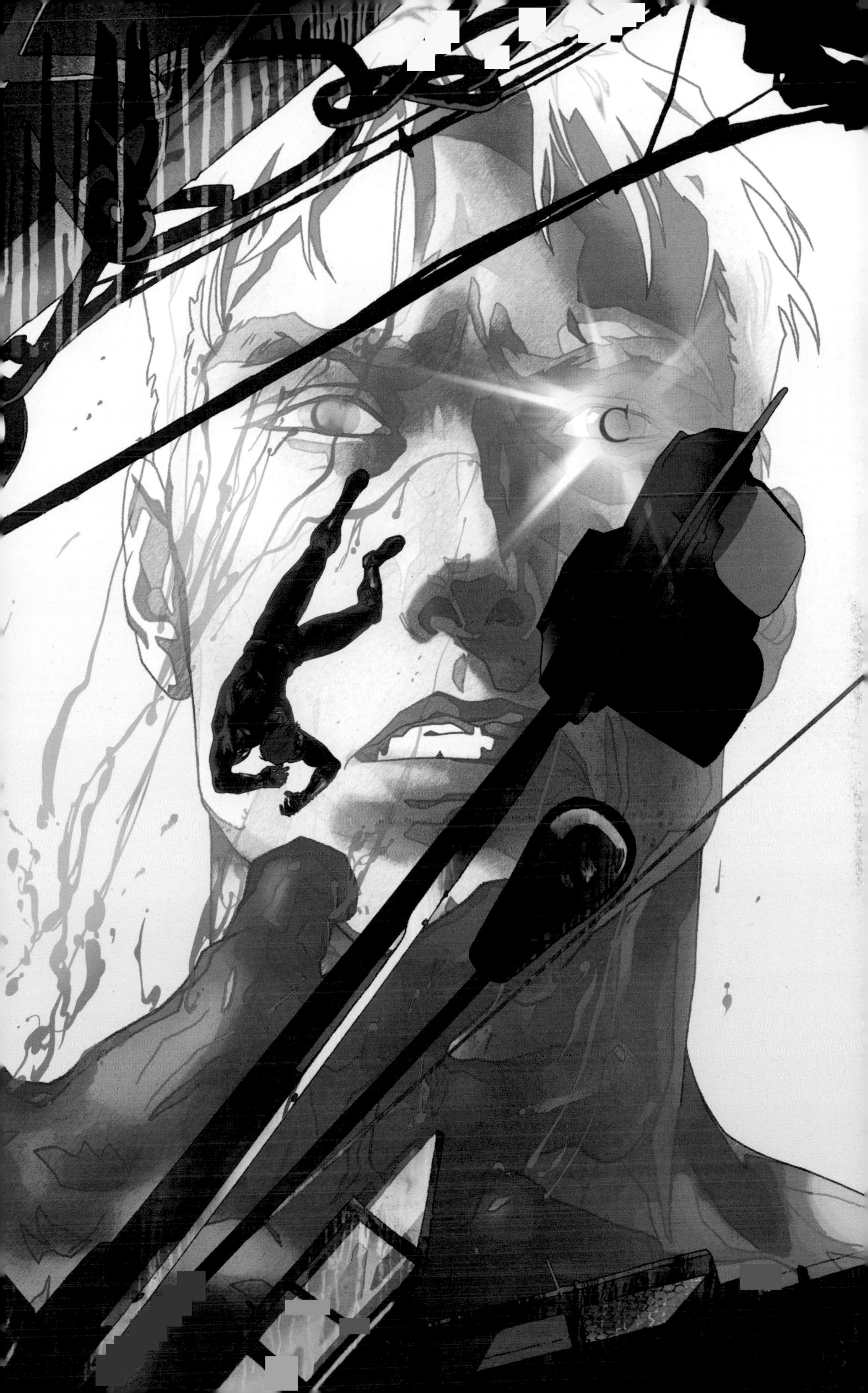

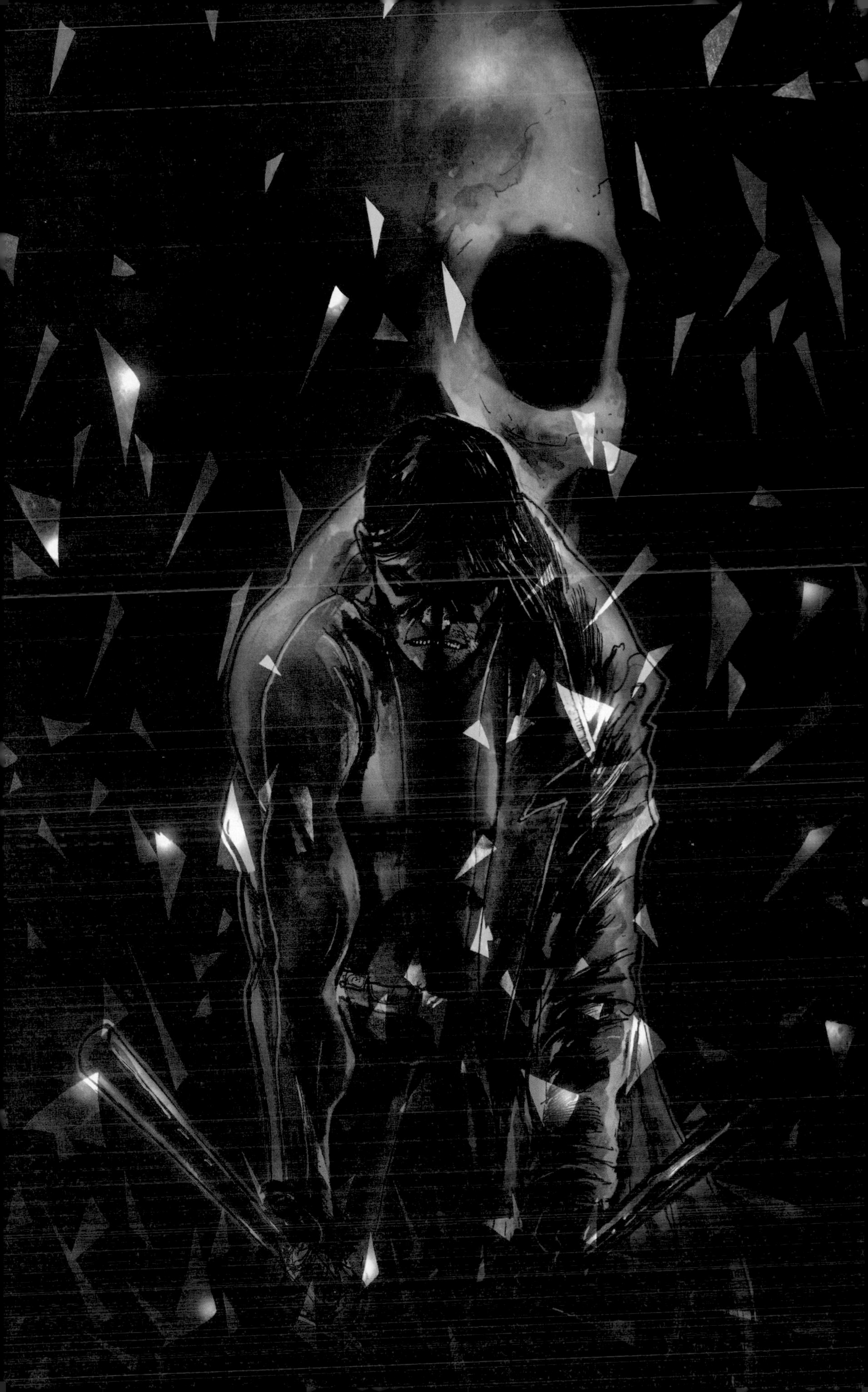

- Evolution of the Trade Cover -

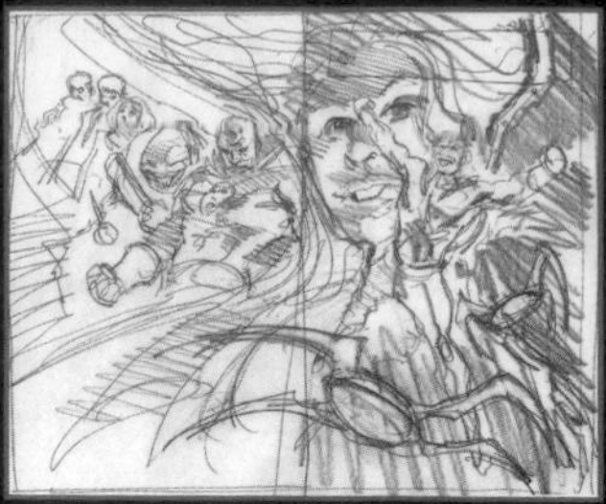

At left initial thumbnail rough

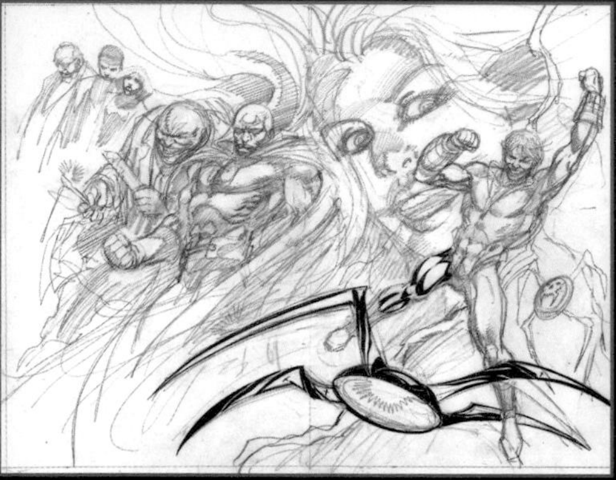

Pencils

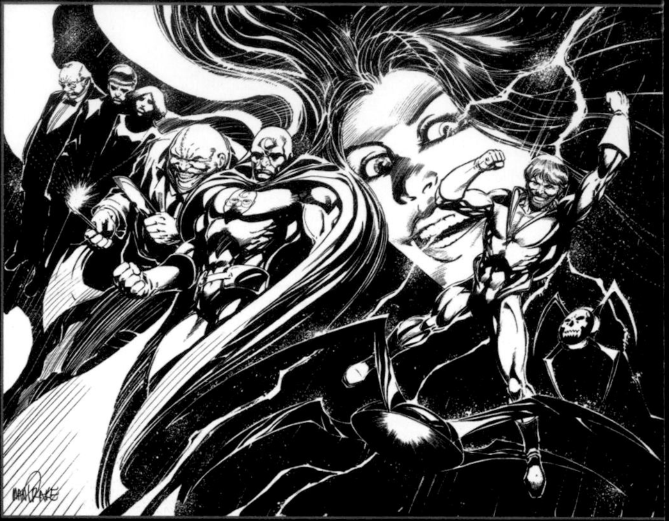

Inks

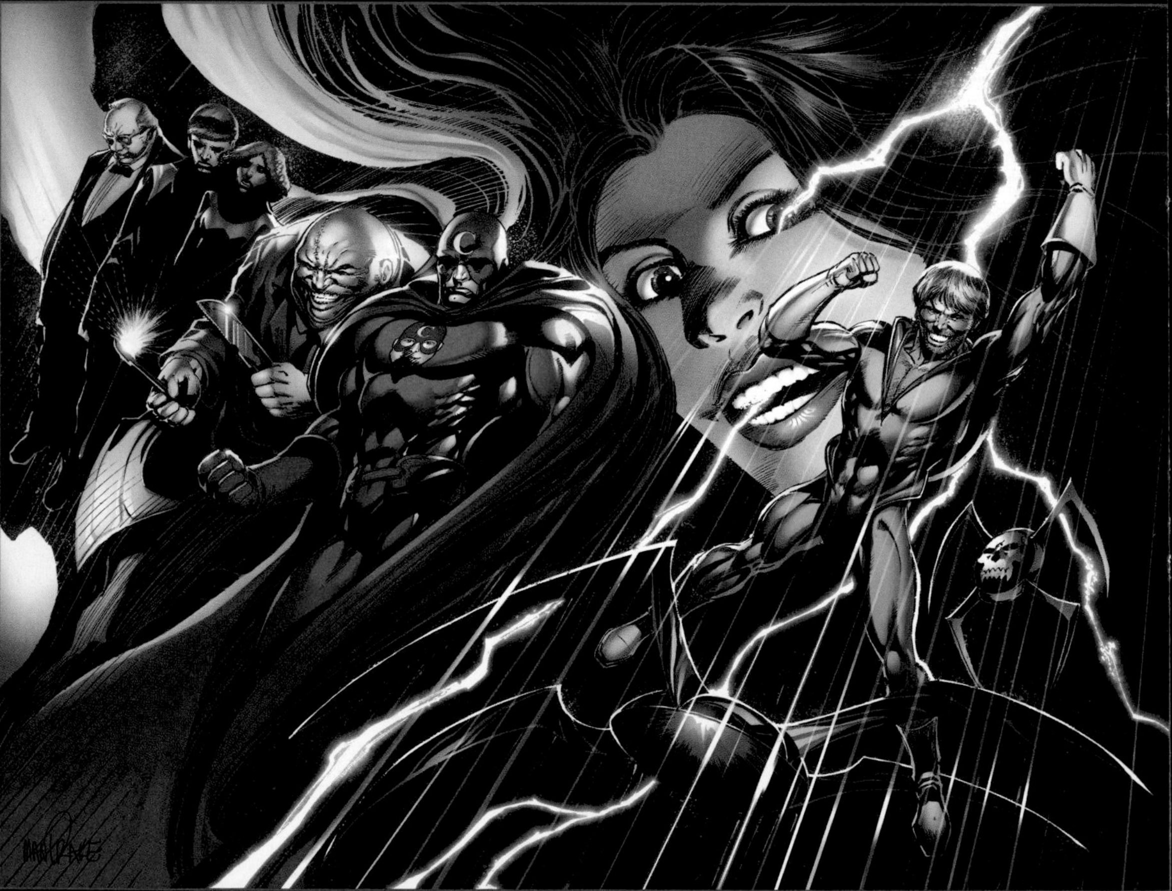

- Behind the Scenes -

"A Moment of Silence"

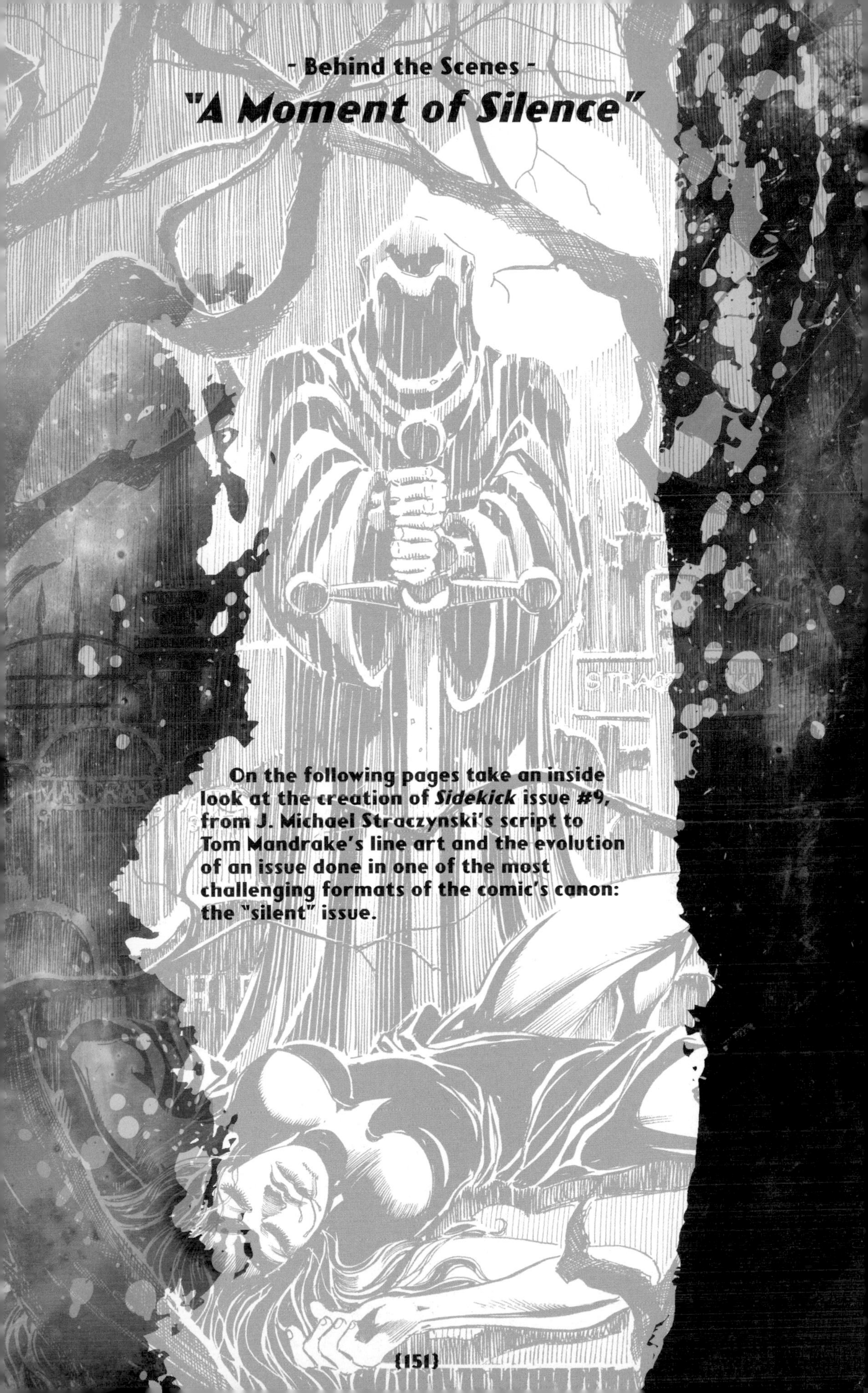

On the following pages take an inside look at the creation of ***Sidekick*** **issue #9, from J. Michael Straczynski's script to Tom Mandrake's line art and the evolution of an issue done in one of the most challenging formats of the comic's canon: the "silent" issue.**

SIDEKICK
ISSUE NINE

"A MOMENT OF SILENCE"

PAGE ONE

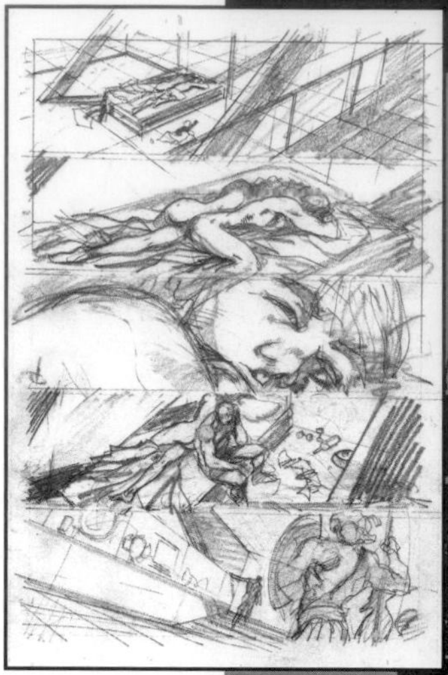

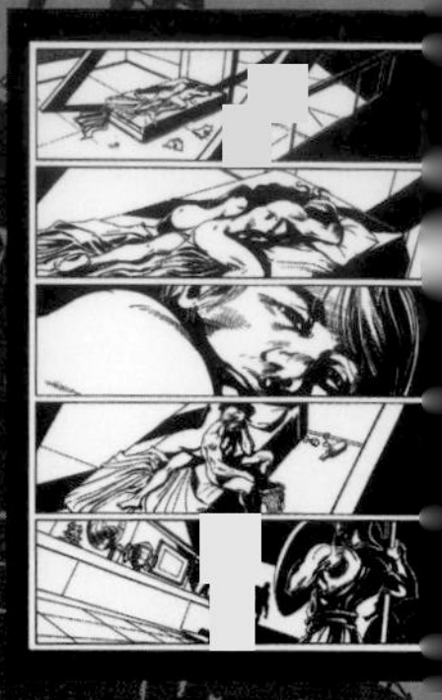

PANEL ONE

Barry in the backup hq, asleep on the bed beside Julia.

PANEL TWO

Closer on him as we hear an os DING-DING-DING-DING.

PANEL THREE

On his eyes as they snap open. DING-DING-DINGDINGDINGDING

PANEL FOUR

He rises, naked from behind.

PANEL FIVE

He walks down the hall, past trophy cases and equipment.

PAGE TWO

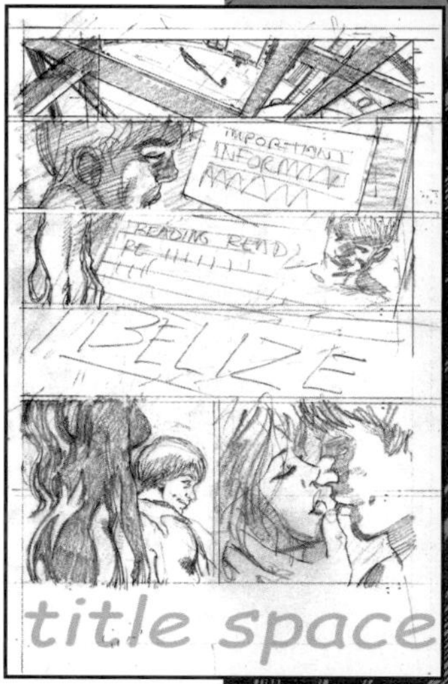
BELIZE
title space

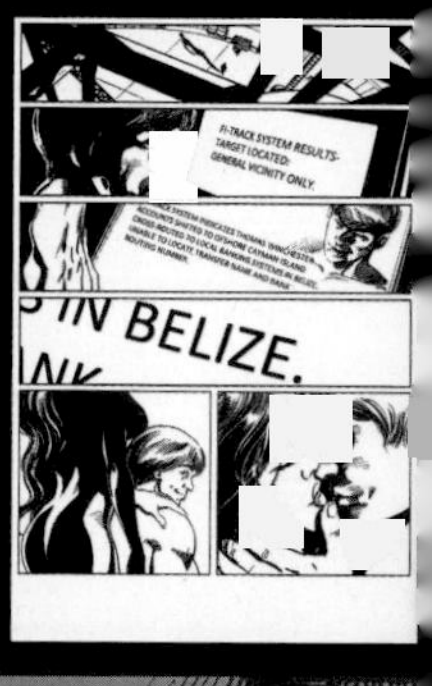
IN BELIZE.

PANEL ONE
He approaches the same equipment he used earlier to try and track the Cowl.

PANEL TWO

Past him where he's sitting to the screen. FI-TRACK SYSTEM RESULTS. TARGET LOCATED: GENERAL VICINITY ONLY.

PANEL THREE

Closer still. FI-TRACK SYSTEM INDICATES THOMAS WINCHESTER ACCOUNTS SHIFTED TO OFFSHORE CAYMAN ISLAND ACCOUNTS CROSS. ROUTED TO LOCAL BANKING SYSTEMS IN BELIZE. UNABLE TO LOCATE TRANSFER NAME AND BANK ROUTING NUMBER.

PANEL FOUR

CLOSE ON the word BELIZE.

PANEL FIVE

He looks to Julia, who has come up beside him.

PANEL SIX

They kiss. TITLE at bottom of page.

PAGE THREE

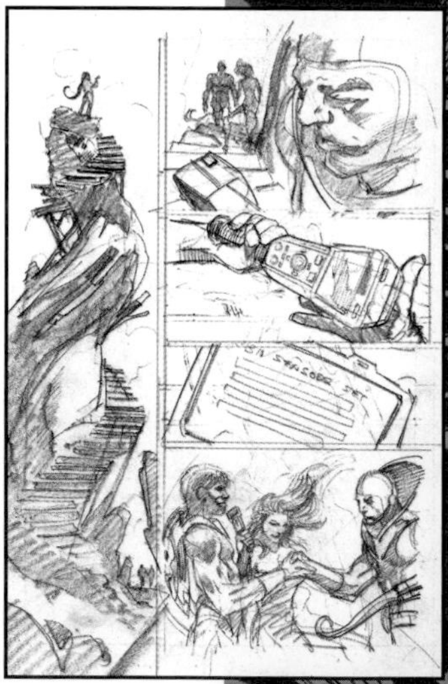

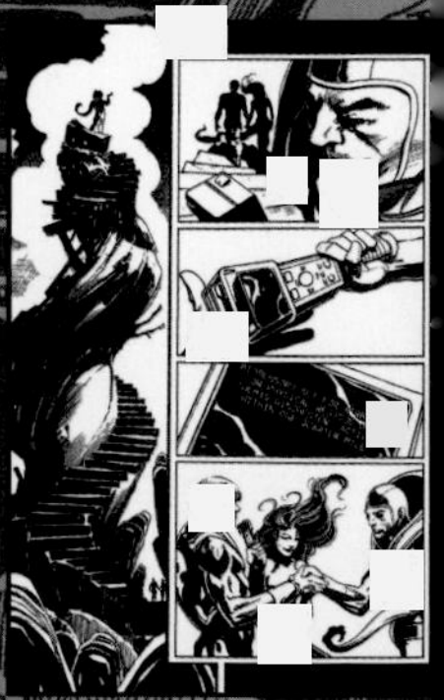

PANEL ONE

Night. Terrorform stands out on a blustery cliff. He's holding a device that looks kind of like the hand-held motion sensors they used in ALIENS.

PANEL TWO

He turns as Barry and Julia approach.

PANEL THREE

He hands over the device.

PANEL FOUR

On the display as Barry holds it. BIOSENSORS SET FOR AIRBORNE OR PHYSICAL DNA RESIDUE OF THOMAS WINCHESTER. ACTIVE WITHIN ONE QUARTER-MILE.

PANEL FIVE

He shakes Terrorform's hand.

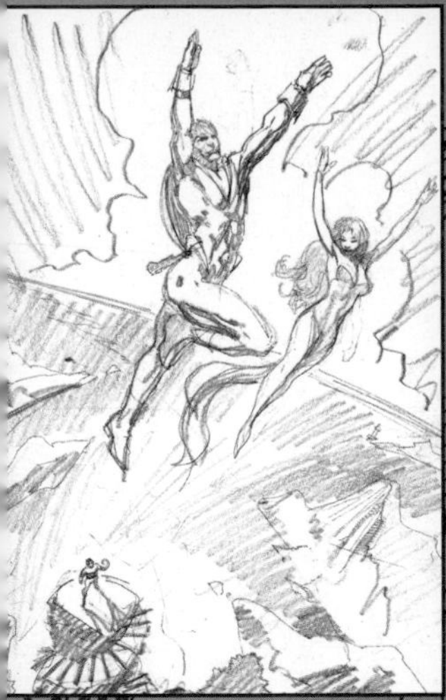

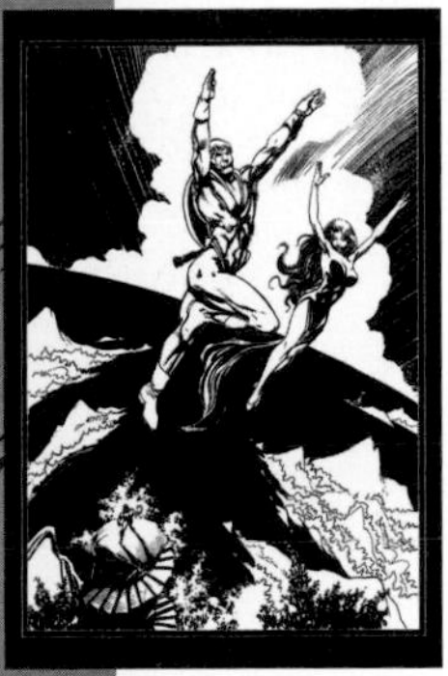

PAGE FOUR

FULL PAGE

They soar up into the night sky.

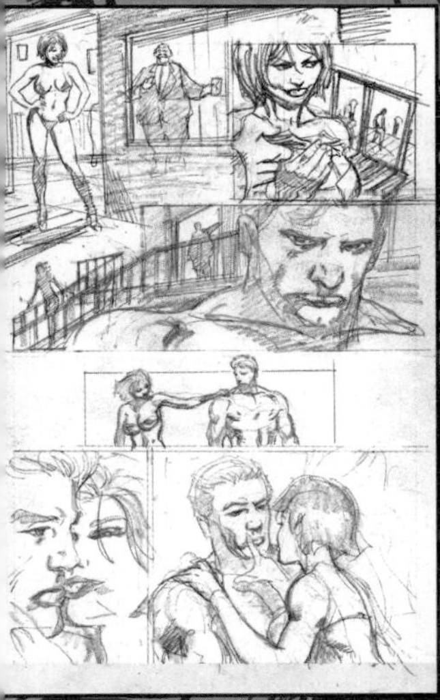

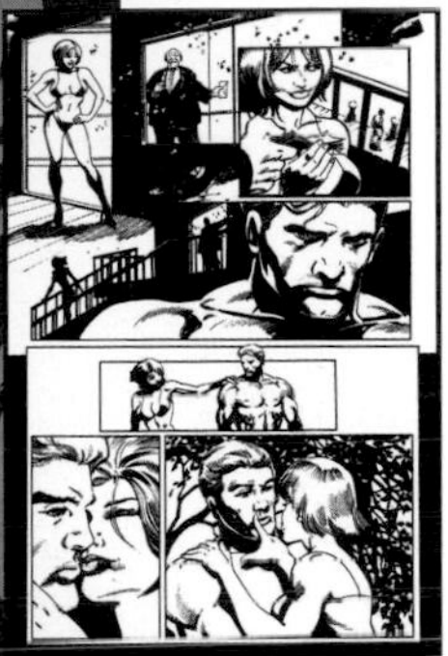

PAGE FIVE

PANEL ONE

Bobby, Thomas' butler/manservant, is handing a fistful of bills to a very attractive woman in an almost-not-there bikini. A window or French doors shows us the beach outside,and a small dock for a boat. We may or may not see Thomas, who is wearing just swimming trunks.

PANEL TWO

She comes out of the house, heading toward Thomas, whose eyes are turned toward the sea, deep in thought. Her attitude is one of "just leave this to me."

PANEL THREE

She comes up from behind him, fingers dancing on his shoulder as she makes the turn.

PANEL FOUR

She kisses him. He barely responds.

PANEL FIVE

She puts her fingertip to his lips.

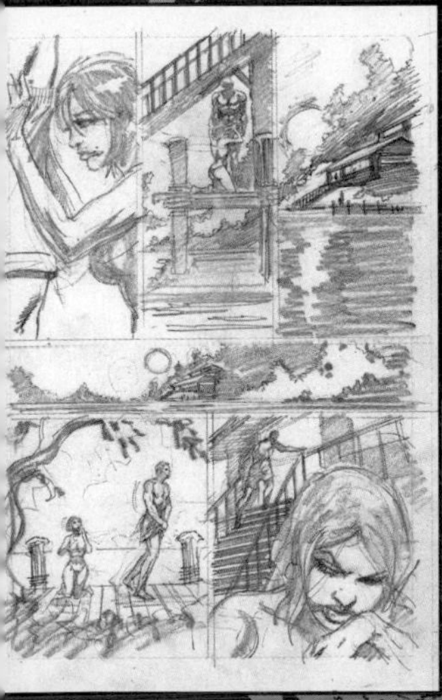

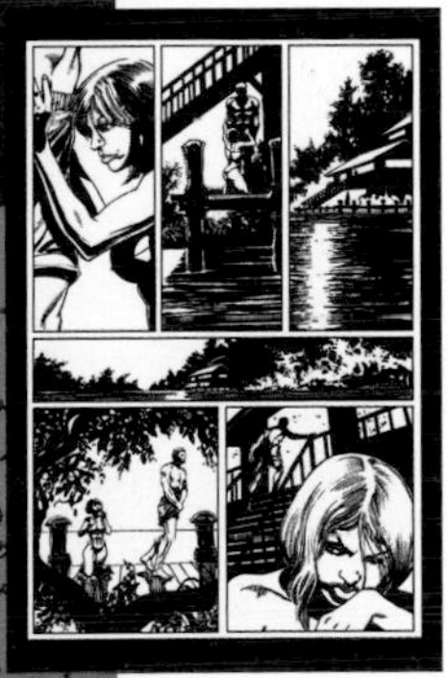

PAGE SIX

PANEL ONE

She starts to descend to her knees in front of him.

PANEL TWO
She reaches for the front of his swimming trunks.

PANEL THREE

A long view, we don't need to see what's going on, we know.

PANEL FOUR

She's still on her knees as he walks away, finished, dismissive.

PANEL FIVE

She stalks off in one direction while Thomas goes back to the house. She clearly doesn't like being dismissed.

PAGE SEVEN

PANEL ONE

Thomas sits at his desk computer.

PANEL TWO
On the screen is the accounts page for FIRST BANK OF BELIZE.We see several accounts listed.

PANEL THREE

On his face.

PANEL FOUR

On the cursor, hovering over a box asking DELETE ALL ACCOUNTS?

PANEL FIVE

He clicks the mouse.

PANEL SIX

On the screen. ACCOUNTS DELETED.

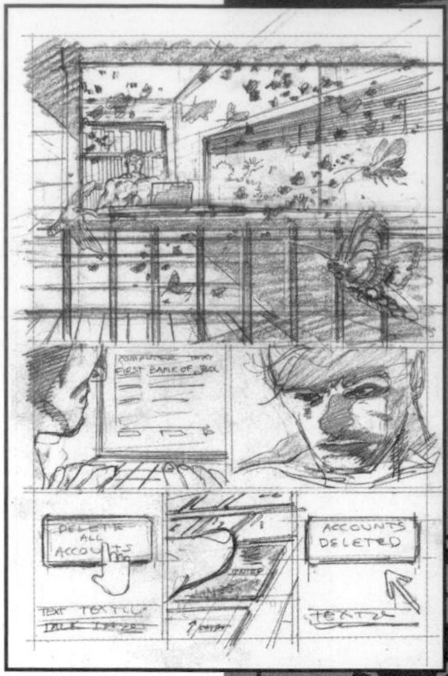

ACCOUNTS DELETED

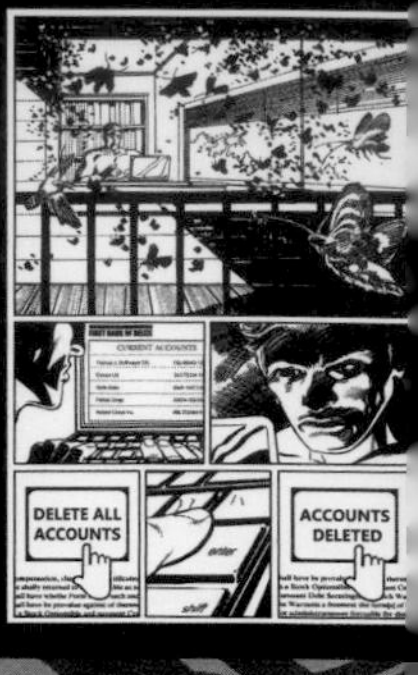

DELETE ALL ACCOUNTS
ACCOUNTS DELETED

PAGE EIGHT

PANEL ONE

A beauty shot of Belize.

PANEL TWO

Barry and Julia, dressed as tourists, move among the crowd as though on vacation.

PANEL THREE

They sit in a restaurant. Barry has the menu propped up on the table in front of him.

PANEL FOUR

Behind the menu, Barry holds the detector.

PANEL FIVE

On the screen: TARGET DNA NOT DETECTED

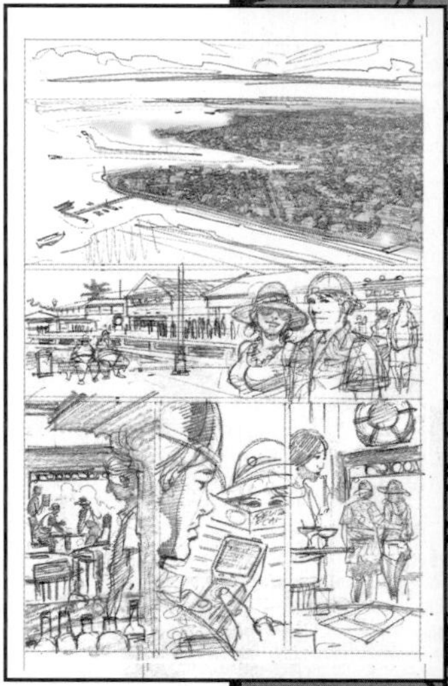

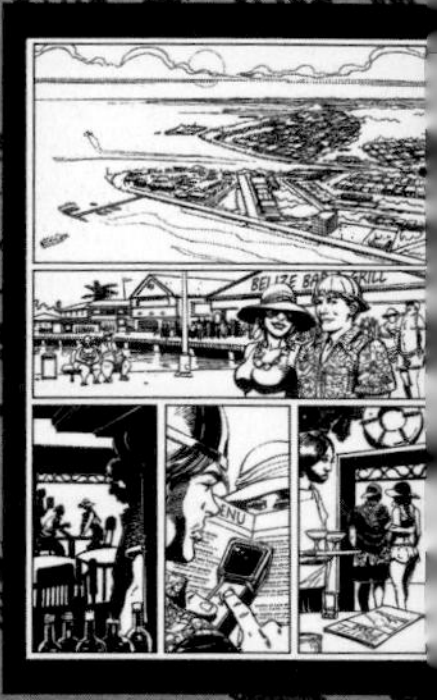

PAGE NINE

PANEL ONE

A swinging nightclub. Exotic dancers on the floor. Hot.

PANEL TWO

Julia dances by herself...as admiring men look on.

PANEL THREE

Barry walks behind the men, their attention elsewhere, using the detector.

PANEL FOUR

Julia looks to Barry.

PANEL FIVE

Barry shakes his head.

PANEL SIX

They join hands and walk out.

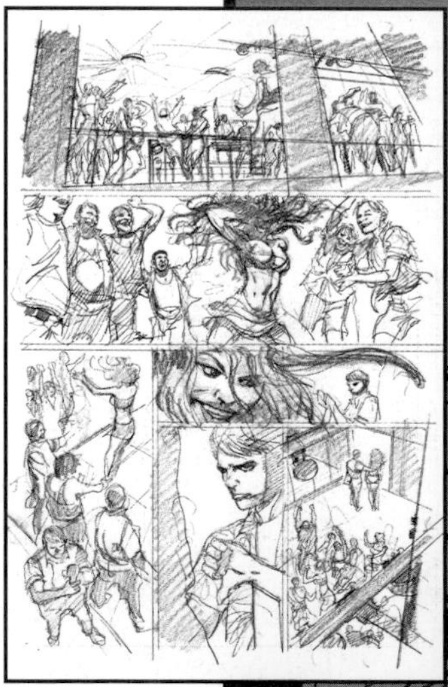

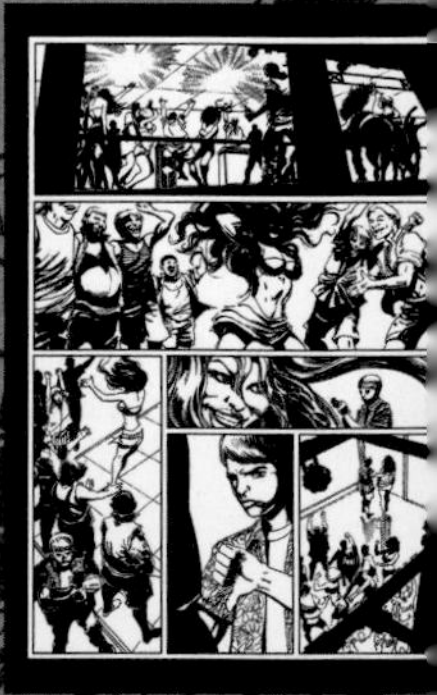

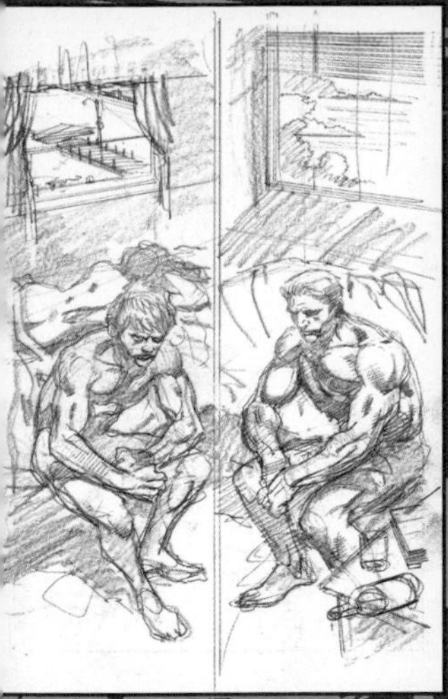

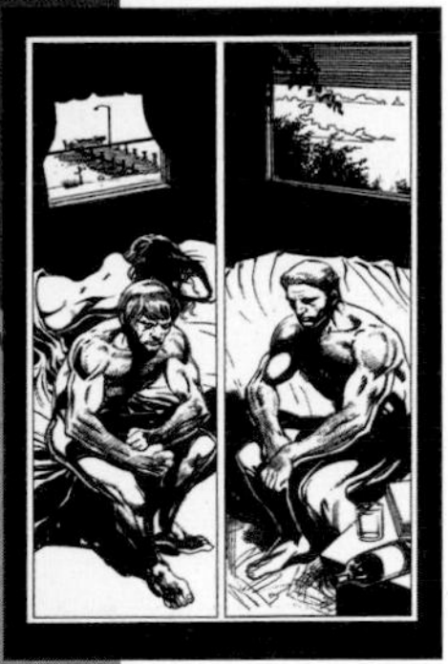

PAGE TEN

PANEL ONE

Barry and Julia are in bed. Well, she's in bed...he's sitting at one end of the bed. Unable to sleep.

PANEL TWO

The same situation for Thomas, but reversed (so if Barry is facing panel right, Thomas is facing panel left.)

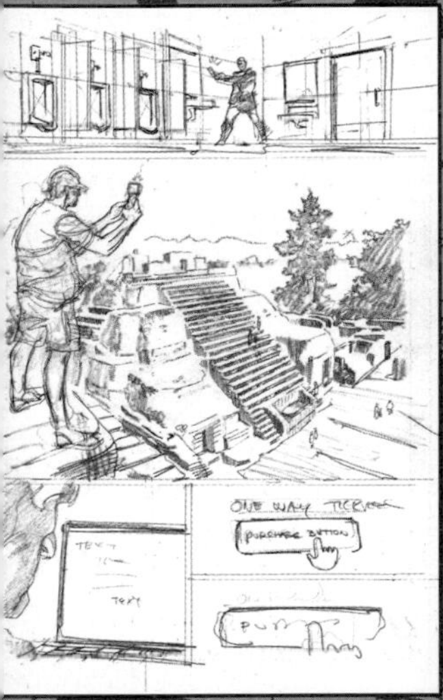

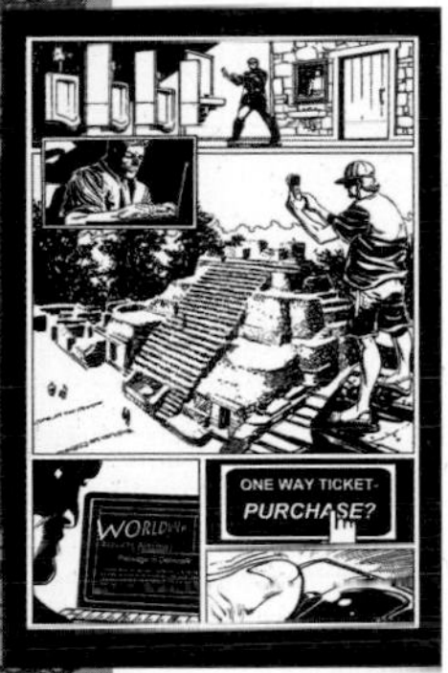
ONE WAY TICKET-
PURCHASE?

PAGE ELEVEN

PANEL ONE

Barry in a fancy restroom, sweeping the detector over the urinals.

PANEL TWO

Thomas in his home office at the computer.

PANEL THREE

Barry in another location (dealer's choice) looking at the screen. TARGET NOT DETECTED.

PANEL FOUR

In Thomas's office as he looks at the screen: a booking page for an airline. WORLDVIEW PRIVATE AIRLINES. PASSAGE TO DENMARK.

PANEL FIVE

The cursor hovers over ONE WAY TICKET. PURCHASE?

PANEL SIX

On the mouse as it goes CLICK!

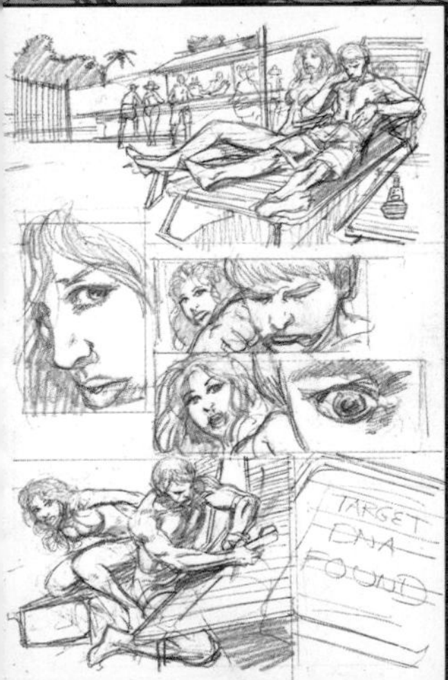
TARGET
DNA
FOUND

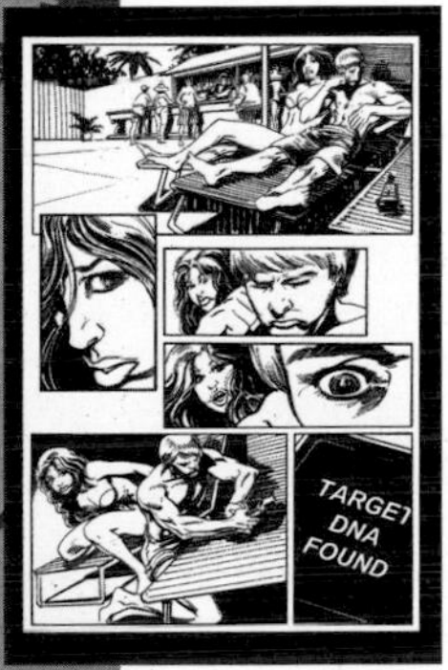
TARGET
DNA
FOUND

PAGE TWELVE

PANEL ONE

Julia and Barry are out on the patio of another club... the place has a pool, lots of women in bathing suits. The device is in Barry's hand, but it's on the seat beside him. He looks discouraged.

PANEL TWO

Julia looks to him, her eyes encouraging.

PANEL THREE

His eyes tell a different story. Giving up.

PANEL FOUR

His expression changes. OS SFX: BRRRRRRRRRRRRRR.

PANEL FIVE

He checks the display.

PANEL SIX

The display reads TARGET DNA FOUND.

PAGE THIRTEEN

PANEL ONE

He holds up the device, so we see him past it, as he aims
it at "us."

PANEL TWO

Past the device to the pool, where a number of beautiful
women in bikinis are hanging out. Nice big panel.

PANEL THREE

There's a rough targeting grid on the device. There's a
blip corresponding to one of the women, though we don't
focus on her until -.

PANEL FOUR

-- as we reveal it's the same woman who gave Thomas a BJ,
in the same bikini. She's walking the pool, looking for
business.

PANEL FIVE

Barry's eyes tell the story. Got her.

PAGE FOURTEEN

PANEL ONE

With a sheer top over her bikini, the young woman walks
along the beach.

PANEL TWO

She sees Julia walking toward her. Smiles.

PANEL THREE

Her pov as Julia approaches.

PANEL FOUR

Sill in her POV: the first hint of Julia taking a swing at
her.

PANEL FIVE

Black panel.

PAGE FIFTEEN

PANEL ONE

Narrow black panel.

PANEL TWO

On the young woman's eyes, opening.

PANEL THREE

Barry's face floats in front of her.

PANEL FOUR

Reveal she's gagged.

PANEL FIVE

Reveal she's hanging by a rope, her arms tied above her,
suspended from a tree above a sheer drop that would
obviously kill her. Barry floats before her.

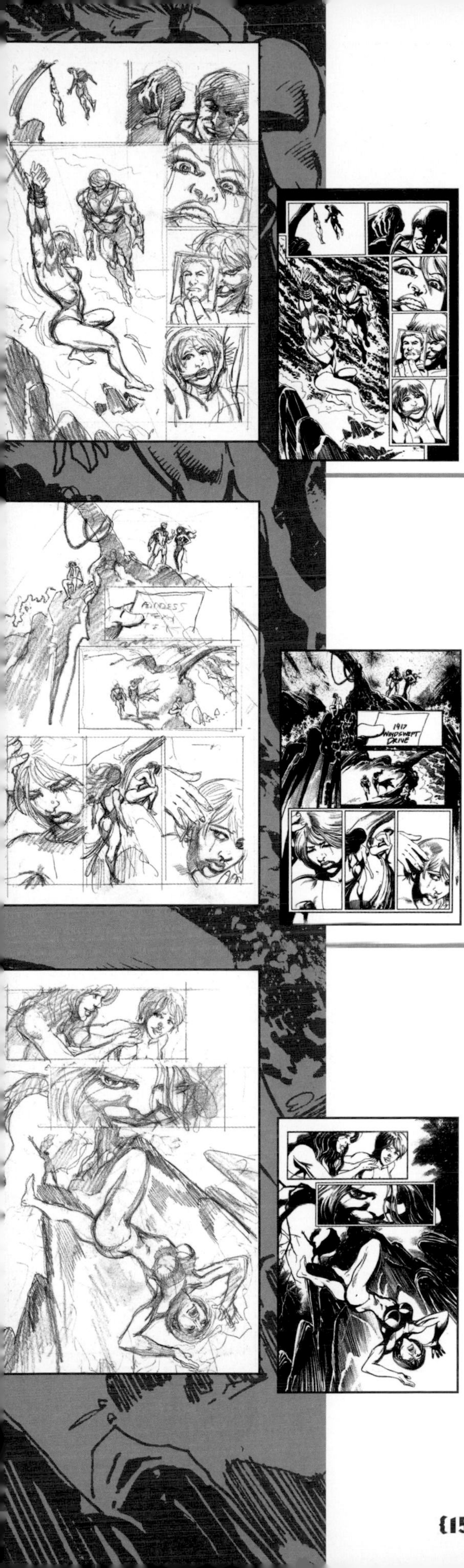
1417
WINDSWEPT
DRIVE

PAGE SIXTEEN

PANEL ONE

The woman begins thrashing.

PANEL TWO

Barry points down.

PANEL THREE

Her pov. It's a long fucking drop.

PANEL FOUR

On her face, terrified.

PANEL FIVE

Barry holds a photo of Thomas in front of her face.

PANEL SIX

She nods frantically...she'll give him whatever he asks.

PAGE SEVENTEEN

PANEL ONE

She now sits on the edge of the chasm or cliff, arms around her knees, shaking. Barry and Julia are looking at a slip of paper.

PANEL TWO

On the paper is handwritten 1417 Windswept Drive.

PANEL THREE

Barry starts away, content to leave the woman alone.

PANEL FOUR

Julia looks from the departing Barry to the woman.

PANEL FIVE

She approaches the woman.

PANEL SIX

She extends a hand to the woman, as though to help her stand.

PAGE EIGHTEEN

PANEL ONE

The woman takes her hand.

PANEL TWO

Julia smiles.

PANEL THREE

She hurls the woman over the edge, to fall to her death.

PAGE NINETEEN

PANEL ONE

Night. Thomas is packing.

PANEL TWO

He goes to a plain wall.

PANEL THREE

He pushes a hidden button. CLICK.

PANEL FOUR

The wall slides away to reveal a hidden room.

PANEL FIVE

It's a resources room: guns, drawers of expensive watches, various other goodies...and framed behind glass on the wall, the Red Cowl uniform.

PAGE TWENTY

PANEL ONE

He opens a drawer containing gold bars.

PANEL TWO

He shoves the bars into a bag.

PANEL THREE

On his face as he looks at something.

PANEL FOUR

He stares at the glass framed uniform.

PANEL FIVE

His face is reflected over the mask.

PANEL SIX

He goes out the way he came, turning off the light, CLICK.

PAGE TWENTY-ONE

PANEL ONE

He continues packing.

PANEL TWO

We come around to see him through the window.

PANEL THREE

We come further out, the room still visible, but further.

PANEL FOUR

We become aware of two silhouettes between us and our view of the house.

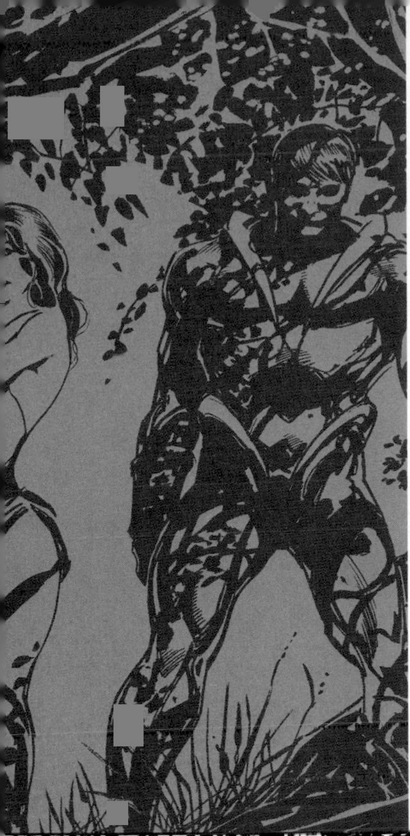

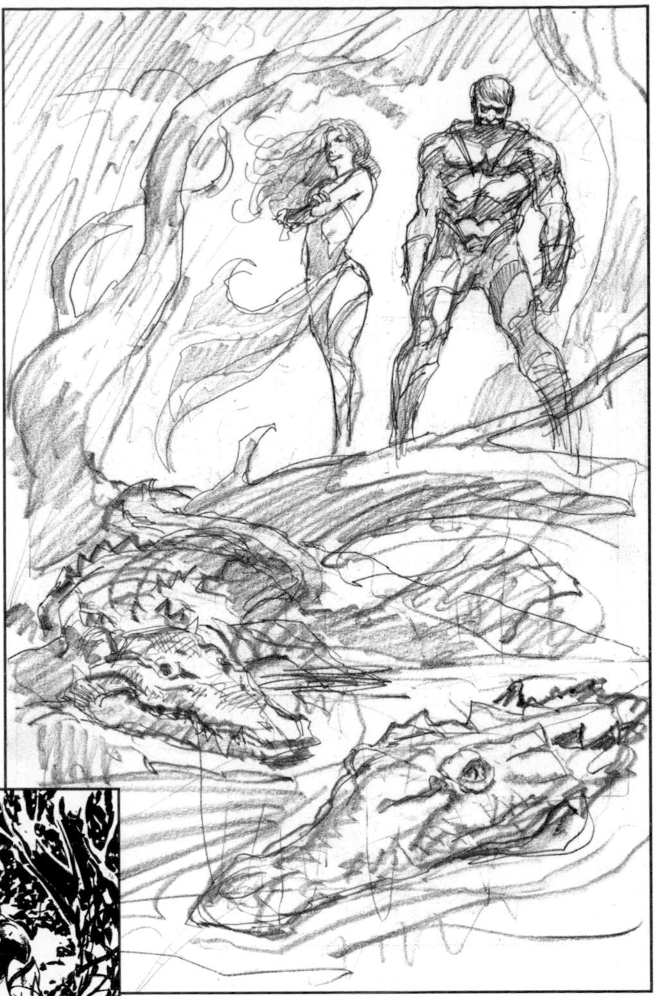

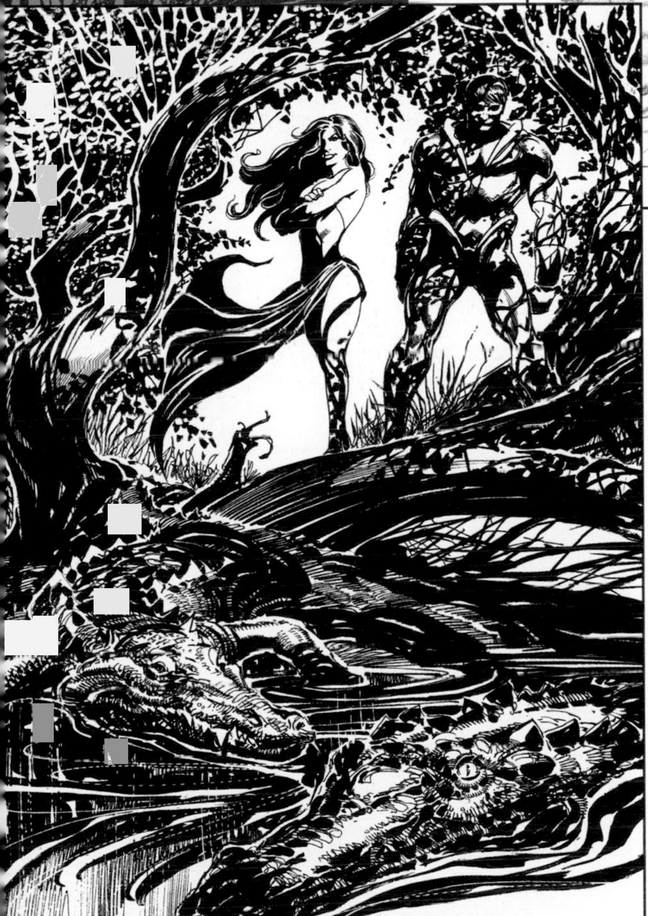

PAGE TWENTY-TWO

FULL PAGE

Barry and Julia hover over the moon-flecked sea, looking at the house...at the room...at Thomas Winchester.

To be continued